The Challenge and Promise of a Catholic University

The
Challenge and Promise
of a
Catholic University

EDITED BY

Theodore M. Hesburgh, C.S.C.

University of Notre Dame Press

Notre Dame and London

Library of Congress Cataloging-in-Publication Data

The Challenge and promise of a Catholic university / edited by Theodore M.
  Hesburgh.
  p. cm.
  ISBN 0–268–00803–5 (alk. paper)
  1. Catholic universities and colleges—Philosophy. 2. Catholic Church—Education—United States—Philosophy. 3. Catholic Church—Doctrines.   I Hesburgh,
Theodore M., 1917– .
LA487.C43   1994
377′ .82—dc20   92–568663
                                                              CIP

The paper used in this publication meets the minimum requirements
of the American National Standard for Information Sciences—Permanence of Paper
for Printed Library Materials, ANSI Z39.48–1984

To
the Faculty and Administration
of the University of Notre Dame du Lac
with deep gratitude
and sincere admiration

Contents

———————

Preface

This book attempts to add another few chapters to the ongoing discussion on the nature of a Catholic university. The discussion goes back to the beginning of the thirteenth century when western universities began—all of them Catholic.

A few centuries later, none of them was Catholic. Then, early in the last century a revival began with the rebirth of Louvain University as Catholic and, a bit earlier, the birth of Georgetown University in Washington, D.C. Since then about 300 Catholic institutions of higher learning, most of them colleges, were created in America. Of the more than 230 that have survived, about a dozen or more are true universities.

But are they really Catholic? Some say that the original vision has been lost, that they are Catholic in name only. Others say that they are more Catholic than ever, in the best sense of the word *catholic.*

To add to the confusion, there are those who say that the whole discussion is useless because the term *Catholic university* is an oxymoron, a contradiction in terms. Their reason seems to be that the church does not really believe in freedom, especially academic freedom. Those who are defensive allege that such anti-Catholicism is the antisemitism of intellectuals.

At this juncture, it would seem helpful to return to the original vision that led to the birth and rebirth of Catholic universities: the promise and challenge of such institutions.

Who can better speak to the promise and the challenge than those who have dedicated their lives to the creation, re-creation, and development of a Catholic university? On the faculty of the University of Notre Dame, I have known many such people, most of them Catholic but some Protestant or Jewish, some clergy but most laymen and laywomen, in all of our faculties of arts and letters, law, science, engineering, and business. I believe that if we could hear them discussing the promise and challenge of this Catholic university, we would advance greatly the wider discussion of the nature of the Catholic university in our times.

I do not think I should ask them to do this without declaring my own position on the subject, since I have spent my whole life, since age seventeen, studying, teaching, and administering in Catholic universities, here and abroad, but mainly at Notre Dame. I would welcome their agreeing, disagreeing, or refining what I have written because it is through the rigorous examination of ideas that truth best emerges. This is in the best tradition of the university— where scholars can disagree without being disagreeable, where the ultimate objective is truth.

In that first Catholic university at Paris, Thomas Aquinas was highly criticized, even threatened, because he used the thoughts and categories of a rediscovered pagan philosopher, Aristotle; but in the end, a deeper and more precise truth emerged, even a wisdom that still enlightens us. I am grateful to my colleagues who add their personal wisdom and understanding to this admittedly difficult task of clarifying the promise and challenge of the Catholic university in our times.

THEODORE M. HESBURGH, C.S.C.

Introduction:

The Challenge and Promise of a Catholic University

THEODORE M. HESBURGH, C.S.C.

A look at today and tomorrow for the University of Notre Dame must take into full account the specific promise and challenges that we face as we try to create here a great Catholic university. Also, we cannot avoid facing frankly the dangers and difficulties that confront us along the road of present and future development. But neither should we be timid, unimaginative, or defensive. In fact, what we need most at this juncture of our history are all the qualities of the pioneer: vision, courage, confidence, a great hope inspired by faith and ever revivified by love and dedication.

I hope that you are not shocked when I say that there has not been in recent centuries a truly great Catholic university, recognized universally as such. Some universities come very close to the reality, but not the full reality, at least as I see it in today's world. One might have hoped that history would have been different when one considers the church's early role in the founding of the first great universities in the Middle Ages: Paris, Oxford, Cambridge, Bologna, and others. They turned to the church for the charters that would guarantee them a freedom and autonomy they could not then have had from the state. Knowledge grew quickly within them because there was that new atmosphere of the free and often turbulent clashing of conflicting ideas, where a scholar with a new idea, theological, philosophical, legal, or scientific, had to

1

defend it in the company of peers, without interference from pressures and powers that neither create nor validate intellectual activity, one of God's greatest gifts to us.

This medieval conjunction of the church and the universities was to undergo a violent rupture in the years following the Reformation and, especially, the French Revolution. Philip Hughes, writing of this period, said:

> Another grave loss was the disappearance of the universities. They had been Catholic, and often Papal, foundations. In all of them there had been a faculty of theology, and round this mistress science their whole intellectual life had turned. Now they were gone, and when restored as State universities, [they became] academies for the exploration and exposition of natural truths alone. Education, the formation of the Catholic mind in the new Catholic Europe, would suffer immeasurably, and religious formation [would] be to its intellectual development an extra, something added on. There would be the further mischievous effect that henceforth not universities but seminaries would set the tone of theological life. The leaders of Catholic thought would not be the professional thinkers whom a university produces but technicians, those to whom the important work of training future clergy is committed and who, among other things, teach them theology. The effect of this destruction of the faculties of theology in the universities of Catholic Europe, the disappearance of the old Salamanca, Alcala, Coimbra, Bologna, Donai, Louvain, and Paris, is a theme that still awaits its historian. Louvain was indeed restored in 1834, but the healthy interplay of the theological intellects of a half a score of Catholic universities, the Nineteenth Century was never, alas, to know.

What we are trying to do today in creating great Catholic universities is, in a sense, a re-creation, so that the twentieth century and, indeed, the next millennium will not suffer the loss that Philip Hughes bemoans for the nineteenth century and most of the twentieth. The comeback has begun in many places, Notre Dame being one of them. But this is happening in a much different world, and in a much different climate of opinion. Moreover, the university, as an institution, has developed in modern times into a much different reality from what it was, even over a century ago when Cardinal Newman wrote his *Idea of a University*. That classic book can no longer be a complete model for the Catholic university of today. Also, one should reflect that Cardinal Newman never realized even in his day what he wrote about so well.

There are timeless principles in Newman's *Idea,* but he wrote about a completely different kind of university in a completely different kind of world. The Pax Britannica and the colonies have given way to the newly independent and largely frustrated Third World. The mainly rural world of the nineteenth century has now become largely urbanized. The population explosion has almost tripled world population in the last hundred years or so. Vatican I has been followed by Vatican II. We have progressively passed through two world wars, a Cold War, and, increasingly, a whole series of ethnic, religious, and brush wars, some unhappily still in progress. We have experienced industrial, communications, nuclear, and space revolutions. Ecumenism supplants some of the ancient and bitter religious and cultural rivalries. Never before has there been so much discussion and action about human rights and human development.

It is not surprising that universities have reflected increasingly in their structure and programs all of these revolutionary developments. Nowhere has this been more striking than in America. We inherited Newman's notion of the British university as an exclusively teaching institution, added on the concept of graduate and research functions from the German university model, and, to further complicate the institution, have elaborated since the end of World War II a new university function of service to humankind on the local, state, national, and international levels.

Apart from tripling the goals, the internal structure of the American university has undergone considerable change as well. Freedom and autonomy are still central to the university's life and spirit here and everywhere, but here they are buttressed by a system of governance that involves diverse layers of power and decision: boards of trustees, faculty, administration, alumni, and students. All do not share equally in the uneasy balance of power, but each group can and does have its say. Sir Eric Ashby has remarked in a classic book that the whole system is very complicated and very imperfect, but somehow it has worked and we have yet to find a better one.

This, then, in the briefest kind of shorthand, is the world into which the Catholic university is being reborn. One must remember that the church did not create the modern university world as it had helped create the medieval university world. Moreover, the church does not have to be present in the modern world of the university, but if it is to enter, the reality and the terms of this world are well established and must be observed. The terms may be complicated and unlike those operative within the church itself. The reality of the university world may make the church uneasy at times; nevertheless, all university people throughout the world recognize this reality and its terms as essential to anything that wishes to merit the name of *university* in the modern context. One may add descriptive adjectives to this or that university, calling it public or private, Catholic or Protestant, British or American, but the university must first and foremost be a university, or else the thing that the qualifiers qualify is something, but not a university.

I should add frankly that many people in the university world and outside it take a dim view of the very possibility of a Catholic university. George Bernard Shaw put it most bluntly when he declared that a Catholic university is a contradiction in terms. I presume that he viewed the church of his day as an essentially closed society and the university as an essentially open society. I shall deal with this considerable oversimplification later, in light of the developments of Vatican II. The core of the answer to Shaw must, of course, be that a university does not cease to be free because it is Catholic. Otherwise, I am not sure an answer is possible. It should also be said that the Catholic university is not the Catholic church. It might be said to be *of* the church as it serves the church and the people of God, but it certainly is not the magisterium, although it does respect it. It is not a seminary, although seminarians may study in it. It is not the church teaching, but a place—the only place—in which Catholics and others, on the highest level of intellectual inquiry, seek out the relevance of the Christian message to all of the problems and opportunities that face us and our complex world.

I would be the last to claim that Notre Dame, or some other Catholic university, will not at times be an embarrassment to the church or the hierarchy because of the actions of some faculty member, administrator, student, or a group of these. Universities have no monopoly on the misuse of freedom; but few institutions on earth need the climate of freedom to the extent that universities do, whatever the risks involved. Moreover, universities since their founding in the Middle Ages have always been unruly places, almost by nature, since the university is the place where young people come of age—an often unruly process—places where the really important problems are freely discussed with all manner of solutions proposed, places where all the burning issues of the day are ventilated, even with hurricane winds at times. Again, by nature, the university—even, or perhaps especially, the Catholic university—has always been dedicated uniquely to criticism of itself and everything else, of those things held most dear.

The university is not the kind of place that one can or should try to rule by authority external to the university. The best and only traditional authority in the university is intellectual competence: this is the coin of the realm. This includes, in the Catholic university especially, philosophical and theological competence. It was great wisdom in the medieval church to have university theologians judged solely by their theological peers in the university.

There will always be times when embarrassment might seem to be avoided by attempting to silence someone of unusual views or eccentric personality. Church and state share this temptation equally, with the church coming off better today, I believe. In most cases where this temptation is indulged, only greater embarrassment ultimately comes, especially to the cause of the university, higher learning, the church, and the state. As Cardinal Newman said so well: "Great minds need elbow room, not indeed in the domain of faith, but of thought. And so indeed do lesser minds and all minds."

By now, it should be clear why we need the pioneering virtues of vision, courage, confidence, and hope, in order to attempt to create what to many seems impossible, a great Catholic university in our times. The time has come to define more positively just what we have in mind, no matter how difficult a task this is.

A great Catholic university must begin by being a great university that is also Catholic. What makes a great university in the ancient and modern tradition that we have been discussing? First and foremost, it must be a community of scholars, young and old, teaching and learning together and committed to the service of humankind in our times. It might be hoped that in a university worthy of the name the young draw perspective from the old and, vice versa, the faculty grows wiser as it confronts the questioning, idealism, and generosity of each new generation of students. Any university should be a place where all the relevant questions are asked and where answers are elaborated in an atmosphere of freedom and responsible inquiry, where the young learn the great power of ideas and ideals, where the values of justice and charity, truth and beauty, are both taught and exemplified by the faculty, and where both faculty and students are seized by a deep compassion for human anguishes and are committed to proffer a helping hand, wherever possible, in every aspect of our material, intellectual, spiritual, and cultural development. I believe that John Masefield, poet laureate of England, had all of this in mind when he wrote that the university is a splendid place. A great university must be splendidly all of this, or it is neither a university nor great. And let us candidly admit that many so-called universities today are neither.

Now the great Catholic university must be all of this and something more. If we at Notre Dame, today and tomorrow, can be all of this and something more, then the bottom drops out of the objections we have been considering. What is the something more? Here we can indeed take a page from Newman's book, where he says eloquently that there must be universality of knowledge within the university. *Catholic* means universal, and the university, as Catholic, must be universal in a double sense. First, it must emphasize the centrality of philosophy and, especially, theology among its intellectual concerns, not just as window dressing, not just to fill a large gap in the total fabric of knowledge as represented in the most modern university curricula. Rather, theology in the Catholic university must be engaged on the highest level of intellectual inquiry so that it may be in living dialogue with all the other disciplines in the university. Both philosophy and theology are concerned with the ultimate questions; both bear uniquely on human nature and destiny. All intellectual questions, if pursued far enough, reveal their philosophical and theological dimension of meaning and relevance. The university, as Catholic, must sustain and deepen this dimension of intellectual discourse that we badly interrupted, to our loss, several centuries ago.

The second sense in which the Catholic university must be universal is related to the first, perhaps a corollary of its philosophical and theological concern. Without a deep concern for philosophy and theology, the intellectual and moral aspects of all human knowledge are in danger of becoming detached and separate. Technique can become central, rather than the human person, for whom technique is presumably a service. Social scientists can close their eyes to human values; physical scientists can be unconcerned with the use of the power they create. Stating all of this is not to say that all knowledge in the Catholic university is ruled by a philosophical or theological imperialism. Each discipline has its own autonomy of method and its proper field of knowledge. The presence of philosophy and theology simply completes the total field of inquiry, raises additional and ultimate questions, moves every scholar to look beyond immediate questions, beyond the immediate field of vision, to the total landscape of God, human beings, and the universe. One might turn the words of Shaw around and say that no university is truly a university unless it is catholic, or universal, in this sense.

Now may I bring all of this back to Notre Dame and our goals as we look ahead? Some may worry a bit about what has just been said if it is phrased in terms of the commitment of this university as Catholic. I submit to you that we have overdone our fears about this word, *commitment,* which has become a kind of dirty word in university circles. Universities that exclude philosophy and theology as integral parts of university education have also made a commitment. Some scholars are committed to agnosticism, atheism, scientism, naturalism, and a whole host of other positions. Is our commitment less sacred or less permissible in the university world? Certainly not, if we make our commitment freely and intelligently. Should those who live peacefully with a host of alien commitments be denied their own? Should a commitment to the wholeness and universality of knowledge by whatever means in an institution that calls itself a university be looked upon as retrogressive? I make no apology for any of my free commitments. I can live and work in a total academic community with all who profess other commitments. I only ask that it not be done in the name of uncommitment, which it is not, and that our intellectual respect for each other be mutual.

At Notre Dame, as in all universities, commitment to be meaningful must be personal rather than simply institutional, must be a matter of one's free conviction rather than institutional rhetoric. I think we have been able to do this at Notre Dame in an inclusive, ecumenical fashion. I have sensed that, whatever the personal faith of each member of our variegated faculty and student body, we are united in believing that intellectual virtues and moral values are important to life and to this institution. I take it that our total community commitment is to wisdom, which is something more than knowledge and much akin to goodness and beauty when it radiates throughout a human person.

If all of this is largely true, then I think that Notre Dame can perform a vital function in the whole spectrum of American higher learning, can do what many other institutions cannot or will not do. We can give living witness to the wholeness of truth from all sources, both human and divine, while recognizing the inner sacredness of all truth from whatever source, and the validity and autonomy of all paths to truth. The Notre Dame community should reflect profoundly, and with unashamed commitment, its belief in the existence of God and in God's total revelation to us, especially through the Christian message; the deep, agelong mystery of salvation in history; and the inner, inalienable dignity and rights of every individual human person. We should recognize at the same time both our God-given freedom and our human fallibility, an uneasy balance dependent upon God's grace that should buttress our every move toward a more profound perception and articulation of truth, as well as a more humane achievement of justice in our times. And Notre Dame must try to do all of this in the most ecumenical and open spirit. The Judeo-Christian tradition should be reflected here at Notre Dame in the very humane atmosphere of this beautiful campus—in a spirit of civility as well as of love, in openness as well as in commitment, in our humble pilgrim search as well as in our enduring faith and hope and love. We may do all of this poorly, but we cannot, if we aspire to be a great Catholic university in our times, attempt to do less. We do not require the Catholic, or even Christian, faith of everyone in the community. We think that most must have this faith or at least respect it, if the vision is to be real, not fictional. Others may have their own Christian, Jewish, Muslim, or other faith and still share, as much as possible, the university's spiritual challenge and vision, as many have already done.

What kind of a place will Notre Dame be, will the Catholic university be, in the years ahead if all of this happens here? First, I think it will be a *beacon*, bringing to light, in modern focus, the wonderfully traditional and ancient adage: *Intellectus quaerens fidem et fides quaerens intellectum.* How to say it for today? Let me begin by saying that modern people stand or cower beneath a mushroom cloud. We have created it, and in a sense it symbolizes all human inclinations toward self-destruction throughout history. Yet we seek a deeper meaning. Life cannot be simply negation and despair, so we seek a faith: in God, in God's word, in God incarnate in Christ our Lord, in suffering and resurrection, in life eternal. These are the only realities that keep us today from the ultimate despair, suicide, either personal or global. This is the faith that we seek in this place, faith as a gift, faith that sets our minds to soaring beyond the limits of human intelligence, on the level of divine intelligence, into the realm of the beyond, the eternal world of faith.

Intellectus quaerens fidem—the human mind reaching out for a faith—this is one side of the coin. The other is *Fides quaerens intellectum:* faith seeking in the university community an expression of belief that will be relevant to the uneasy modern mind. We cannot be satisfied here with medieval answers to modern questions. We cannot, for example, speak of war as if the bow and arrow had not been superseded by the nuclear intercontinental ballistic missile. Faith is unchangeable in what it believes, but, as good Pope John said, there are many ways of expressing what we believe—and today, the words must be directed to the inner complexity of our times, what Manzoni called *guazzabuglio del cuore umano,* "the utter confusion in the heart of humanity." The university is best prepared to understand this human confusion, to speak to it with faithful words that say something, to avoid meaningless formulas, empty phrases, words without weight. If the Catholic university can fulfill this first function of the human mind seeking faith and faith reaching out for an expression adequate to our times, it will indeed be a great light in the all-encompassing darkness that engulfs our world today. Such a university will represent the moral resource of the Catholic tradition, interpreted for contemporary society. Such a university will be faithful to the wisdom of the past, relevant to the present, and open to the future.

Secondly, the Catholic university must be a *bridge* across all the chasms that separate modern people from each other: the gaps between young and old, men and women, rich and poor, black and white, believer and unbeliever, potent and weak, east and west, material and spiritual, scientist and humanist, developed and less developed, and all the rest. To be such a mediator, the Catholic university, as universal, must be engaged with, and have an interest in, both edges of every gulf, must understand each, encompass each in its total community and build a bridge of understanding and love. Only in such a university community can the opposite sides discuss matters civilly, not shout at each other. Only in such a university community can there be the rational and civil discourse that builds bridges rather than widens the gulfs of misunderstanding. If this cannot be accomplished at the Catholic university, then the human situation is hopeless, and we must resign ourselves to hatred, noise, violence, rancor, and, ultimately, the destruction of all we hold dear. Bridges are best built by love and understanding. Peace, not conflict, is both means and end.

Thirdly, the Catholic university must be a *crossroads* where all the intellectual and moral currents of our times meet and are thoughtfully considered. How great is the need today for a place where dialogue is temperate, not strident, where all ideas are welcome even if not espoused, where hospitality is assured for all who sincerely have something to say. Where else, except in the Catholic university, can the church confront the challenges, the anguishes, and the opportunities of our times? Where else can there be an agora such as that in which Saint Paul spoke of the unknown God in Athens? *The Church in the Modern World,* of Vatican II, addressed many problems of the church in the world today. This document is an invitation rather than an ultimate answer. If the ultimate answers are to be found, the church may best find them within the Catholic university community which is in living contact with the faith and the world, with the problems and all of the possible solutions, with the possibilities and the despairs of all of the people of our time. In the modern Catholic university all sincere and thoughtful persons should be welcomed, listened to, and respected by a serious consideration of what they have to say about their belief or unbelief, their certainty or uncertainty. Here should be the home of the inquiring mind, and whatever the differences of religion, culture, race, or nationality, here should be the place where love and civility govern conversation, interest, and outcome. Jacques Barzun called the university the house of the intellect. The Catholic university should, beyond all else, be this house, as well as the house of respect and lively discussion in the cause of truth, which unites us all in its quest and in its promise.

Let us now return to where we began, to the possibility of a great Catholic university in our times, since this is the ultimate challenge for Notre Dame today. I would like to describe one more dimension to the vision glimpsed above. Here my guide is Father Teilhard de Chardin, a modern prophet despite the problems that come with his view. Father Teilhard envisioned two parallel paths of human development: one natural that involved our humanization of all creation, another supernatural that would Christianize the total world. The natural goal was *omega;* the supernatural was called *pleroma,* or the recapitulation of all things in Christ, our Savior. Teilhard believed that we would naturally give ourselves to the process of humanizing the world as we know it. This process would be attended by all manner of human frustration and despair, especially when all of the ambiguities and human negations bear upon us. For Teilhard, there was only one guarantee of human perseverance in the quest of natural progress: the parallel path of salvation history, of the grace of God in Christ, the deep belief that ultimately the omega and the pleroma would merge in the new creation. Otherwise, despite his deep belief in the evolutionary movement upward and onward, Teilhard knew nothing but despair.

I think we can find in the Teilhardian presentation an analogy or a prototype for the Catholic university. All universities are totally committed today to human development and human progress in the natural order of events. This whole endeavor is ultimately a fragile thing and, left to itself, is often laden with frustration and despair. Here in the total spectrum, the Catholic university has something spectacular to offer. Call it faith, call it belief, call it a simple parallel course depending on other sources of strength, other sources of knowledge, a belief in an ultimate goal surpassing all natural endeavor.

The Catholic university must be all that a university requires and something more. It may be that the Teilhardian parallel is the something more, the extra element that defies frustration and despair. However you measure it, we commit ourselves here to the something more, not in a triumphal spirit of superiority, but with the humble realization that at Notre Dame we must be ourselves, in keeping with our tradition, and that being ourselves will mean that we may add something to the full strength of what we most cherish: the great endeavor of higher learning in our beloved America and in our total world. How more splendidly can we be a splendid place?

Reflections on the Mission of a Catholic University

HAROLD W. ATTRIDGE

Father Hesburgh's invitation to reflect on the character and mission of Catholic universities at the end of the twentieth century is impossible to refuse. Father Hesburgh has long shown the kind of visionary leadership that remains an inspiration to all who labor in the environment that he did so much to create. To contribute in some small way to the continuance of the enterprise of Catholic higher education is indeed a privilege. In response to his reflections on the topic, let me offer a few personal reminiscences, some considerations about the present, and some suggestions for the future.

Personal Experience

My first contact with a Catholic university took place more than thirty years ago, when I matriculated as a freshman at Boston College. At that time and place it was not difficult, as least for a neophyte, to say what a Catholic university was. Boston College was a place where several generations of Boston area Catholics, Irish and otherwise, had found the opportunity for a serious higher education. It was the stepping-stone to professional careers, and therefore to the middle class, for many children and grandchildren of immigrants, for the most part first-generation collegians. Yet it was not simply a ladder for social mobility. The university clearly stood for something, a long tradition in which faith and reason had found a harmony.

13

The university, staffed largely by Jesuits, was a part of the extensive network of social ministry of the church, a ministry that extended to health and human services, as well as to education. It was, as the recent papal encyclical suggests, an enterprise born from the "heart of the church." Although some members of the university may have had a view of its role as a center for research, its primary function was educational. While it was a complex educational institution, the university had a mission to transmit the culture of the past and to open a group of philistine youth to the life of the mind. To safeguard young Catholics from the dangers of modernity was perhaps an element of the mission. The Jesuits who sent their students on from high school to Boston College certainly had the expectation that in that environment their former students would be protected from the rampant atheism of secular academe. Yet that defensive tone was not the ethos of the faculty that we encountered at Boston College. Instead we found men—and the faculty in the College of Arts and Sciences was almost exclusively male at the time—who wanted us to think for ourselves, who tried to expose us to the literature, history, philosophy, and theology of western (and sometimes even eastern) culture, and who expected us to respond as intelligent Catholics.

At that time and place, of course, it was not difficult to say what a Catholic was. The boundaries of the religious community were clear, whether they had to do with maintaining high personal standards, with weekly attendance at Mass, or with more trivial matters, such as abstinence from meat on Friday. Everyone inside the community, and most people outside it, knew that Catholics stood for a strict moral code and practiced an esoteric, but aesthetically pleasing, cult, and bore special reverence for the pope. While actual practice of the faith may have been more or less strict, what it was to be a practicing Catholic was clear.

Frequently students found in the attempt to unite faith and reason more piety than hard thought. I well recall a song that some of the wags on campus would sing, to the tune of "There's No Business Like Show Business":

> There's no -ism like Thomism
> like no -ism I know.
> Everything about it is appalling,

everything about it is a fraud;
It will have you on your knees and crawling
until you're sprawling, before God!
There's no -ism, like Thomism, etc.

Despite the students' youthful cynicism, Boston College was a campus where high ideals were in evidence, and the practical implications of Christian commitment pursued. The late sixties were the days of passionate concern with civil rights, and I well remember the leadership of a senior social activist Leo Haley, who died as a victim of crime while serving the poor in Roxbury. Those too were the days of vehement protest over the American involvement in Vietnam, and I well remember the vigils conducted on campus by those students and faculty who found the war beyond the bounds of any conceivably justified use of military force. Whether we wanted to or no, we were part of an intensely Catholic religious and intellectual culture that shaped our reactions to the world in significant ways.

Times obviously have changed, both in the church and in the universities associated with it, as I now perceive from the vantage point of another Catholic institution where I have served for eight years after a hiatus of two decades in more secular academe. As a result of the Second Vatican Council, and of the social and economic changes that swept the American Catholic population in the aftermath of World War II, the Catholic community has become more diverse, less insular, more upwardly mobile, and more outwardly successful. The need for the old avenues to the middle class that Catholic institutions of higher education provided is no longer felt as keenly, at least among some of the traditional constituencies of Catholic institutions. Such Catholics are as likely to be found at Harvard or Stanford, Duke, or S.M.U. as at Notre Dame, Boston College, or Georgetown. At the same time, new generations of immigrants, particularly from Latin America, have swelled the ranks of the Catholic population and have presented new educational needs to which Catholic institutions have tried to respond, however inadequately.

While the Catholic population and its expectations have changed, Catholic universities too have changed by moving to become more comprehensive institutions of higher education. Hence, my experience of a Catholic university now is far different from what it was as a student thirty years ago. Instead of being primarily colleges for the preparation of a new professional class of Catholic doctors and lawyers, at least some Catholic institutions have become universities in the fullest sense, concerned as much for the production of new knowledge as for the transmission of inherited wisdom. Through the process of laicization of formal governance structures that took place in the late 1960s and early 1970s, Catholic universities and colleges have also achieved a large degree of autonomy from ecclesiastical control. Institutional autonomy and an increased dedication to the full range of a university's functions have enabled Catholic universities gradually to assume a more prominent place among American institutions of higher education. They are not yet among the elite, although the graduate of one has now become president of the United States. Even the best of the Catholic institutions remain, by and large, on the second tier of comprehensive research universities in the United States, on a par not with Harvard, Yale, Princeton, Stanford, Chicago, or Michigan but comparable with Duke, Northwestern, Vanderbilt, or Emory.

Despite the changes in the institution and its environment, I see continuities between the environment that I knew as a student and that in which students at Notre Dame now operate. Now as then the Catholic environment breeds a sense of commitment to service that is distinctive in its breadth and intensity. It fosters a genuine concern for those whom society has left behind. Like the Boston College of a generation ago, Notre Dame is also a place that opens horizons to new generations of students. Some of them come to university with a bit more superficial polish than did many of my contemporaries, but all come with the same need to confront the basic issues that a liberal education, an education that is morally committed and open to transcendence, poses.

A Basic Vision

With all the continuities and discontinuities, the transformations within American Catholicism and American Catholic higher education have raised questions in an acute form about the nature and function of Catholic universities. Do they have a distinctive character that differentiates them from other institutions of higher education, a character that makes a difference to the educational enterprise? Should that specific character be fostered, and if so, how?

My own response to all the issues connected with the ideal of a Catholic university in the late twentieth and early twenty-first century would take more space than is currently available. A few broad strokes will have to suffice. Let me begin by citing some of my own remarks addressed to the faculty of the College of Arts and Letters at the University of Notre Dame in my Christmas report of December 1993.

Our identity as a Catholic university is in part a result of the stories that we tell about ourselves. As Catholics we tell a tale that reaches deep into the history of the people of Israel and has an important episode that we commemorate at this season. As we celebrate the birth of Jesus of Nazareth, Christians confess him to be the light of the world. Yet we do so with some trepidation, knowing that after well nigh two thousand years of his shining, light still fails to reach many corners of our world. Our confession is one of hope, ultimately in the "reign of God" which Jesus proclaimed and for which he died. That reign of God is a state of affairs that will, we trust, unite, as Isaiah said, lions and lambs, or, as Paul said, Jew and Greek, slave and free, male and female. We know that such a realm of peace and justice, in both society and church, is devilishly elusive. Yet we dedicate ourselves to that end as we contemplate the image of a young woman, displaced by the requirements of the political order, holding her infant son, wrapped in rags and lying in a stable. Whatever our confessional background, most of us who work in this university share something of this story and the vision it embodies.

All of us who are privileged to work in this university share an-other vision, inspired by another unlikely hero, an Athenian sentenced to death for impiety and the corruption of youth. In many ways he has defined for twenty-four centuries the essential components of the life of the mind: to wit, the ability to give a reasoned basis for belief and the quest to find the truth that lies behind appearances. His practice of asking embarrassing questions, even at the risk of personal loss, and even without hope of an immediate answer, is fundamental to what we are.

The Catholic identity of this university is a matter of how two such fundamental stories relate. At one level there is, as far as I am concerned, no conflict. The commitment to work for the reign of God is entirely compatible with the quest to know the truth and to live in conformity with it. Not to engage in the, oftentimes abrasive, quest for truth is, in fact, to run the risk of setting up idols. At a university, particularly a university that seeks to work for the kingdom of God, the quest of Socrates must be sacrosanct.

At another level the two visions of human endeavor stand in tension. For each vision has a history as well as institutional incarnations. That history and those embodiments may have enriched the visions, but they may also have clouded them. When elements within our environment challenge one or another component of our complex identity we must state clearly and forcefully what we are about, as our academic council did this semester in response to the ordinances proposed by the committee of the National Conference of Catholic Bishops. Yet our task is not a negative one. Our task at a Catholic university, a fundamental feature that differentiates us from similar institutions without a tradition of religious commitment, is our willingness to engage both of our paradigmatic visions in critical awareness of the strengths and weaknesses of each. That is hardly an easy calling. It requires enormous goodwill and thorough honesty, a number of faculty who share both visions, and, at the same time, a willingness to engage all perspectives in an environment conducive to true dialogue. The calling, though difficult, promises to make real a light that can truly be illuminating. For 151 years Notre Dame has let the light of faithful reason and reasoned faith shine. May it always continue to do so.

This set of remarks in effect recognizes the different foci around which the life of a Catholic university, now just as when I first entered one, revolves and calls for a necessary balance in relating them. To maintain such a balance, of course, is easier said than done.

Implementing the Vision

A Catholic university of the twenty-first century must express its fundamental commitments in every dimension of its life. It cannot be content, as was the Boston College of my youth, with a program of instruction developed around a *ratio studiorum* of the sixteenth century. The Catholic university of the present must take account of its function as a locus of research as well as a venue for advanced instruction.

RESEARCH INITIATIVES

Channeling the research initiatives of a major university is not a simple matter. Academic freedom dictates that individual faculty members or groups of faculty should be allowed the autonomy to pursue lines of inquiry that are meaningful to them, and so they must. The institution as a whole, however, can foster and provide incentives for certain kinds of research. One vehicle for doing so is the apparatus of institutes and research centers that are established, sometimes through faculty initiative, sometimes through administrative fiat, usually through some collaborative process. Institutes in the history, structure, and rationale of things Catholic constitute one subset of relevant possibilities. Yet Catholic universities should not devote themselves solely to Catholic traditions. Such a focus is sure to guarantee a provincialism, indeed a parochialism, that belies the name university.

Qua university, and qua Catholic university, institutions such as Notre Dame or Boston College should address the whole range of human problems and issues, from the meaning of literature through the possibility of treatment for blood disorders. It is obvious that not every institution can or should do everything. The basic point is that no Catholic university worthy of the name can afford to devote itself exclusively to Catholic issues; yet none can afford to neglect ventures that are of primary interest to the religio-ecclesiastical tradition.

Of what, then, should a Catholic university foster the investigation? Notre Dame does numerous things more or less well, and more or less related to the university's Catholic character. Its strongest departments in the humanities are theology, philosophy, and medieval studies, and scholars in each pursue the kind of research appropriate to the traditional core disciplines of the humanities: How are we to make sense of divine revelation in the twentieth century? In an age of cybernetics what does it mean to be a knowing mind? What, in our complex society, constitutes human goodness, beauty, truth? In addition, the university supports a center for the study of American Catholicism, a center for the philosophy of religion, an institute of peace studies, and a center involved with science and religion that sponsors an undergraduate concentration in science, technology, and values. These and other research initiatives have a fairly clear, or potentially clear, relationship to interests that have been traditionally Catholic. Other research centers or institutes have a less obvious or immediate relevance to the Catholic character of the university. The Kellogg Institute of International Relations, the Center for the Study of Contemporary Society (with its Laboratory for Social Research), or the Center of Labor Economics would be examples, yet each has sponsored programs that are of interest to many Catholics and of obvious relevance to the social teaching of the church. On another front, the Institute for Pastoral and Social Ministry has focused on continuing education for both clergy and laity; it now has assumed a more research-oriented focus, as befits a major university. One area in which Notre Dame at least has not pursued an active research program through a major institute or research center is the fine arts, and one challenge during the next century for this university will be to enhance the support of research and artistic productivity.

To develop a list of research initiatives is at best illustrative—but is certainly not meant to be definitive—of the kinds of things a Catholic university can undertake. How any Catholic university will respond to the challenge to conduct research appropriate to its identity will depend on its resources and situation. Yet at the heart of its research mission will be a commitment to address the issues that theology and philosophy have pursued.

PROGRAMS OF INSTRUCTION

Education of undergraduate, graduate professional, and graduate research students remains a central element of any Catholic institution of higher learning. The historical roots of all Catholic universities lie in undergraduate instruction, and whatever else they may come to do, these universities will and should continue the educational enterprise on which they were founded.

New generations of undergraduate students need a grounding in those disciplines that have proved their worth over centuries: logic and the arts of reasoning rightly; epistemology and the reflection on what we really know and how; metaphysics and the consideration of what is most fundamentally real; the study of Scripture, the prose and poetry that constitutes revelation in a special sense; ethics and moral theology, the reflection on the values, virtues, and norms that constitute moral reasoning; the history of civilization and of the community of faith, the experience that tests all of the more abstract theories; the literature that celebrates and enshrines human experience. To have encountered these disciplines, to have wrestled with the problems that they treat, is one of the marks of a Catholic intellectual. To provide the opportunity for an encounter with this intellectual experience, indeed to see to it that such an encounter takes place, is an essential function of a Catholic university.

The development of the research dimension of Catholic universities such as Notre Dame requires that equal attention be paid to graduate students, whose goal is to become professional teachers and researchers. This development has involved a shift of effort and has introduced new tensions in the fabric of university life. There is not for graduates any single core curriculum that defines their participation in a Catholic institution. Their participation in the research appropriate to their disciplines should involve at least some of them in the kinds of questions particularly relevant to a Catholic institution. All, however, should be first and foremost competent scholars and scientists, combining the kind of learning and creative insight that will lead to a life of productive research involvement.

One of the oldest functions of a university is the provision of professional education, in law, medicine, and ecclesiastical ministry. To these has been added in modern times graduate professional education in the administration of business and governmental entities and in the principles, design, and execution of engineering systems and architecture. Here too Catholic universities need to excel not only by providing the best possible technical training, but by emphasizing as strongly as possible the ethical standards appropriate to the various forms of professional life.

PROGRAMS OF FORMATION

Not all of the education that takes place in a university, particularly for undergraduates, occurs in the setting of classrooms, laboratories, and lecture halls. As Newman recognized in his *Idea of the University*, the most important educators at any university are peers, and so it should be at any Catholic university. What takes place in and around the residence halls of a university is vitally important to the overall educational experience.

The University of Notre Dame, like other Catholic institutions, attempts to create conditions in its residence halls in which faith and learning can coalesce. The rich social and liturgical life of the student body is a positive result and constitutes one of the fondest memories of many alumni. Many faculty are concerned that there is too rigid a divide between the life of the residence halls and the life of classroom and laboratory, too deep a cleft between the affective life of faith and the reflective life of the mind. That there are dangers is clear, and it is one of the problems that this Catholic institution has yet to resolve. Yet there are clearly strengths in the attention that has been devoted to fostering the life of faith in the context of student residences. These should be preserved and enhanced.

Challenges and Opportunities

BECOMING A TRUE UNIVERSITY

Over 151 years ago a visionary French priest, Edward Sorin, C.S.C., committed an archetypal act of chutzpah by building a log cabin on the shores of a lake in northern Indiana and calling it a university. While Father Sorin's foundation has grown and prospered in the last century and a half, some would argue that a bit of chutzpah remains in the claims that it makes. An anecdote about dinners in Chicago suggests that two common topics of conversation every fall are Who is going to be Chicago's Nobel laureate this year? and Will Notre Dame be number 1 in football? Such anecdotes enshrine a stereotype of the way Notre Dame has been. Yet they also point to a reality of life on this, and other, Catholic campuses. Activities peripheral to those of a real university occupy an inordinate amount of the university's attention. At the same time, the academic core of the university remains in many areas undeveloped. For instance, to have at the beginning of the twenty-first century a minimal program in the languages and cultures of the Far East is not to be in a position to grapple with the global realities that confront us all.

More generally, Notre Dame, like all Catholic universities, has a long way to go to become the center of learning that it aspires to be. Fields of excellence have been developed, but they need to be expanded. Graduate studies and research have become a part of the university scene, but they constitute still a relatively small part of the university's effort. The most basic challenge confronting institutions like Notre Dame is to make their rhetoric about being a university a reality. Notre Dame and its peers have committed alumni and benefactors who share the lofty aspirations of a Father Sorin; they will no doubt make aspirations realities.

During recent years there has been considerable anxiety in Catholic university circles about whether the Catholic heritage of universities like Notre Dame can be preserved in the face of pressures to diversify the student body and to recruit excellent faculty regardless of confessional stance. Some critics have predicted that the university is on the verge of sliding down a slippery slope that many universities with Protestant foundations traveled over the course of the last century.

Such fears are obviously not totally groundless. The student body of Notre Dame remains overwhelmingly Catholic; yet the faculty has become increasingly diverse in recent years. More importantly, even among Catholics on the faculty there is a difference in attitude toward the hierarchy of the church from what prevailed a generation or two ago. Despite the skeptical attitude toward a sclerotic Thomism that I recalled from my student days, there was among Catholic faculty of the sixties a general respect for the clerical leadership of the church. That respect has certainly waned, in part because of the major shocks to the Catholic psyche that have taken place in the last generation: the lack of reception on the part of many Catholics of the teaching of *Humanae Vitae* regarding contraception, the sexual scandals affecting priests and religious over the last two decades, and the failure or refusal of the episcopal leadership of the church to address adequately the concerns of women in the church, particularly women who claim to have a vocation to ordained ministry in the church. Even those who identify with the intellectual or sacramental traditions of the church often find themselves hard pressed to defend certain of the church's official positions. Such disaffection, coupled with the attractions of positions outside Catholic colleges and universities, has made it increasingly difficult to attract strong Catholic faculty.

In the face of such developments a university that wants to remain Catholic must return to the basic principles of a Catholic vision such as I articulated above. The university must continue to identify men and women who share the fundamental vision of the

divine will for humankind that informs the Catholic tradition, who
see their academic career as bound up with such a vision, and who
want to live their academic lives in an environment that prizes their
religious and moral commitments. The university must then make
special efforts to recruit such people to the faculty, with the special
postdoctoral opportunities and enhancements to positions that are
necessary to attract faculty with established reputations. At the
same time the university must insist that all its faculty have the
freedom to conduct research and to teach as their conscience leads
them. They must have the freedom to articulate seemingly unor-
thodox positions. Only when such positions are presented honestly and forcefully will the teaching of the church be what it can
and should be. Only where the freedom exists to defend such positions will the best Catholic faculty be interested in joining the university community.

While there is some cause for concern on the issue of recruiting
and retaining a faculty dedicated to the aims and principles of a
Catholic university, there is no reason for the despondency that
sometimes surfaces in discussions of the issue. The environment
for learning and for the exercise of religious faith that a university
such as Notre Dame provides can and should be an attractive one for
faculty who view their work as a vocation involving significant
components of the moral and religious.

TIES TO THE INSTITUTIONAL CHURCH

The ties of the university to the institutional church remain important but problematic. The source of the most recent problems
has been the attempt of the hierarchy of the church to develop a
more formal and direct relationship between it and all Catholic
institutions. The vehicle for this relationship is the provision of the
Code of Canon Law that stipulates that faculty teaching in the
theological disciplines need an ecclesiastical mandate to do their
teaching in a Catholic institution of higher education. The attempt on
the part of the hierarchy of the church in the United States to enforce
this canon with a series of ordinances that would, in effect, vest the
power to hire and fire theologians in the hands of the local ordinaries is a fundamentally misguided effort. If enforced, it would
do more to dismantle the system of Catholic higher education that
has been developed over the course of the last century and a half

than would all the secularizing tendencies of the contemporary American society. The difficulties in attracting the best and the brightest Catholic faculty to Catholic institutions would be dramatically increased.

The ordinances are clearly a bad idea, as the leadership of Catholic higher education in the United States has emphatically insisted. The concern that motivated them can and should be addressed by the universities themselves, by a reaffirmation of the founding vision that inspired the creation of the system of Catholic higher education, a reaffirmation that looks not to an idealized past, but draws on experience to make the future of Catholic higher education what it has always aspired to be: the vigorous pursuit of knowledge in an environment which values the life of faith.

The Difference of a Catholic University

Otto Bird

Granted that we know what a modern university is in America at the end of the twentieth century. Not that there are not disagreements about its various functions, their relation to one another, and how they are to be accomplished. But a Catholic university as such shares a common commitment to that purpose, or purposes. The question, the problem, is how, in what respects, a Catholic university, would and should accomplish that objective. The question, in short, is one of difference. How is a Catholic university in America different from other universities, and what difference does it make?

The difference is the church, the Roman Catholic church and its magisterium, entrusted with the responsibility to conserve, teach, and promote the understanding of the revelation entrusted to it by its founder Jesus Christ and passed on through his apostles to the pope and his bishops. In short, the difference of a Catholic university is the fact of this presence of the church.

This presence is not just a matter of past history. Many of our colleges had a religious foundation, but that fact of the past has no bearing at all on their functioning in the present. The chapels still present on their campuses are now mainly ceremonial. Robert M. Hutchins, when criticized for closing at night the chapel at the University of Chicago against the express declaration in the founding charter, retorted that it was now being used more for the generation of new souls than for the regeneration of old ones. Things are different at a Catholic university. For there, in church and chapel, the sacraments are celebrated daily, providing channels of divine grace to strengthen and perfect the natural work of the university.

The presence of grace provides the vital difference: in practice, through the actions of liturgy and religion; and in doctrine, through the study and exploration of the theology of grace. Education at every level is a work of nature in that it exercises and develops powers natural to the human being. But for the Catholic university still more is needed. As St. Thomas noted, "man in the state of corrupted nature falls short even of what he can do by his nature, so that he is unable to fulfill all of it by his own natural powers." For this reason we need "a gratuitous strength superadded to natural strength," not only in order "to do and will supernatural good" but also "to be healed" so as to complete our natural work (*Summa theologica* I–II, q. 109, a. 2).

Grace as a presence and an object of study enters into the Catholic university and sets it apart from any secular university by the priority given to theology and to its closest handmaiden, philosophy. Begotten and inspired by the divine source of all truth, this university has as its mission, its responsibility, and its primary aim the pursuit of the truth, and especially of the truth in religion and theology, and in moral as well as theoretical philosophy. In these matters of theology and philosophy the Catholic university stands apart from, and opposed to, the secular schools, where the very idea of the truth, of pursuing and achieving it, is not only denigrated but denied. Our founding principle of *fides quaerens intellectum*, of faith seeking understanding, rests on the conviction not only that there is a truth to be attained, but that the intellect is capable of reaching it.

This commitment to an understanding based on Christian faith, to a natural undertaking blessed by divine grace, influences, flows into, the activity of every major function of the university and identifies the Catholic institution as unique and different from all others. The effect of this commitment can be marked on all three of the major intellectual functions of the university: on the collegiate level of liberal and general studies, on the specialized level of graduate and professional schools, and on the so-called service function of answering special demands put to it from society at large.

The Catholic difference affects all three functions by the priority that it establishes. Christianity is a historical faith that is based on actions, words, and beliefs that occurred in a particular time and place and that constitutes "the faith which has been once and for all entrusted to the saints," as is declared in the Letter to Jude. Thus the data, principles, the primary content, have been given, not discovered, and transmitted through the tradition that has conserved and treasured them in seeking ever deeper and broader understanding of them. From this, as a result, in its intellectual work priority is given to theology, philosophy, history, and the languages needed for understanding the Sacred Scriptures. The intellectual tradition that has been achieved and that continues developing provides many eminent models of Christian thought and practice. They are the giants upon whose shoulders we can stand and thus see farther than we could if we were left to ourselves.

Such is the Catholic difference in the university. What difference does it make in the way that institution functions? Consider first the collegiate function of providing a liberal and general education. Here for the Catholic the distinguishing characteristic is the overriding presence of theology and philosophy. In the secular university theology is reduced to the study of the history and comparison of religions while markedly avoiding any question of truth. The status of philosophy there is also pretty much the same. The Catholic college, however, in its commitment and devotion to the truth of its faith, ever seeks the truest theology as well as the truest philosophy. Within that tradition the theologies of St. Augustine and St. Thomas stand preeminent. They do so because they employ the truest philosophies, those of Plato and Aristotle. Hence in philosophy the work of these two thinkers deserves special and intensive study, just as Augustine and Aquinas do in theology.

Because of his or her faith the Catholic is not ashamed, disdainful, or afraid of tradition. The Bible contains a canon of great books that demand and reward the most intense study. But there exists also a tradition of great books in theology, philosophy, literature, and the natural and social sciences. At the collegiate level these great books should provide the basis of a liberal and general education. They should do so not merely because they provide the basis of our tradition, although that in itself is an important fact as well as a value, but also and even more importantly because they supply the best materials for the development of the liberal arts and the intellectual virtues. And these arts and virtues should be the primary aims of the college.

Recent years have witnessed criticism of, and attack upon, the great books as a canon that must be overthrown. The motive here has been mainly political as based on the charge that this tradition is a product of bias, being male, white, and western. This criticism is further misguided and selective in completely omitting from attack the work of science, which is also almost entirely the product of white, western males. The omission is significant, since if science were criticized for the same reason, science as we have known it, along with the truths it has established, would soon wither and die. But the very same thing would also happen to theology, philosophy, and literature if these critics were successful in the pursuit of their aims. For these disciplines would then be deprived of the essential nourishment that has contributed to developing the arts and virtues of the modern intellect.

This criticism of great books derives largely from two basic mistakes about teaching and reading. The first mistake lies in the claim that each reader constructs his or her own text. It is true that in reading a text each reader performs an activity of his own that results in his understanding of the text. But that this understanding is a free construction on the part of the individual reader is simply nonsense. For then it need have nothing at all in common with other readers of the same text nor be in any way determined by the text itself. In reading a mathematical theorem, one is not free to conclude as one likes. One has not understood, one has not read, the theorem if she has not followed the steps that lead to its particular conclusion. The same is true of a scientific exposition. A philosophical argument allows for greater differences of interpretation, while works of imaginative literature allow for the widest divergence of individual response. For this there are many reasons. One is that the verbal construct of that imaginary world presents human beings with different characters, a wide range of emotions, engaged in many activities to any one of which an individual reader may well respond differently from another. Another cause of different readings lies in the employment of language containing a wealth of metaphor and ambiguity which readily lend themselves to different interpretations.

The second mistake in the criticism of great books lies in the claim that they are culturally determined by the place and time of their origin. According to this claim, great books of the western world are great only in the western world. Yet this charge is simply not true once one considers books in all the arts and sciences. It is not true of books of science, mathematics, and logic which are transcultural in that their truths are recognized and accepted in all cultures. It is somewhat more true in works of religion and philosophy, especially as either bears upon morals or politics. In these fields, different beliefs and practices affect judgment concerning the good and the true; yet even in these matters the relativity is not complete. Imaginative literature, and poetry in particular, is most bound to its culture. This is so mainly because of its intimate dependence upon the language in which it is written. Hence the difficulty of translation and the divergence of attempts at it. Yet cultural dependence even in this area is not complete. For even in translation the excellence has been recognized in the epics of Homer, the *Divine Comedy* of Dante, the Book of Job, and the *1001 Nights.* Even in religion and theology, where reading and understanding depends still more upon the beliefs of the reader, there still remain objective standards of judgment. Thus the charge of cultural dependence and relativity of great books rests on very shaky ground.

Turning now to the graduate and professional schools, we can address the same question and ask what difference it makes for these activities to be carried on in a Catholic university. And fundamentally the answer is the same as it was for collegiate learning. It is the presence of the faith and the primary responsibility for theology. Since the very beginning of the Church, theological speculation has been engaged in exploring the meaning of the faith, identifying its basic doctrines, discerning their relations to one another, measuring and judging the effects that advances of knowledge in other fields may have upon it. The result at the highest state of magnificence and truth was the production of the great summas of medieval fame. Yet the theological task is never finished, never completed, for with the advance of knowledge there continually arise new questions that have to be addressed for their theological bearing. This has been notably the situation in our modern world where science has acted as the demiurge in pushing forward the frontiers of knowledge. For this ever-present task theology can find its greatest help in philosophy. For this discipline possesses the ability, as none of the special sciences does, of detecting, analyzing, and judging the theoretical and practical implications of the discoveries and theories of science.

In the modern world, where pluralism reigns and the university through the fragmentation brought about by specialization has become a multiversity, there is a unifying task to be undertaken. It is one capable of making the university more of an intellectual community than it now is. Intellectual unity can occur at different degrees. At its maximum, it consists in agreement regarding the true and the false, the good and the bad, thus establishing a unity of doctrine. Such a unity existed when theology and philosophy in the Catholic university were based upon the teachings of St. Thomas Aquinas. The minimal degree of unity consists in agreement upon the end that the community is pursuing, thus providing a unity of purpose. Such minimal unity is found now in most of our universities; they provide a common place in which many diverse disciplines as well as different and even opposed philosophies and theologies can all engage in the common pursuit of knowledge. In between the maximal and the minimal there is another degree of unity. This consists in agreement about the differences and the understanding of them.

In the multiversity, disagreement exists not only about conclusions but also about the principles and methods by which conclusions can be reached. So much is admitted, and with that the situation is left to lie. But there is more that can and ought to be done. Difference produces a controversial situation, and this situation can be made an object of study, research, and analysis that aims to identify and formulate the questions that pose the issues that give rise to different and conflicting answers that establish positions related in various ways to one another and involve different points of agreement and disagreement. A center that has the analysis of disagreement and controversy is needed more than ever in our present situation. It could make the fragmentized multiversity somewhat more of a university. A Catholic university in aspiring to be catholic or universal is especially adapted for such a work.

With regard to the service function that the university performs, the effect of the Catholic difference is clear. Any great university serves society in many diverse and different ways. Of these the primary and most important and its own proper responsibility is the conserving, advancing, and imparting of knowledge that are the functions of the college and graduate and professional schools. Apart from this general service, there is a special "service function," as it is now called. This consists in providing answers to particular problems or requests originating from an agency outside the university. Many such requests today come from agencies of the government. The Catholic university along with others performs many such tasks. However, the one service that is uniquely Catholic, and that cannot be supplied except under the responsibility of the Catholic church, is the educating and training of priests for its churches, schools, institutes, and offices. In the past that task has been undertaken mainly by Catholic seminaries. But in today's world that is becoming ever more the responsibility of the Catholic university.

I have said little about the function of the university as a social and cultural institution. That function makes the university a high and noble institution. But the analysis of that I leave to the other essays in this volume. I have concentrated instead on the difference of a Catholic university and the difference it makes. I have done so in the conviction that this difference provides the Catholic university with a mission that is greater, grander, higher than that of any other university.

A Catholic University

DAVID B. BURRELL, C.S.C.

As a Holy Cross priest in my thirtieth year of teaching at Notre Dame in philosophy and in theology, I have been party to countless discussions regarding what makes for a Catholic university. (It would have been smoother to write "what makes a university Catholic," but that would have presumed that the meaning of *university* was already fixed, so that *Catholic* would be an addition. I do not believe that to be so, as will appear.) Most of these conversations have focused on this university, Notre Dame, but the venue has often been a larger one, like the Association of Catholic Colleges and Universities (ACCU) in the United States, or the International Federation of Catholic Universities (IFCU) worldwide. Each time, I have contributed as a humanist, trained in theology at the Gregorian University in Rome (with Bernard Lonergan) and in philosophy first at Laval (in Thomas Aquinas) and finally at Yale (with Wilfrid Sellars, Alan Anderson, and others). During the seventies I also had responsibility for developing our faculty of theology at Notre Dame, so I was involved institutionally with these questions. Yet the most significant steps for me began in Jerusalem in 1980, as I rounded off ten years of reflection on theological education to serve as rector of the Ecumenical Institute for Theological Research (Tantur). Stimulated by Karl Rahner's prescient reflections on the matter, that experience opened my eyes to a broader ecumenism, specifically among Jews,

Christians, and Muslims.[1] It is that interfaith perspective which has shaped my teaching and writing over the past dozen years and may offer a particular perspective on the question of a Catholic university.[2]

Universities are in large part products of their cultures, and we in North America have inherited a hybrid of English and German educational and scholarly expectations. Moreover, Catholic education in North America has been indirectly fostered by a liberal social and political climate in whose ecology independent initiatives found generous niches in which to flourish. As a result many of the institutions of higher education owe their origins to church ventures and their development to the generosity of donors who value the presence of such an educational milieu. In that significant cultural respect, Catholic colleges and universities belong to a larger set of church-related institutions of higher education. Yet there remains an additional shaping feature for Catholic ventures: the religious congregation that initiated and has continued to sponsor most of them. For these families of religious—male and female—have contributed a particular spirit and an affective presence to their schools and even added another aim to higher education: formation. This goal most visibly sets Catholic colleges and universities off from their independent counterparts, so that the erosion of this dimension most often brings charges of secularization (or more literally, worldliness) from interested parties. Moreover, this dimension stands threatened by a view of the university as a place of "purely intellectual" exchange to which concerns like formation in virtue can only appear extraneous. So a Catholic college or university (like Notre Dame) can easily be caricatured as clerical in administration, narrow in outlook, and a French boarding school in practice.

This university had to fight against that caricature in its postwar era of incredible expansion, led by Theodore Hesburgh, C.S.C. Since that period was also punctuated by Vatican II, one can note a clear symbiosis between the American church's emergence from a distinctly parochial culture and Catholic higher education's parallel and sympathetic movement. Since that effort spanned my years here first as a student and then as a faculty member, it is fascinating to attempt a retrospective. (And useful as well, for one cannot silence current queries whether we and others have not adapted all too well to a larger academic climate that will prove arid not only for our religious ideals but even for our educational goals. That question will occupy the bulk of these current reflections.) For students the adaptation consisted palpably in reducing rules! My initial year at the university after ordination and prior to graduate studies found me acting as a liaison between administration committees mandated to carry out such changes and student groups intent on maximizing them. The presence of veterans had rendered earlier French boarding school practices manifestly obsolete, so the university administration responded with a line of accommodation, soon to be reinforced with Vatican II changes in church practice as well.

Yet the administrations of Father Hesburgh and of John Cavanaugh before him had set their sights primarily on educational practices: to enhance the quality of faculty and programs; in short, to make Notre Dame a viable conversation partner in the dialogue shaping American higher education. The religious congregation undergirding Notre Dame—the Congregation of Holy Cross—was a relative newcomer in religious families (1841) and quite without any tradition in higher education. So its intellectual leaders took their bearings from the wider American scene at the time, often citing educational leaders like Robert Hutchins at Chicago and Nicholas Murray Butler at Columbia.[3] A few luminaries stand out, however: from the turn of the century, John Zahm, and from the early decades, James Burns. These men stimulated others to study and to conceive of Notre Dame in terms grander than educating Catholics from the region to take their place in society, although that goal tended to dominate institutional thinking until the years after World War II. The stories of these pioneers and of those who responded to their inspiration remains to be written, however, as institutions like ours have been preoccupied with making their mark in a larger academic world. To that effort we must turn.

Recent developments in American intellectual culture have substantially altered the terms of discussion of a Catholic university, yet we may ask whether institutional goals set in the era of expansion have taken cognizance of them? I am referring to the perspective which sees any intellectual inquiry as fiduciary and so not merely tolerating but actually requiring commitment. Moreover, these commitments may resist direct scrutiny yet they clearly fuel the entire venture. In Alasdair MacIntyre's felicitous expression, all inquiry is "tradition-directed" inquiry.[4] In Alvin Plantinga's words, diverse sets of beliefs are structured by "basic beliefs" which provide a floor for discussion and are not normally themselves up for discussion.[5] The fact that these two are members of the Notre Dame philosophy faculty and that their works are published by the University of Notre Dame Press testifies to the degree of sophistication which has accrued to the central question of this volume and also to its inherently ecumenical perspective. In short, there is no such thing as a *university*, full stop. There are different kinds of universities, beholden to diverse educational traditions. The crucial question for any of them is whether the tradition which they embody respects and fosters freedom of inquiry? Is any question fair game, or are some queries ruled out antecedently?

The very form of this question intimates a conflict with faith traditions, since believers customarily hold certain things to be true as part of their primary response to a revelation which they take to be from God. The primary response is a personal and ostensibly wholehearted one; it may be argued how closely specific beliefs are connected with that response, but some will certainly be germane: God's initiative and providence, for example, as well as human beings' capacity to respond and to be transformed accordingly. So views of human nature or of the cosmos which would leave no room for such a transaction would on the face of it be offensive to such believers. And were faculty members to incorporate views antithetical to the faith of the community in their teaching of students, how could they be tolerated? Since we know that they would not have been tolerated in many church-related institutions of higher education over the years, the question is a live one within a history of conflict. If we are to adhere to the pattern of "tradition-directed" inquiry, the question will become: How open can such traditions be to differences in viewpoint, conviction, and to diversity more generally?

Here a Catholic tradition must be distinguished from later Christian strains, for Catholics can claim a legacy reaching into the high Middle Ages where disputed questions offered the pattern for educational strategy, and where a relative autonomy of such educational endeavors from ecclesiastical authorities had already been negotiated. One institutional vehicle for such relative autonomy has been the religious congregation whose members have customarily taught and administered such institutions. (While religious are certainly subject to ecclesiastical authority, they are so indirectly and hence can often mediate disputes with an ear to both sides.) So the classic American scenario of conflict between church administrators (many of whom have little understanding or sympathy for the openness required for intellectual inquiry) and university faculty or administrators has been less a feature of the Catholic academic environment. Our tradition has rather been bedeviled by the arbitrary exercise of authority on the part of clerical or religious authorities within the institution, or by curricula designed to convey an intellectual formation to complement the moral one. I am better placed to comment on curricular matters, and particularly on the subject of philosophy.

It is significant that Father Hesburgh used to signal our commitment to Catholic education by gesturing to the fact that we had come to require two courses in philosophy and two in theology of every undergraduate student at Notre Dame. And it is even more significant that many felt such a requirement to be scandalously minimal! It had in fact been scaled back in the mid-sixties by a university curriculum reform and thereafter adhered to as a prime feature of our university core. (It is crucial here to speak of a university requirement, for other Catholic institutions would often distinguish students for traditional liberal arts degrees from those in more professional programs, asking more philosophy of the former and very little of the latter.) And the scale-back was complemented by a concerted effort to improve offerings in both disciplines, but especially in theology. For the academic study of theology was a relative newcomer to Catholic higher education, interestingly enough, while philosophy had long been fostered and supported at the graduate level as well.[6] The reason for this apparent anomaly lay in the traditional Catholic separation of the two disciplines, according to whether premises taken from revelation entered into one's argumentation or not, together with the relative monopoly on postgraduate theological training by more formally ecclesiastical institutions such as the Catholic University of America and various European faculties. (It is significant that Saint Mary's College launched a postgraduate program in theology for women, at the initiative of its long-time president, Sister Madaleva, because women were not welcome as students for higher degrees at the ecclesiastical institutions. Notre Dame itself, like many other Catholic universities in North America, did not inaugurate doctoral programs in theology until the late sixties.)

More positively, philosophy had been seen among Catholics as the vehicle for confronting a wider culture, since its premises were presumed to be taken from reason itself while theology involved a particular faith commitment. As we shall see, this presumption was jejune, since all inquiry can be seen to involve commitments of one sort or another, as the history of developments in Catholic philosophy will testify. Yet convictions regarding the relative autonomy of reason fueled investment in philosophy at Catholic institutions, and these were bolstered by the more constructive view of philosophical reason as a positive factor in developing an articulate tradition of faith: "Faith seeking understanding." Both views embody a legacy reaching far back into the early Middle Ages to Anselm and corroborated by later thinkers like Albert and Thomas Aquinas—all of whom have also been celebrated by the tradition as saints as well, so confirming the propriety of argument and disputation as integral to this tradition of faith. (This constructive factor tends to distinguish Catholic from later Christian families of faith, as testified by the relative absence of a philosophical curriculum in most Protestant colleges or seminaries.) Moreover, philosophy in Catholic colleges and universities had been given a specific boost by the encyclical of Pope Leo XIII (*Aeterne Patris*) which sought to direct the attention of the Catholic intellectual and academic community to the legacy of Thomas Aquinas.

Especially that encyclical and the enthusiasm it generated gave philosophy the prominence it enjoyed in the curriculum of American Catholic colleges and universities in this century. Yet ironically enough, the discipline which was supposed to have begun conversation with a wider intellectual and academic culture turned out in fact to isolate Catholics from the American philosophical ethos. For the philosophical tradition expressly promoted by Leo XIII in *Aeterne Patris* seemed to American contemporaries to be antiquarian and antecedently committed to conclusions favorable to Catholic faith. What was supposed to have proceeded from pure reason was quickly seen to be imbedded in a tradition of inquiry whose horizons seemed quite foreign to what others supposed was an unfettered exercise of rational inquiry. Hindsight allows us to see that each side was misled in its assessment of the other, since "pure reason" or its "unfettered exercise" may both be seen to be chimera. But the climate was such that neither group was able to communicate very well with the other, so that Catholics after Vatican II tended to side with the others' assessment of Thomism and abandon the experiment. Before long, however, a set of convictions regarding "tradition-directed" inquiry allowed greater voice to pluralism in intellectual strategies in philosophy, so Catholics found fresh respect for the tradition of Thomas Aquinas, yet this time minus the claims of Thomism to have offered a purely rational account of things. It was perhaps inevitable that such respect came at first from others, but in a relatively short thirty years since Vatican II something of Pope Leo's original promise may be said to have been realized, although in a completely unexpected way.

That development has been acted out here at Notre Dame by the way in which a faculty of philosophy was moved, largely through the initiative of Ernan McMullin during the sixties and seventies, from one with a specifically Thomist focus to a pluralistic faculty which seems to thrive at a Catholic university. Moreover, I would like to examine how the two—pluralist and Catholic—go together, for that may help us learn something positive about the task of becoming a Catholic university. (It is increasingly a presumption of current discussion that a Catholic university is a task; what it is to mean now will take bearings from the past but be realized in ways as yet unexplored.) The first lesson to be learned from the saga of philosophy in Catholic institutions of higher learning in this century is that Pope Leo's initiative was two-edged. While it succeeded on the one hand in giving philosophy a place of honor by promoting and even mandating a specific mode of philosophical inquiry, it also had some deleterious effects. One of these was purely sociological: asking that a specific philosophy be taught to large numbers of students required a proportionately large number of teachers to be trained, with the predictable statistical result that many of them would not be very good.[7] The other is more subtle: How can an ecclesial body foster a particular philosophy? While it would be proper to stimulate scholarship in a particular tradition, it does not seem appropriate to promote specific conclusions. And that is precisely the wisdom we seem to have gained from the historical dialectic of the past thirty years.

So a Catholic university will want positively to promote scholarship in a specifically Catholic tradition in philosophy yet also want to be in conversation with the wider world of academic philosophy.

That dual desire will positively foster diversity within its faculty of philosophy. Moreover, in such a climate the scholarship into Thomist and other Catholic traditions of philosophy will have a chance to interact with a broader stream of discourse—something which the earlier unique focus on Thomist thought in fact prevented. So the tension between a communitarian and a pluralist model for Catholic higher education can be illustrated in the ways in which current faculties of philosophy in such institutions have made this transition. Those of a communitarian persuasion will prefer a distinctive focus; those of a more pluralist bent will encourage diversity. But how can we reasonably hope that diversity will lead to pluralism and not to fragmentation? This question is more pressing in that each of the terms—*diversity* and *pluralism*—are often used in persuasive and ideological ways. In fact, diversity alone need not have any cohesive center; and *pluralism* is often used honorifically to signal one's hope that diversity will lead to fruitful conversation rather than mere standoff. Again, our model at Notre Dame in philosophy has turned on a practice supposedly endemic to philosophy itself, if not to the university more widely: conversation. We have committed ourselves to a weekly colloquium in which faculty and students listen to one another. Diverse viewpoints do not make this any easier, of course, but they can make it more interesting. What has happened in fact is that the history of philosophy has become the lingua franca of our colloquia while a distinctive feature of the philosophical training of our graduate students remains attention to the history of philosophy.

One fringe benefit of attending to the history of a discipline, interestingly enough, is a certain distance from current philosophical fads. History offers perspective, and attention to history is positively fostered, it seems, by our Catholic tradition. Here we have a specific way in which being Catholic can abet being pluralistic. Moreover, this would hardly be worth mentioning if institutions without such a tradition to invoke were not currently bedeviled with intellectual fads. It is hard to know what to make of this, yet without aligning oneself with naysayers and prophets of doom, there are indications that our Catholic moorings can offer us a comparative advantage educationally in the academic world in which we live. The challenge will be to articulate this perspective in terms which will not easily be mistaken as denominational or parochial.

As I mentioned at the outset, contemporary reflection on all inquiry as "tradition-directed" may help us both to foster a particular tradition as well as to open conversation more widely. Both are needed if we are to be Catholic in name and in spirit, and faithful as well to a vigorous tradition of rational inquiry.

I noted that I speak as a humanist. Can anything of this be transferred to other disciplines? Can our experience with philosophy help others to articulate a path for themselves which could lead to an analogous comparative advantage? Are there ecological niches in the wider American academic scene, discipline by discipline, which will allow Catholic universities to foster what is best in our tradition while making a distinguished and distinguishable contribution to a larger scene? If these can be located, it should be clear that our programs will attract the kind of students whom we seek, and we would then be poised to make the contribution which we think we should be making to the American intellectual milieu. Yet locating them will require imagination and conviction on the part of faculty, and faculty are not endowed with these much more than the general population. One feature is particularly promising, however, and that is the shared sense of mission which can be found among people of other faiths. So long as the quest for Catholic identity can be pursued in a sufficiently inclusive manner, calling upon all who see their life as a gift, their work as a call rather than a career, and our relation to the world as conservation rather than exploitation, we will find many people open to the invitation to join such a venture. They will be people of other faiths or of no recognizable faith at all, yet personally searching for something more than standard academe. If our Catholic heritage will allow us to become distinctive in that way, we can find willing and committed allies.

Notes

1. Rahner's essay, "Towards a Fundamental Interpretation of Vatican II," *Theological Studies* 40 (1979): 716–27, has been variously reprinted—e.g., *African Ecclesiastical Review* 100 (December 1980). See my reflections: "Jerusalem and the Future of Theological Inquiry," *Tantur Yearbook*, 1981–1982, 35–55.

2. Specifically, *Knowing the Unknowable God: Ibn-Sina, Maimonides, Aquinas* (Notre Dame, Ind.: University of Notre Dame Press, 1986); *Al-Ghazali on the Ninety-nine Beautiful Names of God*, trans. with Nazih Daher (Cambridge:

Islam Texts Society, 1992); and *Freedom and Creation in Three Traditions* (Notre Dame, Ind.: University of Notre Dame Press, 1993).

3. The volumes of the Educational Conference of the Priests of Holy Cross, published for four decades from the mid-twenties until the early sixties, offer documentation for this observation. Like so many such ventures, Vatican II made them appear parochial, and discussions assumed a wider perspective.

4. The best presentation of this thesis can be found in Alasdair MacIntyre's Gifford lectures: *Three Rival Versions of Moral Enquiry* (Notre Dame, Ind.: University of Notre Dame Press, 1990).

5. Among others, see the essays in *Faith and Rationality: Reason and Belief in God,* ed. Alvin Plantinga and Nicholas Wolterstorff (Notre Dame, Ind.: University of Notre Dame Press, 1983).

6. See the illuminating remarks by Philip Gleason on this role for philosophy, in *Keeping the Faith* (Notre Dame, Ind.: University of Notre Dame Press, 1987), chap. 2.

7. I owe this observation to a conversation with I. M. Bochenski, O.P., some twenty-five years ago, who succinctly formulated what many of us had observed.

Two Faces of Academic Freedom

FREDERICK J. CROSSON

"Academic freedom," wrote Richard Hofstadter forty years ago, "is a modern term for an ancient idea. . . . [I]ts continuous history is concurrent with the history of universities since the twelfth century."[1] That ancient idea is the singular nature of a certain kind of educational institution and the things due such an institution because of its nature, because of the nature of the activity of teaching and learning at a certain level. Given the kind of enterprise in which it is engaged—namely, a communal enterprise of trying to understand and to share an understanding of the way things are—it requires and claims a necessary, if limited, autonomy from outside interference.

Looking at the early years of the University of Paris shows that the awareness of this status was recognized very quickly. That famous Catholic university (the adjective was then redundant) took its origin from the cathedral school of Notre Dame, which grew in size due to attracting masters (*magistri*) and students from all over Europe. The increasing number of masters and students led to classes being taught outside the cathedral cloister (and hence outside the immediate supervision of the cathedral), expanding over to the south bank near St. Germain-des-Prés (hence the "Latin Quarter") and to St. Genviève-du-Mont on the north bank. Following the pattern of the guild movement, the masters had formed themselves into an association by the middle of the twelfth century, and in 1200 the corpora-

45

tion was chartered by the king with certain immunities and privileges vis-à-vis local jurisdictions.

The clarification and consolidation of these immunities took time and was punctuated by protests on the part of students and faculties, in which the most potent power of the latter was a kind of strike, a suspension of lectures until the status of the university was acknowledged. Thus in 1228–1229, several students were killed in clashes with townspeople and soldiers, and the masters suspended lectures in protest. Of course the cooperation and discipline of all of the masters was necessary for this to be effective, and it is significant that they acted together in asserting their collective right to immunity from local jurisdiction.[2] One of the results of this incident was the issuance of the papal bull *Parens Scientiarum* in 1231, which gave the university the right to suspend lectures and confirmed its authority to make its own statutes and punish masters or students who violated them.

By the middle of the thirteenth century, the acknowledged autonomy of the university (and of course Paris was not singular in this regard) was quite extensive:

> It enjoyed, among other exemptions, immunity from the civil and criminal jurisdiction of the local magistrates, from the disciplinary ban of excommunication by the local bishop, from all tolls and taxes. . . . The University had the right to make and enforce rules and regulations for its own members; to set up courses and examinations; to regulate the time, content and method of teaching.[3]

But of course its autonomy was not sovereignty. For example, the degrees were awarded de jure by a delegate of the Roman see, the chancellor of Notre Dame who served as chancellor of the university. There was also a rector, chosen from among the members of the faculty of arts, who was head of the university and who was elected by the masters. But the chancellor awarded the degree because it was a *licentia ubique docendi,* a license to teach anywhere (i.e., at any of the existing universities not just at Paris), and that status had to be granted by a higher authority. However, the chancellor could not refuse to grant a license to anyone recommended by the masters of the respective faculty.[4]

The academic freedom of the university, its acknowledged authoritative competence over its internal affairs, and which was the result of the recognition of its emerging nature as a sui generis institution of society, was not identical with what is today generally called academic freedom. It was not a freedom of individuals but a freedom of the university from external control over its academic undertakings and for the purpose of achieving its natural purpose, namely (as noted before), the determination of the truth in matters of theology, philosophy, law, and medicine, and the preparation of students to share in that work. It bears underlining that the freedom striven for was corporate: it was for the body of masters and students as a whole, as a Universitas Magistrorum et Discipulorum.

A corollary of that corporate responsibility for the academic enterprise was its internal supervision: the regulation of the teaching and learning as it unfolded in the courses, in the methods, texts, examinations, and even of attire.[5] Assuming responsibility for upholding its own standards and keeping its own order—since it won the recognition of that right from both pope and king—the corporate body of the masters was logically led to the regulation of the teaching of its own members.

> For the liberties which enabled them to exercise their intellectual functions made possible also the corporate imposition and enforcement of restrictions. Now it was the institution and its parts which not only claimed freedom but exercised control . . . [and asserted] the right of the corporation to impose restrictions on the teaching of its members.[6]

A control, one might observe, required by the assumption of the responsibility.

It should not be necessary, but it may not be amiss, to observe that medieval universities were not part of the "dark ages."[7]

> The modern lay reader, under the influence of an old rationalist stereotype, often thinks of the Middle Ages only as an age of dogma and suppression. Unless, however, . . . the full vigor of the clash of interests and doctrines in its intellectual milieu, notably in the thirteenth and fourteenth centuries, is seen, neither the remarkable corporate power of the university nor the independence and boldness of some of its outstanding masters will be appreciated.[8]

. . . the liberty of thought permitted within the pale of Catholic Christianity was far greater than has generally been supposed. . . . At the height of its maturity medieval thought displayed a latitude which is truly surprising; the speculation of the twelfth and thirteenth centuries contains a diversity which quite belies the notion of any orthodoxy rigourously imposed from without.[9]

. . . there seems no adequate proof for a single specific instance of persecution of men of science by the church for purely scientific views in the twelfth and thirteenth centuries. The occasions when such men got into trouble and when we know the reason why, are just those occasions when they left science to dabble in theological or ecclesiastical concerns.[10]

The reader will pardon the piling on of quotations (they could easily be multiplied): the point is simply to indicate that the existence of an internal authority over academic matters does not necessarily entail (and did not) wrongful suppression of intellectual inquiry. Rather, the acknowledged autonomy of the university as responsible for its own enterprise obliged the university to oversee the internal operation of teaching and learning.

Hofstadter comments [in 1955]:

The recent tendency among some academic men in the United States to propose more rigorous academic self-discipline or self-censorship in return for an anticipated broader respect for university independence from the community shows a disposition, however unwitting, to move somewhat closer to the medieval equipoise between corporate autonomy and academic freedom.[11]

The language of the final comparison points toward exactly the issue to be addressed from a juridical context in the following section of this essay: namely, the current use of the term *academic freedom* to refer to individual freedom and not to the freedom of the university as a corporate body. It has become customary among academics to use the term only in its individual signification, perhaps largely because an association of university professors has been in the forefront of the battle for academic freedom, i.e., individual academic freedom.

But the brief review above of the early emergence of university autonomy, of the academic freedom of the medieval university, suggests that that autonomy is more fundamental than, and presupposed to, individual academic freedom. If one thinks of the list above of the immunities and privileges acknowledged by tiara and crown to belong to the nature of the (medieval) university enterprise, one will not be totally surprised to find the Supreme Court, in perhaps its most quoted dictum on academic freedom, confirming that nature. Academic freedom is constituted by, as Justice Frankfurter (himself a former Harvard professor) wrote in 1957, "the four essential freedoms of a university—to determine for itself on academic grounds who may teach, what may be taught, how it shall be taught, and who may be admitted to study."[12]

It is important to be clear about the difference of individual academic freedom from institutional academic freedom on the one hand and the citizen's right to freedom of speech, on the other. The first difference should be at least moderately in sight after the previous historical review.[13] The other difference is accessible to the reflection of anyone even vaguely familiar with the first amendment rights guaranteed by the U.S. Constitution. For those rights belong to every citizen and protect the person against (among other things) unwarranted restrictions on the expression of opinion. But individual academic freedom belongs to someone in virtue of a function exercised as a member of a specific kind of institution, namely, an institution of higher education.[14] It is not the same as the ordinary citizen's right to freedom of speech, although much writing about academic freedom does not reflect an awareness of the difference. Criticisms of censorship in an academic context often merge with the appeal to freedom of speech. Of course every faculty member, as a citizen, possesses those rights also, but they are distinct, logically and juridically, from individual (or corporate) academic freedom.

Court cases involving academic freedom can be generally divided into three categories: individuals (professors) against the state; individuals against university administrations or boards of trustees; universities against the state (institutional academic freedom cases). Although cases in the categories have been decided under the first amendment, the appearance of academic freedom in Supreme Court cases is relatively recent: the first mention of the term in a (dissenting) Court opinion dates only from 1952. And, as a constitutional scholar of the issue has written:

> The Supreme Court . . . has not developed a comprehensive theory of academic freedom . . . as a distinctive First Amendment doctrine. The relationship between "individual" and "institutional" academic freedom has not been clarified. Nor has the Supreme Court decided whether academic freedom is a separate principle, with its own constitutional contours justified by the unique roles of professors and universities in society, or whether it highlights but is essentially co-extensive with the general First Amendment rights of all citizens.[15]

The same scholar, after an extensive review of the cases of the last four decades, has offered his own judgment on the normative issues involved:

> Concern about judicial competence and respect for institutional academic freedom . . . should preclude courts from intervening in internal debates between faculty and administrators over the definition of professional quality [tenure issues]. Although peer review, procedural safeguards in tenure decisions, and faculty participation in university governance may all promote individual academic freedom, courts should also be reluctant to impose them on universities as first amendment requirements, particularly because doing so might weaken academic freedom at its substantive core.[16]

One might put it even more strongly: treating the academic freedom of individuals within a university simply as a first amendment right would be to ignore the specific nature of the university and to infringe or ignore the most fundamental academic freedom, that of the autonomy of the university vis-à-vis the state. From this respect, the proper role of the judiciary should be to exclude public officials from interference with properly academic affairs.[17]

A case in the early 1980s involved this issue. Princeton University had a policy requiring outsiders who wished to distribute leaflets on campus to have an invitation from a member of the university or permission from the dean of Student Affairs, and when a person with neither nevertheless distributed materials for a political party, he was arrested and tried. On appeal, the New Jersey Supreme Court regarded it as a case of conflict between the "protections to be accorded private property" and "expressional freedoms" and found against the university. It was appealed to the U.S. Supreme Court (though not decided because the issue was moot before the case was heard), and in its statement, Princeton argued that its academic freedom under the first amendment was disregarded by the state court, which assumed "the ancient right of a university community to determine how its educational philosophy may best be implemented." Princeton claimed that, at least for a private university, its choice of educational philosophy, "however broad, orthodox or eccentric, is immunized by first amendment academic freedom from interference by the state," that no governmental branch is constitutionally competent to adjudicate a private university's educational goals, whatever may be the state's jurisdiction over health and safety standards.[18]

Amy Gutmann, a professor of politics at Princeton, who is critical of the university's position in this case, agrees with their argument on a generic principle:

> If its name is more than a pretext for tax exemption, every college and university in the United States is dedicated to furthering the life of the mind. But universities disagree upon the standards that are to guide that life, and who within them should determine those standards. American universities, public and private, sectarian and liberal, share one, perhaps only one common point of agreement: that the state should not determine what those standards are.[19]

When it comes to the question of individual academic freedom, she comments that the

> idea of academic freedom for scholars, as derived from the German concept of *Lehrfreiheit,* is neither a universal right of citizenship nor a contractual right of university employees. It is perhaps best understood as a special right tied to the particular role or office of scholar, similar in form (but different in content) to the particular rights of priests, doctors, lawyers and journalists.[20]

This seems generally correct, except that individuals in the four latter roles, while they may be members of guilds or professional associations, can have and exercise their office as individuals, in contrast to the university professor.[21]

Adjudicating the possible conflicts of these two kinds of academic freedom, Gutmann concedes that on either the corporatist or liberal democratic models, there could be legitimate grounds for a university to oversee and regulate internal academic freedom. Under either the corporate or the liberal democratic model, she argues, individual academic freedom would come under constitutional jurisdiction only insofar as it was contractually assured at the time of faculty appointment. If a faculty contract of appointment contained guarantees of academic freedom, those could come under the constitutional protection of contracts freely entered into. If a contract of appointment did not contain such guarantees, there might be grounds for regulating individual academic freedom which were constitutionally protected as exercises of institutional academic freedom. That is, "limitations upon academic freedom within universities . . . demand sufficient institutional reasons, which in some cases can be found within the established religious or other ideological purposes of a private university."[22]

Even before the court cases of the last four decades, the American Association of University Professors and the American Association of Colleges jointly issued their 1940 Statement of Principles on Academic Freedom and Tenure. That statement, while it does not mention institutional academic freedom, implicitly alludes to it in the "limitation clause" (as it has come to be known): "Limitations of academic freedom because of religious or other aims of the institution should be clearly stated at the time of appointment."

Twenty-five years after that statement and consistent with it, Committee A (on academic freedom and tenure) of the AAUP declared in 1965, in a case involving a Jesuit university, that "satisfactory conditions of academic freedom and tenure now prevail at Gonzaga University" even though the university required each faculty member to "be careful not to introduce into his teaching controversial matter which . . . is contrary to the specified aims of the institution" and reserved the right to dismiss nontenured faculty for "inculcation of viewpoints which contradict explicit principles of Catholic faith and morals."[23]

But before long (in 1970), a committee of the AAUP issued an "interpretive comment" to the statement asserting that "most church-related institutions no longer need or desire the departure from the principle of academic freedom implied in the 1940 Statement, and we do not now endorse such a departure." In 1988, a subcommittee of

Committee A took a further step in a report recommending that the limitations clause be understood as disapproving any institution's invoking of it, on the grounds that by doing so, the institution would forfeit "the moral right to proclaim themselves as authentic seats of higher learning."[24]

The full Committee A after publishing the subcommittee report sensibly commented that it could not accept that interpretation, "due in part to the belief that it is not appropriate for the Association to decide what is and what is not an authentic institution in higher education." It immediately added, "The committee did not conclude, however, that invocation of the clause does not relieve an institution of its obligation to afford academic freedom as called for in the 1940 Statement."[25] Not only is it difficult to understand what the last comment means for the whole issue (Is there a limitation clause that can be legitimately invoked or is there not?) but it renders obscure what are to be understood as the proper grounds for censure motions in such cases.

There the matter stands, murkily. On the basis of constitutional precedent and on the basis of the reading of the limitation clause for at least twenty-five years, institutions should not be censured for regulating individual academic freedom in the name of institutional academic freedom, so long as that is set out clearly at the time of appointment. One conceivable course of action for the AAUP would be to replace, if its membership so desired, the language of the 1940 statement. However, that course presents awkwardnesses, since not only was the statement issued jointly by the AAUP and the AAC (which has of course approved neither the 1970 nor the 1988 AAUP comments), but the 1940 statement has subsequently been endorsed by some 120 educational and professional societies and to replace it would be to lose, at least at the beginning, that collective endorsement.[26]

Quite apart from these legal-hermeneutical issues, there are other reasons for respecting the primacy of institutional academic freedom with respect to individual academic freedom. It seems very likely that the insistence on the primacy of individual academic freedom would increase the diversity of religious and nonreligious views represented within, for example, a religiously affiliated college or university, since it would in effect proscribe the invoking of any limitation clause. Institutional academic freedom, the freedom of the institution as a community of inquirers to commit itself to the pursuit of truth within a religious tradition, would yield to the right of individuals to decide whether to do so or not.

But while this would be the likely internal effect, it would also lead to the diminishment of diversity among institutions of higher education, since it would, before long, eliminate the distinctive religious character of such institutions. Not only would this be arguably contrary to the free exercise clause, it would be contrary to the philosophical argument that all voices should be allowed to be heard if we are to have a chance at exchanging our limited views of what is true for more ample ones. To eliminate the distinctive voice of the community of inquirers represented by a religious university seems more akin to the suppression of freedom of inquiry than to its fostering. Nor can it be plausibly responded that those individual professors who are religious can always pursue issues from the perspective which concerns them, since the pursuit of truth requires for its stimulation and development the sharing of different points of view within a community and tradition of inquiry. If there is nothing in one's environment which fosters such a community, it is unlikely to flourish. If few or none in one's academic community share the perspective under which one approaches intellectual matters and if the institution does not prize it, it will be difficult to sustain.

Diversity of perspectives is itself a desirable good in the pursuit of truth (quite apart from its consistency with democratic pluralism), and it would be ironic if "a principle born of opposition to dogmatism itself became dogmatic and authoritarian."[27] Perhaps it is worth noting that reference is often made in these discussions to Socrates as an exemplar of the undaunted questioning of conventional wisdom. John Stuart Mill cites him, in the essay *On Liberty*, as one who claimed to know nothing and to ask questions about everything. Mary McLaughlin points to him as one who "defends his right to the free pursuit and utterance of truth."[28] But in fact in Plato's *Apology*, he not only claims to know some things (29b, 37b, 41c), he repeatedly insists that he is resisting the opinion of Athens because he is obeying god rather than man (28e, 29d, 30a, 33c, 37e). It is in fact historically the case that resistance to social and civil authority has generally been motivated by the conviction that one should obey God rather than man, as Martin Luther King argued in his *Letter from a Birmingham Jail*.

As for the idea that truth can be effectively pursued within the context of beliefs that are not themselves completely subject to rational verification, that claim seems not only verified by history (most universities were Christian, after all, until the last hundred years), it is in fact analogous to the normal situation of inquiry even in the natural sciences. The distinguished chemist, Michael Polanyi, relating the story of the decades-long resistance to his new theory of adsorption and how difficult it was to get a fair hearing for it, accepts that as appropriate for scientific method. Contrasting his view with that of Bertrand Russell, he quotes the latter: "The triumphs of science are due to the substitution of observation and inference for authority. Every attempt to revive authority in intellectual matters is a retrograde step." Polanyi comments: "Such statements obscure the fact that the authority of current scientific opinion is indispensable to the discipline of scientific institutions; that its functions are invaluable, even though its dangers are an unceasing menace to scientific progress."[29]

The contention of the argument thus far is not that all religious institutions of higher education should invoke the priority of institutional to individual academic freedom in order to preserve their religious character: some will not be interested in doing so; some will have already lost their religious character, and there are likely to be reasons why it has drifted away. But the argument does aim at defending the legality and the appropriateness of such a claim when an institution wants to preserve its religious nature.[30]

The most critical area for the issue of academic freedom in higher education is in the seminaries or in the departments of theology, and a closer look at some aspects of this area is pertinent to these reflections. To simplify the problematic, we will restrict the discussion to theology in universities.

———

Cardinal Newman's analysis in *The Idea of a University* of the role of theology will serve as a useful point of departure. Written in 1852, these classic discourses address the question of the nature of a university—not of a Catholic university, but of any genuine institution of higher education. Only in the last of the nine discourses does he consider what would distinguish a university under the auspices of the Catholic church.

One of his themes is the need to include theology—knowledge

about God—in the encyclopedia of disciplines and subject matters in the university. If theology is not included as a field of study, what will happen (and this argument applies to the absence of any of the basic fields of study) is that the other disciplines—psychology, literature, philosophy, et al.—will assume the role of making pronouncements about divinity and religion, since the topic is of such significance historically and currently that it cannot and will not be ignored. Theology is an academic discipline, and a university (Newman knows colleges only as parts of a university), i.e., any institution which purports to teach the basic disciplines, must include it to be truly a university.

Indeed it seems to me that in this respect Newman could have subscribed to the comment of the 1988 report of the AAUP subcommittee of Committee A referred to above, which declared, "if theology is an academic discipline, it must be treated as any other discipline. Higher education is not catechesis."[31] Theology, as Newman understands the term, is indeed not catechesis: it is a branch of knowledge (he sometimes calls it "Religion"), independently of any revelation.

But suppose a community of people[32] comes to believe that it is a fact that the object of that discipline, God, has himself spoken to us, has spoken of himself and of latent aspects of the human situation. It would be irrational for such persons not to conduct their theological inquiries in the light of the things revealed, seeking to understand in depth the words that God had spoken. Their faith, their belief, would seek understanding through a theological inquiry basing itself on those words written down long ago. And now if part of that community also believed, as Catholics do, that in order to preserve the clarity and certainty of the meaning of those words, God had constituted a perduring authoritative interpreter to help the theological inquiry by keeping it from errors, then it would be foolish for a university under Catholic auspices to conduct its theological inquiries independently of that aid.

And that is Newman's position:

> though it had ever so many theological Chairs, that would not suffice to make it a Catholic University; for theology would be included in its teaching only as a branch of knowledge. . . . [T]he Church has no call to watch over and protect Science: but toward Theology she has a distinct duty: it is one of the special trusts committed to her keeping.

Where Theology is, there she must be; and if a University cannot ful-
fil its name and office without the recognition of Revealed Truth, she
must be there to see that it is a *bona fide* recognition, sincerely made and
consistently acted on.[33]

So while certain academic subjects such as natural or philosophical theology, history of religion, etc. may be only "branches of
knowledge," a theology based on revealed premises cannot by its
nature be such. And if those premises are not susceptible of unlim-
ited construal but only construal within a tradition of authoritative
hermeneutic, then the conduct of theology in a Catholic university
cannot be independent of the church. It hardly needs to be added
that this does not transform theology into catechesis. Such a claim
can only seem humorous to anyone who has tried to read Aquinas,
say, or Barth or Rahner.

Theology in a Catholic institution cannot but be conducted with
the help of a tradition of inquiry in which some things are assuredly
known. To deny that they are would be effectively to remove oneself
from that tradition of inquiry. Father Charles Curran, who was
dismissed from the pontifical faculty of theology at the Catholic
University of America, agrees that a Catholic theologian must "the-
ologize within the sources and parameters of the Catholic faith" and
that among the grounds for dismissal of a tenured professor as an
incompetent Catholic theologian would be not believing in Jesus or
not accepting a role for the pope in the Church.[34]

But that "some things are assuredly known" does not mean either
that everything is known or even that most of the questions which
understanding can address to faith have been formulated, let alone
answered. That is why even a theology based on the premises of
faith is not and cannot ever be a closed system, for reasons which
Newman argued in *The Development of Christian Doctrine*. And that is
why theologians and Catholic thinkers in general need individual
academic freedom, why they need to be part of a community of
inquiry, why indeed the church needs to assure that freedom so that
the meaning of the premises of faith can be unfolded and their
understanding deepened.

The main thrust of these pages has been to maintain only that on
constitutional, historical, and philosophical grounds, institutional
academic freedom in religious institutions of higher education may
claim priority over individual academic freedom, and that the courts

may and have recognized that autonomy. The other side of institutional academic freedom, namely, with respect to the sponsoring
religious body, needs equally to be clarified. The acknowledgment
by the medieval church of the subsidiary autonomy of the emerging
universities would provide a starting point for tracing a parallel
institutional academic freedom, which must await another time. But
it should be clear that the normative role of the church in setting the
parameters of theological speculation does not entail authority over
such properly academic matters as faculty appointment, curriculum,
and student admission.

Finally, it bears underlining once again that the freedom of the
university defended here is not to establish or preserve some insular
sovereignty: the function of the Catholic university is ultimately to
serve both the political community of which it is a part and the
religious community to which it claims fidelity. It serves them both
by aspiring to determine what is true about nature and society and
art and God, and helping its students to learn to do so for themselves,
for the truth is a good common to both communities. Academic freedom of both kinds is a necessary condition for that quest.

Notes

1. R. Hofstadter and W. P. Metzger, *The Development of Academic Freedom in the United States* (New York: Columbia University Press, 1955), 3.

2. Cf. Hastings Rashdall, *The Universities of Europe in the Middle Ages* (Oxford: Oxford University Press, 1936), 1:334–43.

3. *New Catholic Encyclopedia,* art. "University of Paris."

4. See the interesting account by A. Gabriel, "The Conflict between the Chancellor and the University of Masters and Students at Paris during the Middle Ages," in *Die Auseinandersetzungen an der Pariser Universität in XIII Jahrhundert* (Berlin: de Gruyter, 1976).

5. To be consulted here is the fine study by Mary Martin McLaughlin, *Intellectual Freedom and Its Limitations in the University of Paris in the Thirteenth and Fourteenth Centuries* (New York: Arno, 1977).

6. Ibid., 22.

7. "An extreme form of the view common in the nineteenth century is that of Bury, for whom the middle ages were a millennium in which
'reason was enchained, thought was enslaved, and knowledge made no
progress.' In Bury's treatment of this problem. . . a few instances of resistance to authority are singled out as romantic but ill-fated episodes in the

progress towards an absolute freedom considered accessible to the modern mind" (McLaughlin, *Intellectual Freedom,* 3). John Stuart Mill espoused a similar view in *On Liberty.*

8. Hofstadter and Metzger, *Development of Academic Freedom,* 5.

9. C. R. S. Harris, *Duns Scotus* (Oxford: Oxford University Press, 1927), 1:40.

10. Lynn Thorndike, "Natural Science in the Middle Ages," *Popular Science Monthly* 87 (1915): 279, cited in Hofstadter and Metzger, *Development of Academic Freedom,* 13.

11. Hofstadter and Metzger, *Development of Academic Freedom,* 9–10. He adds, "The difference—and the difficulty—is that the modern American university neither shows the militancy nor enjoys the respect of the medieval university."

12. *Sweezy v. New Hampshire,* 354 US at 263. My phrase "Academic freedom is constituted by" is borrowed from Justice Powell, who, quoting Justice Frankfurter's specifying of the four essential freedoms, wrote that "the 'four essential freedoms' of a university constitute academic freedom" (*Regents of the University of California v. Bakke,* 438 US at 265 [1978]).

13. For an extensive survey of the present juridical state of the question, cf. David M. Rabban, "A Functional Analysis of 'Individual' and 'Institutional' Academic Freedom under the First Amendment," *Law and Contemporary Problems* 53, no. 3 (Summer 1990): 227–301.

14. A good deal of litigation has dealt with the question of the extent to which such individual academic freedom may be extended to primary and secondary education. The issues here are complicated by the state sponsorship of the latter for specific purposes (e.g., the skills required to be a functioning citizen, the "socialization" or "acculturation" of young people), different from those of higher education.

15. David M. Rabban, "Academic Freedom," in *Encyclopedia of the American Constitution* (1986). "No case to date [1990] has presented the Court with a direct conflict between institutional and individual claims of first amendment academic freedom" (Rabban, "Functional Analysis," 281).

16. Rabban, "Functional Analysis," 300–301. Some constitutional scholars perceive the Supreme Court as defining constitutionally protected academic freedom exclusively in institutional terms.

17. "Judicial views of civil liberty may infringe academic principles just as much as executive or legislative views of national security" (J. Peter Byrne, "Academic Freedom: A 'Special Concern' of the First Amendment," *Yale Law Journal* 61 [1989]: 304).

18. Rabban, "Functional Analysis," 258. See the discussion in Amy Gutmann, "Is Freedom Academic?" *Liberal Democracy: Nomos 25* (1983): 257–86, who contrasts the ways in which a "corporate pluralist" and a

"liberal democrat" might analyze the case. The argument is in *Princeton University vs. Schmid,* 455 US 100 (1982).

19. Gutmann, "Is Freedom Academic?" 272. She continues, "The claim that universities should be free from governmental control over determining their academic standards can be understood on the corporate view as an assertion of academic freedom for those private institutions dedicated to furthering the life of the mind. But this is a rather recent and peculiar understanding of academic freedom." As we have argued above, it is, rather, ancient and common.

20. Ibid., 273.

21. Saving a narrow construal of *priest* in contrast to the constitutional category of *clergy.*

22. Gutmann, "Is Freedom Academic?" 261. A certain prejudice seems reflected in "or other ideological purposes."

23. Quoted in Michael M. McConnell, "Academic Freedom in Religious Colleges and Universities," *Law and Contemporary Problems* 55, no. 3 (1990): 308. For this part of the discussion, I am much indebted to McConnell's article.

24. Cf. the discussion of the subcommittee's claim that this interpretation was a return to the original basis of the 1940 statement, in McConnell, "Academic Freedom," 309.

25. "Report of Committee A 1988–89," *Academe* 75:49, quoted in McConnell, "Academic Freedom," 310.

26. Moreover, the 1940 statement is used by some accrediting agencies as part of their assessment process (e.g., the Association of American Law Schools), and their decisions, like those of all authorized accrediting agencies and unlike those of the AAUP, carry significant legal consequences (e.g., loss of government loans).

27. McConnell, "Academic Freedom," 314.

28. McLaughlin, *Intellectual Freedom,* 9. Similarly, Hofstadter and Metzger, *Development of Academic Freedom,* 27.

29. Michael Polanyi, "The Potential Theory of Adsorption," in id., *Knowing and Being* (Chicago: University of Chicago Press, 1969), 94.

30. Of course it would have to be consistent and serious about that preservation across the board. The recent action of the Supreme Court in declining to review a Ninth Circuit case in which a private, self-described Protestant secondary school was required to cease hiring only Protestant teachers, on the grounds that it had evolved into a "primarily secular rather than a primarily religious orientation," is a sign that inconsistency in religious character may make it impossible to claim institutional academic freedom.

31. "The Limitations Clause," *Academe* 74:55. The subcommittee added:

"this is no less true for professional clerical education than for any other professional calling." Newman would not have agreed with this, for reasons to be mentioned shortly.

32. Monotheistic believers in such a revelation number about half of the human race.

33. J. H. Newman, *The Idea of a University* (reprint, Notre Dame, Ind.: University of Notre Dame Press, 1982), 163, 172.

34. C. E. Curran, "Academic Freedom and Catholic Universities," *Texas Law Review* 66:1454. Curran argues there for greater individual academic freedom of theologians in Catholic universities. His article is followed by a response by two law professors at Texas: D. Laycock and S. E. Waelbroeck, "Academic Freedom and the Freedom Exercise of Religion," id., 1455–75.

On Teaching Theology as a Vocation

Lawrence S. Cunningham

> I shall try, to the best of my ability, not so much to show
> you something as to search with you.
>
> St. Anselm, *Cur Deus Homo*

A majority of the contributors invited to write for this volume by Father Hesburgh will speak with some authority about the experience of being a part of a Catholic university. My remarks, however, will spring from a more limited perspective. The larger part of my professional life both as a graduate student and as an academic was spent in state-supported "secular" schools. In fact, before coming to Notre Dame I taught for seventeen years in the state university system of Florida. In that sense, at least, I am, to borrow the self-description of Francis of Assisi, *idiota et subditus omnibus* (unlettered and subject to all) when it comes to speaking of Catholic higher education from any long-term acquaintance.

My reflections, then, revolve around what I discovered in moving from a relatively small department of religious studies in a "secular" school to a large department of theology in a professedly Catholic institution of higher learning. My decision to move, incidentally, derived in large part from my desire to be in a place where the possibility of doing Catholic theology ex professo was possible instead of doing what was vaguely called *Catholic studies*—a rubric flexible enough (and sufficiently methodologically cloudy) to forestall any constitutional problems for a state school.

Which brings me to a first preliminary point. Notre Dame (I use Notre Dame as an example since I know it best, but let it also stand as a synecdoche for Catholic universities more broadly conceived) is radically different from state schools, and it is that precise fact of difference that attracted me. Otherwise, why would one abandon the sybaritic pleasures of a Florida campus for the more austere joys of northern Indiana?

Let me be more precise: In what does this difference consist? Some things are obvious, but not of central concern, in this essay: a smaller student body; brighter, better-prepared students on the whole; the sense of tradition even if, on the negative side, it results in a kind of homogeneity and sort of complacent insularity among many of the undergraduates.

At a deeper level—and this will come as a shock to uninformed readers—a kind of freedom is possible at a Catholic school that does not exist in state schools. The freedom, for instance, to begin a class with a prayer if someone is so inclined; the ability to walk across campus and participate in the liturgy of the church;[1] the knowledge that there are serious scholars across a range of disciplines who would entertain theological discussions seriously—that sort of thing. There was, and is, an ethos at Notre Dame that sees religious faith not as an individual quirk but as a constitutive part of the human experience. I think it was the novelist Norman Mailer, who, on a visit to this campus in the past, remarked that here one could utter the word *soul* and not have people blush. Exactly.

All of this, however, is not to say that the Notre Dame ethos smacks of the cloister or the sacristy. In fact, this university is living proof that gives the lie to those clichéd views of Catholicism as a monolithic reality in which, like the juggernaut, a single body of believers, marching under papal orders, advances in serried ranks against the modern world.

Nor is it correct to think that because Notre Dame is Catholic it is also narrowly sectarian. After six years at this institution I am in a better position to appreciate that Catholicism is a Weltkirche—a world church. In my own area of theological education I feel an obligation to be in dialogue with my fellow theologians (and their students) in all parts of the world. We have educated and been educated by persons from Europe, Africa, Asia, India, the Americas, and Australia during my short tenure here.

Nor is Catholicism all of a piece on this campus. Under the broad rubric of *Catholicism* there ranges a variety of opinions, sensibilities, spiritualities, tastes, and theological worldviews. There are those, to be sure, who fear what Walter Lippmann once felicitously called the "acids of modernity" and circle the wagons in a bastion of "nay saying." Others, beguiled by a hazy dream of some putative golden age of Catholic unity, construct a vision of Catholicism which is equal parts ahistorical Thomism, Chestertonian quips, and a thinly disguised horror at what Vatican II has wrought. Such folks have a menu of institutional options open to them around this university community ranging from the charismatic movement or other restorationist efforts to the sectarian Opus Dei group which has a toehold at the very edge of the campus. On the other end of the spectrum are those liberal Catholics who get nervous every time Rome clears its throat, laud the "preferential option for the poor," and take secret delight every time they are trashed in the pages of *Wanderer* or *Crisis*.

None of these positions at the edge is rigid. Where do we locate on the Right/Left spectrum those who are doctrinally conservative but profoundly radical in their social philosophy (e.g., the supporters of the Catholic Worker movement)? How do we categorize those who are regular communicants, deeply committed to Catholic education, and shaped by their Catholic past, but who have more than a twinge of doubt about the full implications of *Humanae Vitae?* And must we excommunicate (mentally) those who throw up their hands in despair at the whole institutional church but whose very critique is shaped by the Catholic ethos? What do we make of those (we have them on campus) who, rather like George Santayana or Graham Greene, characterize themselves as "Catholic atheists"?

In fact, what strikes me as a tyro here at Notre Dame is how catholic this place is when one understands catholicity in the deepest meaning of that word. There is an identifiable tradition called the *Catholic tradition.* It is characterized by a sense of tradition, a feel for the sacramental, a bond of belonging, a kind of aesthetic, and an articulation of the historic faith of the Great Church. This tradition has been so ably articulated by theologians that I will not rehearse their descriptions here.[2] Such a tradition exists, however, is vibrant, and continues to be a shaping reality in world culture.

The one point I would like to emphasize, however, is the fact that *catholicity* (the term means "of the whole" or "universal"), while a description of the church, is also an aspiration, which is to say, that only in the eschaton will the full catholicity of the church find its realization. The church, in other words, is catholic but it strives towards that future catholicity when, at the consummation of the ages, all things on earth and heaven will be summed up in God (see Eph 1:10).[3] What that means in the concrete has vast implications for the university community.

First, it means that the church as it historically exists in this or that moment of time has not enshrined everything that the gospel proposes, nor does it have full possession of the treasury of truth. Surely, part of the task of achieving catholicity is to be alert to those aspects of the church which militate against greater universalism. A Catholic university must be critical of those varieties of ethnocentrism, nationalism, blindered philosophical paradigms, frozen theological slogans, and prejudices which block our ability to speak the gospel in terms appropriate to the age while—and this is no easy task—being faithful to our inherited tradition.

Such a task demands a place where it is possible to get the facts straight (in areas of analytical research) so as to expose ideologies where they exist and, in the process, clear the way for different formulations. To do this with any sense of sophistication, it is absolutely crucial that we pursue the truth honestly, openly, and courageously even when it is painfully antagonistic to what we have assumed about our past tradition.

Such an assessment of our inherited tradition demands that scholars be allowed to speak just as it demands that they be willing to listen. That listening must occur across disciplines so that the theologian hears the voice of the scientist just as it makes use of the work of historians, sociologists, economists, and others who work in the social and humane sciences.

The university alone provides the place where this important conversation can take place. The traditional home of theologians since the sixteenth century was the seminary, and their traditional audience was the future priest. They still must staff seminaries, but today the public face of theology must be in the university, where the range of intellectual disciplines contextualizes that critical reflection on faith which is the fundamental task to which the theologian sets his or her efforts.

If the "official" church does not value this role of the university as an essential part of the life and mission of the church as a partner in a vast conversation about the faith and its implications for the human enterprise, it inevitably means that the voice of theology will be emarginated and its worldview sectarian. The cliché "the university is where the church does its thinking," like all clichés, carries with it an essential truth—and that truth should not be forgotten.

But the good of the church as an existent historical reality does not sum up the field of inquiry at a truly Catholic university. Thomas Aquinas reminds us that while there are many forms of rigorous knowing (*scientiae*) there is only one wisdom (*sapientia*).[4] A more contemporary cut on this observation would be this: human knowledge is of a piece; we may know in various ways, but our knowing has a final, if inarticulate, goal, which is truth. That truth is, in the final analysis, founded in God.

If we take that framework—a traditional intellectual credo of the Catholic tradition—with utmost seriousness, then we can reach a fundamental conclusion: the work of the university, at its deepest level, is the drive towards God who is the source of all truth. University work may not be (indeed, is not) the only way to ultimate truth, but it is surely one way. In that sense, I would see our common intellectual task as being part of a great conversation whose end should be that clarification of the mind whose telos is God.

A further point: there is something inexorably countercultural about the Christian gospel. That antagonism to the Zeitgeist may be calibrated on a rather lengthy continuum. At one end is that part of the Catholic tradition which hymns *fuga mundi*—a flight from the world which is transitory and whose allures are evanescent. Monasticism, perhaps, stands as the single oldest institution in the Christian tradition which testifies to the perennial gospel value of resisting the world. At the other end of the spectrum are those attempts—represented historically by the various efforts to construct a Catholic humanism—to affirm the essential goodness of the redeemed cosmos and the continuity of the gospel with human achievement.

Somewhere in the center of that imaginary line the Catholic university must place itself. Its very reason for existing would be undermined should we negate human achievement or doubt the human capacity to know and learn. On the other hand, the Catholic university must nurture within itself a prophetic strain by which it can critique those elements of culture which carry within them antihuman impulses or destructive surges of sheer hubris. That means that the Catholic university cannot simply be an unreflective part of the reigning consensus.

One sees moments of such prophetic alertness when, at a place like Notre Dame (which has been blessed with much success in its endowment, its students, its distinguished faculty), we stop and ask ourselves (or are queried by others) if we have insulated ourselves from the poor of the world; if we are only in the business of cranking out people with the M.B.A. or J.D. who look for success without some sense of social purpose; if our students use their education as a ticket to glamorous careers; etc. Such alertness should give us worries about the kind of research we do; the courses we teach; and the areas of study we enter (or fail to nurture). None of us—who are, after all, middle-class people with intellectual pretensions—can escape a certain happiness with the status quo, but to the degree that we are not self-critical we fail in catholicity.

A final point. I have always loved Chaucer's line in the prologue to the *Canterbury Tales*, where he describes the Oxford scholar: "Gladly wold he lerne; gladly teche." I take that as a motto for who I am and what I do.

First of all, I am a learner. After nearly thirty years as a teacher-writer I consider myself a learner (i.e., a researcher). I learn best within a community which is made up of other learners. For that reason it is a privilege to be at Notre Dame where there are persons who can both encourage and criticize me in my attempts to gain some mastery over the vast tradition of reflection on the faith which is the enterprise of theology. Our common discussions, seminars, exchange of writings, etc. hone my own perceptions and advance me as a learner. The fact that my department, while self-descriptively Catholic, is also ecumenical keeps my work from being too narrowly denominational or self-congratulatory.

Secondly, I am a teacher. It has always irritated me that we refer to our teaching as a *load* or that people will say that they could not "get their work done" because of their teaching responsibilities. At Notre Dame, all of our faculty, from chaired professors to assistant professors, are expected to teach across the curriculum—from required introductory courses for newly arrived first-year students to advanced seminars for doctoral candidates. With rare exceptions we do not exempt our faculty from such obligations. Nor should we. When young people come here for their undergraduate education they should have the possibility to learn from those of our faculty "stars" whose names are on every serious bibliography of theological studies.

In fact, I deem it both a privilege and an opportunity to face a class of first-year students and tell them (this is part of my opening salvo each year) that my subject is intrinsically interesting and will be fascinating for them. Some actually come away with that conviction and, although they may not remember the details of my theological discourses, they might acquire the most precious gift that was given to me as a young person: love of learning.

In this regard, I take as another motto the one which belongs properly to the Dominicans and, especially, to the greatest of their order, Thomas Aquinas: *contemplata aliis tradere*, "to hand on to others matters once contemplated." The great ideal of a serious theologian is to be in a community of scholars in which they can think and speak; think over those things which are new and old; speak to those who come to this material fresh. To teach is to share what has been learned.

In a setting like Notre Dame we might aspire to connect learning with the pursuit of the Christian life itself. We may not always do that in a conscious fashion, but it is a goal towards which we should strive. What is important is that a place like Notre Dame provides the home where such an exercise of joining life to learning is possible, even if we fail to exercise that possibility to its fullest.

For some time I have been collecting reflections by writers and thinkers who have reflected on the relationship of scholarship and spirituality.[5] I have in mind such meditations as that of Simone Weil on school studies and the love of God, or Edith Stein's observations (in her letters) on learning and holiness, or Thomas Merton's reflections on the similarities of monasteries to universities. All of these sensitive writers keep one thought forcefully before their minds: that the pursuit of learning is a spiritual quest and that the end of the quest is God. One need not be in a religious school to enter into that quest; many, in fact, are on the way who do not belong to such schools. The point is, however, that a place like Notre Dame invites its community to make that journey in an open and explicit fashion.

In extending that invitation the university is part of a very old tradition. I doubt that most of us always think of our work as a vocation to holiness or feel ourselves quite up to the demands that such a calling makes on us. As he began his university career, Thomas Aquinas must have felt the same way. It is fitting, then, that we utter the same prayer with which he ended his inaugural lecture at the University of Paris in 1256:

> Although no one is adequate for this ministry by himself and from his own resources, he can hope that God will make him adequate. "Not that we are capable of a single thought on our own resources, as if it comes from us, but our adequacy is from God" (2 Cor 3:5). So the teacher should ask for it: "If people lack wisdom, they should beg it from God and it will be given them" (James 1:5). May Christ grant this to us. Amen.[6]

Notes

1. At one campus in Florida the Newman chaplain was denied the right to celebrate Mass on the campus while renovations were done to the campus chapel off campus, on the grounds that state law forbade the consumption of alcoholic beverages on state property. Whether the chaplain had the wit to elaborate on the doctrine of transubstantiation is not known to me.

2. The most comprehensive study of catholicity is Avery Dulles, S.J., *The Catholicity of the Church* (Oxford: Clarendon, 1983).

3. Dulles notes, correctly, that the closest New Testament word we have for catholicity is *pleroma*, "fullness."

4. *Summa Theologiae,* I–IIae, q. 57, 2c. In that same question Aquinas notes that wisdom (*sapientia*) is the highest of the intellectual virtues.

5. I have been inspired in this enterprise by the classic work of the late Jean LeClercq which has been so much a part of my own intellectual development: *The Love of Learning and the Desire for God* (New York: Fordham University Press, 1961).

6. Complete text in *Albert and Thomas: Selected Writings,* ed. Simon Tugwell, O.P. (Mahwah, N.J.: Paulist Press, 1988), 353–62.

A Catholic University, Maybe;
But a Catholic Law School?

FERNAND N. DUTILE

Father Hesburgh knows how to ask tough questions; in twenty-seven years as a faculty member on university campuses and especially lately, I have heard no issue debated more regularly, more contentiously, and yet less conclusively than that addressing the essence of a Catholic university.[1] I mean to discuss in this piece not only that issue, but the related—if not subsumed—one of the nature of a Catholic law school.

Perhaps these issues loomed less daunting some decades ago. The climate for religion in America may have been better then,[2] and, accordingly, people less likely to challenge the desirability, indeed the very notion, of a Catholic university. When such challenges arose, they were less likely to come from faculty members who themselves worked at Catholic universities. Several forces joined to alter this situation.

First, until about a quarter-century ago, ownership largely told us which universities were Catholic; if the Congregation of Holy Cross or the Society of Jesus "owned" a college or university (and they literally did), the place was Catholic. Moreover, the control the owners exercised precluded, for a variety of reasons, much overt discussion of whether the place was truly Catholic, whether Catholicity was important, and, as part of that question, whether religious affiliation hampered the intellectual thrust of the institution.

Today, ownership of the institutions has itself often wandered

71

from the religious orders to so-called lay boards of trustees. Even though these orders may have reserved, through governing documents,[3] some voting powers that constrain a move to full secular status, undoubtedly the loss of ownership, both symbolically and substantively, created opportunities for questioning the Catholic nature of the institution. After all, such dramatic changes in governance made the university more like other universities in American life.[4]

As institutions of higher education, and especially universities, have sought to make their mark on the world of research and writing, many faculty members—and, indeed, many departments—have felt threatened by the notion of a Catholic university. Whether that threat stemmed from the specter that less academically qualified Catholics would displace better scholars or that academic freedom would somehow weaken in a Catholic university, we have had, of late, no scarcity of faculty members on Catholic campuses willing, if not eager, to dispute both the nature and the desirability of a focus on Catholicity.

To be sure, this movement has been buttressed by an egalitarian spirit, a spirit that owes much to the civil-rights movement of the sixties. That spirit tempts one to see any preference for Catholics in a university's hiring process—especially when such preference is advanced as the sine qua non of a Catholic university—as merely the flip side of discrimination. Also, the rapidly improving academic reputations of many Catholic universities have, in a sense, made them victims of their own success: more and more non-Catholics (and perhaps Catholics as well) are drawn to these universities less by their Catholic, or even religious, affiliation than by their academic excellence. At many institutions, the parallel phenomenon has dramatically changed the religious intensity of the student body, as well. People for whom the religious nature of the institution provided little if any attraction will likely, once on campus, ignore, if not resist, the institution's religious heritage.

Traditionally, the more campus positions the governing religious order could fill with its priests, sisters, or brothers, the more intense, both substantively and symbolically, the religious feel of the institution. Alas, even as many institutions swelled their faculty ranks during the heady expansion of the late seventies and the eighties, fewer members of religious orders became available to occupy faculty positions. The decline in religious vocations (and the concomitant departure of so many from religious life) thus contributed markedly to the dilution of commitment on campus to the religious attachments of the Catholic university.

But what makes the institution Catholic? Ownership of the institution can no longer—if it ever did—provide the litmus paper for testing true Catholicity. Is intuition, or impression, or formal affiliation the only standard left? Discussions of this issue have often assumed that some magic factor, if only we could articulate it, determines the Catholicity of the institution. That magic factor remains elusive. Capsule definitions of the Catholic university inevitably oversimplify or rely on relatively meaningless abstractions.

Many complex things, however, are not given to a simple answer. What constitutes a happy marriage? What provides the best opportunity for a child to grow up happy and productive? What should be our public policy toward the poor? We no longer, if we ever did, expect facile answers to such difficult questions. Why should we expect a facile description of the Catholicity of as complex an institution as a university? It might be easier to describe the nature of an American university, but even that project would yield no simple answer.

Recently, during an interview, a prospective member of our faculty stated that Notre Dame's Catholicity constituted for him a large part of the university's attraction. To compel an elaboration on this, I asked him, "What makes Notre Dame Catholic, the crucifixes in the classroom?" To my surprise, he answered, "Exactly!" At first, I took his answer to be merely glib. But, in retrospect, I believe he saw those crucifixes as symbols of a multitude of factors—a few indispensable, but none sufficient—that make an institution authentically Catholic. Moreover, in the truly dynamic Catholic university these factors may continually change or at least develop. What Joseph O'Meara, former dean of the Notre Dame Law School, said of the law seems equally true of the Catholicity of an institution: "[It] may be compared to a tapestry which is being woven always, which repeats many of the patterns of the past but is constantly adding new patterns and variations on old patterns. . . . [It] is always an unfinished product."[5] No one color, figure, or design establishes this tapestry, and certainly not with finality. A confluence of many forces, forces that, as Father Hesburgh stresses, adapt to changing times, yields the Catholic university.

It begins, of course, with the sense of mission.[6] The truly Catholic institution must see its destiny in terms of Catholicity. Catholicity is difficult enough to develop wittingly; it clearly will not happen accidentally. Many institutions have set out to be religious but ended up far wide of that objective; none, to my knowledge, set out to be secular but ended up truly religious.

Perhaps next in importance comes a faculty that includes a critical mass[7] of Catholics. Of course, the preference would be for committed Catholics, but almost no way to effect this seems practical. Background checks (analogous to those performed by governmental institutions regarding loyalty and the like) would send unacceptable signals. Moreover, even if such checks took place, what would they look for? Weekly or even daily Mass attendance? Periodic confession? Support of the parish? Even good marks on these tests may not reveal the committed Catholic. (Some Catholic institutions do look askance at the prospect of hiring divorced or cohabiting individuals, but surely this screen, even should it be desirable, is inadequate). Screening for felonies and other comparable misfeasance, moreover, may be little more than any employer, religious or not, would do.

Accordingly, a commonly voiced objection to seeking Catholics for the faculty invokes the impossibility of screening for anything more than formal religious affiliation ("checking the box," as it is sometimes called). This objection, it seems to me, misses the point. Although the institution cannot be sure that all—or even most—of those formally Catholic faculty members it hires will be committed Catholics, an institution, and especially a large one, can expect that the pool of Catholics hired will include many such Catholics. What trumps all is the undeniable fact that a failure to hire formally Catholic faculty members will result in few faculty members committed to the Catholic nature of the institution; that result, in turn, will unerringly presage the demise of that institution's religious character.

How many does a critical mass require?[8] Obviously, this difficult question is further complicated by the fact that the market for Catholic academics may vary according to the discipline. Currently, for example, it may be more difficult to secure academically outstanding Catholics in the field of mathematics than in theology or philosophy. Of course, it will be more important, as well, for the theology and philosophy departments to attract Catholics than for the mathematics department to do so. In any event, the truly committed Catholic university will reach out to recruit to all its departments not only promising Catholic scholars but also Catholics with established academic reputations.

We can expect much of the leadership, official and otherwise, of an institution to come from the faculty. Wherever it comes from, however, it is crucial that it, including especially the president and the chief academic officer,[9] be committed to a Catholic university. Otherwise, the vigilance required to ensure a sufficient number of outstanding Catholics on the faculty and the continuation of religiously oriented components and activities on campus will dissipate. Tight budgets, for example, make it all too convenient for administrators to reduce, if not eliminate, many "ancillary" items that truly give the Catholic campus its texture. After all, a religiously affiliated university will most likely become secular not through some dramatic decision of the governing board but through erosion:

> The movement from religious commitment to secularity was the result most often not of any secularist plot but rather of a fit of absence of mind . . . . [T]he critical steps down the slippery slope to secularity were almost always initiated by administrators and faculty members who did not intend secularity at all . . . . Almost all of the formerly Christian institutions that capitulated to secularity lost their religious identity incrementally and by inadvertence, not by one critical step or conscious policy.[10]

Once gone, the Catholicity of an institution will be irretrievable.

The Catholic university reveals itself too by the religious affiliation of its students. Often, this will be a function more of its attractiveness to Catholic high school seniors than of its considered selection of Catholic students; it would be surprising if a Notre Dame, a Santa Clara, or a Marquette would not draw large numbers of Catholic applicants even without any attempt to do so. Of course, recruiting at Catholic high schools and preferring, at least to some extent, Catholics in selecting among applicants will further increase the campus population of Catholics. Together, Catholic students and faculty, themselves and through campus organizations, keep alive in class and elsewhere not only intellectual dynamism but also social activism and worship related to their Catholic affiliation.

Not only will Catholic faculty and students enrich the Catholic university; the Catholic university will provide the resources, the curriculum, the support, and the comfort that will help such faculty and students fulfill themselves personally and academically. This will be true especially for those whose academic interests focus on the religious. But this important network of Catholicity will remain important for many others whose academic work and personal lives the Catholic atmosphere will markedly enhance. This atmosphere will include not only the central campus church but also chapels in residence halls,[11] priests and religious brothers and sisters as residence hall counselors, and a sophisticated department of campus ministry. At times of crisis, for example when a student dies, campus Masses and counseling will bring solace. The promise of the Catholic university, therefore, must include not only the good things done for religion by the institution and its employees but also the good done for society generally by those whose personal and professional formation the Catholic university so dramatically affects.

A Catholic institution will choose areas of inquiry important to religion in general and Catholicism in particular: "Religious universities justify themselves in the larger academic world by raising and contemplating questions that are not elsewhere engaged."[12] The various disciplines, of course, relate differently to Catholicity. The Catholic university would be expected to emphasize philosophy and, especially, theology. These two disciplines relate centrally to Catholic doctrine, thought, history, and worship. Moreover, other departments might focus on matters related to religion and Catholicism. The music department might stress liturgical music; the architecture department might pay special attention to the design of churches. Institutes and centers with religious focal points will inevitably arise on campus. Notre Dame lists, for example, the Medieval Institute, the Center for Ethics and Religious Values in Business, the Center for Pastoral Liturgy, the Center for Philosophy of Religion, the Institute for Church Life, the Jacques Maritain Center, and the Center for Continuing Formation in Ministry. In turn, these components and others sponsor courses, publications, symposia, lectures, and other activities related to religion. In this total construct, "Catholics and others, on the highest level of intellectual inquiry," as Father Hesburgh puts it earlier in this volume, "seek out the relevance of the Christian message to all of the problems and opportunities that face us and our complex world."

The point is not that some of these activities could not occur on secular campuses; the point is that all of them surely will not, at least not with the concentration, integration, support, and attention they garner in the full network that is the Catholic university. At the truly Catholic university, these activities will not serve as mere accessories but rather will occupy the core of the institution's mission. And these will in turn cause countless ripples of Catholic and otherwise religious impact throughout society.

Moreover, there are strong indications that religiously influenced thought has become increasingly unwelcome on American campuses. "For the most part," one scholar has asserted, "the idea that one's religion might shape one's scholarly perspective is simply unknown in mainstream academia. That absence is so much taken for granted that even academics who are themselves religious often think that they must keep quiet about their faith."[13] Accordingly, providing institutions that will be hospitable to religious perspectives may now be more important than ever.

How does a Catholic law school fit into all this?[14] Obviously, there is no "Catholic law" of torts, contracts, or criminal procedure. Nonetheless, most of what I have stated regarding the university applies as well to the university law school. At Notre Dame, the mission statement of the Law School proclaims in the very first sentence both the school's Catholicity and its dedication to the "integration of reason and faith in the study of law."[15] The statement commits the school to preparing attorneys "whose decisions are guided by the values and morality which Notre Dame represents."[16]

The Law School seeks to maintain a critical mass of committed Catholics and, indeed, includes two priests of the Congregation of Holy Cross. The student body includes a large number of Catholics. The curriculum contains aspects one would not expect at a secular law school. For the Catholic law school, jurisprudence plays the role of both theology and philosophy. Jurisprudence allows the exploration of the human person's relationship to other persons, to government, to the world, and, ultimately, to God. Notre Dame, unlike almost any other law school, requires each student to take a course in jurisprudence. Some among its several jurisprudence courses focus on Roman Catholic or other religious perspectives.[17]

What about other courses? The instructor's jurisprudential view of the relationships among human beings, government, the world, and God will influence dramatically the issues, considerations, and discussions brought to the course. The Judeo-Christian conception of the dignity of the human being, for example, tells us much regarding the appropriate role of government, a thematic concern in the study of law.

A course entitled "GALILEE" exposes students firsthand to "the legal needs of the urban poor," allowing these students "to incorporate their religious value systems into their future practice of law."[18] Much of the faculty's scholarship reflects religious values and interests.[19] Members of the faculty conduct pre-Cana instruction for law (and other) students planning to marry. The *Notre Dame Law Review* boasts that it is "Dedicated to Our Lady, Mirror of Justice." The annual retreat for faculty culminates in community worship. The law building features a beautiful chapel; Masses are said there, in the student lounge, and in the courtroom. Students find support for, and occasions to implement, their faith in organizations such as the Christian Legal Society, the St. Thomas More Society, the Social Justice Forum, and the Right to Life Society.

This pervasive religious orientation itself occurs in the context of an intensely religious university. Faculty, students, and staff make heavy use of the university's conduciveness to academic pursuits, worship, and other activities supportive of religious outlook and interest. Too, faculty members and students in other disciplines on campus find invaluable the resources the Law School provides for interdisciplinary study, study often implicating religiously related values. Members of the Notre Dame community, both within and without the Law School, find in the Law School an enriching, fulfilling religious tapestry, one that is friendly to both professional and personal life. The impact, direct and indirect, on their lives and on those with whom they come into contact here or elsewhere will inevitably be enormous.

I do not mean to say, or even to suggest, that Notre Dame Law School in particular, or religious law schools in general, exercises a monopoly regarding the importance of "values." The great number of law teachers at secular universities whose teaching, research, and personal lives reflect the noblest values makes any such claim not only inaccurate but arrogant as well.

To the extent that the nature of a Catholic law school relates differently to values, the difference, I believe, is twofold. First, a religious law school may emphasize a quite different mix of values. We can imagine a four-level pyramid whose bottom layer we label "values in general." We might label the next higher layer "religious values." We might label the still next higher layer "Christian values"; and the top layer, "Roman Catholic values." Whatever we might decide each of these layers includes, it seems clear that values reflected in the upper layers will likely include, interpret, implement, and generally inform many of the values reflected in the lower layers; indeed, the religious values at the top of the pyramid may well provide special life, insight, or sources to the values included in the lower levels. Mother Teresa provides a helpful analogue; although many nonreligious people do wonderful things for the less fortunate, surely her faith-driven devotion to the sick and poor manifests a special dimension. On a university campus, a scholar might, for example, focus on the history of Catholicism in Canada, thus enriching the study of history at all levels of the pyramid. The lower layers will—though less often—include, interpret, implement, or generally inform those values occupying the upper layers.

The second difference, closely related, involves the comfort with which, at a truly religious law school, professedly Roman Catholic, Christian, and other religious values can be unabashedly discussed, defended, and, I daresay, even challenged. These challenges, even as they question the interpretation of such values, recognize their importance.

Nor do I mean to suggest that the truly religious law school reflects an orthodoxy of thought; no one who has participated in (or even heard) the discussions of the Notre Dame law faculty at its regular luncheon table would make such a claim. Those who expect a rigid orthodoxy on the Catholic campus forget that the truly Catholic university is much more a vehicle than a destination. As Father Hesburgh makes clear, such orthodoxy precludes the notion of a university. Indeed, the religious ideology of any Catholic on the Notre Dame Law School faculty will have more in common with that of some Catholics at state universities than with that of some Catholics on the Notre Dame faculty. A common faith does not preclude the diversity of thought that lends intellectual ferment to the lives of teachers and scholars.

The first challenge, then, of the Catholic university and of the Catholic law school will be to develop effective Catholic leadership and to attract the requisite numbers of committed and talented Catholic scholars even as the numbers of committed Catholics in the general population seem so steadily to decline. This will undoubtedly require, in many situations, favoring Roman Catholic scholars in faculty appointments; given the importance of religious freedom under our Constitution and otherwise, however, this should be seen not as discrimination but as affirmative action, which is anything but a new concept in American higher education.

A second challenge will involve protecting the academic freedom of those who teach, do research, and study at Catholic institutions. Faith has nothing to fear from ideas. Properly understood, the Catholicism of an institution should liberate, not regulate. A religious institution may justifiably expect members of the community to respect the religious traditions of the institution and to adhere to behavioral norms of which those members had notice prior to accepting employment. Beyond this, university officials and faculty must resist attempts, from either within or without the institution, to impose religious orthodoxy.[20] As incidents at some institutions have indicated, such attempts result in the intellectual marketplace discounting the scholarly reputation, aspirations, and production of the institution involved. Scholarship tempered by intellectual constraints inevitably loses its persuasiveness. Ultimately, universities that are inhospitable to free inquiry will become inhospitable, and therefore unattractive, to serious scholars, whether Catholic or non-Catholic.

Of course, religious campuses, reflecting human frailty, will inevitably develop some particular orthodoxies. But these may be less threatening to academic freedom than orthodoxies—different ones, to be sure—prevailing at secular campuses.[21] The total freedom to discuss, from a religious perspective, issues spanning the intellectual spectrum may more than offset whatever orthodoxies eventuate on the religious campus. Of course, it is crucial as well that agencies involved in the accreditation process, such as the American Bar Association and the Association of American Law Schools, recognize the right of religious institutions to exercise their religious freedom. There is no gainsaying that a "religiously affiliated law school cannot account for itself theologically by being . . . like law schools maintained by the state or by non-religious sponsors."[22]

The Catholicity of a university or of a law school cannot, I have submitted, be captured by a definition, let alone a slogan. Catholicity is a culture, a culture that provides a lens through which a community views not only its academic life, but all aspects of existence. If the institution remains truly Catholic, the world itself will come to view that community through that same lens.

The challenges facing both Catholic universities and Catholic law schools remain formidable. If these challenges are met, however, the promise is clear and great: institutions in which the true interests of Roman Catholicism find fruition through the intellectual, professional, and personal development of their faculty members and students, whose lives will enrich this world and, one hopes, the next.

Notes

1. Father Hesburgh's introductory essay raises, among other questions, the issue of whether a Catholic university is possible. To that extent, use of the phrase *Catholic university* begs the question. Nonetheless, for convenience's sake, I will use that phrase to allude to institutions that profess to be Catholic.

2. On the climate for religion in America, see Stephen L. Carter, *The Culture of Disbelief: How American Law and Politics Trivialize Religious Devotion* (New York: Basic Books, 1993).

3. See P. Moots and E. Gaffney, *Church and Campus* (Notre Dame, Ind.: University of Notre Dame Press, 1979), 7; see generally at 5–9.

4. See, e.g., J. Conn, S.J., *Catholic Universities in the United States and Ecclesiastical Authority* (Rome: Editrice Pontificia Universita Gregoriana, 1991), 166: "Probably the most significant actions taken by Georgetown University to conform to American standards of university governance were the expansion of its Board of Directors, the inclusion of laymen on the Board, and the exclusion from the Board of internal officers of the institution with the exception of the President."

5. Joseph O'Meara, "An Introduction to Law and How to Study It," *Notre Dame Lawyer* 48 (1973): 7.

6. For Notre Dame's mission statement, see Edward A. Malloy, C.S.C., *Final Report: Colloquy for the Year 2000*, 2–3 (1993).

7. Of course, non-Catholics who support the Catholic mission of the university must be not only tolerated but welcome. "The danger in affirming the centrality of Notre Dame's Catholic mission and character is that some members of the University community may feel excluded or unappreciated.... [T]he first word that must be spoken is that all are welcome and honored here.... [The University] benefits from and brings to public recognition the contribution of individuals from a wide variety of backgrounds, religious or not" (ibid., 4).

8. Notre Dame's most recent long-term planning document speaks of "a

proper balance in which . . . the number of committed Catholics predominate" (ibid.).

9. The president, if not the chief academic officer as well, will be appointed
by the board of trustees; obviously, therefore, the board itself must be
committed to the Catholic dimensions of the university's mission statement.

10. James Nuechterlein, "The Idol of Academic Freedom," *First Things* 38
(December 1993): 16.

11. Students, faculty, and staff at Notre Dame, for example, may attend
any of about 175 Masses offered on campus each week.

12. Nuechterlein, "Idol," 16.

13. George M. Marsden, "Religious Professors Are the Last Taboo," *Wall
Street Journal*, December 22, 1993, A10. The same scholar maintains that the
exclusion of scholarship with religious viewpoints encompasses especially
that involving traditional Christianity. See Peter Steinfels, "Scholar Calls
Colleges Biased against Religion," *New York Times*, November 26, 1993, A22,
col. 1. Stanley Hauerwas, a theologian at Duke University Divinity School,
has asserted that "religiously committed scholars are 'scared' to declare their
beliefs" (Steinfels, "Scholar," A22, col. 1). See also Thomas L. Shaffer,
"Erastian and Sectarian Arguments in Religiously Affiliated American Law
Schools," *Stanford Law Review* 45 (1993): 1859, 1863: At state universities,
"religion is generally regarded as something to be kept private."

14. That a religious law school makes sense in America today may not be
a foregone conclusion. See Shaffer, "Arguments," 1878: "I suppose a group
of religious people has a reason for maintaining a school for the training of
lawyers." Shaffer discusses what he sees as the "three positions in the
Christian theology of legal education": the secular, the Erastian, and the
sectarian. He "tend[s] to favor the sectarian" (ibid., 1860, note 13).

15. "Notre Dame is a Catholic law school dedicated to the integration of
reason and faith in the study of law and committed to developing Judeo-
Christian principles within systems of jurisprudence" (Notre Dame Law
School, *Mission Statement*).

16. Ibid.

17. One such course examines "the relation between the human law and
the higher law as that law is seen in the natural law and Revelation. Primary
emphasis is on the Treatise on Law of St. Thomas Aquinas . . . . Other sources
[include] Pope John Paul II." The course examines important issues "with
reference to the social teachings of the Catholic Church." Another course
"[e]xamines jurisprudence in light of divine revelation and Christian philosophy . . . with a strong . . . Biblical component" (see Notre Dame Law
School, *Bulletin of Information*, [1993–1994], 20).

18. Ibid., 22. GALILEE is an acronym for Group Alternative Live-In Legal
Education Experience.

19. See, e.g., Gerard V. Bradley, "The Enduring Revolution: Law and Theology in the Secular State," *Emory Law Journal* 39 (1990): 217; Gerard V. Bradley, "Church Autonomy in the Constitutional Order: The End of Church and State?" *Iowa Law Review* 49 (1989): 1057; F. Dutile and E. Gaffney, *State and Campus: State Regulation of Religiously Affiliated Higher Education* (Notre Dame, Ind.: University of Notre Dame Press, 1984); Fernand N. Dutile, "God and Gays at Georgetown: Observations on *Gay Rights Coalition of Georgetown University Law Center v. Georgetown University*," *Journal of College and University Law* 15 (1988): 1; Douglas Kmiec, "The Higher Law Background of the Notre Dame Law School," *American Journal of Jurisprudence* 37 (1992): 213; Douglas Kmiec, "America's Culture War—The Sinister Denial of Virtue and the Decline of the Natural Law," *St. Louis University Pub. Law Review* (forthcoming 1994); Robert E. Rodes, Jr., *This House I Have Built: A Study of the Legal History of Establishment in England,* 3 vols. (Notre Dame, Ind.: University of Notre Dame Press, 1977–1991); C. Rice, *Fifty Questions on the Natural Law* (San Francisco: Ignatius Press, 1993); Thomas L. Shaffer, *Faith and the Profession* (Provo, Utah: Brigham Young University Press; Albany, N.Y.: State University of New York Press, 1987); and Thomas L. Shaffer, *On Being a Christian and a Lawyer: Law for the Innocent* (Provo, Utah: Brigham Young University Press, 1981).

20. Some would urge for religiously affiliated institutions a notion of academic freedom quite different from that prevailing at other universities: "The hesitancy of most church-related universities to define academic freedom in terms relevant to their distinctive purposes stems from their thralldom to the reigning norms of the secular academy" (Nuechterlein, "Idol," 16). For an example of the tension that can result from conflicts between orthodoxy and dissent, see Carolyn Mooney, "Conservative Brigham Young U. Contends with Small but Growing Movement for Change," *Chronicle of Higher Education,* June 30, 1993, A13; and Denise K. Magner, "President of Brigham Young U. Rejects Professor's Plea to Stay," *Chronicle of Higher Education,* December 8, 1993, A26.

21. "Del Gardner, an economist who has written about water-management policies, says that at [Brigham Young University] he has never felt the pressures from the agricultural establishment that he felt while teaching at public land-grant colleges" (Mooney, "Brigham Young," A13). See also Alfred J. Freddoso, "On Being a Catholic University: Some Thoughts on Our Present Predicament," *Fellowship of Catholic Schools Newsletter* 17, no. 1 (December 1993): 47: "I know beyond the shadow of a doubt that I personally have much more intellectual freedom [at Notre Dame] than I would at a . . . secular university."

22. Shaffer, "Arguments," 1859.

The Sins of the Cornishmen:
A Parable

SONIA G. GERNES

One February, on a day so blustery the rain came in spiteful pellets, and the wind was like a hatchet blade against the back of my head, I walked across the sea to an island off the coast of Cornwall. That's an unusual claim—walking across the sea—but much is unusual on that jagged, wind-eroded peninsula where once the flat world was thought to end.

I had taken the train from London two days before, dozing my way through an early twilight as the train slid along the coastline toward Penzance. Suddenly, an apparition glided into my peripheral sight. Across a beach silvered by the peculiar blue of dusk, across a band of silver water, a high, spiky island rose, and upon it a castle, turreted like an archetype of childhood dreams. I sat up straight and rubbed the glass to see if it were real—this strange, unearthly silhouette. I watched in full wakefulness until dusk and distance had blurred the image into the sea again, and the train began to slow for arrival in Penzance.

Whatever this vision was, I knew I had to go there. There are still a few romantic bones in my sensible, mid-life body, and they crave the remote, the mysterious, the lonely and wind-hewn, the secret of lives tucked into odd corners of the world. My host at the B & B gave a more mundane explanation: St. Michael's Mount, he said, was an eleventh-century monastery, built by the Benedictines who built Mont St. Michel off the coast of Brittany. Unlike its French counterpart, however, this monastery was seized and secularized, first being given to an order of British monks, then becoming in turn a fort, a crown property, and finally the stronghold of the local lord. It's open to the public, my host said—if you're persistent enough. Guided tours go up, but only on certain days in the off-season of February, and only at low tide when the sea recedes enough to expose a causeway of ancient stones—perhaps a third of a mile in length—which will get you more-or-less dry-shod across the expanse of water.

The day I went was a nasty day. I had gone with friends that morning on a little one-car train to the village of St. Ives, an artist colony strung out along a ragged bay, and between intermittent squalls and sunshine, we dodged the wind from gallery to gallery. My friends wanted to stay in St. Ives, so I went to St. Michael's alone, taking a series of local buses which set me down in increasingly more isolated spots with the promise that another bus would come along to claim me. When I finally reached the village, I sat on a bench until the tide was low enough to use the causeway.

The island is larger than it appears from the mainland—a support village of low-lying houses and outbuildings and military supplies surround the rocky outcrop on which the monastery was built. An elderly Cornishman was selling tickets in one of the outbuildings, but when I tried to buy one, he was reluctant to sell. "The tour doesn't go until three," he said in the pungent accent of Cornwall, "and there's danger today—the wind's too high. If the tour goes at all, you'll be on your own risk."

"Why is there danger?" I said. "Because I might blow off the rock into the sea?"

The Cornishman nodded. "Explore the bottom first," he said. "Think about it, Lass, and then decide."

I decided. I didn't want to blow into the sea—a rather melodramatic end to my semester in London—but I knew I wouldn't rest if I just turned away. I watched people stagger across the causeway, talk to the Cornishman and then turn back, but as three o'clock drew near, some of them stayed—even families with half-grown children.

Before the guide opened the gate to the path up the mount, he huddled us all in a bunch. "Stay together," he said. "Form a solid wall. Put the children toward the center and hang on to them." We did. We weren't taking any chances. We marched up that hill and into the wind in a phalanx, shoulder to shoulder, in a quasi-military step.

Why am I telling you this? What has my little travel tale to do with the question of Catholic character at the Notre Dame? Not much, probably, but I am neither theologian nor philosopher nor logician. I am a poet and storyteller; I deal in the language of emotion and the truths of human experience, and what I have to say about the issues themselves can be said in two sentences: Teaching at a Catholic university gives me, in one sense, a greater academic freedom than I would have at a secular or public university—the freedom to raise questions about belief and to create an atmosphere where my students are free to do the same. However, unless this institution acknowledges the other freedoms I possess (as a citizen of a democracy, for example, or a member of the academy) it's not a real university—it's not catholic or universal.

What has concerned me more this past year, as I've listened both to friends who fear that we are trading our heritage for a secular bowl of pottage, and to friends who fear that parochialism (and perhaps ecclesiastical censorship) will push out the less-than-orthodox and constrict intellectual inquiry, is the prevalence of the word *fear* in our discourse. We have as yet no story to tell us how this will all turn out, and while some of us fear that we will not be allowed to explore the castle and see the view for ourselves, some of us fear that anyone straying from the solid phalanx (especially those taking students with them) will blow into the sea.

As one who harbors both of those fears (though more of the former), I've been hard put to find consolation. What little I have comes from story itself (for story conveys truth without the exclusions that definition implies), or from storytellers who've come before me. One of the most potent of these in twentieth-century America was Flannery O'Connor, a skillful observer of the truth of human experience, who was also a flat-out, absolutely orthodox, pre–Vatican II Catholic. (She had no opportunity to be a post–Vatican II Catholic since she died in 1964.) O'Connor was not shy about asserting her religious stance: "I see from the standpoint of

Christian orthodoxy. This means that for me the meaning of life is centered in our Redemption by Christ and what I see in the world, I see in relation to that" (*Mystery and Manners*, 32).

However, O'Connor was equally adamant about artistic freedom and the necessity of individual vision: "The Catholic fiction writer is entirely free to observe. He feels no call to take on the duties of God or to create a new universe. He feels perfectly free to look at the one we already have and to show exactly what he sees. He feels no need to apologize for the ways of God to man or to avoid looking at the ways of man to God. For him, to 'tidy up reality' is certainly to succumb to the sin of pride. Open and free observation is founded on our ultimate faith that the universe is meaningful, as the Church teaches" (*Mystery and Manners*, 178).

O'Connor maintains that it is an abuse to think "that we can close our own eyes and that the eyes of the Church will do the seeing. They will not. We forget that what is to us an extension of sight is to the rest of the world a peculiar and arrogant blindness and that no one today is prepared to recognize the truth of what we show unless our purely individual vision is in full operation. When the Catholic novelist closes his own eyes and tries to see with the eyes of the Church, the result is another addition to that large body of pious trash for which we have so long been famous" (*Mystery and Manners*, 180).

Defending the integrity of the specific discipline, O'Connor insists that "the novel is an art form and when you use it for anything other than art, you pervert it. I didn't make this up. I got it from St. Thomas (via Maritain) who allows that art is wholly concerned with the good of that which is made; it has no utilitarian end. If you do manage to use it successfully for social, religious, or other purposes, it is because you make it art first" (*Habit of Being*, 157).

––––––––––

My own story of St. Michael's Mount is, however, about utility— about the uses of the imperfect. When we finally gained the top that blustery February day—past the trees, past the cannons, past the mounted guns—we had a magnificent view of the coastline. The wind tore at us above the battlements, but the configuration of jagged land revealed itself as something entirely new. We saw something else as well. Our guide pointed back the way we had come and said, "See the stone causeway—the one you crossed on. You were walking on the sins of the Cornishmen."

In the one of the early centuries, the guide explained, the abbot wanted a causeway built so that the monastery would be more accessible—at least at low tide—to pilgrims and those bringing gifts and supplies. Crafty as these old abbots often were, he offered to forgive one sin for every stone the Cornishmen cut and brought and put into place. (Assumedly Cornish women were included in the deal as well.) Obviously the locals were not a saintly lot, the guide pointed out, for the causeway is both long and wide.

Our little group chuckled in appreciation, then moved out of the wind and toward the castle door. I found myself lingering, however, watching the sea butt against these failings turned to stone. Something about the old abbot's idea pleased me, smacking of simony though it did. I realized standing there that in life I've never known quite what to do with failures and negative experiences, and as an academic I've never known what to do with partial or ever-changing truths. Aside from occasional (and usually short-lived) triumphs, I deal constantly with artistic judgments that are partly subjective, with research that may already be outmoded, with the sense that all of us can fall prey to premature conclusions, toadying to the latest trend, an excessive desire to shine. Half the statements I make today may be proved untrue tomorrow, and self-doubts pile up like stones rooted out of a garden, and like stones, they can trip and bruise and make people fall. But the old abbot was on to something. A university is made of many stones. Taken together, cut and fit and leveled by all the other stones, balanced against each other, they can pave—they can lead to a mountain—they can keep you dry.

When I finished my tour of St. Michael's Mount that day in February, the storm clouds over Cornwall had not abated, and the wind had not died down. The guides who had been so concerned that we march up in a solid phalanx seemed to have forgotten the danger now that the tour was over, so we straggled down the mount in ones or twos or threes. I was alone with no one and nothing in particular to hang on to, and sometimes I staggered from the force of the gale, and sometimes I had to pause to keep my balance, and sometimes on the causeway of stones I took a little ocean spray. But I don't remember being really afraid. The wind was still a hatchet at the back of my head, and my stout wool coat seemed made of the thinnest gauze, but I walked firmly and with a fair degree of confidence. I was walking on the sins of the Cornishmen, and I did not fall into the sea.

What Made Catholic Identity a Problem?

PHILIP GLEASON

Being an old-timer, I have personal recollections of Catholic academic life since the late 1940s when I was an undergraduate at the University of Dayton. And being a historian with a special interest in the development of Catholic higher education, I have recently learned a good deal about the subject that I did not know in the earlier phases of living with it since the 1940s. In what follows, I want to treat the Catholic identity issue from that combined perspective—as a long-time participant-observer and as a historian. The two dimensions have become so intermingled that it would be impossible for me to say which has been more important in shaping my present understanding of the subject. But what follows does not pretend to offer a systematic history. Its far less ambitious goal is to highlight some of the changes bearing on the issue that have taken place in my lifetime.

Considered from the vantage point of the present, the most striking thing about the Catholic identity issue in the 1940s and 1950s is that it did not exist. The reality, of course, existed—in the sense that Catholic colleges and universities definitely had that identity, were Catholic, and made no bones about professing their Catholicity. What did not exist was the "problem" of Catholic identity. That did not exist because the Catholicity of the institution was so much of a given—seemed so clearly a fact of nature—that no one regarded it as a problem any more than they regarded it as a problem that a college was a college and not a filling station or a furniture factory.

In other words, the Catholic identity (or Catholic character) of places like the University of Dayton in the 1940s was a reality that could be—and was, indeed—taken for granted. But there was a kind of paradox here, for the main reason Catholic colleges of that era could be unself-consciously Catholic was that Catholics were still self-consciously different. To be more precise, American Catholics were so conscious of holding distinctive religious beliefs that it seemed perfectly obvious that they needed their own schools to perpetuate the outlook on life that flowed from those beliefs.

So long as Catholics continued to constitute that kind of distinctive religious subculture, the Catholic identity of Catholic colleges would not emerge as a problem. For as Thomas LeDuc said in discussing the displacement of a religious orientation by a secular one at Amherst College, "The very acceptance of an idea operates to make exegesis needless and apology supererogatory. Only when its validity is challenged will there appear a body of definition and discussion."[1] The challenges that eventually started people talking about the problem of Catholic identity were only beginning to take shape at mid-century. They were still much weaker than the internal and external factors reinforcing that identity as a given quality whose existence could be taken for granted.

The chief internal factor reinforcing it was the continuing momentum of self-confidence produced by several decades of fabulous growth in numbers of faithful, in organizational energy, and in spiritual vitality. The Catholic intellectual revival of the interwar period—called by some the Catholic renaissance—carried over strongly into the post–World War II era. So did the various apostolic movements inspired by what was known at the time as Catholic Action. The closely related battle against "secularism," which had gotten under way in the thirties, reached its climax in the late forties. Thinkers like Jacques Maritain and John Courtney Murray, S.J., gained a respectful hearing for the Catholic tradition in philosophy and theology; on a less rarefied level, journalists like John Cogley applied natural law reasoning to the problems of the day. Catholicism attracted intellectual converts, and Thomas Merton's *Seven Storey Mountain* (1948)—the story of his conversion and vocation to the priesthood as a Trappist monk—became a minor publishing sensation. Monsignor Fulton J. Sheen, who was a famous convert maker, reached a wider audience as a lecturer, spiritual writer, and media personality.

In a word, the American Catholic subculture seemed to be in good shape, intellectually speaking. It was plagued by no doubts about having a distinctive religio-intellectual tradition, about the contents of the tradition, or about the responsibility that fell on Catholic colleges and universities to articulate the tradition, present it to young people, and represent it in the larger world of learning.

Externally, the religious identity of the Catholic college was reinforced by certain features of the national cultural scene. The war had sparked a revival of religion, for there were, as the saying had it, "no atheists in foxholes." On a deeper level, totalitarianism and war discredited secular liberal ideas of human perfectibility and rehabilitated "Christian realism." That expression was particularly identified with Reinhold Niebuhr, who infused his influential social and political commentary with the spirit of Protestant neo-orthodoxy. By the late 1940s, observers were calling attention to evidence of a major revival of religion. That, along with the country's Cold War repudiation of communism, was well calculated to bolster the morale of Catholic educators and reinforce their commitment to integrating faith and learning in their colleges and universities.

At the same time, however, countercurrents were beginning to build up that would at length render problematic the hitherto taken-for-granted quality of these institutions' Catholic identity. The subtlest was the continuing social assimilation of the Catholic population and the concomitant acceleration of the process by which Catholic colleges and universities adjusted themselves to prevailing standards in the larger world of American higher education (especially after they took up graduate work in earnest). This twofold process of social and academic acculturation took place gradually and—especially in respect to social assimilation—more or less beneath the surface. For that reason it went unnoticed for quite some time. Indeed, it was not until the 1960s that social scientists began to publicize the finding that Catholics had experienced dramatic upward mobility and by then surpassed their Protestant fellow citizens "in most aspects of status."[2]

As they became less distinguishable from other Americans in terms of income, occupation, residential location (for they, too, moved to the suburbs), and educational aspiration—and as the sense of ethnic distinctiveness faded for the grandchildren of immigrants—Catholics, especially the young people who came of age after World War II, began to wonder whether they were so different from everyone else that they had to have their own separate institutions, and why they were expected to hold different views from other people on matters such as divorce and birth control.

The earliest indication of this tendency was the intra-Catholic criticism of "Catholic separatism," "ghettoism," and the "siege mentality" that erupted around 1950 and continued strongly for several years. No doubt it was in part a response to hostile external criticism. For while the Catholic critics defended the church from foes like Paul Blanshard, who portrayed Catholicism as intrinsically un-American, they also wanted to eliminate whatever features of Catholic life gave needless offense to others. This made good sense in the highly charged atmosphere of interreligious conflict over issues like aid to parochial schools, which Protestants and secular liberals regarded as examples of arrogant aggressiveness on the part of Catholics. To defuse this kind of hostility, Catholic liberals urged their coreligionists to participate more actively in "the mainstream of American life" by joining "pluralistic" movements for social betterment along with Protestants, Jews, and nonbelievers.

The advice was perfectly justifiable in the circumstances, but it was also inevitably assimilationist in tendency. Insofar as it was assimilationist—and the confusing terminology of *pluralism* served to obscure the fact that it was[3]—intra-Catholic criticism of ghettoism implicitly endorsed the underlying social processes that were making Catholics more like other Americans and simultaneously weakening their distinctive identity. But even if this had been pointed out at the time, the critics would probably have dismissed it as unimportant. For they were objecting to what they considered unduly exaggerated forms of Catholic distinctiveness. Catholicity as such, they would have said, was far too deeply rooted to be at all threatened by eliminating these extremes.

This view of the situation was implicit in the most famous critique of American Catholic academic performance ever published—Monsignor John Tracy Ellis's "American Catholics and the Intellectual Life." Delivered first as a lecture at the spring 1955 meeting of the Catholic Commission on Intellectual and Cultural Affairs, published a few months later in the Fordham quarterly, *Thought,* and reprinted as a small book the next year, Ellis's blast set off a chain reaction of self-criticism that continued into the early 1960s. His target was not ghettoism as such, but the appallingly poor showing made by American Catholics in scientific research, scholarly publication, and intellectual leadership generally—all of which of course reflected very unfavorably on Catholic institutions of higher education. Ellis did, however, hit hard at ghettoism in his conclusion, which was that Catholic scholars' indolence and their "frequently self-imposed ghetto mentality" were primarily responsible for this dismal record.[4]

Yet despite his unsparing criticism, despite his coming down hard on ghettoism, and despite his urging Catholics to "mingle" more freely with "their non-Catholic colleagues," it was quite evident that Ellis regarded the Catholicity of Catholic scholarship as being too deeply rooted to be in any way threatened by a public airing of its deficiencies or by closer association with outsiders. On the contrary, it was only by following his counsel that Catholic scholars could "measure up" to their responsibilities as bearers of "the oldest, wisest and most sublime tradition of learning that the world has ever known."[5]

But as the chorus of self-criticism mounted in the late fifties, much else besides laziness and ghettoism was causally linked to "Catholic anti-intellectualism." Thomas F. O'Dea, for example, identified formalism, authoritarianism, clericalism, moralism, and defensiveness as the five "basic characteristics of the American Catholic milieu which inhibit the development of mature intellectual activity." And Daniel Callahan carried the logic of criticism to its seemingly inevitable conclusion by announcing that "the real culprit" was "the American Catholic mentality" itself.[6] At this point, one might reasonably have asked whether Catholics had any solid basis for thinking they had an intellectual tradition that was even respectable, much less one that was "the oldest, wisest, and most sublime" in the history of the world.

Though self-criticism was thus intended as an assault on Catholic smugness—which did, indeed, furnish a very large target—it could not help but raise deeper questions about the content of the Catholic intellectual tradition. That in turn posed an implicit challenge to the identity of Catholic institutions of higher education, for it was their ostensible dedication to that tradition that gave them their distinctive character. Increasingly sharp criticism of neoscholastic philosophy had the same effect, since it had previously been considered the intellectual centerpiece of the Catholic renaissance and the most essential element in the undergraduate curriculum. By late in the fifties, however, Catholic educators had largely abandoned their earlier preoccupation with integrating the curriculum around a core of neoscholastic philosophy and theology. Instead, they devoted themselves to the "pursuit of excellence"—with excellence being understood as the way things were done at places like Harvard and Berkeley.

Of course, most professors in Catholic colleges were too much absorbed in their own work to keep abreast of the Catholic intellectualism discussion, or to pay much attention to curricular developments that did not impinge directly on their own concerns (or the self-interest of their departments). But they were being affected by more subtle changes. One such change was heralded by growing opposition among Catholic sociologists to the older view that there was such a thing as "Catholic sociology." This was significant because sociology was different from mathematics or chemistry. No one had ever prescribed "Catholic" approaches to those subjects; but the founders of the American Catholic Sociological Society insisted that their discipline was different because the teacher-researcher's personal worldview and value commitments entered directly into the way sociology was studied and taught. The fact that a new generation of Catholic practitioners regarded the "Catholic sociology" approach as outmoded and embarrassingly parochial reflected a degree of academic acculturation that foreshadowed more pervasive identity problems to come.[7]

Those problems were to burst forth in the 1960s, but they did not do so right away. Pope John XXIII, who issued his call for *aggiornamento* in 1959, and John F. Kennedy, who was elected president the following year, seemed the bellwethers of a new and better day for an American Catholicism that had "come of age" (to use a phrase popular at the time). Indeed, the last of the strictly Ellis-inspired critics of Catholic higher education verged dangerously close to a new kind of smugness by asserting that, thanks largely to the younger lay professors who had absorbed professional standards in graduate school, Catholic colleges were in "transition from a prolonged intellectual adolescence to a point where they can face the challenges of maturity."[8]

By that time (1964), the pace of *aggiornamento* had picked up so markedly that the same author, John D. Donovan, could refer to "fundamental challenges to the validity and viability of the theological, structural, and historic warrants of the pre-1950 system" of Catholic higher education.[9] But this abstract, stuffily academic way of putting the point corresponded to the muffled and obscure state of the question at that time. The fundamental challenges were still latent. No one—or at least no Catholic—had come right out and said in plain language that just as there could be no such thing as Catholic sociology neither could there be such a thing as a Catholic university.

What precipitated that crucial next step, raising the issue in the starkest terms and causing it to be stated with brutal directness, was the explosion over academic freedom set off in December 1965, when St. John's University in New York summarily dismissed thirty-one professors. In the aftermath of that gross violation of academic due process, and as other academic freedom cases erupted, George Bernard Shaw's dictum that a Catholic university is a contradiction in terms was quoted repeatedly. John Cogley, who said a Catholic university was as outmoded as the papal states, also paraphrased Gertrude Stein in insisting that a university is a university is a university.[10] A faculty committee at my old alma mater (which had its own academic freedom crisis) issued a report, part of which proposed outright secularization as the goal to be achieved. But the unkindest cut, which was also the most revealing of changing attitudes, was delivered elsewhere. It came in 1966 from two Catholic professors at Fordham (one a layman, the other a priest) who said that urging people to take up an "intellectual apostolate"—a staple of earlier self-criticism—was tantamount to recruiting "holy panderer[s] for the Catholic Church."[11]

Catholic intellectuals—and therefore Catholic institutions of higher education as well—were obviously undergoing a severe crisis of confidence. A generation earlier, this would have been called a "failure of nerve"; by the mid-sixties, people spoke instead of "identity crises." At Notre Dame (where I had come as a graduate student in 1953 and joined the faculty six years later) the identity problem did not emerge directly from the uproar over academic freedom, although we did stage the first scholarly symposium on the subject ever held at a Catholic institution.[12] Notre Dame's awakening to the academic identity problem as such was a by-product of the more general identity problem that overtook American Catholicism after Vatican II. And that, in turn, took place against the background of the national crisis of confidence caused by racial violence, antiwar protests, and campus disturbances. Adding to the social and political turmoil were unsettling shifts on the cultural front, most notably the counterculture and the women's liberation movement.

The religious identity of Catholic colleges and universities thus emerged as an explicitly recognized problem when three powerful forces came together in the mid-1960s. The first of these was the social and educational assimilation of American Catholics that had been building up since World War II. Besides making them think and feel more like their non-Catholic neighbors, this progressive acculturation had been accompanied by self-criticism that made Catholic academics positively ashamed of the past and determined to break out of its mold.

How long it would have taken for these internal pressures to bring the Catholic identity issue to explicit formulation is a moot question, for the other two forces—Vatican II and the national cultural crisis of the sixties—intervened. In combination they popped the cork on the pent-up internal forces and multiplied the shattering effect of the resulting explosion. Their influence was especially marked in reinforcing and generalizing the tendency to reject the past that was already present as an element of the situation created by the internal pressures. *Change* was the talismanic word in those days. The past, as I heard the president of a Catholic women's college say, was irrelevant because the future would be entirely different!

Obviously this was not the only reaction to the council and the domestic upheaval, but it was of crucial importance for our topic. Why? Because the Catholic identity of Catholic colleges and universities was an inheritance of the past, and in the postconciliar climate that made it an ipso facto candidate for change. How could it remain a taken-for-granted assumption—an unself-consciously held and therefore unexamined given—when everything else in Catholic belief and practice was being scrutinized, challenged to justify itself, reinterpreted, modified, or even rejected? That their religious identity would now become an explicit problem was made even more inevitable by the fact that the colleges had been subjected to so much preconciliar criticism for weaknesses said to flow from clericalism, authoritarianism, and other characteristics associated with their being Catholic.

The emergence of the problem did not, of course, mean that those who discussed it—even those highly critical of the past—wanted Catholic colleges and universities to reject or abandon their religious identity. Outright secularization was an extreme option recommended by very few and followed by even fewer. The great majority of Catholic educators wanted their schools to remain Catholic. At the same time, however, they realized that being Catholic in the future could not be exactly what it had been in the past. For two reasons: because the self-understanding of the church as a whole had been transformed by the council, and because ongoing changes in Catholic higher education itself had reached a tipping point that required some fundamental readjustments.

Thus the Catholic identity problem was (and is) precisely that—a problem. It is a problem because, though Catholic identity is prized as something to be cherished, nurtured, and preserved, neither its substantive content nor the means to be employed in maintaining it are anything like as clear as they were in the preconciliar era. For we must remember that it was the clarity of Catholic religious beliefs in the 1940s—and the conviction that the church would never change her teaching—that made the Catholic identity of Catholic colleges a taken-for-granted given. After Vatican II, when the church's teaching had undeniably been changed, Catholic belief was not nearly so clear as it had been. How then could Catholic educators continue to take for granted what was no longer there as a given?

If the problem "surfaced" (as people used to say in the sixties) roughly three decades ago, how has it developed since then? That is too obvious a question to ignore, but too big a one to try to answer. Let me conclude with a few informal comments based mainly on what has happened at Notre Dame.

First, it is striking how much attention the subject has received. Thus when the new lay board of trustees took over its duties in 1967, the revised by-laws of the university included an explicit commitment to maintain Notre Dame's Catholic character and that commitment has remained an active concern of the board ever since. Each of the three major university self-studies since the early 1970s has also placed preserving Notre Dame's religious identity first among institutional priorities. And the issue has been discussed in many other campus forums over the years.

The prominence of the issue flows naturally from the shift from its being something that could be taken for granted to something that needs to be self-consciously articulated. Hence the discussion seems to me not only appropriate but vitally necessary. Even the disagreement that the discussion causes, potentially damaging to the internal harmony of the university community though it be, shows at least that the matter is being taken seriously.

The disagreement itself flows from the two sources mentioned above: the transformation of the church's self-understanding wrought by Vatican II and subsequent developments; and ongoing changes internal to Catholic colleges and universities. Illustrative of the first are differences between conservative and liberal Catholics over issues like academic freedom, theological dissent, the role of the magisterium, the relation of colleges and universities (especially the latter) to ecclesiastical authority, and the degree to which education for justice can serve as the core element in an institution's Catholic identity.

Among ongoing internal developments bearing on the Catholic identity issue the most important, in my opinion, are changes in the composition of the faculties of Catholic colleges and universities. Thirty years ago, Donovan drew attention to changes in outlook and orientation accompanying the growth of the lay faculties whose younger members were mainly recruited from leading secular graduate schools. The shifts he sketched have become more noticeable in recent years. Priests and religious have virtually disappeared as a numerically significant factor on many faculties and no longer dominate the ranks of academic administrators as they used to. Even more significant, however, is the operation of a generational transition that has all but completely displaced faculty members (lay and religious) who were formed when the earlier mentality held sway. Not all of the older generation were equally articulate about, or committed to, maintaining the religious character of their institutions, but it is a fair generalization that a good many more of them were so disposed than is the case with the generation that has replaced them. In addition, many of these younger faculty members consider it unprofessional—indeed, improper—to take a candidate's religion into account as a consideration in hiring. As a Jesuit writer has observed, by 1970 it had become déclassé to show any interest in that dimension of a candidate's background.[13]

The growth of this kind of feeling among faculty members, along with the disagreements already mentioned about what Catholic identity entails in substantive terms, adds up to a serious problem indeed. And its seriousness is heightened by the fact that overreaction to it, especially on the part of ecclesiastical authorities who feel an understandable concern for the future of Catholic colleges and universities, could easily make matters worse instead of better. Continued discussion is of course necessary, for what can no longer be taken for granted has to be raised to a new level of self-consciousness and articulated in more explicit terms.

It will not be easy for all parties to that discussion to combine the requisite degree of clarity and frankness with the equally essential qualities of moderation and—perhaps most important of all—respect for the goodwill of the opposition. For despite the depth of feeling involved, the suspicions aroused, and the polemics that too often accompany exchanges on the subject, there is, I believe, a great reservoir of goodwill still shared by all the parties to the discussion. Being a historian, I would like to think that the reservoir of goodwill is fed, at least in part, by the realization that what is at stake is the continuity of a tradition venerable in age, rich in humane associations, and honorable in its achievements, which it is our obligation to hand on in the form best suited to future needs.

Notes

A slightly different version of this paper was delivered as the Marianist Award Lecture at the University of Dayton, Dayton, Ohio, January 17, 1994.

1. Thomas LeDuc, *Piety and Intellect at Amherst College, 1865–1912* (New York: Columbia University Press, 1946), vii.

2. Norval D. Glenn and Ruth Hyland, "Religious Preference and Worldly Success: Some Evidence from National Surveys," *American Sociological Review* 32 (February 1967): 73–85.

3. For discussion of the conceptual confusion associated with the term *pluralism,* see Philip Gleason, *Speaking of Diversity: Language and Ethnicity in Twentieth-Century America* (Baltimore: Johns Hopkins University Press, 1992), 63–69.

4. John Tracy Ellis, "American Catholics and the Intellectual Life," *Thought* 30 (Autumn 1955): 351–88.

5. Ellis, "American Catholics and the Intellectual Life," 386–88.

6. Thomas F. O'Dea, *American Catholic Dilemma* (New York: Sheed and Ward, 1958), chap. 7; Daniel Callahan, *The Mind of the Catholic Layman* (New York: Scribner's, 1963), 98.

7. For more on this shift, see Philip Gleason, *Keeping the Faith: American Catholicism Past and Present* (Notre Dame, Ind.: University of Notre Dame Press, 1987), 67–70; and the articles in the fiftieth anniversary issue of *Sociological Analysis* 50, no. 4 (1989).

8. John D. Donovan, *The Academic Man in the Catholic College* (New York: Sheed and Ward, 1964), 193. The study on which this book was based was the last one commissioned by the CCICA as a follow-up to Ellis's critique.

9. Donovan, *Academic Man*, 195.

10. John Cogley, "The Future of an Illusion," *Commonweal* 86 (June 2, 1967): 310–16.

11. Edward Wakin and Joseph F. Scheuer, *The De-Romanization of the American Catholic Church* (New York: Macmillan, 1966), 261. The call for secularizing comes from "Academic Freedom at the University of Dayton: A Report of the President's Ad Hoc Committee for the Study of Academic Freedom at the University of Dayton, July, 1967" (copy in author's possession), esp. 25, 27–28. For background on the case, see Erving E. Beauregard, "An Archbishop, a University, and Academic Freedom," *Records of the American Catholic Historical Society of Philadelphia* 93 (March–December 1982): 25–39; this article does not, however, take note of the recommendation for secularizing.

12. See Edward Manier and John W. Houck, eds., *Academic Freedom in the Catholic University* (Notre Dame, Ind.: Fides Publishers, 1967).

13. Joseph A. Tetlow, S.J., "The Jesuits' Mission in Higher Education: Perspectives and Contexts," *Studies in the Spirituality of Jesuits* 15–16 (November 1983–January 1984): 33.

Scientific and Engineering Excellence in a Catholic Context

WILLIAM G. GRAY

This time in history is a period of exciting scientific and technological advancement. Journals, newspapers, and television report developments in space exploration, nuclear fusion, biological degradation of toxic waste, medicine, and a myriad of other remarkable areas. This expansion in knowledge is based on an increased fundamental understanding and application of chemistry, physics, biology, and mathematics. Individuals who are having the greatest impact in technological development are well educated in these basic sciences and in related aspects of engineering. Reports of scientific achievement typically refer to the investigator responsible as a "physicist," a "chemist," or an "engineer" according to his or her educational background. On the other hand, these reports rarely, if ever, make mention of the individual's religious affiliation, philosophy of life, or understanding of morality. In contrast, when a person becomes noteworthy in politics, literature, or the arts, that person's religious upbringing, practices, devoutness, code of ethics, and social history are scrutinized in great detail. A subjective description of personal and spiritual qualities is treated as providing more insight into ability to contribute in these fields than an objective listing of educational experiences.

As a consequence of comparing the classes of characteristics deemed to be important in defining scientifically and nonscientifically oriented individuals, one might infer that a discussion of the promise and challenge of a Catholic university will not have much relevance to departments in colleges of science or engineering. Indeed, one might be led to conclude that the role of Catholicism in science and engineering today should be very small. In addition, the church's past unwillingness to assess scientific data objectively, to view scientific findings as insights into God's creation, has caused it to play a negative role in the development of scientific knowledge. In the classic case illustrating the long-standing conflict between science and the church, Galileo's condemnation by Rome in 1663 for holding that Earth is not the center of the universe was not lifted until 1992. The fact that this final determination came at such a late date and only after a thirteen-year study of the case by experts appointed by John Paul II may cause some to place the insightfulness of the church in scientific matters on a par with that of the Flat Earth Society. As a consequence, consideration of the possible role the Catholic nature of university should have in education and scholarship might lead to the conclusion that Catholicism is an obstruction, or at best tangential, to the scientific education of young minds or in the development of new scientific knowledge. In reality, a tendency to conclude that a Catholic perspective may contribute to the orientation of a university's activities in a theology, philosophy, English, or other liberal arts department seems to exist. However, in structuring a curriculum in engineering or science, Catholicity is often viewed as impeding or, at least, in no way adding to the kind of education the engineer or scientist will receive.

If this view can withstand scrutiny, it has serious consequences for development of science and engineering in the context of a Catholic university. These disciplines will not be central to the mission of the university and will be only tolerated as expensive irritants that divert resources from the primary educational endeavors. Yet for a great Catholic university to exist, it must be a true university with teaching and research missions in diverse fields; it must be a great university providing the highest possible quality education and developing new knowledge and truths that have a significant impact on humanity's ability to improve the world; and it must be a Catholic university, imparting its knowledge of truth about God to animate rather than suppress all areas of intellectual inquiry. The view that Catholicity has no role in science or engineering at a university is merely an indicator of the failure of that institution to be great, of its failure to be Catholic, and of its limitations as a university.

The discussion at the University of Notre Dame that centers on whether it, or any other university, is, or can be, a "great Catholic university" seems to have taken on a new urgency in recent months. At the same time, the discussion tends to become stalled with much hand-wringing and angst but little enthusiasm for embarking on an adventure. One of the most common proclamations, in fact so common that it has taken on the aura of a cliché, is George Bernard Shaw's claim that *Catholic university* is an oxymoron. In the current local discussion, comparisons are also made with other universities, institutions said to have failed in remaining faithful to the religious orientations of their founders, a failure that cannot be tolerated here. Safeguarding the Catholic character of Notre Dame often centers around the actually trite condition of maintaining a Catholic majority on the faculty and then defining just exactly what this condition means. These arguments, in my view, do not get at the actual important issues that must be considered in assessing the character of Notre Dame or any other university.

Education at a Catholic University

The primary responsibilities of a university are to educate its students, to expand the base of knowledge, to seek truth, and to foster the intellectual life. The measure of the greatness of a university is the success with which it carries out these responsibilities. For a university to have an opportunity to be truly excellent, it cannot arbitrarily eliminate areas of knowledge and truth from study. Secular universities, however, have eliminated religious elements from their overall mission. Education and the search for knowledge at these schools are carried out in an environment that does not ask about or seek any supernatural implication to the areas of study. In fact, in many universities, the secular approach is not only areligious; it is anti-religious. Notre Dame, on the other hand, was founded with a religious dimension, with an explicit mission to incorporate the truth of God as understood in the Catholic tradition into its programs. The incorporation of a religious dimension, in fact, broadens Notre

Dame's mission and responsibilities in comparison with its secular counterparts. Achievement of excellence at a Catholic university is more daunting and difficult than achieving excellence at a secular university because it is a more general task. It requires excellence in a wider body of knowledge and truth than is considered at a secular institution. In the same way that a liberal arts college has defined its mission by excluding disciplines such as engineering from its curricula, secular colleges have defined their mission by excluding faith and the spiritual dimension of humanity from their curricula. Thus the phrase *Catholic university* is far from being an oxymoron but is rather a generalization of *secular university*. This generalization declares the institution's recognition of, and desire to incorporate in its curricula, the truths found in Catholicism, as well as its intention to study the incomplete or secular truth that exists when the spiritual aspect of life is denied. Furthermore, a Catholic university must also accept the responsibility to seek and develop truths about God and the church, a responsibility that may, at times, put it at odds with church hierarchy. Thus inherent in a Catholic university is a tension, a tension between adherence to church teaching of truths and responsibility to question accepted concepts for the purpose of enhancing understanding. This tension evidences itself in any Catholic university and will become even more significant in a truly great Catholic university.

In accepting the challenge of educating the young, a university endeavors to teach them to make decisions. These decisions may lie in the business arena, in chemical analysis, in any area of intellectual inquiry. In addition, students must learn to make decisions about their personal life, about freedom and responsibility, about a code of ethics that will guide them through life. For many students at Notre Dame, the college years are their first time away from home. These students are free to select when and how to relax, study, or recreate. A day in college is structured differently from a day in high school. Living in a dormitory is much different from living at home. College is a time of transition from being dependent upon one's parents to being more fully independent and responsible for oneself. A school that bills itself as a Catholic university has a serious responsibility at this time of its students' lives to challenge them to make decisions based on truth, knowledge, and prudence. A university must challenge its students to make responsible and informed decisions about disciplines for study, career options, personal morality, social behavior. At a secular institution, this guidance, if it exists at all, is offered in the vacuum of the absence of God's word and of the teaching of the church. The challenges in decision making that can be made to young people beginning to find their way can be made well in a university that is truly Catholic, that makes this challenge in the context of religious truth while adapting to the realities of the modern world.

Intellectual Freedom and a Dogmatic Church

In a university, although some changes occur very slowly, with important goals requiring tens of years to achieve, the rhythm of undergraduates progressing through their studies is such that the student body is renewed every four years. Phasing in a new educational program or fully implementing a new mode of interacting with students takes four years. In the Catholic church, the time required for change tends to be much longer than four years. Many Catholic faculty are products of the pre–Vatican II educational system that stressed conformity and orthodoxy over scholarly, or even thoughtful, consideration of church teaching. The old *Baltimore Catechism* taught young Catholics to regurgitate memorized answers to questions without comprehension or even knowledge of the words used. The Bible was not studied, or even seen, in Catholic grammar schools of the 1950s; it was considered to be too complex, too easily misinterpreted, beyond the ability of students (and their teachers) to understand. Rather, Bible history, consisting of sanitized narratives about the Bible, was a common part of the grammar school curriculum. Religious education was designed to conform the mind to the mold desired by the church, not to engage the mind in the early steps of a lifelong search for God. Catholicism was reduced to blind obedience to the laws of God and the laws of the church. For many, Catholicism was a regulated way of life that did not involve the intellect. For some, this regulation did lead to piety and deep faith. For others, the regulation produced a fear of God that interfered with coming to know God.

This tension between lock-step conformity and intellectual inquiry may also be viewed as a tension between the cause of faith and the effects of faith, between training and education. The church of thirty-five years ago seemed to operate on the principal that if a young person were regularly exposed to the rituals of Catholicism, he or she would continue the habit into adulthood. This strategy for building the church was most completely implemented in the Catholic schools. It was successful in some instances but in others was little more than the application of behavior reinforcement of the same order as teaching a trick to a pet. Attendance at Mass on First Fridays and on Sundays was an obligation monitored by Catholic school authorities with the idea that repetition at a young age would give rise to an unbreakable habit in maturity. Altar boys would memorize their Latin responses, typically with no understanding of the meaning of the dialogue with the priest that would take place at Mass. Many children passing through the parochial school system abandoned their faith shortly after the sister-trainer turned her attention to the next group of children. The mentality of religious education seemed to rest on the assumption that by training the young to participate in rituals designed to express faith, faith would develop. At most, faith was treated as an effect of participation in religious actions. At least, faith was merely equated with regular participation in the rituals of religion. A converse approach whereby faith developed through thought and inquisitive study of God would lead to a vibrant participation in religious rituals was not employed.

The movement away from heavy-handed authoritarianism in the church has been slow. The length of time over which changes occur is such that thirty more years must pass before most Catholic bishops will have spent their youth in the post–Vatican II era. Old habits die hard, and the current hierarchy is struggling with loss of the ability to obtain mindless adherence to their demands. The fact that change in leadership in the church takes more than a lifetime is at odds with the four-year residence time of a student in a university. A Catholic university of the old style in which ideas are not sifted and faith is measured by adherence to declarations by the hierarchy will never be a great university. Such an institution, by stifling the intellectual study of God, will be unable to generate new under-standing, or new knowledge, or enriched and truly deepened faith. This atmosphere of control must give way to an environment where a student comes to comprehend more about faith, to form his or her conscience, to come to grips with the life of faith that encourages decision making but is cautious about the great responsibility to make decisions based on knowledge rather than hearsay, whim, or peer pressure. A Catholic university that can foster this development of a young person will be consistent with a great university's challenge to foster the intellectual life and to educate its students. The propensity of the church to become exasperated with thought by the young and by the scholars who teach them leads it to revert to old form and simply demand conformity. Such demands threaten all Catholic universities' opportunities for true greatness. The promise of becoming a great Catholic university can only be fulfilled if the intellectual life at that university is nurtured so that this life incorporates and explores the widest possible body of knowledge including knowledge of God.

Although the church of today makes a greater effort to involve the minds of the faithful, the penchant for confusing the causes of a person's adopting Catholicism with the effects of adopting Catholicism remains. This is, perhaps, most clearly seen in the fact that enumeration of the characteristics of a Catholic university leads to statements such as the following, found in the Apostolic Constitution *Ex Corde Ecclesiae:* "In order not to endanger the Catholic identity of the university or institute of higher studies, the number of non-Catholic teachers should not be allowed to constitute a majority within the institution, which is and must remain Catholic."[1] Although this statement and philosophy may seem reasonable at first blush, in fact serious flaws exist. This restriction is incapable of making any distinction between nominal and practicing Catholics. It fails to take into account the personal commitments of individual faculty, Catholic or otherwise, to the truth-seeking goals of the institution. It fails to consider the uniqueness of the various disciplines represented on the faculty and their particular needs for excellence. In fact, a litmus test for Catholicity of an institution based on the claimed religious affiliation of the faculty hints at a mentality seeking conformity and an unwillingness to examine thoughtfully and to contribute meaningfully to an ongoing discussion of a university's success in achieving its educational goals. The call for a Catholic majority would seem, rather, to be a call for a controllable set of conforming Catholics, a set insuring that the hierarchy could impose its will if necessary. In distinction to this approach, the actual composition of the faculty, in terms of religious affiliation, should turn on the ability of the administration to articulate the goals and objectives of the university. In other words, a Catholic-oriented faculty will be a result achieved by defining the educational, research, and teaching goals of the university and then acting purposefully to see that those goals are achieved. In that context, the percentage of faculty who identify themselves as Catholic becomes irrelevant.

Leadership and Consistency within the University

A key element to assuring the Catholicity of a university through definition and achievement of educational goals while providing the possibility for greatness is leadership. The leadership must be successful at both articulating the goals of the institution and in assuring that the goals are accomplished. Important in this is the need for consistency. A university that desires to be a great Catholic university cannot compromise its principles. It must seek excellence in all it does and not swerve from the path it has taken for any expediency. Father Hesburgh has stated that one does not honor God with mediocrity, so indeed a Catholic university must seek excellence in its faculty, its students, its curricula, and its extracurricular programs. Similarly, the message it conveys to its faculty and students must also be conveyed to its friends, alumni, and the world at large. All entities with whom the Catholic university interacts must hear the same message, must know that the university is engaged in a search for truth and knowledge that includes the truth about, and knowledge of, God. Students who are in various stages of moral formation must not be presented one set of norms while others who interact with the university are presented a different set.

As an example of the difficulty in providing a consistent message, consider the very practical educational challenge facing Notre Dame in encouraging moderation among its students in the use of alcohol. This challenge is particularly important for universities because students undergo the transition to legal drinking age during their time in college and must be able to make responsible decisions as that transition occurs. The encouragement must come through social and moral educational programs, by example of the faculty, through leadership, and from the campus social environment. As a policy of the university, abuse of alcohol is to be discouraged. For such a policy to be real and to illustrate the commitment of the university, abuse of alcohol by faculty, alumni, and friends, as well as by students, must be discouraged. Nevertheless, excessive use of alcohol before, during, and after football games at Notre Dame is commonplace. The university, particularly as a Catholic university, has a responsibility to discourage such behavior. Catholicity implies an informed choice, so simply banning alcohol from campus is not the appropriate tack. Aggressive educational programs coupled with statements of policy aimed at convincing those who visit campus to use alcohol in moderation, if at all, are important elements of a consistent effort to educate students in truth. A policy encouraging moral behavior must not be compromised for benefactors or in such a way that morality might seem to be irrelevant on football weekends. The need for consistent presentation of principles and leadership promoting those principles is required, particularly in programs involving family life, social justice, technology for developing nations, personal honesty—all issues in which the university has the opportunity to apply its Catholic perspective.

Scientific Research in a Catholic Context

Some faculty or graduate students may argue that the Catholic character of the university, consistency between teachings and action, will limit their ability to conduct research because some topics will not be allowed. At this time, research in areas related to biological sciences involving human reproduction and fetal tissue research is among the most controversial. A recent article in the *Chronicle of Higher Education* argues in favor of research on the cutting edge of genetic science:

> Researchers have a right to conduct research that they find to be of medical or scientific interest. They may not have a right to federal, state, or university funds but if they find money from other sources, university administrators or boards should not stop research because it is ethically controversial, because it will bring bad publicity, or because guidelines are lacking.[2]

In the past, Galileo might have argued that celestial mechanics research was hindered by church involvement. Despite the close-minded zeal with which Galileo's research was suppressed and the resulting deep-seated fears harbored by modern-day scientists, the need to provide a context in which research can be done is incontrovertible. Several examples may help to illustrate this point.

One of the fundamental principles upon which fluid mechanical investigations are based is the equation of mass conservation. This principle states that the rate of accumulation of mass in a volume is equal to the net influx of mass into the volume across its boundary plus the rate of generation of mass within the volume. In the absence of nuclear reactions, the generation term will be zero. This principle can be expressed mathematically for infinitesimally small volumes and for deforming and moving finite volumes, as well as for simple volumes fixed in space. The ability to relate changes in mass within a volume to processes occurring at its boundary is extremely useful and is applied to virtually all engineering problems involving flow, such as canning of food, oil reservoir exploitation, rocket propulsion, sewer design, computerized weather prediction, etc. If one were to set up a research program, for example, involving the numerical prediction of tidal flows but decided to exclude overtly conservation of mass as one of the principles upon which the computer models would be built, the models developed would be able to predict fantastic processes. Moderate flows into San Francisco Bay might be shown to inundate the entire state of California. Massive public works projects might be advocated by the researchers to protect the state from this threat. Despite the freedom experienced by performing research without requiring that the equation of conservation of mass be satisfied, the scientific community at large would reject the results. Although this scenario may seem far-fetched, many tidal models do exist that fail to satisfy the constraint of mass conservation. However, these models do not overtly exclude the principle of mass conservation, they merely subvert the ability of the model to impose this constraint accurately. The ability of a computer model to conserve mass is, in fact, one of the standards that must be used in determining the quality of the model. Denial of the existence of the principle of mass conservation in consideration of tidal processes does not provide greater freedom and latitude in research; rather, work performed in which this principle is not effectively imposed is research that should not be performed.

Although this example may seem somewhat fanciful, one might make an argument that research, even in the humanities and social sciences, needs to be conducted with an awareness of basic scientific principles. This fact is implicitly recognized by the presence of science departments at liberal arts colleges and the traditional requirement made of all college students that they fulfill some science requirement as part of their degrees. Conversely, engineering and science students must have an awareness and appreciation of the humanities and the social sciences and fulfill a requirement in these disciplines as part of their degrees. Recognition that since the time of Erasmus of Rotterdam it has been impossible to be expert in all fields does not imply that an individual can work in his or her particular discipline oblivious to all other repositories and generators of knowledge.

A second case worth considering is the research done in Germany during World War II. At that time, controlled experiments designed to determine the ability of humans to survive in the absence of food, in the absence of drink, or when subjected to extreme cold were conducted. These are important questions, and knowledge in this area can contribute to determining the scope of a rescue operation that might be conducted for people lost at sea, in optimizing logistics for Antarctic exploration, or in determining the supply load requirement for future deep space exploration by humans. Indeed, research designed to improve understanding of the capabilities and limitations of the human body is important. The scientists who conducted the human experiments in the 1940s were working to make contributions in biological sciences. Despite this fact, the German research has been almost universally condemned. This work showed a complete disregard for the value of human life by the research teams and of the rights of those individuals subjected to the tortuous, life-ending tests. This research proceeded because of the absence of a strong voice calling for an ethical approach to scientific study, because scientific research was promoted while denying the existence of certain fundamental principles. Scientific research performed in isolation from other important principles may also run amok. All research performed in denial of fundamental truths shares that same risk. Indeed, some research that may be carried out at a secular institution would be of a different scope from that carried out at an institution that recognizes truths about God. The ability of a Catholic institution to provide perspective and a larger context to the work that is carried on within its confines is a strength not a weakness.

Lest there be misunderstanding, let me emphasize that the role of the Catholic aspect of a university is not to intrude in disciplines without respect, to dictate appropriate areas of knowledge for study, to restrict intellectual inquiry. Departments at a Catholic university must not attempt to align their disciplines such that each has a distinctively and narrowly Catholic flavor defining Catholic chemistry, Catholic literature, Catholic engineering, or even Catholic theology. The Catholic nature of a great university provides a context, a set of truths, a tension that challenges, enriches, and broadens all areas of inquiry. This type of impact is not unique to the Catholic side of a university in that history, language, physical principles—any body of truth—will also have an impact on all research, education, and service activities of a great university. Incorporation of Catholicism in a university is the expression of a desire to include a store of truth in the life of the university that is considered nonessential in a secular university. However, a Catholic university should not treat its Catholic nature as an extra appendage that requires particular consideration and attention to prevent it from being amputated. Catholic character must be woven into the fabric of the university. Unfortunately, the unfulfilled development of a great Catholic university at Notre Dame and at all other institutions of higher learning has led to a defensive posture whereby departments are asked to single out how the Catholic character has an impact on them; statistics on percentages of Catholics on the faculty are studied scrupulously; and faculty express concern that conformity will be imposed. For a university to develop towards greatness, its Catholic character must be developed and proclaimed consistently by a visionary administration as an additional opportunity for the study of truth. It cannot be erected as a wall designed to constrain and exclude.

Excellence in a Catholic Context

Activities in science or engineering may be thought to be stepchildren in a discussion of, or effort to develop, a great Catholic university. Indeed, the content of courses such as thermodynamics, paleontology, ecology, or structural analysis at a Catholic university will be essentially indistinguishable from their counterparts at any other quality university. However, the Catholic character provides an overall context for education such that the technology learned can be better placed in the perspective of societal needs and deeply understood as a manifestation of God's provisions for humanity. Technology is relied on by society to cure a great number of its ills. Technology has been used for economic development, to design weapons alleged to insure peace, to improve farm productivity, to eradicate disease, and to preserve buildings, writings, and art that constitute our cultural heritage. Naudascher has observed that science and engineering are often relied on to remedy ills even when those ills exist precisely as a result of technological realizations of earlier hopes.[3] Many of our attempts to solve societal problems by technological or social programs have failed because they simply address material need; they do not consider the need to capture and engage the human spirit, to incorporate Truth. Students educated to consider technology and science as components, and not necessarily the most important components, of the array of truths that contribute to human well-being are apt to be more able to contribute significantly to the solution of the world's problems. In no case can Catholic character be a rationale for inferior education in science, engineering, or any other identifiable discipline. Indeed, Catholic character requires more of students and researchers than the omission of the truth that is implied by promotion of secular character only. Those who participate in developing excellence in a Catholic context should clearly recognize that the standard for excellence is higher and more difficult to achieve than in a context that does not consider the total spectrum of truths. This realization must not be a deterrent from striving for the goal of a truly excellent Catholic university nor may it be an excuse for compromising or settling for anything less.

Notes

This essay is offered with deep appreciation to the people of St. Brigid's parish, San Francisco, who have worked for the last 130 years giving of themselves and their resources to build a community of faith. As a child, I benefited greatly from the generosity, kindness, and Christianity of the parishioners of St. Brigid's. This community is now faced with the forced closure of their historic church in June of 1994. The closure seems to be driven by a mentality that values funds over faith, power over piety, conformity over Catholicism, a mentality that threatens universities as well as parishes—and men and women of goodwill everywhere, in all walks of life, who strive to build excellence and Catholicity into their endeavors.

1. John Paul II, Apostolic Constitution of the Supreme Pontiff, *Ex Corde Ecclesiae,* article 4, item 4.

2. John A. Robertson, "Protecting Research on the Cutting Edge of Genetic Science," *Chronicle of Higher Education,* November 24, 1993, A40.

3. Eduard Naudascher, "On a New Dimension in Our Engineering Work," contribution to the Symposium on Megatrends in Hydraulics Research for the Future, Fort Collins, Colorado, July 1985.

Some Theological Reflections on
Ex Corde Ecclesiae

CATHERINE MOWRY LACUGNA

In 1979 Pope John Paul II published *Sapientia Christiana*, a document governing the relationship between ecclesiastical faculties and institutions (those established by charter with the Vatican and that grant degrees in the name of the Vatican). This was followed by the 1990 Apostolic Constitution on Catholic universities, *Ex Corde Ecclesiae*, which applies to all other Catholic institutions of higher learning and is directed to all those who either govern them or have any interest in them, including bishops, religious congregations, and laity. The majority by far of Catholic colleges and universities come under the norms of *Ex Corde Ecclesiae* rather than *Sapientia Christiana*, so the focus of this essay is *Ex Corde*.

Ex Corde Ecclesiae is a substantive reflection by the pope on the religious ethos that lies at the heart of the Catholic university. As such it provides a welcome occasion to think about the mission and identity of Catholic universities from an explicitly Catholic perspective, and in that way to think also about the relationship between the Catholic university and the Catholic church. Unhappily, *Ex Corde* has recently become controversial, largely because the norms proposed by the Committee on Education of the U.S. National Conference of Catholic Bishops for its implementation appear to most educators to be quite unworkable and indeed detrimental to the academic freedom and legal standing of universities. (As of this writing, the ordinances are merely proposed and have not become juridically binding, thus it would be out of place to comment on them here) The most prudent course is to approach *Ex Corde Ecclesiae* in a spirit of genuine intellectual inquiry and honesty and to examine the present pope's vision of the university in relationship to the church. After a brief overview, I will focus on two principal theological proposals in the document: first, the title and opening line, the claim that the Catholic university is born *ex corde ecclesiae,* from the heart of the church; and second, the view that the Catholic university is *in* the church. Each of these is a significant theological claim, as distinct from, say, an exhortation to university administrators or to bishops. By *theological claim* I mean a statement pertaining to the nature of some theological reality, in this case, the church. Underlying these two principles is an ecclesiology (view of the nature of the church) that can legitimately be scrutinized by a theologian from an explicitly theological point of view.

Brief Overview of Ex Corde Ecclesiae

Work on the apostolic constitution began in 1985, when the Vatican Congregation for Catholic Education initiated a process of consultation with educators to prepare a pontifical document on Catholic universities. The document went through several drafts, incorporating recommendations and suggestions from specialists in Catholic higher education. On various occasions delegates from Catholic colleges and universities worldwide met with the pope to discuss preliminary schemas and further drafts.[1]

The constitution is divided into two parts. The first treats the Catholic university's identity and mission, and the second contains general norms for application to "all Catholic universities and other Catholic institutes of higher studies throughout the world" (no. 1.1). The document emphasizes the consecration of the Catholic university to the cause of truth and acknowledges the need for institutional autonomy and academic freedom to carry out this aspect of its mission. Four essential characteristics make a Catholic university Catholic: inspiration of individuals and of the whole university community; continuing reflection in the light of the Catholic faith upon the totality of human knowledge, to which it also seeks to contribute; fidelity to the Christian message as mediated by the [Catholic] church; service of the people of God and of the human family. *Ex Corde* also examines the role of theology in the Catholic university and vis-à-vis the magisterium; the importance of the laity in carrying out the mission of the Catholic university; the relationship of the university to the local bishop; the university's service of the human community; the need for pastoral ministry; dialogue with culture and with science; ecumenism; and evangelization.

The Catholic University: Born Ex Corde Ecclesiae

Two unique theological claims frame the document. The first is that the Catholic university is born *ex corde ecclesiae,* from the heart of the church. The historical origin of the universities was indeed the Catholic church. In the mid-thirteenth century the University of Paris was established out of the cathedral school of Notre Dame; shortly thereafter universities flourished at Bologna, Oxford, and elsewhere. There is also a philological connection between the terms *catholic* and *university.* In Latin the words for university are *universitas studiorum,* the universality and totality of studies. *Catholic* already means universal.[2] Despite this history, in the contemporary academic world *Catholic* and *university* are at times seen as contradictory terms, especially when being Catholic has entailed a lack of genuine intellectual freedom because of limitations imposed by ecclesiastical authorities on intellectual inquiry.

But the pope is making more than a historical or philological observation. For him, the Catholic university is *ex corde ecclesiae* because the university participates in, and indeed activates, the mission of the church. The unique vocation, characteristics, and tasks of a Catholic university, and the particular way it pursues its commitment to research and teaching, are, for the pope, *means by which the church preaches the gospel.* To be sure, through teaching and research the Catholic university fulfills its own nature, which he describes as "confronting the great problems of society and culture" (no. 13). But for the pope, teaching and research are means by which the Catholic university also proclaims the gospel of Jesus Christ. While the pope clearly adverts to the autonomy and academic freedom of the Catholic university, he also describes the Catholic university as an instrument that the *church* offers to our age; the Catholic university assists the *church* to find cultural treasures *nova et vetera;* the Catholic university enables the *church* to initiate dialogue with people of every culture; the Catholic university is essential to the growth of the *church* and the development of Christian culture.

Clearly the pope envisions the Catholic university as entirely in the service of the church, even if the university in some sense inhabits its own proper sphere. For the pope, the Catholic university is by definition not a neutral or generic institution; precisely what makes it Catholic is its ecclesial character and connection. In *Ex Corde* the Catholic university is explicitly charged to proceed in a manner consistent with Scripture, with tradition, and with the hierarchical magisterium which is described as the authentic guarantor of divine revelation. The document states that all academic disciplines fit in the context of a vision of the human person and the world that is enlightened by the gospel and by faith in Christ, the Logos, who is at "the center of creation and human history" (no. 16). Presumably this applies as much to mathematics and electrical engineering as to literature and theology.

People working in higher education in the United States are unaccustomed to thinking of the Catholic university as born *ex corde ecclesiae*, as an institution that is church-sponsored in the sense that the church offers the university to society, or in the sense that the ultimate responsibility of the university is, through its research and teaching, to serve the gospel of Jesus Christ. More likely, we think of the mission of the Catholic university as complementary to the mission of the church. To use the document's own language, the Catholic university is indeed shaped by the religious and intellectual traditions of Catholicism; committed to the dialogue between reason and faith; concerned for the ethical dimensions of knowledge; diligent in the teaching of students; active in dialogue with all cultures and with other religious traditions; and concerned about the formation of the whole person. Most educators would probably see a happy coincidence between these dimensions of a Catholic university's life and the tasks that belong properly to the church's life and ministry.

But does any of this necessarily mean that the Catholic university originates out of the church? Could we not just as well say that the Catholic university is born *ex necessitate scire omnia*, born from the need of the human mind and heart to know everything, the need of faith to understand itself, the need of the human spirit to make sense out of the human condition and the world by bringing to bear on these mysteries all the fields of knowledge and inquiry, including theology? For example, the document states that research at a Catholic university includes (1) the search for the integration of knowledge; (2) a dialogue between faith and reason; (3) an ethical concern; (4) a theological perspective. Probably many of those involved in Catholic higher education are in agreement with *Ex Corde* that the mission of the Catholic university to search for ultimate truth is not at all inconsistent with the Catholic beliefs that all truth derives from God and that there is a fundamental unity of all human knowledge. But is this true because the Catholic university is born *ex corde ecclesiae*, or because the human heart and mind, shaped by the traditions of Catholicism and Christianity, seek to understand the human person and the world from a religious and indeed an explicitly Catholic perspective?

The critical point seems to be the meaning of the word *church*. As it stands, the document very nearly equates the church with the institutional church or with the hierarchical magisterium. But the church is the whole people of God, all members of the Body of Christ. While it is impossible to say exactly what the pope has in mind with the word *church*, there is certainly a widespread reflex to read the word, especially as it appears in pontifical documents, as if it means only the hierarchy. As a theologian and an educator, I would suggest that it would be possible and indeed fruitful to rescue the phrase *ex corde ecclesiae* by interpreting it in a way more consistent with contemporary theology and ecclesiology. To say the university is born *ex corde ecclesiae* should mean, from the heart of the people of God whose quest for knowledge is genuinely religious. What is the heart of the church? The heart of the church is the Holy Spirit who is leading the church into the fullness of truth. But the institutional church does not control the Spirit, nor does the church control the human need and desire for knowledge, which is why the Catholic university is not simply an extension of the church.

In other words, the desire to know all things religiously is not bestowed by the church, as if the church were the sole source of the gifts and presence of the Spirit. From a theological standpoint, on the one hand it would be a mistake to drive a complete wedge between the church and the Catholic university and see no connection between their missions, but on the other hand, it would also be a mistake to collapse the identities of church and university and sacrifice the genuine autonomy of the university vis-à-vis the church.

These qualifications on the phrase *ex corde ecclesiae* help to explain, for example, why so many Catholic institutions open the academic year with a Mass of the Holy Spirit. These institutions aspire to be an instrument of the Holy Spirit who brings all things to truth; presumably if the Catholic university authentically searches for truth and does so from a self-consciously Catholic perspective, then it may indeed be a vehicle for the Spirit. This perspective also explains why the mathematician, to use a common example, need not be Catholic to work productively and harmoniously within the aims and mission of the Catholic university. The vocation of the mathematician is to seek mathematical truth according to the methods provided for by that science; from the perspective of Catholicism, this search for truth is an inherently religious enterprise, regardless of how the individual mathematician regards her discipline.

The University Is in *the Church*

The second central theological claim in the document is that "the university is *in* the church." This is jarring for those of us who think of the Catholic university as having its own proper sphere—however much there might be points of commonality between the missions of the Catholic church and of the Catholic university. According to the document, the Catholic university's relationship to the church is essential to its institutional identity qua university. The university is said to participate in the life of the local church where it is situated, and in the life of the universal church by virtue of its role in a worldwide community of scholars. This connection between church and university creates "a special bond with the Holy See" (no. 27) and entails adherence to the teaching authority of the church in matters of faith and morals. Individual Catholics are called to personal fidelity to this same teaching authority; non-Catholics are required to respect the Catholicity of the university.

It should not be overlooked that the document also claims that bishops are to participate in the life of the Catholic university and "to promote and assist in the preservation and strengthening of their Catholic identity, including the protection of their Catholic identity in relation to civil authorities" (no. 28), even if the bishops do not do so through internal governance. In the norms given in *Ex Corde Ecclesiae*, as well as in the norms proposed by the American Catholic bishops for implementation of this document, the local bishop is given an unprecedented responsibility for guaranteeing the catholicity of Catholic universities, along with an astonishing and disturbing degree of control over the license of Catholic theologians to teach theology. The university is even required to report periodically to the competent ecclesiastical authority about the university and its activities.

To say that the Catholic university is *in* the church is quite a different matter from saying that the mission of the Catholic university is consonant in certain, but limited, ways with the mission of the church. The Catholic university and the Catholic church inhabit their own proper spheres. It is not the role of the magisterium to define the mission of the Catholic university. At best this is a work of the whole people of God who undertake to seek truth with an explicitly religious purpose. The implication being drawn from the two precepts that the university is born *ex corde ecclesiae* and that the university is *in* the church is that the magisterium has jurisdiction over the Catholic university. This cannot be correct, since the need of the human spirit to know the truth, and the human creativity and ingenuity at work in the construction of a university, do not derive from the church narrowly understood; these result from the way God has created us: with limitless desire for knowledge and understanding. The search of the human heart for truth is beyond the power of the church's magisterium to bestow or to control. The search for truth and knowledge is not inconsistent with the mission of the church; however, the autonomy of the university, to which the document adverts explicitly, requires freedom from ecclesiastical jurisdiction. Of course *Ex Corde* assumes that communion with the church will never be incompatible with academic freedom and autonomy. Perhaps in an ideal world this would be true, but there is too much in the history of the church to indicate that the hierarchical magisterium sees itself authorized to interdict, interfere with, censure, restrict, or terminate the employment of scholars and professors.

In the field of theology in particular, theologians are mandated to submit to the teaching authority of bishops and to assent to Catholic doctrine. It is unclear what the word *submit* means here; the mechanism suggested by the proposed ordinances for implementation would require theologians to seek a mandate from the "competent ecclesiastical authority," usually a local bishop. It is also not clear what *competent* means here, since fewer than a handful of American Catholic bishops have been trained as theologians.

Certainly authentic Christian and Catholic theology requires an explicit ecclesial—not ecclesiastical, but ecclesial—connection. Theological scholarship is motivated by love for the church and the desire to serve the church through intellectual work; but theology is also an academic enterprise proper to the university. As such, theology has its own proper dynamics and methods that cannot be circumscribed by the magisterium. Theology can serve the church only if the theologian is truly free to search for truth wherever she finds it. (I am presuming, of course, that the theologian is appropriately conscientious about her or his responsibilities to Scripture and tradition.)

Furthermore, bishops are not necessarily competent in academic matters or in matters requiring theological expertise, any more than academic theologians are necessarily competent in pastoral matters. Consecration as a bishop does not grant infused scientific or theological knowledge. Indeed, not every spiritual or theological insight comes through the institutional church. There are legitimate advances in knowledge (religious and other) that come through trained experts in universities. This should alarm no one, since, according to the Catholic vision, all truth is the fruit of the Holy Spirit, who blows where the Spirit wills. To be sure, *Ex Corde* assumes that there is no truth to be found, scientific or theological, that could possibly be inconsistent with revelation. "While each academic discipline retains its own integrity and has its own methods, this dialogue [between faith and reason] demonstrates that 'methodical research within every branch of learning, when carried out in a truly scientific manner and in accord with moral norms, can never truly conflict with faith. For the things of the earth and the concerns of faith derive from the same God'" (no. 17). Again, in an ideal world, perhaps this would be true, but the hierarchical magisterium has shown itself on many occasions all too ready to foreclose topics that deserve vigorous discussion within the academy, or to pronounce on matters that require genuine scientific or theological expertise.

The Catholic university is *in* the church only in the limited sense that the Catholic university is the undertaking of members of the church. As such, the university arises out of the charism (gift of the Spirit) of a whole people. But the Catholic university is not *in* the church in the sense that it is subject to ecclesiastical jurisdiction; nor can the Catholic university be subject to limitations about what questions and issues scholars may legitimately pursue, or, worse, what conclusions may be reached.

I have drawn attention to two principal ideas in the document: that the Catholic university is born *ex corde ecclesiae,* and that the Catholic university is *in* the church. I have argued that while there is a legitimate and even inherent connection between the mission of the church and the mission of the Catholic university, it is improper to see the Catholic university as derived from, and therefore subject to, the jurisdiction of the institutional church.

In the case of the discipline of theology in particular, the theologian at one and the same time contributes to the missions of both church and university. For most of us who work as theologians in an academic setting, these two dimensions of our work are inseparable. We desire to serve both church and academy through our scholarship. It would be ironic, and unfortunate, and it would diminish the well-being and ultimately impede the mission of the church, if, in the struggle to maintain the theologian's freedom and intellectual integrity, she or he were forced to choose between serving either the church or the academy. By the same token, it would be tragic if the Catholic university were forced to relinquish the nomenclature *Catholic* in order to be free from ecclesiastical interference, free to be itself, and thereby to pursue truth in a truly Catholic way.

Notes

1. For a complete account of the origins of *Ex Corde Ecclesiae,* see *Origins* 20/17 (October 4, 1990): 266–76; and John P. Langan, ed., *Catholic Universities in Church and Society: A Dialogue on* Ex Corde Ecclesiae (Washington, D.C.: Georgetown University Press, 1993).

2. George Tavard, "Comment," in Langan, *Catholic Universities in Church and Society,* 65.

The Catholic University:
Living with ND (Necessary Dissonances)

DAVID C. LEEGE

They gathered as they do, four thousand strong, each night, four nights hand running, for the annual Christmas festival at St. Olaf College. Pilgrims, they sat hushed and expectant in Skoglund Center Auditorium, not really an auditorium with amenities, just a gymnasium with folding chairs on the floor flanked by uncomfortable bleachers. And despite the lingering sweetness of lefse and lingonberries on their lips, the annual ration of lutefisk rumbled in their stomachs. Then, to the orchestra's lead, five choirs processed, banners flowing, crosses lifted high.

Almost as tall as the crosses, the campus chaplain strode forward and intoned, "Those who dwelt in deep darkness—on them the light has shined. What wondrous love is this, O my soul!" The choirs and orchestra lifted their bowed heads, seven hundred of them, one-fourth of the students—mathematicians, economists, political scientists, biologists, elementary education majors, philosophers, and some music majors. Pat, my wife, looked at me and I at her. We teared over. Well, not just tears, great suppressed sobs. God is present in this community of learners and pilgrims! There is meaning to life here, among these searchers of every kind, because they know God is present in history, in them. And despite its differences of ethnic heritage, that is where we also live our daily lives, in a Catholic community of searchers under the patronage of our Lady.

127

As if to affirm our article of faith, the massed choirs followed a brass fanfare with the poetry of Richard Crashaw in the music of Richard Dirksen, first in unison, then in mysterious dissonances:

> Welcome all wonders in one sight!
> Eternity shut in a span.
> Summer in winter, day in night,
> Heaven in earth, and God in man.

The strings and the woodwinds conversed, while the choirs continued, once with a lone soprano section asserting itself, often, all humbled in awe:

> That he, the old eternal Word,
> Should be a child and weep.
> Each of us his lamb will bring,
> Each his pair of silver doves,
> Till burnt at last in the fire of thy fair eyes,
> Ourselves become our own best sacrifice.

Then, beyond their dissonances, their awe-full pleas, their well-scored individualisms, they restated the theme in an ornamented chorale:

> Welcome all wonders in one sight!
> Eternity shut in a span.
> Summer in winter, day in night,
> Heaven in earth, and God in man.
> Welcome all wonders in one sight!

The hope that is the Catholic university is celebrated over and over in the liturgies of Word and sacrament, the liturgies of learning, the liturgies of life. Liturgy has as its primary function the celebration of oneness, of unity, of community. Liturgies find expression in both consonance and dissonance. They challenge the cacophony of babble, of individualisms so loud that other voices cannot be heard. While the confident community occasionally needs the strength of the chorale, even then it relies on an ornamented line to play off of the stable harmonies and give the chorale depth. Liturgy responds to the challenge of the new, not with ossification, but with examination and often incorporation. The altar is brought out to the people; the Gospel is read in their midst.

And to this confrontation with old stone and old paper the people bring new expression and new understanding. They sing the ornamented line of the chorale.

Nowhere is this process more elemental, more vivid, than at the university that springs from, and struggles with, its founding faith. There is the potential for enormous academic freedom at the Catholic university. The confidence that God is made flesh, that God is not only creator but one of us, within us, and is our redeemer and sustainer, makes all learning possible. No question—of mechanism, of meaning—is out of bounds at this university, for it is all a wonderment. No orthodoxy of current or past magisterium or of political correctness dare stand in the schoolhouse door. The hypothesis unentertained is the failure of the student, the scholar, or the church leader to find current meaning in the three articles of the Creed. The fear of exploration betrays a flagging confidence in the robustness of God's grace. God is patient with the searcher, God guides, God can and will judge. Some wags sport a marvelous sweatshirt that reminds us:

> God is dead.
> —Nietzsche
> Nietzsche is dead.
> —God

This obligation of each of us to our creator, redeemer, and sustainer is a scandal to Jew, Greek, and Christian, to extend Paul's terms. For the Christian humanism that impels the Catholic university pushes the individual scholar alternately between exhilarated highs and dejected lows. I think of it, in my extension of Ogden Nash, through the mystery of incarnation:

> If odd of God
> to choose the Jews,
> More odd of God
> to be in me.

The highs of this freedom come from the insatiable search for knowledge, from solving the puzzle, whether it be in tectonic movements, in energy in matter, in genes and mutations, in voter realignments, or in moral reasoning. The lows come not only from the intractable problem, but also from the profound disease, that the creature may conclude he or she is more powerful than the creator. That is why we have universities and colleagues and students instead of solo practitioners. If not sufficiently humbled by a spouse or a child, we are quickly brought to our knees by colleagues and students who observe our stupidities and dismiss our published flatulence.

Responsible peers are the best protection against our excesses. They can administer blows to the ego—were it not for egos, we could not survive the academy—far more effectively than a bishop armed with ordinances or some other well-intentioned extension of *Ex Corde Ecclesiae.* Colleagues remind us when we have not taken covenant, Christ, or Socrates seriously. If they fail to do so, we fail to be a Catholic university. If a bishop feels obligated to perform in this role, we place him in an unfamiliar setting where he does not belong. He will bungle it worse than did our peers. In my eighteen years at Notre Dame I have yet to feel that external intervention is even remotely necessary.

Other highs and lows come from our contacts with our students. The highs almost always are the products of deferred gratification. To be sure, most students overrate us on teacher-course evaluations. They could not possibly know we were that good—yet. And we know we are not that good because we are not routinely producing Rhodes, Marshall, and other prestigious fellows. But they do leave Notre Dame literate—even the athletes, the children of faculty and staff, and the Domer legacies. Most of them have outstanding verbal skills—although like a conversation like with a student on like campus about like anything will have more likes in it than it like needs. Many students are ethically sensitive, both in a personal and in a social sense; that is a tribute not only to the religious life on campus, the Center for Social Concerns, the Hesburgh Program in Public Service, the Kroc and Kellogg institutes, the faculty, classmates, dormmates, and rectors, but also to one or both of their parents. A few students are skunks, but then, I have met their fathers and I understand a home environment that nurtures cheaters, self-aggrandizers, and opportunists. Their fathers were that way when they were here, my older colleagues explain. So we fail at times—intergenerationally. Some of our students even enjoy learning—which is different from liking entertainment by teachers—and they will continue to engage faculty in correspondence and conversation.

That is where the deferred gratification comes. It is not uncommon to receive a Christmas letter from a student five or ten years out who says, "You know that project you made me do" (or "that technique I had to master," or "those arguments I had to abstract")—"and how I resisted it? I now do that for a living and I love my job. In fact, I love Notre Dame because you understood what I needed and wouldn't let me get by with less." Those are the nicest Christmas presents a teacher could receive, and our former students are gracious enough to send them. That is the sense of community, of responsibility, we have to each other in the Catholic university. I once had a student, an English major, who had to rewrite his research paper four times before I would accept it. He got angry with me. But he did a second major, took extra courses, returned to the Freshman writing laboratory, and is now in a highly respected graduate program in international studies. I anticipate his gift some day: he will be writing foreign policy addresses.

To be sure, these are teaching highs not unique to a Catholic university. But the struggle, the deferred gratification, and the gracious follow-through result from a process of taking well-meaning but spoiled Catholic kids to the woodshed. Not all state universities have the time, or take that time, with students. We must. They are a gift of God to their parents and to the world. What we are as a university will live through them.

The lows of teaching are nagging problems at Notre Dame and, I suspect, other Catholic universities: (1) many students are too deferential to pursue independent learning and (2) most students grasp little of the Catholic faith. I think both have their roots in Catholic elementary and secondary education and in functioning American Catholic families.

Deference to elders and experts is a wonderful virtue. It gets good grades. It yields invitations to be a junior Rotarian or nominations for the National Honor Society. It makes parents beam and grandparents dote. It may make the difference in a letter of recommendation to Notre Dame's admissions office. It also contributes to intellectually careless study habits. It makes faculty more impressed with themselves than they deserve to be. And it is especially stultifying of either the student's intellectual or religious maturity when the teacher also speaks with the authority of the shared faith.

Higher education, and especially a Catholic university, needs a critical mass of freaks and intellectual bomb-throwers in its classrooms. Too many 1250 SATs, A– GPAs, student body officers, multiple letter winners—all with a high level of deference—contribute to education-as-hoop-jumping. Young people need to learn early the importance of challenging the textbook, chasing down an idea different from the teacher's, and arguing through religious doubt. We do not live in a revealed world of ideas. We must through much tribulation enter into the kingdom of God. Creative confusion, followed by search, and progressive understanding in fits and spurts—that is the nature of intellectual life and Christian maturity. At times I deliberately include in a lecture material I know to be cockamamy; when students gullibly write it into their notebooks, I challenge them to think first and write later, instead of write first and memorize later. A little edge, a touch of pugnaciousness, is a sign of health in school and church.

Illiteracy of the Catholic faith I trace to the process of assimilation. Catholics were once a persecuted minority in this country. These underdogs now disproportionately provide the leadership for government, Fortune 500 companies, and civic organizations. To be sure, the latercomers—the recent waves of Mexican Americans, Southeast Asians, and EIPs (expatriate Irish priests)—are going to have to fight their way up, but most ethnic Catholics have moved into leadership posts commensurate with their educational attainment a quarter century earlier. (The presumed prejudice against Catholics in the boardroom, a reality earlier, is now a methodological artifact created by sociologists who should know how to estimate a time-lagged model.) But when many Catholics made their peace with America, they swallowed the whole American dream, forgetting that Christians (i.e., Catholics) are indeed different.

Their offspring confuse being a faithful Catholic with being a good American. They stress the virtues of patriotism, thrift, diligence, and the avoidance of homosexuality, abortion, or felonious conduct—just as their parents and grandparents did when we studied them in the Notre Dame Study of Catholic Parish Life.

I once began my undergraduate seminar on religion and politics by describing several religious experiences I had had and asking students to relate theirs. A young woman, a Notre Dame senior, I believe from Orlando, described a Sunday Mass on July 4th where her parish members processed from church onto the street with the American flag held high, singing the "Star Spangled Banner." She said she knew it was a religious experience because she got goose bumps all over and was short of breath! I terminated that exercise, fearing that someone would mention the half-time show at the Orange Bowl. Religion for American Catholic young people is often civil religion. Even Notre Dame's baccalaureate ceremony blesses the American flag before the Mass is pronounced over.

While the young people's prayer life is more likely to be Christocentric than their forbears' reliance on saintly intercessors, they have little understanding of sin and grace, the efficacy of sacraments, the desirability of liturgical prayer, or of the nature of Christian freedom and authority. At a minimum they have not yet learned that faith is both an individual and community property.

Like previous generations they pick and choose social, and even doctrinal, teachings, emerging with strange composites of theological liberalism and conservatism. Invariably they make prescriptive teachings of some proscriptive teachings, and they think they have found the essence of Catholicism in one or two rules of conduct. Alas, what suffers is the rich mosaic of Catholic worldviews shaped by centuries of inquiry. Something must be accepted or rejected, in their minds, because pope and bishops promulgated it. As a result, they are confused by differences between Augustine and Aquinas, Maritain and Teilhard de Chardin. It is a formidable task to reconstitute the Catholic intellectual life in the university when its pre-university form is based on acceptance or rejection of formulaic authority.

Many church leaders, sensing loss of consensus in the culture, have acted very much like those in the Reformed tradition. Together with evangelical Protestants, they seek statutes and decisions to protect us from ourselves. The models of the godly life are to be enforced by the state. Prescription loses out to proscription; clarity of gospel message, confession, and grace play second fiddle to legislative majorities or court decisions. Again students define faithfulness by involvement with the Right to Life chapter or hours spent in the soup kitchen. Action and will replace understanding, mind, and soul. The goal of "enculturation" is short-circuited by the goal of electing the right public officials and holding Catholic public officials accountable to whatever their bishop felt they should have done on this or that piece of legislation. The example of some church leaders does not suggest to young people that the Catholic intellectual life involves a long search for understanding and wisdom in a complex world. And even bishops who hear out other voices—such as Rembert Weakland who sat down with women to listen to their perspectives on women's issues—are "disciplined" by their brethren. The freedom realized in the Catholic university affords a setting for listening that the church sometimes is unwilling to tolerate.

Still another feature of the Catholic university that holds great promise for the future is the international nature of the church. Catholics are everywhere and have been for centuries. A world church reminds its universities of the paradox that learning is a product of a culture, while the search for truth is universal. That is why a Catholic university must invite into the quest for truth those shaped by non-Catholic western cultures and non-Christian non-western cultures. This includes both faculty and students.

Models of the Catholic university that rely on the proportion of the faculty who are Catholic are closer to European-style partitions—the Catholic sector, the liberal sector, the red sector—than to the assumption that truth for our time and for all time involves an ongoing search. A Catholic university would be foolish not to be attentive to replenishing the supply of Catholic intellectuals in its faculty ranks. That is at the core of its identity. It must search high and low and, in the parlance of the day, use affirmative action to locate and attract Catholics who share the vision of Christian humanism. At times that may mean rejecting Catholics for faculty appointments when they want to make of the university a base for church or state political operations. At times it means giving little credence to the Catholicism of those baptized but for whom the religious struggle has long since ceased. And at times it may mean hiring Protestants or Jews or Muslims or Hindus who find the universality and unique freedoms of the Catholic university something that attracts them and in whose conversations they will join. A Catholic university should be a many-angled traffic circle, nay a plaza, where scholars the world over contribute to the flow of ideas.

Internationalism should also characterize the education of students. Nowadays, an American university or college which does not encourage more than two-thirds of its students to study abroad for at least a semester is doing them a disservice. Students who present themselves for a university education without reading and speaking a language other than English are ill prepared for higher education. Unfortunately, not enough Catholic elementary and secondary schools build foreign languages and cross-cultural understanding into their curricula. But then, neither do the public schools which are looking for places to balance the budget. The Catholic university can send clear signals to its feeder schools about the importance of language skills and foreign study. The religious communities which have historically run these universities have recognized the role of foreign languages in their training and assignments of men and women in earlier times. Their models should be transferred to the laity for whom we faculty are now responsible.

There is considerable controversy among the faculty of a Catholic university about the nature of the curriculum and of the scholarly specialties for which faculty should be recruited. For example, a department of economics may argue that, given the social encyclical tradition, it should eschew the hiring of Chicago-school economists, monetarists, or econometricians. Instead, it should focus on Third World development and institutional economics, and on topics like welfare policy and labor. There is little question that the encyclicals find both capitalist and socialist models of development wanting and, until John Paul II's most recent social encyclical, were less than impressed with the need for centers of power outside church and state to encourage democracy, or with the possibility that economic liberty might be a strong instrument for meeting human need. "Liberty, rightly understood," to borrow a term from Tocqueville, was until recently a foreign concept to Vatican social thinkers. Its origins are in Reformed thought and it found its deepest expression in the Scottish Enlightenment—both some distance from Rome.

The financial centers of New York and London and the headquarters of the Federal Reserve Board in Washington are also some distance from Rome. While it is true that Chicago-school economic theory and econometric estimation procedures have served the macroeconomies of capitalist countries, that is no reason a priori to shun scholars adept with such theories or tools. European Catholic economists have not only not shunned, but often embraced, Vienna-school economics. Students at American Catholic universities need to comprehend all the tools that states and private actors use to create viable economies, for human needs are met in many ways. That equations are employed to estimate terms of that model economic reality does not mean the loss of human concern any more than the use of magnetic resonance imaging will render the physician incapable of remembering that it is a human's condition she is diagnosing. A curriculum that consists of "Ethics of ———" in course after course forgets the substantive subject matter that requires ethical focus. The teaching of ethics, carefully inserted into a strong substantive curriculum, is a little like the use of brandy in Christmas fruitcake: if it were the main ingredient it would spoil the cake but, used strategically, it gives the fruitcake its distinctive flavor as it ages.

Frankly, I think the reasons Catholic economists sometimes are tempted to limit the curriculum to encyclical-inspired concerns have more to do with the underdog roots of American Catholic ethnics and even the fear of mathematics as a strong logic, than they have to do with Catholic social teaching. Outside the U.S., Catholic universities and Catholic economists are less constrained, but they had social standing much earlier.

Similar arguments can be made for diversity in the gender studies and marriage and family courses, for example, in sociology or psychology. A Catholic political theory program that ignored poststructuralism, Nietzsche, or Foucault, for example, would assume that critique of the canon and deconstruction have no place in the search for truth. The other side of the coin is that a language and literature department, English or otherwise, that for several years hired only faculty operating from the race–class–gender paradigm would not be meeting its obligations to explore the full range of literary theory. Such a personnel design would impede the academic freedom on which it is based. While at one time or another, many Notre Dame departments have flirted with options similar to those illustrated above, they have generally sought balance, or at least have faced tough questions from colleagues in cognate fields, from a dean, or a provost. The result is still a responsible use of intellectual diversity.

Now to a personal note: I, a confessing Lutheran, came to Notre Dame by choice. I came to direct a large research holding company developed originally by George N. Shuster that had as its mission encouraging faculty to balance sustained inquiry with strong teaching. I worked myself out of that midwifing job when the colleges made their transitions toward "a national Catholic research university" that continues to take teaching seriously. I have since directed the Notre Dame Study of Catholic Parish Life, established other fledgling programs, and served as a full-time teaching and research faculty member.

There were times, as I dealt with deans, provosts, vice-presidents, or alums, or raised monies, when I felt a little like *The Godfather*'s Irish accountant at a Mafia family wedding. There are cultural differences between Catholics and Lutherans, far more related to their American experiences than to doctrinal differences. Father Theodore Hesburgh and Father James Burtchaell who hired me welcomed me to Notre Dame's altars at Sacred Heart. The dioceses and religious communities where I have spoken on the parish study have always asked me to Communion and included my work in their intentions. In eighteen years, only one faculty member has questioned me about why a Lutheran would receive the Eucharist in a Catholic church, not because Catholic faculty do not care but because they understand fully the sacramental and symbolic powers of Christ's presence among the faithful. I cannot imagine another way to initiate the academic year than through the opening Mass. For all our orneriness as faculty, liturgies unite our many members into one body. More personally, it affirms that my vocation is here, that God can use my ministerial gifts among Catholics, and that Catholics will embrace me. That common confession is, after all, the rock on which the Church is built.

At the same time there are differences at the margins. I appreciate being a Lutheran because Lutheranism is a confessing evangelical movement within the holy, Catholic, and apostolic Church. Some day we shall come to that unity for which Christ prayed in his most priestly prayer. In the meantime we recognize the wonderful charisms the Spirit has gifted on the religious orders, communities, and particular Christian traditions through the ages. The church is no less diverse and pluralistic, all things considered, than the Catholic university in North America.

I do not share the progressive vision of Teilhard which Father Hesburgh finds compelling. I am still mired in my Augustinianism, Lutheranism, and neo-Niebuhrianism. I am constantly reminded of the presence of evil, of the demonic in the world and even in the church. It asserts itself in the misuses of power that abuse the vulnerable. It stinks from the rotting bodies of ethnic cleansing, genocidal warfare, and the drug and gun businesses of our inner cities. It still exists in nuclear stockpiles, among racial supremicists, in the human woe that finds a Hitler or a Zhirinovsky attractive. I am not confident that the world is evolving toward humane ends. No matter how much we learn from history, we turn around and repeat the mistakes. We still may blow ourselves to smithereens or blithely take health risks that result in AIDS in pandemic proportions. Evil is its own scourge, but it brings down with it many innocent parties. Yet I do not despair. We live under the cross, by the grace of God. We do the work to which we are called in the communities to which God directs us. We live to serve. Yes, Garrison Keillor understands Lutherans.

My father, who once lived in Elkhart and now in heaven, was gladdened by my return to the Midwest from Washington, D.C., but saddened that I would be working at a Catholic university. He greeted me with the lament, "Surely a Lutheran university would hire you." In time, one almost did—as its president—I was of the right ethnic background but I was by then the wrong kind of Lutheran. Tribalism always separates us from our common ministries. Only occasionally have I experienced tribalism at this

Catholic university. We have a mission that runs deeper than the tribe, a mission anchored in the centuries. It enlightens and transcends prejudice, it respects authority but resists the mailed fist.

In the end I return to music and poetry to express the purpose of the Catholic university. The editors of the *Lutheran Book of Worship*—who my Catholic liturgical friends claim committed only one fault with the book, adding the modifier *Lutheran* to the title—included a wonderful contemporary hymn of celebration that understands the Catholic university. It is called "Earth and All Stars." Its first four stanzas take us through the universe and nature, commerce and industry, and music; stanzas five and six, to the university and wisdom:

> Classrooms and labs!
> Loud boiling test tubes!
> Sing to the Lord a new song!
> Athlete and band!
> Loud cheering people!
> Sing to the Lord a new song!

> For he has done marvelous things.
> I too will praise him with a new song.

> Knowledge and truth!
> Loud sounding wisdom!
> Sing to the Lord a new song!
> Daughter and son!
> Loud praying members!
> Sing to the Lord a new song!

> For he has done marvelous things.
> I too will praise him with a new song.

What a thrill to contribute to the ornamented line of the chorale, to have a hand in new understandings, new songs, in this world of wonderment!

I have no triumphal pretenses about the products of our efforts. Knowledge is the product of an agnostic stance, building on others but always restless to push us beyond our current limitations of theory, concept, measure, or logic. Knowledge, even religious knowledge, is pragmatic; it gets us by. In "Love Divine, All Love Excelling," sung to Hyfrydol, Charles Wesley concludes:

> Finish then thy new creation.
> Pure and spotless let us be;
> Let us see thy great salvation
> Perfectly restored in thee!
> Changed from glory into glory,
> Till in heaven we take our place,
> Till we cast our crowns before thee,
> Lost in wonder, love, and praise.

The Hebrew Union book of prayer retells an old Jewish story. At the end of each day, God looked over what he had created and pronounced, "It is good." At the end of the sixth day, he did not make that pronouncement—first a man, but he was incomplete, then a woman, then assignments for them, but still God did not say, "It is good!" The lesson the story draws is that it was the human imperative to convince God that this new handiwork was not a failed project. Sacred Scriptures tell the sagas of human action and divine intervention. The Church celebrates that history.

In the Catholic university, while we maintain the pretense that our stewardship assignment makes of us cocreators, we know the task is unfinished. Despite our new creations, we plead with God, in Wesley's words, to "finish then thy new creation" and, in Augustine's insight, to let our souls find rest in God. The Catholic university and Catholic character to the university are never finished creations. That is why we must continue the endless conversations. The process is its own reward. It was human conceit that created the new Soviet citizen, and it is human conceit that creates the perfect follower of the magisterium. But we stand in wonder of the creation, untangling its mysteries, as we live daily in God's grace.

In luce tua videmus lucem

Becoming a Great Catholic University

CRAIG S. LENT

Angels, as far as I understand, do not have universities. Universities are for humans. The doctrine of the incarnation is perhaps surprisingly relevant to an understanding of what a great Catholic university might be about.[1] Jesus came in the flesh to redeem not just human souls but all that is authentically human. We are not, as the Gnostics thought, spiritual flames trapped in fleshly bodies. Through the incarnation Jesus validates our humanity as corporeal, finite, and limited. We need to learn the truth; it is not implanted within us. Jesus presumably learned to read by being taught. In a Catholic view, human cultures, our learning, arts, and sciences, are part of our humanity and objects of the redemption of Jesus (and in need of redemption because of the effects of sin). A Catholic university is a human activity, a creative intellectual activity of teaching and learning, that is dedicated to God. As is so true, dedication to God means working for the betterment of others—our students, our colleagues, the church, and society.

When I came to Notre Dame as a postdoctoral fellow in 1984, I did not think I was coming to a Catholic, or even Christian, university in any important sense. I thought Notre Dame was a post-Christian university with some vestigial trappings of faith, now relegated mostly to student residence halls and ceremonial events. It was, I assumed, on the same path to secularization that Princeton, Harvard, and Duke had taken, just moving a little slower because of the pace to which Catholic institutions were accustomed. I have been delighted to discover that I was wrong in this assessment, though others will argue it was merely premature.

I awakened to possibilities not yet extinguished through working on a large, long-range planning project called the "Colloquy for the Year 2000." My principal focus was on upgrading the infrastructure required to enable serious research and scholarship to progress at Notre Dame, a task to which I remain committed. In the course of attending the many meetings of the Academic Life subcommittee, however, I noticed that a few people around our very large table spoke about the Catholic character of Notre Dame seriously and in the present tense. One even mentioned the Holy Spirit as an agent actively at work on our campus.

As part of the information gathering phase of the colloquy, the Academic Life subcommittee launched a series of task forces to gather input from the various departments and units of the university. As a member of two such task forces, I had the opportunity to visit each department in the colleges of science and engineering. Aside from gathering valuable comments regarding the state of the research infrastructure, I was struck by the potential that still exists within the faculty for realizing a genuinely Catholic and Christian university. A great number of committed Catholics and other Christians are here. Interestingly, they understand their faith to be entirely irrelevant to their life at the university. It is, for them, a private matter, much as it would be if they worked for any large corporation. That the Catholicity of the university is a matter for others—in residence halls, in the theology department, and in the administration building—is what many faculty members have understood the leadership of the university to say. They have no part in it because, as everyone knows (correctly), there is no "Catholic physics" or "Christian mathematics." Yet given a glimpse of the vague possibility of some sort of integration of their personal commitments with their professional lives, many warmed to it immediately.

Still, many on the faculty are "uncomfortable" with the resurgence of talk about the Catholic character of Notre Dame. Some state unequivocally that the university should secularize, that entanglements with "religion" are entirely inappropriate for a modern university. Others see, not without reason, concern about Catholicism as an excuse for turning back from an emphasis on serious research and scholarship toward a level of comfortable mediocrity. Some are convinced that the whole discussion is a cloak for a power struggle between the Congregation of Holy Cross and the predominantly lay and newly energized faculty.

In this interesting environment, several of us in the spring of 1992 sent around a letter inviting faculty whom we had reason to believe might be interested to meet and discuss these issues. Our intent was to have an unsponsored and unofficial conversation among Notre Dame faculty on the topic of the Catholic character of the university. We were surprised to find that in response more than 60 people appeared on a Wednesday night during finals week. The group decided to have monthly meetings with somewhat formal presentations followed by a lengthy and lively discussion period. These meetings have continued, frequently drawing more than 130 participants, and remain ad hoc and unofficial. I am deeply indebted to all those who have participated in them; I have learned a lot and continue to learn from these discussions. My contribution to this volume I view as an opportunity to reflect on some of what I have learned so far from conversing with my colleagues.

Education at a Great Catholic University: A Parent's Perspective

We humans are not born with enough preprogrammed instincts to allow us to survive without contact with other humans. We must rely on others to teach us. Parents are, of course, the primary educators of the next generation. We also learn from others in the community in which we grow up. We learn skills and techniques, we learn what our obligations are, and we learn some of what other people have discovered and thought. Through this we acquire a sense of place in our society and in our history. That we may subsequently call these into question presupposes our initial acquisition of them.

The fact that our brains hold more information than our genes is an aspect of our created nature. In this we see that our creator designed us for this sort of dependence on the previous generation and our responsibility toward the next. This is another aspect of God's design in creating humans to live socially, in community with one another. In a sense, part of God's creative act in forming each individual is still unfinished at birth. God's creativity is mediated through the ongoing nurturing and education of parents and the broader community. Moreover, as individuals we ourselves participate in this cooperative process with God, increasingly becoming more responsible for our own formation.

Our obligation to listen to preceding generations and teach subsequent generations is an aspect of our created nature that we must take seriously. Catholic Christians have responded to this responsibility in part by forming Catholic schools, colleges, and universities as instruments through which we can better fulfill our obligation as a community to educate our children. Such Catholic institutions are on the one hand an extension of the parental task of education and on the other hand represent the involvement of the community as a whole toward this end. In universities, students with requisite abilities can pursue advanced learning, appropriating what has been discovered by others and learning to think clearly and creatively and to communicate effectively. The Catholic university must be understood to be first and foremost a response to this intergenerational obligation which has as its source the one whom we call Father.

In our day, the university experience has to do with more (but not less) than education traditionally conceived. The four years of undergraduate work function as a transitional phase in the passage of young adults from more or less complete dependence on their parents to a state of financial and personal autonomy. At the university they enjoy more independence than when they lived under their parents' roof but less than they will have once they leave and begin adult careers and responsibilities. It is a time of maturing, testing, and setting up one's approach to life. When I look back on my time as an undergraduate, it was clearly a period when many of my own basic approaches to life crystallized. I came to some important conclusions which I still hold today, took some paths and foreclosed others, formed some intellectual commitments which are still in place; and even when issues were not resolved then, that is when they were framed. This process is of course part of education in the broadest, and perhaps best, sense.

A Catholic university offers its students the opportunity to work through this pivotal phase in intellectual and moral development in the context of a community whose fundamental commitments are those of Catholic Christianity. This has innumerable consequences, small and large, for the way undergraduate life is experienced. This is a community which worships and prays and does so in the open. Masses in the student halls are part of the normal rhythm and are well attended. When a student dies, the community grieves in the Basilica of Sacred Heart—we bring our grief to God. Campus Ministry conducts a variety of seminars and programs and does an excellent job. Problems exist, certainly, but they are more or less those that beset any college-aged group. As a parent I would be pleased to send my children to study and learn in such a faith-filled environment.

But as a parent I also know that the faith my children leave home with will not alone be enough to sustain them as they enter the adult world. I want them to be armed with strong and disciplined minds. They will need to be able to think, to think carefully and rigorously, to discern the subtle distinctions and uncover the subtle lies the world will throw at them. I want them to think as Christians. I want them to develop an attraction to what is good and true and beautiful. They must, to a greater extent than when they lived in my house, take responsibility for forming their own character. What I want for them is an environment in which their minds are fully challenged and engaged, sharpened to their fullest potential, and formed by the bedrock truths of the gospel of Jesus Christ.

At Notre Dame, people with serious intellectual "credentials" still speak openly about Jesus Christ, not just as an interesting historical religious figure but as Savior and Lord. This is a community that takes faith seriously, not just as a private and personal source of solace, but as intellectually consequential. Here a world-renowned scholar can be heard to say that "the Catholic faith is the best thing that ever happened to the human mind because Jesus is the best thing that ever happened to humanity." It is important that such a statement could be made here, but also essential that it was an intellectual heavyweight who made it. It will not do to settle for intellectual mediocrity or for intellectual secularization.

The promise of Notre Dame is that it might become at the same time a first-rate university and a vibrant Catholic intellectual community. Only in such a community, constantly challenged by the twin demands of academic excellence and faithfulness to the gospel, can generations of young Christian minds be formed to engage and leaven the world. To such a university I, and many others, would like to send our children.

Research and the Intellectual Life
at a Great Catholic University:
A Faculty Perspective

If the educational mission of a great Catholic university requires the presence of a lively Catholic intellectual community how does one create and sustain one? Here the faculty is certainly the key.

In the hands of the faculty rests directly the task of teaching students. Teaching I understand to mean inviting students into a fuller life of the mind, introducing them to the thoughts and accomplishments of the past, and engaging them in the present inquiry. It is through the faculty that students make contact with the ideas of Aristotle, the art of Picasso, the theories of Maxwell and Heisenberg. While students are finally the principal agent of their own education, the faculty synthesize and present a coherent framework in which that education can proceed. Great teaching entails presenting the known to students in such a way that they not only can comprehend what has gone on before but also are drawn on to new investigations. A great university requires excellent teachers.

Universities are characterized by more (but not less) than great teaching. A university is about learning and it is in the nature of a university that the faculty are learners as well as teachers. *Research*, the name we give to learning at this level, is as central to the concept of the university as is teaching in the classroom. Research and scholarship are not just faculty perquisites. To be a great university, Notre Dame must have a faculty of the highest caliber, capable of advancing knowledge not simply transmitting it.

In fact, the synergy between research and teaching is one of the most exciting dynamics of university life. It should not be eclipsed by the occasional abuses or apparent tensions that receive sometimes excessive attention. As an undergraduate I chose to attend a research university despite the fact that I knew the classes would be larger and the professors less accessible than at a four-year college. I went because I wanted to be close to those people who were actually on the cutting edge of their discipline, to learn how they thought. Even though the undergraduate curriculum was fairly standard for my field (at that time, physics), there is no doubt in my mind that I got what I was seeking. I learned how to think about physics from people who did physics. They were practitioners. Their excitement at the subtle insights that their field afforded was clear and contagious. As a parent, I want my children to have that kind of opportunity also. A great university requires excellent teachers who are also excellent researchers.

Having assembled a group of first-rate teachers and researchers, one does not yet have the faculty of a great university, much less a great Catholic university. If the students are indeed to be invited into the life of an intellectual community, a community must be functioning. If each excellent professor interacts only with his or her students but not with other faculty, then there is no intellectual community. The fact that the university brings people together in physical proximity is then just a matter of convenience. Then we might just as well all be in separate scattered institutions, were it not for the difficulty of getting to class on time! To have a community, even an intellectual community, there must be some glue that binds us together.

Three elements seem to me to be essential to forming any community. Let me illustrate these using as examples at two extremes, the community of stamp collectors in South Bend and an Amish community in northern Indiana. The first essential element is that something is held in common by all members of the community. For the stamp collectors this is a common interest in stamps; for the Amish, a common set of beliefs about how to live an authentically Christian life in the modern world. The second element is that the community members gather and associate with each other. Stamp collectors meet at stamp shows and exhibits; the Amish, in regular religious assemblies. Without gatherings, each would just become a set of individuals with (accidentally) common interests. The third element is some form of obligation that is binding for the community members' behavior. For stamp collectors, this is simply civil and fair dealings with one another; if counterfeiting, cheating, and theft were prevalent, the community would disintegrate. For the Amish, the obligation takes the form of comprehensive financial and familial commitments to live life together, aiding each other and working for the common good.

For a university faculty an intellectual community consists of similar elements. The faculty hold some intellectual commitments in common. These are minimally a commitment to the goals of education and research and to the academic virtues of honesty and intellectual integrity, without which a university cannot function. The faculty assembles as a whole on various annual occasions and in departmental and group meetings at many levels. The meetings serve both pragmatic and symbolic ends. The obligations undertaken by faculty are, in addition to those directly related to job performance, summarized in the notion of *good colleagueship*. A good academic colleague is one who can be counted on to listen to ideas and discuss them, to interact creatively and fairly, and to contribute to the commonweal. We have all known people whom we might describe as fine teachers and fine researchers but poor colleagues.

The intellectual community at the center of a Catholic university is characterized by holding in common a certain respect for Catholic intellectual tradition. One would expect many members of such a community to be Catholics. As has been said often, however, the essential requirement is not a particular creedal affiliation but a respect for Catholic intellectual tradition. Absent such respect, the whole enterprise of a Catholic university must appear foolish. Many have observed that much of the on-campus hostility to the discussions of the Catholic character of Notre Dame comes, not from non-Catholics, but from Catholics who view Catholic intellectual tradition as oppressive and dangerous.

What we hold in common enables us, faculty and students, to engage in a conversation. Without some common ground, conversation is impossible. This conversation links the participants together into a genuine intellectual community. It is a conversation about everything—about nanoelectronics and political development, about diplomatic history and insect navigation, about truth and error, justice and injustice, vector computation and groundwater contamination. It is a conversation about right and wrong, about beauty and ugliness, about the human good and human debasement, about Aristotle and Aquinas and Ross Perot and Irwin Schrödinger and Jesus. This conversation is surely animated by particularly Christian and particularly Catholic concerns. But it just as surely includes all who are interested, and all are invited to be part of it. The character of this conversation is the hallmark of a great Catholic university. The conversation is the core of the intellectual community. What we should look for in prospective faculty members, in addition to excellence in teaching and research, is a desire to be a part of *this* conversation. Holding a common respect for Catholic intellectual tradition is not insignificant, it means we can have a conversation in these terms. We can talk about virtue and creation, about sin and redemption, about right and wrong. As Norman Mailer is said to have observed, "Notre Dame is the only university where one can use the word *soul* without blushing."

The Catholicity of Notre Dame should be a positive factor in the intellectual life of each faculty member. If it is a difference that makes no difference in the concrete experience of the faculty, then the Catholic character of Notre Dame becomes at best only a description of the religious residential experience of undergraduates and at worst, false advertising. If the intellectual life of a faculty member is not enriched by being at a Catholic university, why come here? Excellent scholars who are Catholic seem often to choose to take university positions elsewhere. This is entirely understandable if Notre Dame in fact offers faculty an intellectual life essentially identical to that at other universities of our size and stature. We then compete for talent in the same way other schools do. If instead Notre Dame was perceived as a unique, interesting, active Catholic intellectual community, we would attract far more highly qualified people. There is no "Catholic physics" or "Catholic mathematics" but there are physicists, mathematicians, historians, and engineers who would like to do their work as part of a vibrant Catholic intellectual community.

One key to understanding how the Catholic character of the university might contribute to making the faculty experience distinctive is the Catholic conception of the unity of truth. Catholics believe God is the author of all truth and the creator of reality. Further, the rational capacity of humankind has not been so corrupted by the Fall that it is incapable of apprehending truth. In uncovering each small truth we can discover something of the fingerprints of its creator. Each act of intellectual creativity mirrors the boundless creativity of the God in whose image we were made. Human knowledge, which in other contexts appears hopelessly fragmented and disconnected in the postmodern landscape, has in the Catholic view an integral wholeness and connectedness.

This intellectual coherence should have consequences in the intellectual life of faculty at a Catholic university. While the demands of specialization are real, there should be opportunity for a broader life of the mind than research in one's specialty. As one mathematics professor said to me, "I am a mathematician but not a mathematical machine. I am a human being. I have other intellectual, and even spiritual, interests as well." I am not suggesting a faculty of would-be renaissance men and women, or, worse, of dilettantes. There should simply be some counterweight to the centrifugal forces of specialization which pull us away from each other and deeper into our own sub-sub-sub-fields. Life at a Catholic university should offer the opportunity for a measure of reintegration of one's intellectual life. Actually, what may be the most helpful program in this regard is already in place. I have twice now availed myself of the opportunity to take a course in the summer. My wife and I took an evening course on the Gospel of John which was taught by the renowned biblical scholar Raymond Brown. Another summer I took a short course on Plato and Aristotle. It was at the undergraduate level, but did me more good than I can say. Neither was a great drain on my normal summer regime of research, conferences, and proposal writing. Both have enabled me to converse with more understanding with my colleagues in other departments. The integrative role of philosophy and theology in the intellectual life of the university was pointed to by Newman and is reflected in the governing statutes of Notre Dame.

The Animation of Catholic Intellectual Life

A great university has a role in seeking truth and understanding that goes beyond its immediate sphere of faculty and students. It has a role in the larger society as a place where new ideas are developed and old ideas reexamined. The way universities have an impact on the intellectual climate of a nation, its politics, self-understanding, and aspirations, is complex and subtle, yet substantial. Ideas are still more powerful than armies.

A great Catholic university can leaven in a unique way the thought of a society with the perspective of the gospel. This happens in two ways—through its graduates who move into positions of responsibility in society, and through the force of its own intellectual culture on the climate of thought. Only a few universities are in a position of leadership in intellectual circles which lends them this kind of weight. None are Catholic. To put it most crudely, we should have *our* "talking heads" on McNeal-Lehrer, on David Brinkley's show, and on CNN; *our* experts writing on the editorial pages of the *New York Times* and the *Wall Street Journal.*

Not too long ago it would have seemed unlikely that a university committed openly to Christianity would have been taken seriously by its intellectual peers (assuming it had attained peer status). This seems no longer to be so. In the current climate, having clear up-front commitments, be they Marxist, feminist, or progressive, is perceived by many as appropriate, even necessary. This may be transitory or may simply be a delayed realization of the fact that to ask a sensible question one must at least provisionally accept some things as settled. We may be at an opportune point in history for the emergence of a great Catholic university and a renaissance of Catholic intellectual life.

Nor is the task so herculean as to seem impossible. The effect of a few individuals in forming whole new intellectual movements is remarkable. Of one of my colleagues I have heard it said that he virtually single-handedly recreated the field of Christian philosophy (and this from a definite non-fan). Another has been credited widely with restoring to respectability the whole theory of virtue. I submit that one does not need to be a large university to have a very large influence.

How does one transform a Catholic college into a great Catholic university? I think several steps that are clearly necessary have already been taken. The first is the professionalization of the faculty. Much of the improvement of the past twenty years, which has been considerable, is due to increasing faculty salaries and aggressively recruiting outstanding candidates both for junior positions and for chaired professorships. (In applauding these developments I in no way want to minimize the remarkable accomplishments of earlier decades.) A great university also must have an infrastructure capable of supporting research and scholarship at a world-class level. I would say we are in the middle of this process now. It involves upgrading library resources, laboratories, grant administration, technical support staff, computing facilities, the bookstore, and a host of other areas. It takes all this just to get in the game of serious university-level academics. There is a justified concern that teaching, particularly at the undergraduate level, not be undervalued as the stakes in research and graduate education are increased. As might have been anticipated, all this activity may have diverted attention from a focus on the Catholic character of the university, at least as far as the faculty is concerned. At this critical moment, we must reanimate that discussion at a new level. The notion of the Catholic character must be appropriated by the faculty if it is to survive. Without retrenching in any of the areas of academic excellence where so much progress has been made, we must flesh out what it means for a faculty to be part of a Catholic intellectual community.[2] Perhaps we have some clues from the ideas of the unity of knowledge and the metaphor of conversation. Admittedly these ideas, at least as I have been able to articulate them, are somewhat vague and tentative now. But a conversation is always a work in progress.

The human search for truth, propelled as it is to questions of ultimacy, is most at home in a community of inquiry open to discussing those ultimate questions. The human intellect is drawn in both directions: toward the particular and detailed, and toward the broad and fundamental. We want to understand truth in its specific and concrete forms and yet are also moved to questions of purpose and meaning. A great Catholic university could be an intellectual community engaged in the search for truth in all areas of human understanding, teaching and learning in the light of the gospel and our Catholic intellectual heritage. A great Catholic university would be a unique gift to the world, to the church, and to our children.

Notes

1. For an interesting discussion of this connection, see John F. Crosby, "Remarks on the Christian Humanism of a Catholic University," *Fellowship of Christian Scholars Newsletter,* June 1993.

2. The climate for this project is not helped by recent well-intentioned, but potentially disastrous, moves by the American Catholic bishops to insert themselves into university governance.

What Is a Catholic University?

Richard P. McBrien

The various contributors to this volume bring to the subject a great variety of experiences in Catholic higher education. At this writing I have served for almost twenty-five years as a faculty member and administrator in two major Catholic universities: Boston College (1970–1980) and Notre Dame (since 1980). At Boston College I was a professor of theology and, for five years, the director of the Institute for Religious Education and Pastoral Ministry; at Notre Dame I served for eleven years as chair of the Department of Theology. Before 1970 I was a member of the faculty and dean of studies at Pope John XXIII National Seminary in Weston, Massachusetts. Except for the six years of grammar school, all of my education from junior high through seminary and graduate studies at the Pontifical Gregorian University in Rome has been in Catholic institutions. In addition, I have been a priest since 1962, having been ordained just a few months before the opening of the Second Vatican Council, and I am the author of a two-volume work entitled *Catholicism*.

I make a point of all this, not to blow my own biographical horn, but to highlight what I take to be obvious: I am so thoroughly Catholic in background and experience, as well as in ministerial and professional commitments, that it would be more than a little bit superfluous for me to spend any significant amount of time and energy speculating about my Catholic identity. I should devote almost all of my time and energy to *being* Catholic rather than wondering about what it *means* for me to be Catholic—unless, of course, I have begun to have doubts about my Catholicity.

I make a point of my lifelong Catholic background for a second reason as well. Just as it would be needless for me to be wondering constantly about my Catholic identity, so, too, there seems to be something superfluous and even diversionary about Catholic universities' and colleges' constantly asking themselves about their own Catholic identity—unless, again, they have begun to have doubts about it (or their founding religious communities have begun to worry about their continued presence and influence within these institutions).

I cannot speak for other Catholic institutions of higher learning (I have been away from Boston College for nearly fifteen years), but I can speak from my experience at the University of Notre Dame. I know of no comparable institution that is so completely, so thoroughly, and so unequivocally Catholic as Notre Dame is. One simply has to spend a few days on the campus to recognize that. And it is not subtle. It hits you like the proverbial ton of bricks.

It is a place marked by conspicuous Catholic symbols: from the statue of our Lady on the golden dome to the grotto, from Sacred Heart Basilica to "touchdown Jesus" painted on one entire side of the towering Hesburgh Library, to various statues of priests and biblical figures scattered across the campus.

In every student residence hall there is a chapel or some space set aside for the celebration of the Eucharist—and it is well attended, not only on Sunday but during the week. The academic year opens with a Mass presided over by the president. The baccalaureate Mass at the end of the academic year is celebrated in the presence of some fifteen or sixteen thousand parents, relatives, and friends of graduates, with the local bishop occupying a prominent place in the sanctuary. Honorary degrees each year are conferred upon renowned church figures. Public events begin with prayer: faculty banquets, the dedication of buildings, the installation of new chairholders, the president's annual fall address to the faculty.

One has only to look this way or that on campus to catch sight of a priest, a nun, or a religious brother—some in traditional ecclesiastical garb. Even those in so-called secular dress are generally known as priests, sisters, and brothers nonetheless.

To ask if Notre Dame is Catholic, or still Catholic (as various grim critics, including a few recent converts to Catholicism and some conservative Protestants, like to put it), makes about as much sense as worshipers at St. Patrick's Cathedral in New York asking if St. Patrick's is Catholic, or still Catholic. All they would have to do is "take a look" (as the late Jesuit theologian Bernard Lonergan used to say)—at the stained-glass windows, the confessionals, the candles, the statues, the stations of the cross, the crucifixes, and particularly the main altar. And if they are patient, they would probably witness a Mass, with the priest in full vestments, the choir in full voice, the prayers recited by the people in full unison.

Therefore, while I heartily applaud Father Hesburgh's initiative in gathering so many disparate essays together in a single volume in order to help shape and advance the discussion of Catholic character within Catholic higher education, I should nonetheless count it a mark of this volume's success if it proves to be the last such effort for a long while. But I shall not make any bets on it.

By way of response to Father Hesburgh's invitation, I shall attempt to state as clearly and as succinctly as I can my own understanding of Catholic identity as it applies to Catholic institutions of higher learning. Although I shall refer hereafter only to Catholic universities, I do not intend thereby to exclude colleges and other comparable academic institutions from the discussion.

My presentation is in two parts. In the first, I shall attend primarily to the adjective *Catholic* in posing the question: What makes a university Catholic? In the second, I shall attend primarily to the noun *university;* therein, I shall touch upon issues of academic freedom and institutional autonomy.

What Is a Catholic *University?*

By way of an answer to the question What is a Catholic university? I offer three criteria, followed by three qualifications:

First, both communally and institutionally the university consciously and explicitly identifies itself with the Catholic tradition and with the wider Catholic community.

Second, both communally and institutionally it intentionally embraces and attempts to live by Catholic values, which are, at the same time, humane values that can be shared by non-Catholic

Christians and by non-Christians alike. Those values, it should be noted, include the values embodied in one hundred years of Catholic social teachings. Therefore, the Catholic university has to practice what the church preaches and teaches about such close-to-the-bone issues as the right of employees, particularly nonfaculty, to unionize and their correlative right to a just wage.

Third, in a Catholic university there exists a critical mass (but not necessarily a large majority, or even a simple majority) of faculty and administrative leaders who are committed and active Catholics and of non-Catholics who respect the Catholic tradition and who support the university's intention to be and to remain faithful to that tradition.

Three criteria. Now three qualifications:

First, to say that the Catholic university identifies itself with the Catholic tradition does not mean that it identifies with the Catholic tradition in some uncritical, extrinsicist, or purely cultural way. The interpretation of the Catholic tradition is not left totally in the hands of the official teachers, or magisterium, of the church. The appropriation of the Catholic tradition is the work of the whole Catholic community, including its scholars, in dialogue with others, especially in a university context. As Father Michael Buckley, S.J., of Boston College, pointed out in an address at LeMoyne College in Syracuse, "No other institution in contemporary culture can offer this continual and dialogic academic reflection to the church." Or, as Father Hesburgh has insisted on many occasions, "a Catholic university is the place where the church does its thinking."

A second qualification: to say that the Catholic university identifies itself with the wider Catholic community does not mean that it identifies with the hierarchy or the official church only. The church is the whole people of God, as the Second Vatican Council made clear. The wider Catholic community is the whole people of God, in all of its rich pluralism and diversity.

Third, it is also important to insist here, again, that the commitment to Catholicity is not inconsistent with a profound and abiding commitment to ecumenicity. But ecumenicity cannot be confused with nondenominationalism. It is a matter not simply of welcoming and then juxtaposing different religious traditions but of integrating them within a Catholic core or center. The core is enriched by the other traditions while they, in turn, should be enriched by their contact and interaction with the Catholic core.

But to understand the Catholicity of a university one must go beyond ad intra considerations and also take into account the multiple ways in which that university relates to communities beyond itself, ad extra.

Just as theology has three publics (I refer here to David Tracy's schema in his book, *The Analogical Imagination*, chapter 1), so, too, does the Catholic university. One of its publics is the *church*. The Catholic university exists within the church, is part of the church, serves the church, and participates in its own distinctive way in the wider mission of the church. But, again, it is crucial that we not interpret the word *church* to mean only the hierarchy or to reflect only the uncritical and unhistorical ecclesiology of certain ultraconservative Catholics, within or without the university's faculty and alumni/ae. On the other hand, the church cannot be excluded from the university's concern and mission. Like theology itself, the Catholic university must attend to the ecclesial, pastoral, ministerial, and spiritual dimensions of the academic enterprise.

A second public of the Catholic university is the *academy*. Since the Catholic university is an academic institution with the explicit intention of observing and being judged by the recognized canons of academic activity, everything it does and fosters must be rigorously scientific. In other words, the Catholic university cannot be so ecclesial in orientation that it compromises its academic integrity. The Catholic university cannot be a first-rate Catholic university without also being a first-rate university. If any principle guided Father Hesburgh's thirty-five-year presidency at Notre Dame as well as his concurrent leadership of the Catholic higher educational community, it was that one.

The Catholic university's third public is *society* itself. The Catholic university must be engaged in ongoing conversation with the wider social, economic, political, and cultural world, especially regarding moral and ethical issues. But when the Catholic university does become engaged, it must have done its homework. It must be willing to listen and to learn as well as to instruct and to exhort. One of the best models of how the Catholic university should interact with the wider society was provided by the U.S. Catholic bishops in the process by which they put together their two major pastoral letters, on peace (in 1983) and on the economy (in 1986), that is, through an open and public process that welcomed and responded to input from across the entire spectrum of relevant specializations and informed opinions.

In the end, however, the question of Catholicity can only be answered dialectically. There will always be some tension between faith and science, between revelation and reason, and between religion and the academy. But as Father Hesburgh has never tired of saying, ultimately there can be no conflict between science and theology because they have a common source of truth. If there is an apparent conflict, it is because there is either bad theology or bad science.

The same tension exists within every Catholic university as it strives to remain at once faithfully Catholic and rigorously academic. To be a Catholic university, we must attend to both the adjective and the noun.

Some on the Left may perhaps be too willing to sacrifice the values associated with the adjective *Catholic* in order to preserve the values associated with the noun *university.* Others on the Right may be too willing to sacrifice the values associated with *university* (like academic freedom and institutional autonomy) for the sake of the values associated with *Catholic.* Both are mistaken, although I think the greater danger at the moment comes more from the latter group than from the former.

We can only have a Catholic university if the two values—religious and academic—are maintained in a creative, dialectical tension that always remains open to change and development. In other words, it is not a matter of either–or but of both–and. And that principle applies whether one is in a Jesuit-sponsored university like Boston College or a Holy Cross–sponsored university like Notre Dame.

What Is a Catholic University?

On April 15, 1985, the Vatican Congregation for Catholic Education released its "Proposed Schema for a Pontifical Document on Catholic Universities." (For the full text, see the April 10, 1986, issue of *Origins,* published weekly by the National Catholic News Service in Washington.) In essence, the document claimed that the Catholicity of a university is juridically determined. That is, only those universities are Catholic which the hierarchy says are Catholic and over which the hierarchy—whether the Vatican, an episcopal conference, or the local bishop—has some significant measure of control.

"The promotion and the safeguard of the 'Catholic' character of the Catholic university," the proposed schema stated in paragraph 21, "is certainly the duty of the members of the university itself and of those who direct it or who support it in any way. It is equally the special task of the pastors of the church who are responsible for the faith in their own particular churches."

Later on, in the norms (II, 9.1), the schema asserted that "the episcopal conferences and the diocesan bishops concerned have the duty and the right of seeing to it that in these universities the principles of Catholic doctrine are faithfully observed." Indeed, "Those who teach theological subjects in any institute of higher studies must have a mandate from the competent ecclesiastical authority" (V, 31). Teachers who lack the requirements of "doctrinal orthodoxy and uprightness of life . . . are to be dismissed" (IV, 26.1,2).

Catholic college and university presidents in the United States, where the overwhelming majority of such institutions exist (235 in all, enrolling over 600,000 students), gave a very negative response to the Vatican proposal. (A synthesis of the responses from 110 presidents was published in the same April 10, 1986, issue of *Origins*.)

These presidents, including Father Hesburgh, objected to the Vatican schema on several counts. The following objections are offered by way of example only. It is not a complete list. Indeed, I am deliberately leaving aside the question of federal aid, because too many conservative critics seem to think that this is the only concern of Catholic college and university administrators and faculty. Government financial aid to Catholic institutions would surely have been subject to court challenge if these Vatican norms had been adopted, but there were (and are) many other arguments against the schema and the thinking behind it. Among them are the following:

First, the Vatican document's ecclesiology was faulty. In almost every instance where the Vatican schema used the word *church*, it meant the hierarchy, or the official church, rather than the whole people of God. Indeed, the proposed schema assumed that Catholic universities were founded by the hierarchy. They were not. They were founded almost exclusively by religious communities who sought charters from the state. They were neither founded nor chartered nor funded by the hierarchy.

Second, the Vatican document assumed that institutions which have legally approved statutes dating back many years can easily rewrite them and get new state approval. This is not so and would arouse considerable opposition. In the present arrangement, according to the presidents, "the safeguarding of the 'Catholic' character of the university is the responsibility of the duly elected board of trustees, and we have never before asserted that it is 'equally the special task' of the pastors of the church. This shift of responsibility has nothing to recommend it."

Third, certain key recommendations in the Vatican schema would have been simply unenforceable. For example, how precisely would a bishop see to it that professors in a university or college within his diocese "observe the principles of Catholic doctrine"? What does that mean precisely? Who would make the determination? By what process? Would there be any provision for an appeal beyond the judgment of the local bishop? The proposed schema was silent about such questions.

Fourth, a close reading of the Vatican text indicated that, according to the proposed schema, there are only four ways of being Catholic: (1) the institution is erected or approved by the Holy See (among institutions in the U.S., only the Catholic University of America in Washington, D.C., fits here); (2) the institution is approved by an episcopal conference (this would apply to no U.S. Catholic university or college); (3) the institution "depend(s) on" or is "administered by a religious family or some other canonical entity" (this used to be true but is no longer so for most U.S. Catholic colleges and universities which are governed by lay boards of trustees); and (4) the institution has a "juridical connection with the diocesan ordinaries concerned." If the finally approved Vatican document on Catholic universities (the Apostolic Constitution, *Ex Corde Ecclesiae,* issued by Pope John Paul II on August 15, 1990) had allowed only these four ways of being Catholic, then only a few of the 235 Catholic colleges and universities in the United States might still be considered Catholic.

Fifth, the real crux of the document, according to the 110 Catholic presidents, was its assertion of a power on the part of the bishop to control theologians and to assure "orthodoxy" in their teaching. "What is proposed here," the presidents insisted, "is contrary to the American values of both academic freedom and due process, both of which are written into most university statutes and protected by civil and constitutional law." Indeed, the 110 Catholic college and university presidents further insisted, the norms proposed by the Vatican were self-contradictory. "There is no way *within* the statutes of our universities that teachers or administrators who lack something as vague as 'doctrinal integrity and uprightness of life' could be dismissed."

Sixth, and finally, the proposed Vatican schema was unnecessary. This issue had already been addressed and satisfactorily dealt with in the past: in a 1972 document issued under the auspices of the International Federation of Catholic Universities, in a 1976 document issued by the National Catholic Educational Association's College and University Department (at the invitation of Cardinal Gabriel Garrone, of the Vatican Congregation for Catholic Education), and in the U.S. Catholic bishops' pastoral letter of 1980, *Catholic Higher Education and the Pastoral Mission of the Church*. What emerges from all three of these documents is an explicit concern and respect for two major values: academic freedom and institutional autonomy.

The 1972 document of the International Federation of Catholic Universities (the product of nine years of work, much of it contributed by Father Hesburgh himself, as president of the international organization) went directly to the heart of the matter: "A Catholic university today must be a university in the full sense of the word, with a strong commitment to and concern for academic excellence. To perform its teaching and research functions effectively a Catholic university must have true autonomy and academic freedom." This autonomy, the document continued, must touch such matters as the selection of faculty, the planning of academic programs, the organization of teaching and research, the establishment of chairs, and the like.

The 1976 position paper of the College and University Department of the National Catholic Educational Association followed a similar course:

Freedom from outside constraints is the very breath of life for a college and university. An authentic Catholic institution of higher learning must be free to be Catholic. If the integrity and freedom of the academy is attacked, undermined by "an academic law of the Church," the Church will be the first to suffer. Its enemies will contend derisively that truth cannot be upheld and defended without resort to penalties and outside sanctions, confirming for some the suspicion that Catholic institutions cannot be true universities.

So, too, did the U.S. Catholic bishops' pastoral letter of 1980 on Catholic higher education: "The Catholic identity of a college or university is effectively manifested only in a context of academic excellence. Policies, standards, curricula, governance and administration should accord, therefore, with the norms of quality accepted in the wider academic community."

These three documents reflect exactly the position Father Hesburgh has consistently adopted and which he reiterated in an important article in *America*, "The Vatican and American Catholic Higher Education" (November 1, 1986).

The central concern about the [proposed Vatican] norms is that they basically run counter to the central reality and requirement of *any* university, namely, that it possess academic freedom and autonomy to do what universities do and what they alone do. . . .

"Obviously," Father Hesburgh continued,

if church or state or any power can dictate who can teach and who can learn, the university is not free and, in fact, is not a true university where the truth is sought and taught. It is, rather, a place of political or religious indoctrination. The latter is perfectly fitting for a catechetical center, but not for a university.

The underlying, although highly unoriginal, argument of this brief essay has been that a Catholic university is a dual reality. It is at once religious and academic. Therefore, it has to honor, preserve, and nurture both its Catholic identity and its academic integrity. Anything done to promote the one while compromising the other is unacceptable. It is not a matter of either–or, but of both–and. As Father Hesburgh himself put it so well in his own contribution to this volume: "A great Catholic university must begin by being a great university that is also Catholic."

In my judgment, we are farther away from achieving the goals associated with *university* than we are from achieving the goals associated with *Catholic*. But others will surely disagree, and that is why we have symposia of this sort: to give all points of view their moment in the sunlight of public scrutiny and discussion. And is that not what universities are for as well—*Catholic* universities included?

What Is a Great Catholic University?

RICHARD A. McCORMICK, S.J.

What is a great Catholic university? may seem an otiose question, the type of thing that burned-out emeriti professors eagerly dissect when conversation falls mum at wine and cheeses. It may yet turn out to be that. But I hope not. If we cannot achieve some minimal clarity on the matter, we shall never know what we are to aim at; we shall never know our goal. Without a clear goal, confusion, stumbling, and failure are all but guaranteed. There may be isolated little victories here and there—almost accidental in their occurrence—but there will be no coherent and unifying dynamic that structures policies, shapes decisions, and guides the entire enterprise as a whole. We shall never arrive.

The dangers encountered in trying to answer the question stem from its terms *great, Catholic,* and *university.* There is the temptation to understand these terms with one-sided, dictated, or inaccurate criteria. For instance, there are those who would interpret *Catholic* in terms of a rigid, narrowly defined orthodoxy, or in terms of the number of sponsoring religious priests and brothers and sisters on campus, or in terms of episcopal and/or Vatican approval. This last criterion was given some recent support in the encyclical *Veritatis Splendor.* In no. 116 we read: "It falls to them [bishops], in communion with the Holy See, both to grant the title *Catholic* to church-related schools, universities, health-care facilities and counseling services, and, in cases of serious failure to live up to that title, to take it away."[1] Similarly, it is quite possible to collapse the notion of *university*, especially a great one, into its research component, or its connectedness to the business or professional world, as if ease of entrance into these worlds is synonymous with university excellence.

To avoid these and similar dangers I have decided to travel a different route. It strikes me as a legitimate contention that a great Catholic university should be measured by its product. Several clarifications are in order if this contention is to survive scrutiny. First, I do not argue that all graduates must manifest certain qualities. There will always be some students who will manage to slip through even the best of schools untouched by its excellence. It should suffice if significant numbers of graduates show these qualities. *Significant* cries out for specification, but I have no nonarbitrary measure. Would it be at all plausible to suggest that at least the same percentage of students as we find on the dean's list would constitute a significant number?

Second, we could go about this negatively and assert that if a university regularly graduates large (majority) numbers of students lacking certain qualities, it is not a great Catholic university. It may get good grants, have famous researchers and enthusiastic teachers; it may have a fine library and an equally fine reputation; and it may make *U.S. News and World Report*'s top five. But if its product is deficient regularly and in large numbers, I fail to see how it can be called a great Catholic university.

What, then, are the qualities we should look for in graduates of a great Catholic university? Before attempting to profile such qualities, I want to mention four qualifiers.

First, by listing certain qualities as defining the excellence of the institution that produced them, I do not mean to imply that the institution alone is responsible for engendering such qualities. Students come to a university with formative family and educational backgrounds that have very often nurtured many of the qualities I shall list. The university should nourish, solidify, and deepen these qualities.

Second, as in most matters, it is possible to err by excess and defect. We can put expectations so high that no university could ever reach them. That is unreal. For instance, we could demand a level of excellence in every student before greatness can be claimed. We could also lower expectations in a way that makes it possible for virtually any university to call itself great. That, too, is unreal because it empties the word *great* of any meaning and trivializes the question.

Third—and this is closely related to the previous point—the profile I propose should not suggest that we are looking for clones. Students will undoubtedly manifest these qualities in different ways and varying degrees. We are assessing human beings, not computers.

Finally, any listing of desired qualities should reflect the world, culture, and country in which we currently live. At other historical moments it is quite possible that a different profile of desirable characteristics, or at least an altered hierarchy, would be appropriate.

That having been said, I now turn to the qualities I would hope to find in the graduates of a great Catholic university. I will list eight.

1. A Catholic vision. There are persons who can be described accurately as *animae naturaliter catholicae.* They have assimilated Catholic culture so personally and deeply that their attitudes, habits, and values are thoroughly stamped by it. This stamping reveals itself in their spontaneous reactions, judgments, and actions. They are walking symbols of a way of viewing the world and relating to everything and everyone in it.

What is this "way of viewing the world"? There are probably many ways of describing such a perspective, no one of which is exhaustively adequate. One very common way, however, is to view Catholicism in terms of sacramentality. Michael Himes and Kenneth Himes, calling it the hallmark of Catholicism, explain the sacramental vision as follows: "Sacraments are experiences which uncover for us the presence of the radical mystery of God's self-gift which is the ground of experience."[2] They continue:

> Sacraments are not intrusions into the secular world; they are points at which the depth of the secular is uncovered and revealed as grounded in grace. Accordingly, any true and just estimation of the secular world is dependent on an appreciation of sacramentality. If one does not have an openness to the sacramental depth of one's everyday actions and choices, one's relationships with others, and the places and things with which one comes into contact on a daily basis, then one fundamentally misunderstands who one is and what the world is like.[3]

The "points" to which the brothers Himes refer are persons, places, things that allow us to experience all reality as grounded in God's gracious self-communication (grace). This sacramental vision is impoverished when "the mediation of God's grace is restricted to special rituals which are formally designated 'sacraments.'"[4] In the Catholic vision, all of reality is sacred, and the seven sacraments seek to "evoke awareness" of this sacredness and ultimacy.

If the college graduate may be expected to share in this vision, then clearly there must be persons, places, events in the university that function as mediations of the vision. University liturgies must function in this way. So must instruction, providing that one does not understand this as paranetic overlay. If these and other university experiences are to mediate the Catholic vision, then clearly there must be on campus persons captivated by this vision, persons whose lives, actions, and words are sacraments of it. I think it was something like this that Lawrence S. Cunningham had in mind in his Warren Lecture when he discussed the importance of sages and wisdom in the Catholic tradition. He refers to "figures who have been able to make their own lives so transparent to grace that they become able to offer a good word (or gesture or story or example) to others in order to bring forth the *nova et vetera* of the Gospel message."[5]

It would be unrealistic to expect to find large numbers of such figures at a given university. But unless there are some, I doubt that the Catholic sacramental vision can be communicated or reinforced.

2. Sensitivity to justice and injustice. It might at first seem farfetched to see this as a quality that a university would be expected to inculcate. Universities exist, it is argued, for growth in understanding and knowledge. They are academic institutions. Do not expect them to do everything.

Arguments like that are separatist. They separate—and isolate—the university from the world in which it exists and which it seeks to understand. In effecting this separation, this attitude also separates the university from the full richness of the gospel. How so? The synodal document *Justice in the World* put it as follows: action on behalf of justice is "a constitutive dimension of the preaching of the gospel."[6] Why? Because in the Christian message, love of God and neighbor are inseparable and love of neighbor is inseparable from justice to the neighbor. The thirty-second General Congregation of the Society of Jesus put it this way: "The Christian message is a call to conversion: conversion to the love of God, which necessarily implies conversion to love of men, which necessarily includes conversion to the demands of justice."[7] It boldly states: "The mission of the Society of Jesus today is the service of faith, of which the promotion of justice is an absolute requirement."[8] Now, if a university claims to be Catholic yet exempts itself from a constituent dimension of the very gospel that inspires its existence, it is involved in self-contradiction.

How can a university be a sensitizing factor to issues of justice and injustice? Above all, I believe, by symbolic witness. That refers to acting out in its own life the values of justice. There are many ways that this can be done, both curricular and noncurricular. For instance, at Notre Dame there are summer service programs, urban plunges, service-oriented seminars, seminars on women, church, and society, etc. There is a free-standing structure in the middle of the campus called the Center for Social Concerns. There is the Center for Peace Studies.

Within theological instruction and campus ministry organization, the words of Archbishop J. A. Plourde, to the synod of 1972, should be carefully heeded: "Its [the church's] moral teaching must at all costs stop giving privileged treatment to private ethics, wherein sin is seen primarily as a private matter, rarely as association, conscious or not, with the forces of oppression, alienation, and physical violence."[9]

But when all is said and done, the most powerful form of symbolic witness is example. What the U.S. Catholic bishops' pastoral letter *Economic Justice for All* said of the church must be said of the university: "All the moral principles that govern the just operation of any economic endeavor apply to the church and its agencies and institutions; indeed the church should be exemplary."[10] Indeed, the Catholic university should be exemplary if it hopes to sensitize its students.

3. Appreciation of, and thirst for, knowledge. There will always be students, perhaps the majority, who will attend college just to get a degree and eventually a job. Many of these people will pick their way through the curriculum with a dominant concern to avoid challenges. Perhaps even a great university cannot do much to, or for, such people. But it should attempt to screen them out before admission and reduce their number after it. They are drags to those who want a true college education.

A true college education? There are many ways of defining that. One I like is this: an exposure of mind and heart that leaves one convinced that education has only begun after four years and desirous that it should continue for the rest of one's life. Implied in such a conviction and desire are experiences of joy, pleasure, and satisfaction in the learning process yet also of incompleteness and inchoativeness. Together these experiences lead one to continue to search, question, read. The curious and inquiring mind is not purely the product of a college education. It has a lot to do with family training and peer and sibling influence. But a great university will nourish and deepen it.

4. *Facility in spoken and written word.* The ability to put one's thoughts in clear spoken and written words remains at the heart of any decent education. The basic reason is that we are social human beings whose flourishing is dependent on each other. One of the basic cements of this interdependence is communication. Without verbal facility, or with it in very hampered form, communication is eroded. And when that happens, we begin to deal with each other in less than human ways. Most often these ways are violent. That is why language is at the very heart of civility.

Language is a sign of our attitudes and thoughts. It is the medium through which we show respect, gratitude, support, anger, love, etc. Through language we educate, build families, participate in the democratic process, share the Good News, and on and on.

The graduate of a great university will reflect the centrality and importance of language by a certain facility. If significant numbers of students state after graduation that "him and me are going to dinner," that university has to be indicted. Henry Higgins would know what I mean.

5. *Open-mindedness.* Open-mindedness is not a mere posture. Nor is it an emptiness reflecting a lack of conviction. Openness combines a respect for others with a respect for complexity. This respect for complexity has roots in a knowledge of history and of one's own limitations. The enemy of openness is ideology, the stubborn and one-eyed insistence on a single perspective or point of view, whether

that perspective be religious, political, philosophical, legal, historical, etc.

In the university context, openness concerns above all the search for truth. The American bishops have provided us with a powerful example in the open and revisionary process used in the development of their recent pastoral letters on peace and on the economy. They have welcomed all points of view, even dissenting ones. A similar example should be provided by the Catholic university. The word *campus* is really the Latin word (*campus*) meaning "field." It designates the arena where armies settled disputes with lance and sword. College campuses exist in part to render such incivility obsolete. The vigorous exchange of ideas by the open-minded in the university setting is the way to reconcile our differences. That is why colleges have campuses, open forums for the discussion and clash of ideas. The word *campus* should stand as a reminder that the clash of swords, the targeting of missiles, and any use of force represent human failure, that vigorous but civil exchange is a form of loyalty to, and protection of, our humanity.

In this respect I should like to note that it always saddens me to meet people thirty to forty years out of college who view the contemporary church and world and their challenges in terms of what they were taught forty years ago by Father X. This means that what Father X gave them was not *philosophia perennis* but *philosophia paralizans*. To that extent, the university was defective.

6. Critical capacity. By *critical capacity* I mean the ability to think through a problem (event, possibility, piece of writing, policy, procedure, etc.), lift up the pros and cons, develop coherent reasons and arguments, and situate one's conclusions (or opinions) within a sufficiently broad context of human and religious values. So often, our convictions, solutions, actions, and policies root in biases, narrow self-interest, cultural distortions, etc., without our ability to recognize these origins. Unless and until these origins are recognized, our ability to think through events clearly is hampered. An excellent university education should leave a student at least several long steps down the road of critical thinking.

7. Ability to listen. The ability to listen is an absolute essential for continuing the educational process throughout life. The person who emerges from a truly great Catholic university should have picked up the art of listening because she or he saw it happening on a daily basis for four years on the part of educated and wise professors. I refer to the fact that an outstanding professor necessarily listens: to other professors, to her or his students, to people from other countries and cultures, to those with hands-on experience, etc.

From a student's perspective, one of the most supportive and confidence-building things a professor can do is show the student, by listening, that she respects the student and takes him seriously. In my own doctoral studies, I remember putting a question to the renowned moral theologian Josef Fuchs, S.J. He paused then stated that my question was an excellent one, that he would think about it and I should too, that then we could discuss it later. Perhaps more than any single event in my graduate studies this incident was educational. In a very practical way it told me that I should trust my insights and have the courage to take my doubts and questions seriously. That taught me a great deal.

This kind of thing should be a daily experience in a fine university. When it is, the products of these universities will be listeners—and learners—in the world they inhabit.

The process of dialogical listening is threatened by authoritarian approaches, especially those that would attempt to stifle dissent. That is the danger in the current ecclesial context. The atmosphere is one of coercion. Elsewhere,[11] I have noted that a coercive atmosphere has the following effects: (1) weakening of the episcopal magisterium; (2) weakening of the papal magisterium; (3) marginalization of theologians; (4) demoralization of priests and other ministers; (5) reduction of the laity; (6) compromise of ministry; (7) loss of the Catholic lesson.

Coercion represents the cessation of the listening process. It represents a practical takeback of Vatican II's assertion: "Let it be recognized that all of the faithful—clerical and lay—possess a lawful freedom of enquiry and of thought, and the freedom to express their minds humbly and courageously about those matters in which they enjoy competence."[12] This affirmative assertion implies that authorities in the church need to listen. A coercive atmosphere takes it back. Where the church should be an exemplar of listening, its actual example moves in a different direction.

8. Willingness to serve. A university education in a Catholic context ought to foster a certain generosity of spirit that seeks opportunities to come to the aid of others in a multiplicity of ways: by education, by defending rights, by relieving suffering, by affecting public policy. This quality is close to the second noted above (sensitivity to justice and injustice) but is much broader and implies more (than sensitivity). The Catholic university will foster and deepen this willingness by recognizing and honoring it, by supporting it spiritually and materially, by providing satisfying outlets for its exercise, and by reflecting it in its own structures and priorities.

These, then, are the qualities I would hope to find in the graduate of a great Catholic university: a Catholic vision; sensitivity to justice and injustice; appreciation of, and thirst for, knowledge; facility in spoken and written word; open-mindedness; critical capacity; ability to listen; willingness to serve.

Is this a hopelessly utopian recipe? Possibly. But I cannot see a single item I would remove from the list of qualities that a great Catholic university ought to inculcate. Indeed, if a Catholic university simply omitted or gave up on any one of these qualities, whether by oversight or intent, it would, I think, forfeit its claim to be a great Catholic university.

Two intriguing questions remain: Are there qualities that need to be added to the list? Are there any universities that meet the demands of the list? My mischievous intent in writing this essay was to provoke your entanglement in these questions.

Notes

1. John Paul II, "Veritatis Splendor," *Origins* 23 (1993): 331.

2. Michael J. Himes and Kenneth R. Himes, O.F.M., *Fullness of Faith: The Public Significance of Theology* (Mahwah, N.J.: Paulist Press, 1993), 82. This analysis is also found in Richard P. McBrien's *Catholicism* (San Francisco: HarperCollins, 1981), 1180. It is developed even more fully in the revised edition of *Catholicism* (1994).

3. Himes and Himes, *Fullness of Faith*, 83.

4. Ibid., 85.

5. Lawrence S. Cunningham, *Sages, Wisdom, and the Catholic Tradition* (Tulsa, Okla.: University of Tulsa), 7. This is no. 27 of the Warren Lecture Series.

6. *Catholic Mind* 64 (1971): 29–42.

7. *Documents of the Thirty-Second General Congregation of the Society of Jesus* (Washington, D.C.: Jesuit Conference, 1975), 26.

8. *Documents of the Thirty-Second General Congregation of the Society of Jesus,* 17.

9. J. A. Plourde, "Making Justice a Reality," *Catholic Mind* 70 (1972): 7.

10. National Conference of Catholic Bishops, *Economic Justice for All* (Washington, D.C.: United States Catholic Conference, 1986), para. 347.

11. Richard A. McCormick, S.J., and Richard P. McBrien, "Theology as a Public Responsibility," *America* 165 (1991): 187–88.

12. *Documents of Vatican II* (New York: America Press, 1966), 270.

The Advantages of a Catholic University

RALPH MCINERNY

One of the happiest events of Notre Dame's sesquicentennial celebration was the publication of Father Sorin's journal, a circumstanced account from 1842 on of the founding and early difficult years of Notre Dame. The book was edited by Father James Connelly, the archivist of the Congregation of Holy Cross, and published by the University of Notre Dame Press. This chronicle reminds us of the soil and seed out of which one Catholic university grew and the intrepid zeal of its first generation. To read it is to be made proud to have anything at all to do with the continuing history of an institution founded by such a giant, a gruff, devout, single-minded, holy giant. It is also to have a vivid image of what the Holy Father meant when he began his document on the Catholic university with the words *ex corde ecclesiae*—from the heart of the church.

I hope you will not find it chauvinistic if I approach our topic from the vantage point of my own four decades as a professor of philosophy at Notre Dame. For better or worse, Notre Dame has emerged as a ready symbol of Catholic higher education. When I came here in 1955, there were still people who thought it must be a Jesuit university. Under the long and historic presidency of Father Hesburgh, Notre Dame's ascendancy was constant and dramatic.

I want to reflect on what happened over those decades, not as a disengaged critic, but as a participant. Many, many good things happened; others have been less happy. I shall also be concerned with the present and where we all go from here.

The Quest for Excellence

In the 1950s, John Tracy Ellis, a church historian, wrote an essay that had wide reverberations ("American Catholics and the Intellectual Life"). Ellis cast a cold eye on Catholic higher education and wondered why our Catholic colleges and universities had not produced the intellectual leaders of the age. They were, he suggested, mired in mediocrity.

Out of this discussion arose the drive for excellence.

So far so good. It has been pointed out that Ellis chose to judge Catholic universities on the basis of something they were not trying to do. They were not research universities, after all, but places where a largely immigrant church moved upward, both culturally and socially. In a 1946 essay in *Life*, Evelyn Waugh, not the most sanguine of writers, praised the American Catholic system of higher education. Nonetheless, the suggestion that we do our job better, indeed excellently, was salutary advice.

Ellis did not ask how Catholic universities could be better Catholic universities, however; he asked how they could be more like their secular counterparts, many of which had been founded under religious auspices and then drifted away. This was a fateful comparison. The history of Notre Dame over the past forty years or so can be seen against the background of the debate Ellis initiated.

Notice how the problem was stated. Not: How can Catholic universities do their job better, even excellently? But: How can Catholic universities become more like their secular counterparts?

There was nothing sinister in this, of course. You and I can construct the implicit argument.

1. Catholic universities should become excellent.
2. The great secular and secularized universities are excellent.
3. Catholic universities should become like the great secular and secularized universities.

THE RENAISSANCE OF THE LIBERAL ARTS

We continue to talk about a liberal education, we call one college within our institution the college of arts and letters, we speak of the humanities, but students are not initially clear what the origin of such talk is. If asked to name the liberal arts, what would they answer? Historically, there were seven, divided into a trivium and a quadrivium—grammar, rhetoric, logic; and arithmetic, geometry, music, and astronomy. In the great entry hall of O'Shaughnessy the arts are represented in stained glass, the trivium over the doorway, the quadrivium on the north wall. They are, of course, the point of reference when we speak of a liberal education, or of colleges of Arts and Letters.

Historical excursus. It would be possible to give a sketch of education from antiquity to just the other day in terms of the liberal arts tradition. The liberal arts were those that made persons free, freed us from ignorance, and were dispositional in emancipating us from slavery to the senses, the passing moment, the vagrant pleasure unrelated to the examined life.

When the liberal arts passed from antiquity to the Middle Ages there were of course linguistic barriers. If the influx of barbarians (our ancestors) into the empire involved assimilation to a Latin culture, Greek was no longer part of the picture, and that closed off Greek learning by and large, unless it were translated into Latin. The portion of Greek learning that got translated into Latin before the Dark Ages closed in formed the spine of medieval education.

The liberal arts tradition was shaped by that fact; it could be argued that the liberal arts were the fragment of Greek learning destined to have a career in Latin. In any case, in the Dark Ages, monasteries become repositories of learning and continuators of the liberal arts seen as good in themselves but also as propaedeutic to the study of Holy Writ.

Toward the end of the twelfth century, vast amounts of Greek literature (most notably the works of Aristotle) began to be translated into Latin, and this transformed the educational system. Liberal arts education had long since moved from the monasteries into towns, the cathedral towns, where a bishop appointed a scholastic to educate future clergy. With the influx of Aristotle and Arabic commentators, the schools of Paris formed themselves into a university at the beginning of the thirteenth century.

Few things are more intellectually exciting than the story of the founding and flourishing of the University of Paris. Dr. Astrik Gabriel, who was my predecessor as director of the Medieval Institute, has devoted a long career to this study and a year ago, at the age of eighty-five, published a book on the university, or *studium*, of Paris which gathers together a lifetime of learning.

The first universities were of course Catholic, and for centuries that was the case. I will come back to the significance of this curiously overlooked historical fact.

Hutchins and Adler. Not twenty years before John Tracy Ellis wrote the article to which I referred above, something very exciting had happened in American higher education. It was a reaction to the fairly recent practice of letting students treat the curriculum as a cafeteria, selecting courses with increasing freedom, putting together their own programs.

It occurred to such figures as Robert Hutchins and Mortimer Adler to wonder why, if to be educated was a specifiable thing, colleges did not present a program to be followed. Both Hutchins and Adler were further motivated by what they thought to be defects in legal education. If being a lawyer means primarily knowing precedents, legal education is largely an exercise in memory. But how much time is spent reflecting on the principles of jurisprudence?

Mark Van Doren, a legendary teacher at Columbia—you will find an account of him in Thomas Merton's *Seven Storey Mountain*—wrote a book called *Liberal Education*. I read it in a service paperback while lying on the gull wing of an F4U Corsair at El Toro in the mid-1940s (when it was on the ground, of course). Van Doren told of the efforts at St. John's College in Annapolis, Maryland, and the University of Chicago to provide a liberal education for students.

This reforming interest brought many of these figures closer and closer to Catholicism and to Catholic institutions of higher learning. Why? Because they saw in Catholic colleges at least a remnant of the tradition of liberal education. There was mutual influence. The General Program of Liberal Education at Notre Dame (now the Program of Liberal Studies), whose first director was Otto Bird—see his memoir published by Ignatius Press, *The Center Does Not Hold: Confessions of a Great Bookie*—introduced a liberal arts program based on reading the great books of that tradition. Bird reveals that this was meant to be, not just a special program, but a pilot that would eventually include the whole college.

The Moral. Recalling this renaissance of liberal education is a very important corrective to the attitude engendered by John Tracy Ellis's critique. There was as a matter of fact a good deal of admiration for Catholic higher education on the part of these reformers. They were reformers because they did not think everything was hunky-dory with non-Catholic higher education. In fact, they thought it had lost its soul, or was in proximate danger of doing so. And these reformers looked both to the tradition of liberal education and to institutions— the Jesuit ones, and Notre Dame—whose curricula were some kind of effort to carry on a tradition meant to emancipate young people from ignorance and acquaint them with the best our culture had achieved, along with reflection on the principles of that culture.

So one could say both (1) that Ellis was criticizing Catholic universities for not doing something (viz., what the secular and secularized institutions were doing) but that something was not what they were trying to do; and (2) that what they were doing seemed to many outsiders the very thing that was needed in non-Catholic universities to bring them back to life.

THE NOTRE DAME EFFORT

One of the charming things about the history of Notre Dame is that, almost from the beginning, there is self-examination going on, effort after effort made to rachet up the quality of the performance. Father John Zahm, whose life bridged the nineteenth and twentieth centuries, a man of enormous personal culture (the Dante collection at Notre Dame is just one of his achievements), wanted Notre Dame to raise its sights and strive harder. Father Andrew Morrissey is said to have opposed him and to have prevailed. It is difficult to imagine anyone prevailing in an unequivocal fashion over Father Zahm.

Before the Ellis essay, first Father Cavanaugh and then Father Hesburgh urged the university to reach its full potential. The discussion that Ellis engendered became part of our conversation. The drive toward excellence is something we associate peculiarly with Father Hesburgh, rightly called the second founder of Notre Dame.

As I have indicated, the Ellis article could give rise to some such thought as: How can we become more like them? The Hesburgh project was essentially different from that. Rather, it was this: How can we do better what we are doing by adding to our mix the best that is going on in non-Catholic institutions?

The Hesburgh or Notre Dame notion of excellence incorporated one of the fundamental assumptions of Catholic culture—nothing true, nothing good, nothing beautiful, can be alien to our tradition. St. Augustine spoke of taking from pagans, as from unjust possessors, their philosophical achievements and incorporating them into the larger whole that is Christian culture.

The Philosophy Department. Let me illustrate how this was implemented in my own area, the philosophy department. I was hired for two reasons: First, I had written my dissertation on Kierkegaard, the great Danish thinker often called the father of existentialism; second, I was a Thomist.

All members—save perhaps one—of the philosophy department were Thomists. This appellation had both a wide and narrow meaning. In the narrow meaning, a Thomist was a student and scholar of the texts of Thomas, their medieval setting, their influence, etc. Colleagues of mine who had been trained at the Pontifical Institute of Mediaeval Studies in Toronto were Thomists in this narrow and very demanding sense. In its broad meaning, a Thomist was interested in combining the achievements of Christian culture, an assimilated Thomism, to whatever developments of a positive kind were going on in contemporary philosophy.

Thus, the question put to me would have been What can we learn from existentialism? Not, notice, How can we become existentialists? but What of value have existentialists added to the ongoing effort to grasp the truth about ourselves, the world, and God?

The ideal of the philosophy department was to have a group of teacher-scholars who shared a common patrimony and were interested in assimilating to it all that was valuable in contemporary thought. The result would be an amalgam or synthesis that would be genuinely new. This was to be Notre Dame's peculiar contribution.

In pursuing this ideal, we added more and more philosophers knowledgeable in different things. Some of them were not at all well versed in the Catholic tradition; some were not even Catholics. Nonetheless, they were eager to take part in the common effort to create something new.

Somewhere during the past forty years this ideal has withered away. No one ever rejected it as such. It was not repudiated. If indeed things fly apart because the center does not hold, I think what happened was that we were inadequately concerned about keeping a central critical mass of philosophers who incorporated in their personal work the collective ideal of the department. Gradually we had senior colleagues who simply did philosophy in some contemporary way and were not interested, personally or professionally, in relating it to traditional philosophy. We have now reached the point where what was once the collective goal of the department can only be a personal one, because a majority of Notre Dame philosophers are uninterested in, or even hostile to, that original ideal of making a new synthesis *ex novis et veteris.*

I suspect that something similar happened to the university generally. One day we looked around to discover the absence of the original ideal of excellence.

The danger now is that we might adopt the first interpretation of the Ellis agenda: How can we become more like them? There are some who feel we have already succumbed to this danger.

The Closing of the American Mind. A few years ago, in *The Closing of the American Mind,* Allan Bloom lamented the decline in achievement in students over the course of his academic career. Since Bloom taught first at Cornell and then at Chicago, he had scarcely labored in fallow fields. His book is a powerful indictment of what is wrong with American higher education. Unlike an earlier generation of critics, Bloom saw no reason to regard Catholic colleges and universities as exceptions to the problem or as pointing the way to a solution. He never even mentions them. Had we become so much like our secular counterparts that the only difference was the stage of decline we were in?

My serious point is this. Anyone who feels a temptation to what I am calling the Ellis conception of excellence had best take a close look at the models he would emulate. The secular universities were only equivocally regulative of educational excellence long before Ellis wrote; since, they have become what Bloom took them to be.

What was the overriding characteristic of his students' outlook? There is no truth. Or, you have your truth, and I have mine. There is no objective measure of truth or falsity. I will return to this.

The Catholic University

What is certain for many is that it has become problematic whether a university can be at the same time Catholic and excellent. Imagine. It is seriously asked whether or not the Catholic faith is an impediment to educational excellence. "Can Notre Dame be a great university although Catholic?"

THE SOCIAL GOSPEL ROUTE

Sometimes when it is asked whether or not Notre Dame still is a Catholic university, the inquirer is told of the Masses said almost around the clock on campus, as well as of the heightened sense of social responsibility on the part of Notre Dame students. Needless to say, these are essential elements of being a Catholic—the Eucharist and a sense of justice and charity which manifests itself in deeds. Call them necessary conditions for a university's being Catholic. But they are not sufficient conditions.

A university is chiefly concerned with the mind and imagination. If the faith has no influence on what goes on in the classrooms and laboratories, studios and stages, of the university, the university is not Catholic.

THE RESEARCH UNIVERSITY ROUTE

A research university is one in which the scholarly work of the faculty takes precedence, where one's essential contribution is discovery, pushing a discipline into new realms, where the aim is to publish and bring renown to oneself and one's institution. Teaching, save in the sense of training assistants, is not a prominent part of the picture.

This cannot be the route of Notre Dame. Our historical mission is to teach young men and women, not for entry into academic ranks—they are not apprentices in the faculty guild—but principally to carry on as educated Catholics in the wider world. To do this excellently, they must be given opportunities to reflect on their faith, chiefly by studying the documents of Vatican II, to consider the philosophical presuppositions of belief, to read the great literature which is by and large Christian and Catholic in inspiration, to grasp the main lines of our history. . .

If we were a research university, we might have six members of the philosophy department. We have nearly forty members because we all teach undergraduates, not as a grudging concession, let us hope, but as the very heart of our professional activity.

Research, publications? Of course. I recently compared university reports of faculty publications of more than twenty years ago with that of a year ago. There has been no dramatic change in publications, prestige of publisher or journal, research grants received, as a result of the de facto minimizing of teaching which is manifest in the risibly light teaching loads of the junior faculty. If a trade-off was envisaged, it looks like a bad bargain all around.

THE HESBURGH IDEAL

It was under the stimulus of the Hesburgh ideal of excellence that the activities of several decades ago went on. I think we should return to that. I described it in microcosm in the philosophy department; the university's pursuit of it would be the macrocosm.

But it is just here that it can be suggested that there was a fatal flaw in the Hesburgh ideal. After all, that ideal presupposed that a Catholic university as Catholic could be excellent. Alas, it may be objected, there is enmity between the university ideal, properly understood, and an institution formally and publicly committed to the truth of the Catholic Faith—named after our Lady!—and its relevance for the work of the university. That assumption, the suggestion continues, collides with the key assumption of the university, which is academic freedom.

ACADEMIC FREEDOM

Pope John Paul II's letter on the Catholic university—*Ex Corde Ecclesiae*—is must reading for anyone who wishes to think with the church on the matter of the nature of Catholic universities. In this letter, the pope refers again and again to academic freedom, but he usually adds "properly understood and respectful of the common good." If nothing else, this suggests that academics are free only up to a point, that their freedom to teach and/or advocate has its limits and can indeed be trumped by other considerations. To this it might be objected—in fact, the objection is frequently made—that a constrained freedom is no freedom and that academic freedom as it operates in the modern university recognizes no constraints.

This is of course a misdescription. I know of no institution of higher learning where an academic's freedom to teach is not bounded by some restraints. And restraints from outside as well as inside the university. Accrediting associations will punish a university if its faculty are not properly trained, if they are ineligible for membership in relevant learned societies, etc. If you insist on teaching Ptolemaic astronomy as the last word on the universe, you are unlikely to get tenure. The fact that not everyone gets tenure alone suggests that assessments and appraisals of academic performance are made, and to complain that one is free to be incompetent is an irrelevance. If you urge your students to burn down classroom buildings, academic freedom will not save your job.

This is all obvious and nonproblematical. Every institution distinguishes between responsible and irresponsible uses of academic freedom. There must then be standards and criteria of acceptable free performance. Being free is not the last word.

If then, academic freedom is always constrained in some way or another, such that appraisals of free performance are possible, the real question is: What are legitimate and illegitimate restraints on academic freedom?

Political Correctness. If there is anything that characterizes the contemporary secular university it is the thought police who roam about the campus seeking whom they might silence.

Until it was declared unconstitutional, the faculty at the University of Michigan were subject to this threat: any student who claimed to have been offended by something a professor said had the right to define that offense. In short, to say one had been offended was sufficient for establishing that one had been offended.

In many places the freedom not to use gender-free language is absent. (I am told that a woman professor of theology at Notre Dame takes points off papers if a student refers to God as *he*. Let us hope this is an aberration rather than a harbinger.)

The charge of *homophobia*—let us pass over the linguistic illiteracy this neologism incorporates—has almost silenced the commonly recognized (and authoritatively taught) truth that homosexuality is a perversion and a sin.

Not too many years ago, it seemed almost mandatory in academe to snicker when the name Ronald Reagan was mentioned.

Every academic knows of such things. New colleagues of mine, coming from secular universities, often comment on the freedom they feel at Notre Dame and did not feel at the place from which they came.

One of the characteristics of the restraints on academic freedom operative in secular universities is their arbitrariness, their shiftiness and alterability. They were not part of any unspoken, let alone spoken, agreement when one was hired, yet they seek to govern the daily activities of the campus.

Conclusion: there are both legitimate and illegitimate restraints on academic freedom in the secular university. To suggest that academic freedom "properly understood and respectful of the common good" disqualifies the Catholic university is nonsense. There is no other defensible kind of academic freedom.

The Advantages of the Catholic University

The genius of the Catholic university resides in the fact that faith and reason are taken to complement and reinforce one another. It is shameful for a believer to regard the truths God has taught us through his Son as impediments to arriving at new truths. Christ is the way, the truth and the life. Nothing we can know about the world or ourselves can possibly conflict with divine revelation.

More importantly, the faith is a powerful stimulus to the search for truth. Faith is an obscure knowledge, a glimpse through darkened glass, but it encompasses as well truths about the world and ourselves. No Catholic scientist could accept the claim that the world is self-explanatory such that all talk of its having a cause is superfluous.

What is both increasingly obvious and insufficiently celebrated is the fact that the faith, the Catholic church, has become the great champion of reason in a time when, on all sides, reason is downgraded, or dismissed, or both. In the practical order, it is the Catholic church almost alone which asserts and defends the very principles of practical discourse, the very possibility of meaningful communication among human beings as to what is to be done. I have in mind the church's championing of the natural law, most recently in John Paul II's magnificent encyclical *Veritatis Splendor*. (Remember Bloom's description of his relativistic students.)

The same can be said of the theoretical order. It has become fashionable to be Nietzschean and see all alleged truth claims as power moves. There is not, we are told, any criterion (or criteria) which would enable us to determine whether, for example, slavery or freedom is the better condition for human beings. Or whether tyranny or liberal democracy is the better form of government. There

186 / RALPH MCINERNY

is no better because there is no objective basis for the good. Or for truth. Richard Rorty is one of the more debonair purveyors of this utterly destructive theory— hardly a theory at all, since presumably its rejection is equally valid.

Universities took their rise under church auspices in the thirteenth century. This country is blessed with hundreds of institutions of Catholic higher learning founded by religious orders of men or women, by dioceses, by the bishops collectively in the case of the Catholic University of America. They are grounded on the assumption that faith fosters knowledge and knowledge supports the faith. They are not everything they might be. No college or university is everything it might be. But if one asked whether the ancient and ever-new ideal of learning stands a better chance of survival in Catholic than in non-Catholic institutions, the answer I think is clear.

In times like these, let us thank God for the Catholic university. Not only is it a place where faith and reason complement and mutually help one another, it is also a seemingly last redoubt where reason and truth can be honored.

And of course where national championship football is played.

What Can Catholic Universities Learn from Protestant Examples?

George M. Marsden

Are there historical forces operating that make it virtually in-evitable that Catholic universities will follow the path taken by formerly Protestant universities in moving away from meaning-ful religious identities? One thinks, for example, of Northwestern, Duke, Boston University, Syracuse, Vanderbilt, and the Universi-ty of Southern California, all formerly Methodist universities, none of which has much more than vestigial Christian identity. Will Notre Dame become, say, within two generations, another Duke or Syracuse? Should that be its goal?

A good case can be made that Catholic universities today are a-bout where their Protestant American counterparts were between the world wars. As late as the 1930s the presidents of schools such as Duke, Syracuse, or even denominationally independent Yale, spoke openly of their schools' Christian heritage and mission. The issue of Christian identity was then often debated. Older faculty had been shaped in the days when their schools had encouraged strong-ly Christian, even evangelical, commitments, and many still had an explicit sense of Christian calling in their work. Others had no nostalgia for the old days and saw the increased openness as purely a gain. In retrospect, we can see that the handwriting was on the wall; but at the time the subject of keeping a place for Christianity on campuses was a subject for conferences, symposia, and books of essays. For many it was difficult to imagine private universities without some Christian identity.[1]

One theme that emerges from the study of Protestant universities is that the loss of distinctly religious identity is not something that the Christians who led those universities directly chose. Rather, the long-term changes were largely the results of choices that in the short run promised to improve not only the university but also the quality of the Christianity on its campus. So even from the perspective of attempting to sustain Christian identity, the choices were often the right ones for the immediate future. Schools became more open, more inclusive, and less coercive, all in the name of the Christian spirit of the institutions. During the era of transition, such universities enjoyed what from a religious perspective might be regarded as a golden age. For more than a generation (for American Protestant schools, typically from the 1890s to the 1950s) they were far more open than they once had been, but they still retained enough momentum from their church heritages to sustain at least a discernible Christian presence.

During that transitional stage a revealing question that was sometimes asked was, Should a church-related university first of all serve the church or the wider public? Typically the answer would be, Both. The two interests, they confidently believed, could be balanced. Part of the duty of the church after all was to serve the public, particularly through such agencies as universities. Furthermore, Protestants in the United States had a long history of cultural hegemony and hence of equating the interests of their churches and those of the culture at large.

By about the 1950s the church part of the equation had become largely nominal. Church-related universities could still point to their impressive chapel buildings and to voluntary religion on campus. Religious activities, however, had become thoroughly peripheral to the main business of the universities. In the classrooms, almost as much as in research, the dogma was widely accepted that science was autonomous in its own domain.[2] Religious truths had their own supplementary values and might be taught in divinity schools, churches, or campus ministries. Religious perspectives might occasionally be offered by a professor here or there, especially in fledgling religion departments, but such outlooks were largely peripheral to the main business of university education.

The assaults on the WASP establishment beginning in the 1960s easily routed most of the vestigial religious aspects of Protestant higher education. By the 1980s most major campus chapels were no longer exclusively Protestant but were into serving interfaith constituencies. Beginning in the 1960s, mainline Protestant campus ministries declined dramatically. Many of the more traditional student moral regulations were casualties of the cultural revolution of the 1960s. In the classrooms, explicit Christian teaching, which already had been rare, disappeared almost entirely, excepting what might be offered by a few of the older professors or in divinity schools. By the 1980s religion departments typically focused on detached study of the history of religions,[3] and the Christianity taught at the handful of major university divinity schools seemed increasingly anomalous in the context of the dominant dogma that religious perspectives should have nothing to do with the highest education.

American University Culture

The example of what has happened to Protestant universities is important not simply because it provides an example of a course that the future Catholic experience might parallel; more fundamentally, the formerly Protestant schools continue to set the standards for the rest of higher education. Essential to any understanding of the current situation is that there is a dominant American university culture that dictates the standards for all who want to be recognized as true universities. This dominant university culture, in turn, has distinctly Protestant origins.

In attempting to understand how that dominant university culture has been defined, the most relevant observation for our present purposes is that American universities had distinctly anti-Catholic origins. The men who established American universities in the late nineteenth century were mostly New Englanders who had roughly the same set of interests as did their compatriots who built American public schools. Education was an essential component for building an advanced and unified national culture. Higher education would be, like the common schools, *nonsectarian*, but that meant broadly Protestant. It would be based on democratic moral ideals into which all peoples could be assimilated, thus unifying the nation.

Furthermore, it would be *scientific,* with science defined as inquiry free from sectarian prejudice. This truly scientific education would also help unify the nation on the basis of what all educated persons might agree on.[4] As Andrew Dickson White, the founding president of Cornell, made clear in *A History of the Warfare of Science with Theology in Christendom* (New York, 1896), authoritarian Catholicism was the antithesis of this scientific ideal.

Freedom was a primary watchword for both the moral and the scientific ideals on which university culture was being built. Faculty would be free from outside political or religious control. Science would be free from external authority. Students would be free to choose most of their courses and would be taught the values of a free and tolerant society and choosing one's own standards to live by. Once again, to those who first defined American university culture, Catholicism seemed the antithesis to all they stood for. In their view, Catholic political views were undemocratic and Catholic education was hopelessly authoritarian and repressive of free inquiry.

At the same time, the shapers of American university culture excluded the more conservative parts of their own Protestant heritage. Theology, which was considered divisive, was removed as a reference point in other academic inquiry, so that religious viewpoints, such as there were, had strictly to do with morality. John Henry Newman had identified this trend in Protestant higher education even before American universities came on the scene. Morality detached from theological reference might be a means for promoting cultural unity, but it would soon make Christianity as such irrelevant.[5]

University culture has changed a great deal in the past hundred years, but not at all in the direction of welcoming distinctly Christian viewpoints into the classroom. While Catholic schools and colleges are accepted far more than they were a century ago, they typically are accepted in spite of their Catholicism. Prejudices against Catholicism have, of course, moderated, but they have hardly disappeared. One only has to look at the history of the prestigious Phi Beta Kappa honor society to document this point. No Catholic school was granted membership until the late 1930s, and by 1960 the total number of schools so honored was two. By 1989 that number had risen only to twelve.[6] Catholic schools that wished such recognition had to be careful about letting Catholicism intrude on academic life. Loyola University of Chicago, for instance, was judged to be qualified in every other respect to have a Phi Beta Kappa chapter, but in 1985 was turned down because of objections to a statement in its faculty handbook that forbade faculty from "attacking and ridiculing authoritative Catholic teachings" when speaking as a representative of the university.[7] Other universities might ban ridicule of other groups and traditions, but banning attack and ridicule of the teachings of one's own church tradition was considered a violation of academic freedom.

Government funding has also been made contingent in part on reducing religious emphases. Many of the court cases testing state aid to religious colleges, especially during the 1960s, had to do with Catholic institutions. Catholic faculty typically testified in such cases that their Catholic beliefs had little influence on what they taught, thus attempting to establish that Catholic schools had essentially secular purposes.[8] Academic freedom was also an issue for the courts. Chief Justice Warren Burger, for instance, wrote in *Tilton v. Richardson* (1971) on the question of state funding for buildings at Catholic colleges that one reason that the colleges involved could be funded was that they were "characterized by an atmosphere of academic freedom rather than religious indoctrination."[9] Whatever one might think of the stands of Catholic colleges on these points is a separable issue; the historical point is that they have been facing immense pressures to be less Catholic if they are to be widely accepted.

A disturbing sequel is the recent court ruling denying the rights of a Protestant elementary school in Hawaii to hire only Protestant teachers. (Again, one's views on the wisdom of the school's policy should be separated from the legal issue involved.) The U.S. Court of Appeals for the Ninth Circuit, in a ruling that the U.S. Supreme Court declined to review, found that since the Kamehameha Schools were not directly church related and had a "primarily secular rather than a primarily religious orientation," they could not use religion as a criterion for hiring. If such principles were to be applied to colleges and universities, the logic of the courts would be that if schools with religious traditions wish to receive government funding they must prove that they are essentially secular. If, however, they wish to continue to use religion as a consideration in hiring, they would have to prove that they were not essentially secular.[10]

Almost all the pressures seem to be in the same direction of imposing academic uniformity at the expense of religious identity. Even a partial list of such pressures suggests how formidable they are: pressures for separation of church and state; pressures for greater academic freedom; ideals of pluralism and diversity; demands for technological excellence; pressures to meet standards of professionalism defined as excluding religion; faculty and departmental demands for autonomy (especially in hiring); reactions to fears of external control; aspirations for recognition of excellence (How will the *U.S. News and World Report* ratings be affected?); pressures from accrediting agencies; pressures of the market to broaden the base of students and contributors; resulting pressures from increasingly diverse faculty, contributors, students, and alumni; changing student mores. With so many forces arrayed in the direction of producing a standardized academic culture, one must wonder whether there is any place for institutions that are substantially shaped by religious identities, unless they are willing to remain in a second-class status.

Searching for Middle Ground

One way of understanding the issue is as a question about pluralism, and diversity, and multiculturalism—ideals that the dominant academic culture claims to value highly. The way these ideals are currently conceived is to emphasize that institutions should include representatives of as many diverse cultures as possible. That is a laudable ideal. As it is typically implemented in the dominant academic culture, however, it amounts not to creating diversity among institutions but rather toward making them all look alike. Particular traditions of institutions, including religious traditions, are expected to give way to representing the variety of currently accepted viewpoints.

It should be asked, however, whether our culture has room for diversity among institutions as well as within them. Can it encourage diversity of institutions? Can multiculturalism include concern for the religious heritages that have been at the hearts of most cultures? Can it tolerate the distinctive institutions of such heritages? Schools should indeed still be encouraged to be as internally diverse as they can be, consistent with their heritages and traditions. But are not the institutional expressions of those heritages and traditions just the sorts of things that concerns for diversity should be protecting?

So far as the future is concerned, the most crucial area where these issues play themselves out is in faculty hiring. Once a church-related institution adopts the policy that it will hire simply "the best qualified candidates," it is simply a matter of time until its faculty will have an ideological profile essentially like that of the faculty at every other mainstream university. The first loyalties of faculty members will be to the national cultures of their professions rather than to any local or ecclesiastical traditions. Faculty members become essentially interchangeable parts in a standardized national system. At first, when schools move in the direction of open hiring, they can count on some continuity with their traditions based on informal ties and self-selection of those congenial to their heritage. Within a generation, however, there is bound to be a shift to a majority for whom national professional loyalties are primary. Since departmental faculties typically have virtual autonomy in hiring, it becomes impossible to reverse the trend and the church tradition becomes vestigial. The Protestant experience thus suggests that once a school begins to move away from the religious heritage as a factor in hiring, the pressures become increasingly greater to continue to move in that direction.

Such a conclusion becomes particularly perplexing if one weighs it against the good reasons that schools may have for increasing faculty diversity. Some of the stricter religious schools may exclude valuable faculty perspectives or they may unduly inhibit academic freedom and creative scholarship. Or a strong case might be made that they would better fulfill their Christian missions by serving broader constituencies. Yet, despite the merits of these concerns,[11] both the historical precedents and analysis of the forces that drive historical change suggest that opening the doors for such valuable and refreshing breezes soon lets in gale-force winds that drive out the religious heritage altogether.

So the puzzle is how to hold the middle ground. How is it possible, short of reverting to repressive strictures of earlier days, to maintain a vital religious presence, including an intellectual presence, in a modern university? Is there any way to retain the balance of being a university that is both Catholic and open to many other points of view?

The Catholic Difference?

One way to get at the answer to these questions is to ask whether there is anything that distinguishes American Catholic universities at the end of the twentieth century from their Protestant counterparts in the early decades of the century. As one who is new to a Catholic environment, I am not the best person to make such comparisons, but I can suggest the following impressions:

First of all, the most obvious difference between American Catholic and Protestant universities is in typical forms of governance. Most Catholic universities traditionally have been governed by religious congregations whose members have been part of the university faculty and administration. Even though direct control by religious orders has been much weakened in recent decades, the role can still be considerable, as at Notre Dame. For one thing, it guarantees the continuance of a Catholic religious presence for worship. That such a presence is marked especially by the regular celebrations of the Mass points to a central feature of Catholicism that distinguishes it from most of Protestantism. At least vestiges of these features seem likely to persist even if the rest of a university loses its Catholic identity.

Priests, sisters, or brothers in the classrooms also provide a religious dimension in the academic life of Catholic universities. Such a presence may, however, diminish if the supply of clerics and members of religious orders continues to diminish or if pressures to abandon preferential hiring become too strong.

Whether religious orders can continue to play a decisive role in the administration and oversight of Catholic universities is a significant question. That role reflects an oligarchic tradition of governance, rather than a democratic one. Of course, all universities are governed by oligarchies of some sort. Nonetheless, pressures are strong in university culture to incorporate more democratic procedures into governance. For instance, faculties tend to insist on virtual autonomy in hiring and in determining curricula.

A second difference between Catholics and Protestants is that in elite American culture, such as academic culture, Catholics long have been outsiders. Formerly Protestant schools, on the other hand, have always thought of themselves as simply American. Thinking of themselves as simply part of general American culture meant that, as the culture changed, they had to change to keep up with it. Hence as the privileged place for Protestantism declined in twentieth-century culture, these schools had to abandon their religious identities, or else lose their insider status.

Having been outsiders to the larger culture has fostered in Catholics some tradition of resistance to conformity to American cultural trends. On the other hand, it has also fostered something of an inferiority complex and also a strong tradition of Catholic Americanism. Since Vatican II, Americanism has triumphed in much of the church and in American Catholic academic culture. Americanism, of course, has many attractive features, but it can become erosive of Catholic identity if it overwhelms traditions of critical resistance to dominant cultural standards. That may be what is happening to much of Catholic academic culture in recent decades. Such trends are reinforced by many Catholics who were brought up in what they saw as an oppressively restrictive atmosphere of pre–Vatican II Catholic schooling and who have reacted by regarding any emphasis on a distinctly Catholic viewpoint as merely a step backward.

The crucial question now is whether there is a willingness in the American Catholic church and its academic culture to be different or whether the trend toward ever-increasing conformity to non-Catholic American models will continue. One way in which Catholics are now different from Protestants is that they have their own major universities. From the point of view of a Protestant who values the distinguished heritage of Christian learning, the presence of such universities is something to be valued and preserved.

A final, and most important, difference from the earlier twentieth-century cases of Protestant universities is that we now live in a postliberal and postmodern era. By *postliberal* I simply mean that most of the promises of a liberal consensus, supposed to provide a scientific basis for shared moral ideals, have not been fulfilled. Rather, our culture is built around the question of how to live with moral anarchy and emptiness. That raises the question of whether Catholic universities should aspire to be just like the rest of elite academic culture. Why should Catholic schools wish to be like Vanderbilt or Northwestern? Is there anything about the coherence of the ideals of such universities that Catholic institutions should wish to imitate?

Furthermore, we are in a postmodern era. By that I mean that we are in an intellectual environment in which we do not need to be intimidated by the intellectual shibboleths of liberalism. We ourselves do not have to hold to postmodern epistemologies to see the force of their critiques of old-style liberalism. Much of the old critique of the very idea of Catholic education was based on naive liberal ideas about positivistic science and the possibility of building a consensus of moral ideals. As Catholics said at the time, it is impossible to establish such ideals on purely naturalistic premises. Now postmodernist critics are saying what leads to the same conclusion: There is no adequate intellectual basis for the moral ideals that most contemporary academics hold most dear.[12] All they have left is campus politics. So, even if we view the case in contemporary academia's own terms, there is much to be said today for being willing to be different.

Not Just Holding Our Own

The question remains, however, whether any of these Catholic distinctives is sufficient to offset the massive forces in academic culture that push for a homogeneity that marginalizes Christianity. The current state of Catholic universities is in many ways attractive. The Catholic presence, even if diminishing, is still substantial. Yet at the same time the universities are open to wide varieties of opinions and constituencies. Once this opening up has occurred, it is not realistic to think that the process can be reversed on any large scale. Faculty, for instance, who were hired under more open terms can not reasonably be required to conform to more narrowly defined expectations. Rather than setting an institutional goal at reversing the trends, however, it makes more sense to address the problem of how to preserve and build on the present balance between tradition and openness. That in itself will take formidable efforts, since all the momentum and most of the external pressures are on the side of increasing openness. Building from where we are, however, is a far more realizable goal than is turning back a flood that has already risen.

While some specific steps, such as guaranteeing a certain percentage of Catholic faculty, can be taken in attempting to maintain such a balance, they are likely to be only artificial holding actions unless they are accompanied by something far more positive. That positive program must include building a respected tradition of

Catholic, or I would prefer to say Christian, scholarship. That would involve getting beyond the stage when the principal options, other than in theology itself, seem to have been neo-Thomism or nothing. In other words the continuing neo-Thomist tradition needs to be supplemented by other vigorous efforts to explore the implications of Christian faith in scholars' explorations of reality. The degree of importance of those implications varies widely among disciplines and will have far more to do with major interpretative issues than with technical questions. Nonetheless, the point remains that Christian faith can have important bearing on major interpretive issues if scholars are only open to asking such questions.

To build positively an intellectual community that asks such questions will involve consciousness raising and recruitment. Serious Christians who are scholars need to overcome their inhibitions, bred by a century of positivist academic dominance, against asking questions about the intellectual implications of their faith. Furthermore, Catholic universities should recruit scholars at all levels who have shown a willingness to ask such questions. Such recruiting might require special funding so that it could be pursued on an affirmative action basis that would not jeopardize positions or varieties of perspectives already in place. Universities should also establish centers, institutes, and postdoctoral programs for encouraging explorations of the relationships of faith to scholarship.

Such programs will require major funding, but if the program of building a first-rate Catholic university is worth pursuing, it is an ideal that might catch the imagination of potential contributors. No such program to move in a direction counter to major historical trends is going to be accomplished with pocket change left over from normal university activities. It will require a major commitment. That commitment, however, should be directed neither toward retreating to the past nor to simply holding one's own. It should be directed, rather, toward the positive goal of building a new model for the contemporary university that would demonstrate that Christianity can have a vital and positive impact on academic life itself.

Notes

1. My documentation for the historical generalizations in this essay can be found in George M. Marsden and Bradley J. Longfield, eds., *The*

Secularization of the Academy (New York: Oxford University Press, 1992); and George M. Marsden, *The Soul of the American University: From Protestant Establishment to Established Nonbelief* (New York: Oxford University Press, 1994). On the immediate issue, see, for instance, Bradley J. Longfield, "'For God, for Country, and for Yale': Yale, Religion, and Higher Education between the World Wars," in Marsden and Longfield, *Secularization*, 146–69.

2. On this point, see the excellent discussion in Douglas Sloan, *Faith and Knowledge: Mainline Protestantism and Twentieth-Century American Higher Education* (Philadelphia: Westminster Press, 1994).

3. See especially D. G. Hart, "American Learning and the Problem of Religious Studies," in Marsden and Longfield, *Secularization*, 195–233.

4. Alasdair MacIntyre offers a telling critique of this outlook in *Three Rival Versions of Moral Enquiry: Encyclopaedia, Genealogy, and Tradition* (Notre Dame, Ind.: University of Notre Dame Press, 1990).

5. John Henry Newman, *The Idea of a University*, ed. Martin J. Svaglic (Notre Dame, Ind.: University of Notre Dame Press), 20–22.

6. Richard Nelson Current, *Phi Beta Kappa in American Life: The First Two Hundred Years* (New York: Oxford University Press, 1990), 210–18, provides a very frank account of such policies.

7. Based on telephone interviews with Joyce Wexler, March 5, 1993, and Frank Fennell, March 16, 1993, and *Faculty Handbook,* Loyola University of Chicago, 1983, 30.

8. Joseph Richard Preville, "Catholic Colleges, the Courts, and the Constitution: A Tale of Two Cases," *Church History* 58 (June 1989): 197-210. For a discussion of the impact of the pressures at the time, see Walter Gellhorn and R. Kent Greenawalt, *The Sectarian College and the Public Purse: Fordham—A Case Study* (Dobbs Ferry, N.Y.: Oceana Publications, 1970).

9. Quoted in Preville, "Catholic Colleges," 209.

10. Scott Jaschik, "Hiring at Religious Colleges," *Chronicle of Higher Education,* November 17, 1993, A30. Notre Dame joined a number of schools in a "friend of the court" brief to the Supreme Court on behalf of the Kamehameha Schools.

11. A frequently heard argument of less general applicability is the claim that the only way to get "the best people" is to drop all considerations of religion. Doubtless that is correct in some instances. However, the other side of the issue is that some leading scholars might be inclined to come to, and to stay at, less highly regarded institutions just because of a religious emphasis. If a lower-ranked institution relies simply on the open market to get the best people, it must reckon with the fact that more prestigious institutions will always have the upper hand in such competition.

12. Charles Taylor, *Sources of the Self: The Making of the Modern Identity* (Cambridge: Harvard University Press, 1989), 515, makes this point.

Diversity and Change:
A View from the Margin

Naomi M. Meara

Many images come to mind when one thinks of the University of Notre Dame, its intellectual life, its Catholic identity, or its legendary spirit. An image that does not come easily to mind is a practicing Roman Catholic feminist, female, full professor in psychology: hence the title of this essay. I believe, however, that perspectives and contributions from such a person, and others who represent equally unlikely images, are necessary, albeit certainly not sufficient, components in the process of developing a great Catholic university which can lead and serve society, academy, and church. Apparently the editor of this volume shares this belief.

There is some comfort in being at the margin, for maybe we spend too much time and effort in debating what is essential to university life or Catholic identity and in worrying about who, or whose role, is at the center of things. Maybe it is more productive to think about all the diverse elements that are included in the very untidy construct of a church-related university and to focus on the substance of our contributions rather than evaluate their importance or centrality. Those judgments are best made by the women and men who will steward the university long after we who are now here have completed our service to Notre Dame. For in truth, the life of the mind and the life of faith—and their interaction—cannot proceed without all of us, our mistakes and foibles as well as our fine minds and generous hearts. What follows are some personal perspectives about the contemporary nature of Catholic identity and university life. I present them as an invitation for discussion, not as an argument for how things ought to be, nor as a set of observations I believe are, or should be, universally shared.

The Role of Change

Creating, developing, and maintaining a great Catholic university, or for that matter any institution, is a process which is never complete. In any given period of time those who work at and for this process build upon what went before, try to make sense of what is now before them, and try to find time to look thoughtfully toward the future. While in fact we are rooted in a specific time and space, we function intellectually in the past, present, and future. And we always cope with change and uncertainty and often with contradiction. In the midst of such ambiguities we try to create threads of coherence and meaning in the context of current realities.

The church changes, the demands of the academic life change, and the needs of students change. Examples of such changes are everywhere. For instance, departments of psychology and their related intellectual offerings are relative latecomers to the structure and curricula of Catholic universities. Notre Dame has recently celebrated its 150th year; its department of psychology has recently celebrated its 25th. Changes regarding women are well known. Notre Dame was founded in 1842; the first class of undergraduate women entered in 1972. Or to cite yet another example, when I was growing up, women were allowed in the sanctuaries of Catholic churches to clean them and to receive the sacrament of matrimony. Now they serve the needs of the community as communion ministers, servers, and lectors. Many would argue that these changes have enriched our traditions, not detracted from them; have enhanced our core values, not eroded them.

These and other changes have occurred, I believe, because of contemporary interpretations of implicit and explicit assumptions of both church and academy. These interpretations, of course, are influenced by the current demands of everyday life. Since the rise of science in the modern world, the official church has come to understand what Catholic and other intellectuals long knew: that the life of faith has nothing to fear from the life of the mind. There will be no more Galileo affairs. For many years in Catholic colleges and universities, if psychology was taught at all, it was a course in the philosophy curriculum, and the professor was usually a priest with little or no formal training in the discipline. A major concern in excluding psychology from courses of study was what has been termed the *free will–determinism question,* as if there is only one question here. The environmental determinism of behaviorism or the biological determinism of psychoanalysis seemed incompatible with traditional Catholic teaching on free will. We have come to understand that there is more to psychology than determinism, and more to Catholicism than free will, and, even if there were not, the nuances of meanings of those constructs and how they are implemented in daily life are not as far apart as a polarized discussion could lead one to believe. Priests and other pastoral counselors discovered that they needed to know much more psychology in order to assist their parishioners, much as psychotherapists are now discovering that religion is an important aspect in the lives of many of their clients and they need more understanding about it.

For its part, the academy has nothing to fear from the life of faith. A pivotal conviction of university life is that truth emerges through the free exchange of ideas. No idea is off limits for discussion, discussions which may be heated or disparate, but which are expected to be conducted with civility and respect for others and their ideas. So it is with ideas of faith, agnosticism, or atheism. All are welcome, perhaps more so in this Catholic university of our Lady than in classrooms elsewhere. As a psychologist, I do not fear such discussions, nor am I discouraged by the church's history related to psychology. Along with others I am concerned about learning from the past and participating thoughtfully in the present and future of my discipline and my faith.

As an academic I must resist the temptation to think that intellectual life is rooted in my discipline, although that is where my intellectual life lives. That having been said, however, I think Notre Dame would be less of a university if there were no psychology department. This is a department which has well over three hundred undergraduate majors, sixty graduate students, and twenty professors, and provides service courses to hundreds of students each year. The research that goes on here and what students learn in this department about such things as human behavior, mind, child development, work, interpersonal relations, or helping others will enhance, not detract from, their lives as parents, professionals, citizens, and church members. The changes in thinking about human nature prompted by academia and accepted by the church have made this rich resource possible for our students and for others who benefit from the research, teaching, and service of our faculty. In my judgment, having psychology at Notre Dame has added different dimensions to what we offer and has enriched our traditions. A Catholic university needs to be ever open to possibilities for change.

Another assumption of academic and Catholic life is that knowledge is better than ignorance. Indeed, education has long been a value for U.S. Catholics: cleric, religious, and lay. Catholic schools were founded to educate an immigrant people, to keep these new citizens and their offspring firm in their faith, and to provide them the bases for competing in the economic life of this rich country. Of late we have come to believe that educational opportunities should be equal for all, in particular for women and minorities as well as for Caucasian men. Notre Dame's undergraduates, now approximately one-half of them women, and the university's recent intense efforts to attract a more diverse faculty and student population, are the university's testament to the assumption that knowledge is better than ignorance for others besides white men. This change, too, has had a bumpy ride, as it has been and is still seen by many to conflict with the church's values regarding the role of women and their unique responsibilities for family life. A change of view in who needs to be educated has caused all of us—women, men, members of majority and minority alike—to think about many hard issues and to question traditional assumptions.

One assumption being questioned is how institutions such as the church are organized. I think few would argue with the notion that the Roman Catholic church represents a hierarchical form of organization. And although we like to delude ourselves that universities are collegial or democratic, few untenured professors or undergraduate students would argue that the university is a democracy. My purpose here is not to make a brief for how church or academy should be organized. Many who have ever attended a parish council or a faculty meeting might argue that perhaps it is impossible to organize either. A look at the consequences of trying to accommodate equality of opportunity in the current organizational structures, however, gives us some idea of the kinds of things we need to think about.

Let us take the case of women. It is the one with which I am most familiar; and the one that is the most delicate with respect to the church. If one has a restricted role, an added or special responsibility, or a position for which she is not eligible, then de facto there is not equality of opportunity. Roman Catholic women meet every one of these conditions. Their church holds them primarily responsible for the success of family life, the moral virtues of their children, and the welfare of their spouses. Ambition in many domains, particularly in service for the church as priests, is seen by many in official positions at best as untoward and at worst sinful. If these official church views are correct and necessary for the perpetuation of the culture or of the faith, then we should be educating women very differently than we are here at Notre Dame. If these views are incorrect, maybe the way we are educating women and men here together at Notre Dame is on the right track. But of course that puts us in conflict with a large segment of the church's teaching authority.

Changing roles for men and women, regardless of the church's views, create ambiguities and disappointments for both. If one is in the hierarchy or another favored position, there is reason to believe one is entitled to be there and therefore it is easy to be threatened by change. If one is, or perceives oneself to be, in the lesser role or position, there is reason to believe that one is devalued or not appreciated, and it is easy to believe those in power are simply preserving undeserved entitlement. These are issues that must be recognized and discussed by students as they plan their family and work lives. The university can provide the setting for young men and women to decide these matters for themselves, taking into account a variety of viewpoints about them. Having women in increasing numbers as undergraduates, graduate students, and faculty has provided more opportunities than an all-male institution would for considering these and other important issues. Again, we have a change that has added to the conversations in the university and to the education and awareness level of both men and women not only at the university but also in the church.

These examples of the role of psychology and women within a

Catholic university illustrate how university life is different from and yet a part of church life, and different from and yet a part of contemporary culture. The time one spends at a university, particularly one's undergraduate time, is a special time to learn free of other responsibilities. The life of the mind can accommodate change and can entertain possibilities that corporate life or church custom often cannot. Without this freedom the academy will die; just as the church will die if fear of ideas replaces reason, or certitude or coercion is mistaken for faith. By definition, faith means conviction not certitude. The church's long-standing respect of one's individual conscience formed by thoughtful reflection in community is at home in the university, particularly a Catholic university. So while at one level these examples illustrate change, at another level they represent old values, e.g., the compatibility of faith and reason, the importance of individual conscience, and the free exchange of ideas.

The Future of the Catholic University

The success of American Catholic education is all about us. Both women and men who received all or parts of their education in these schools are successful as lawyers, physicians, corporate executives, and the like. They have heeded the gospel's call to service and devoted much energy to their communities, churches, and families. They have given talent and treasury generously to others; the University of Notre Dame in particular has been blessed with extraordinary financial benefactors. With such success in our midst why now are we calling special attention to the role of the Catholic university? What is it that we perceive is now needed, that might be different from what we have done in the past? One concern is the status of intellectual life; another, the status of the Catholic church.

It is no secret that in the U.S. much more value is placed on financial success than on intellectual life. We discourage individuals from entering the academy, and by our pay and treatment turn them away from the teaching profession in general. Research or knowing for the sake of knowing is not as valuable as knowing so we can market a faster computer or a better camera. Ordinary citizens do not support the ideals of a university as they did fifty years ago. Education has become confounded with increased earning power, competitive edge, or financial success. The values of a liberal education are no longer salient. When major universities attempt to enhance their western civilization curriculum with work from other cultures, they are criticized for promoting inferior or irrelevant knowledge. The academy and its authority to make curricular decisions are not well respected. The values of knowing, teaching, serving, and inclusion are not only part of the U.S. academic tradition but also are clearly part of the gospel message of Jesus. These values, however, are no longer assumptions whose significance and importance we can take for granted. We need to encourage more undergraduate students (women, men, minorities) to choose the life of the mind as their profession and to make it possible for them to do so.

If I am correct that in principle (whatever the job market realities may be) we need more scholars and professors, then graduate education needs to become a higher priority than it has been in the past both here at Notre Dame and at other Catholic institutions. This priority cannot be achieved at the expense of any other priority, least of all at the expense of our traditional strength, a fine undergraduate education. Nonetheless, the life of the mind is a revered part of Catholic heritage, and it is the life of the mind that will move our faith and culture into a more enlightened and less commercial future. We cannot become a great Catholic university without superb graduate education, which will prepare scholars for the academy in the finest institutions in the world.

The second concern is the status of the Catholic church in the U.S. Many individuals, particularly young women and men, are leaving the established church. This circumstance means we run the risk of losing not only numbers but diversity. We need to study and to understand why church life is not as important anymore, particularly for the young. What kinds of individuals are leaving and why? How can we converse with such individuals and learn what they are trying to tell us about religion, authority, institutional organization, personal relevance, and the like? People leave and stay in an organized religion for a variety of reasons; we need to know what those are and, if possible, be responsive to them.

The concerns about the Catholic identity of Notre Dame are part of a larger picture of U.S. Catholicism. Catholics who are college educated are used to the more collegial (albeit not democratic) and open ways of the academy. Many have responsible positions in home and work, where their judgment is sought after and respected. They lead exemplary personal and family lives, and they respect authority and value it as a necessary part of cooperative community. Authority, however, has to be credible: no one respects the unreasonable professor or the tyrannical boss. Subordinates may comply with their wishes, but they will not believe or value what they say. In the current climate one can argue whether the authority is credible or whether after so much national delusion (e.g., Vietnam, Watergate, Iran-Contra) many simply are unable to trust it. Discussion regarding the role of authority in modern life needs to happen. With respect to the teaching authority of the church, such discussions surely need to happen soon, both here at Notre Dame and at other Catholic universities. In fact, the academy may be the only place where such conversations can occur without a preconceived notion of how they should be resolved.

Common Ground

I have tried to demonstrate my beliefs that there are many perspectives on the Catholic identity of Notre Dame; and that all can be helpful in attempting to build a great Catholic university and to serve the church and the world. To focus on what is central misses the point and perhaps derails us into conversations of importance or self-importance rather than leads us to the substance of our potential contributions. Through the examples of the development of the psychology department, the admission of women to undergraduate study, and the entrance of girls and women into the sanctuaries of some churches as assistants, I have tried to dispel the notion that the church does not change. I have tried to argue that the academy is an ideal place for some of those changes to be contemplated and implemented, as well as for others to be rejected. I see at least two important future tasks of a Catholic university: educating scholars for the academy; studying why many young Catholics are leaving the church.

We can dwell on extreme stereotypical differences between church and academy, for example, blind obedience thought to be demanded of clergy and other Catholics, or total chaos and ineptness thought to be fostered by academic freedom and tenure. When we do that, we miss most of what church and academy are about. We also miss the important, and not coincidental, fact that the history of western university education is inextricably tied to the Roman Catholic church. There are conflicts and differences in the way the two institutions go about their work; but there are many similarities as well. At their best both are institutions with visions about the betterment of mind, soul, and heart. While both abide by certain authority structures and customs, both also value individual persons and their freedom as well as their right and responsibility to form individual conscience, to dissent, and to live with civility in community. Both leave to the ages ultimate judgments, to God in the case of the church and to the wisdom of the future in the case of the academy.

Both church and academy contain within them wide differences of opinion and perspective. Officially, each sanctions such diversity in their call and their welcome. The church is open to all who seek faith; the academy, to all who seek knowledge.

Most importantly, perhaps, both are about change; and both have changed dramatically over the years and will undergo changes none of us can yet envision. Events such as the establishment of psychology departments and the opening of equal education for women, not to mention hiring women on the faculty with compensation commensurate to that of men, were ideas unthinkable in both academy and church not many years ago. While not without their difficulties, both are rather commonplace today. Not incidental to this state of affairs is that the higher education that many of these women received was funded by their Catholic religious communities. We expect education to change individuals; and we expect a spiritual life to do the same; and we do not always know where the change will lead us or what it will call us to do.

One hundred and fifty years ago Father Sorin had a dream and began a journey to build a great Catholic university. As visionary and wise as he was, it is doubtful he could have envisioned the strength and quality of the Notre Dame of today, not to mention the many different kinds of individuals who study and work here. Be that as it may, it is clear that Father Sorin succeeded magnificently with his segment of the journey or process of building a great Catholic university. Let us not be afraid to add to that journey by using our gifts of faith and intellect to discern the changes of the future and to provide for them. For in fact, each perspective, and each of us who holds it, is equally important in this journey, and each is central. While my perspectives or those of others may not readily represent common images of Notre Dame, no perspective is marginal to the process of developing a great Catholic university unless the credibility of that perspective is fully and fairly considered and then dismissed by the community of scholars. Let us trust in these scholarly deliberations and encourage participation by those who represent the widest possible diversity in the spectra of religious faith and human knowledge.

Meeting the Challenge and Fulfilling the Promise: Mission and Method in Constructing a Great Catholic University

WILSON D. MISCAMBLE, C.S.C.

In 1968 Christopher Jencks and David Riesman published *The Academic Revolution*, their influential study of American higher education, in which they described the "Harvard-Berkeley model" of the research university as the academic pacesetter. When examining Catholic universities, they observed that "the important question" was not "whether a few Catholic universities prove capable of competing with Harvard and Berkeley on the latter's terms, but whether Catholicism can provide an ideology or personnel for developing alternatives to the Harvard-Berkeley model of excellence." They speculated, with some prescience, that "the ablest Catholic educators will feel obliged to put most of their energies into proving that Catholics can beat non-Catholics at the latter's game. But," they noted, "having proved this, a few may be able to do something more." Throwing down a gauntlet of sorts before Catholic educators, they asserted that "there is as yet no American Catholic University that manages to fuse academic professionalism with concern for questions of ultimate social and moral importance" and challenged Catholics to make "this distinctive contribution to the over-all academic system."[1]

It would be pleasant to report that in the ensuing quarter century a number of Catholic institutions have met the challenge put forth by Jencks and Riesman and that flourishing Catholic universities now exist that are committed to the pursuit of their distinct mission in American higher education. Alas, this is not the case. For many Catholic institutions, the past two decades have witnessed a substantial diminution of their Catholic identity. Sadly, some of the oldest and most respected Catholic schools are well advanced down a course to secularization similar to the one to which Protestant institutions of higher learning like Duke and Vanderbilt succumbed and which my distinguished colleague, George Marsden, has described so well.[2] The rapaciousness of the forces for secularization—made all the more so by their complexity and subtle allure—leads to predictions of their effective triumph in the major Catholic institutions. Vestiges of Catholic identity might remain in campus ministry, or in residential life, or in the supposed influence of a religious order's tradition, but the central academic project will simply ape the "Harvard-Berkeley model." Faculties will be dominated by those who have no interest in, or allegiance to, the Catholic mission of the institutions, who, in fact, might be deeply hostile to it.

One might undertake a *tour d'horizon* of Catholic universities and speculate on which ones have passed a virtual point of no return and are marching inexorably to complete secularization, but such an undertaking would serve no good end here. It suffices to say that no Catholic institution—neither Notre Dame nor any other—has cause for complacency about its own situation. Nor can any institution take a back-handed pleasure that another has advanced further along a secularist path. Indeed, Catholic institutions need to cooperate more effectively to support, encourage, and challenge each other. Nonetheless, there is in Catholic higher education today a "dividing line," as Peter Steinfels has put it, "between those institutions determined to face these questions [regarding secularization] and those who prefer to avoid them, proceeding with a calculated ambiguity or by simple default."[3]

The University of Notre Dame, I am thankful to say, is an institution in which the questions regarding Catholic identity and mission are still posed, whatever the limitations of the institution in settling upon answers and acting upon them. Admittedly, facing these questions honestly is not the easiest of tasks, and the temptation to gloss over crucial issues has not always been avoided. But at Notre Dame, men and women have wrestled, at times with some intensity, with the myriad of questions involved with becoming a notable Catholic university. I merely watched this discussion as an interested observer during my time here as a doctoral student in history in the late 1970s. However, my direct involvement in the discussion has increased steadily from the mid-eighties as a seminarian in the Holy Cross order and student in the theology department to the present time, when I serve as a priest-teacher and scholar in the department of history. I understand part of my vocation and responsibility as a priest of Notre Dame's founding religious order to contribute to this debate and to aid in strengthening Notre Dame as a Catholic university. If God and my provincial are willing, I hope to be about this undertaking for years to come. Fortunately, this will not be a lonely work. My own involvement in the conversation on these matters at Notre Dame has revealed to me colleagues—Catholics and non-Catholics alike—who are eager for Notre Dame to fulfill its true promise as a Catholic university and to reject the easy temptation of the secularism which characterizes most American universities. They, like me, want Notre Dame to pursue its distinct mission, to avoid the essential uniformity accepted by most American private and public universities, and to contribute notably to American higher education, the church, and society at large.

The task will not be easy—of which more anon—but Notre Dame has some distinct advantages in its pursuit: the strong resolve of its fellows and trustees; the continuing involvement and commitment of its founding religious order; the loyalty and support of its alumni and friends; the appeal of the university to Catholic parents and students; the faith of Notre Dame's students; the special place of Notre Dame in American Catholicism; the enduring vision of Theodore M. Hesburgh, C.S.C., calling Notre Dame forth to be a truly great Catholic institution; the commitment of faculty members dedicated to the undertaking; the resources of the rich, if somewhat neglected, Catholic intellectual tradition; and the recognition that emphasis on subjects appropriate to a Catholic university means no tempering of academic excellence but instead an opportunity to achieve real intellectual distinction, as Notre Dame's focus on the philosophy of religion and on American religious history aptly demonstrates. The very existence of these elements has given to Notre

Dame a special opportunity and responsibility to meet the Jencks-Riesman challenge and, in the process, to blaze a trail for other religious institutions of higher learning. Indeed, the times demand that Notre Dame thoroughly reject the timid and unimaginative path to secularization and pursue its authentic development as a Catholic university.

The Great Need

It is a curious and ironic reality that some of the significant features of contemporary society and academe simultaneously present formidable obstacles to the development of Catholic universities yet reveal the desperate need for just such institutions. This is not the place to take the pulse of this society or its academic world in any detail, but a brief excursion will reveal both the necessity of Notre Dame's fulfilling its promise and the potential of its contributing to the world beyond its beautiful campus.

A mere recitation of the serious problems which confront our society makes for depressing reading—social disintegration and the dissolution of the family structure; rampant individualism and the decline of community; the drug and violence and death culture; the pervasiveness of crime, alienation, and isolation; the breakdown of moral standards; materialism; limited confidence in government, and so forth. Such realities have prompted President Clinton, no less, to decry "the great crisis of the spirit that is gripping America." A Catholic university, which is concerned to ask questions of ultimate social and moral importance, will address such questions authentically. It will be able to diagnose more clearly the true nature of the societal ills and to prescribe appropriate remedies without the restrictions which secular institutions place upon themselves. It might address the full needs of men and women—material and spiritual—by injecting morally and religiously grounded viewpoints into the public square. It will speak to the development of a more just and moral society.

The American academy is enormous, and secular research universities, which set the direction for the whole enterprise, have many strengths, especially in their research achievements.[4] Major American universities benefited enormously from the beneficence of the federal government in the Cold War era. Large-scale governmental-scientific collaboration and the development of a military-industrial-academic complex (as exemplified by an institution like MIT) helped power the great achievements of American science and technology. American universities also became the location for much of the nation's intellectual life and the source of many of the ideas and proposals—both good and ill—that influenced the society. The important place of universities in the society could hardly be contested. Yet, while conceding their influence and enormous technical accomplishments, American universities are beset by substantial problems. They are for the most part fragmented entities, lacking an intellectual coherence or sense of unity and given to moral relativism and postmodern intellectual fads in which truth becomes a mere expression of power. And, as George Marsden has argued persuasively, they "have jettisoned the most important of human concerns."[5] A genuine Catholic university, with its conceptions of universal truths and the unity of knowledge along with its willingness to accord theological and philosophical investigations a central place, holds out hope both of overcoming this debilitating intellectual fragmentation and examining seriously the most fundamental moral, social, and religious issues.

The challenges set forth in the preceding paragraphs are much more easily outlined than met. This is especially so because we live in a time, as the liberal Yale Law School professor Stephen L. Carter recently has pointed out, when the elite culture—that which dominates the national news media, policy making, the courts, and the universities—is programmed to trivialize religion.[6] Other astute observers would portray the elite as more profoundly and explicitly hostile to religion.[7] Whatever the case may be, a Catholic university cannot necessarily expect a friendly reception because its very existence, if authentic, represents an implicit critique of the intellectual presuppositions of this highly secularized elite culture. So be it. We must be aware of this situation and yet avoid a defensiveness which limits our engagement with the academy and the society at large. And, if Notre Dame pursues its course with integrity, we may be surprised at the friends and admirers located in other institutions and sectors of society who cheer for us because they recognize the importance of our venture and the need for a renewed participation by Christianity in this nation's public and intellectual discourse.

A Mission Renewed

Most Catholic universities have mission statements of one sort or another. For the most part they are harmless and little-read documents, although each should encapsulate its university's purpose and commitments. Some Catholic universities, perhaps reflecting their approach of calculated ambiguity, have adopted increasingly tepid statements such that the astute Jesuit theologian, Michael Buckley, has observed that "the very vagueness of language and the indeterminacy of the general commitments leave one with the sense that the decline in some Catholic institutions may be already advanced, that the conjunction between a vibrant Catholicism and these universities seems increasingly faint, that the vision is fading."[8] A clear statement of mission and purpose is essential, however, if a Catholic university is to hew its distinct course rather than follow meekly in the wake of the "Harvard-Berkeley model."

The final report of the Colloquy for the Year 2000, submitted by Notre Dame's president, Edward A. Malloy, C.S.C., to the trustees of the university in May of 1993, contained a mission statement for the university which, whatever its other limitations, was not received as tepid. It described Notre Dame as "a Catholic academic community of higher learning . . . dedicated to the pursuit and sharing of truth for its own sake" and set forth as one of its goals the provision of "a forum where through free inquiry and open discussion the various lines of Catholic thought may intersect with all the forms of knowledge found in the arts, sciences, professions, and every other area of human scholarship and creativity."[9] If the mission statement had been limited to such general goals, it might have been benignly received and quickly shelved. But it went further and outlined some practical requirements deemed essential to achieving these goals. Specifically, it stated that "the Catholic identity of the University depends upon, and is nurtured by, the continuing presence of a predominant number of Catholic intellectuals" and it asked that all faculty—both Catholics and non-Catholics—respect the university's objectives and willingly enter into "the conversation that gives it life and meaning." These statements gave some sense that the overall mission statement might be more than mere words, that it might be meant and acted upon.

These more practical objectives have prompted debate. The revelation that the mission of the university might have implications for matters such as faculty hiring provoked a negative reaction among certain faculty members, who gave evidence of being embarrassed to be part of a Catholic university which takes its commitments seriously. Such individuals apparently assumed, perhaps as a result of confusing earlier signals from the university administration, that Notre Dame would maintain at most a calculated ambiguity towards its Catholic identity.

The debate at Notre Dame over the mission statement, and especially over the matters of faculty commitment and faculty hiring, has for the most part been healthy. The issue was at least raised to what John Courtney Murray termed "the level of disagreement." The debate over the mission statement, however, revealed that, while this document serves as a statement of intention and a guidepost of sorts, it still needs to be fully owned and internalized. Commitment to the mission of the university will be essential for Notre Dame to fulfill its real promise. Only when the mission has been successfully embodied in its central components will the identity of a Catholic university be firmly established. This is why the leadership of the university must articulate forcefully the essential and distinctive goals of the university. The vision of Notre Dame as a great Catholic university must capture the loyalty of all its elements. The religious character of the institution should come as no surprise to any who would study or teach here. Indeed, it should influence the decisions of all, from freshman students to endowed chairholders, who seek to enter this intellectual community.

Theory and Practice

Preparing a mission statement is relatively easy compared to the task of implementing it in the life of the university. It is in this area of implementation—of devising strategies which answer the question, How?—that Catholic universities have been especially confused and weak in recent years. Reasons for this situation are not hard to identify. Since the collapse of the neoscholastic synthesis in the 1960s, no overarching theory has emerged to replace it as a source for intellectual coherence for Catholic universities and as a method for faith and reason to engage.[10] Catholic universities have manifested rather poorly the unity and integration of knowledge claimed in their self-definitions.

The story of this intellectual failure is undoubtedly a complex one, but surely it can be attributed in part to the failure of contemporary theology to serve the Catholic university well. Pope John Paul II's apostolic constitution on Catholic universities, Ex *Corde Ecclesiae*, accords theology "a particularly important role in the search for a synthesis of knowledge as well as in the dialogue between faith and reason." Theology is called to serve "all other disciplines in their search for meaning, not only by helping them investigate how their discoveries will affect individuals and society, but also by bringing a perspective and an orientation not contained within their own methodologies." But, if Notre Dame is any guide, theology has assumed a rather insular posture within the Catholic university. It operates rather like any other discipline and contributes little to intellectual synthesis or integration. The fundamentally incarnational and sacramental nature of Catholic theology is occasionally mentioned but is rarely explicated effectively by theologians in a way that a physicist or architect or historian would note or care about. I hasten to add that the cupboard is not completely bare, however. In sharp contrast to the relative barrenness of theology stands the Catholic philosopher Alasdair MacIntyre, whose provocative argument that all universities teach out of a particular intellectual tradition and whose powerful presentation of the Thomist mode of inquiry provides much fuel for reflection for serious Catholic universities.[11]

The present absence of an overarching synthesis to serve as detailed guide for Catholic universities need not paralyze us. There is no need to wait for a great architect to come along to provide specific plans and instructions for building the structure of a Catholic university. The university is a living entity and an evolving one. Fortunately, if the appropriate and willing on-site artisans can be assembled and can converse and cooperate, they can build on the established foundations and fashion in remarkable ways an educational institution prepared to face ultimate social and religious questions. In this sense, willing faculty contributors in the venture are an essential component. They can compensate effectively, if you will, for the absence of a guiding theory. With the guidance of the

Spirit, their discussion and debate—their conversation—will aid in forging a new synthesis. For this reason Notre Dame must enlist men and women willing to commit their lives to the undertaking. Recruiting and retaining such a faculty is the most important task which Notre Dame faces at present.

Faculty Hiring: The Crucial Issue

The faculty is located at the heart of a university. When a faculty is hostile to the mission of the institution, its attenuation is likely. When a faculty is passive, the mission is likely to be anemic. When a faculty is committed, there is every likelihood that the mission will be fulfilled.[12] These observations are so obvious as to be banal. Yet it is surprising how many Catholic institutions have ignored these commonsense insights over the past two decades. Engaged upon a needed effort to improve their quality and eager to gain a form of academic respectability, Catholic universities across most departments increasingly hired in a manner similar to their secular peers. Sizable numbers of scholars joined the faculty ranks who had little or no interest in the university's mission. At Notre Dame, the majority of these individuals have been passive towards the university's mission, a few have been hostile and appear to accept George Bernard Shaw's canard about *Catholic university* being a contradiction in terms. Their increasing presence has led to occasional expressions of concern from administrators about "the long-term maintenance of the Catholic identity of the university" but to few creative and workable answers to the question of how to recruit committed faculty across the whole range of disciplines who will embody and express the fundamental purposes of the institution.

It is understandable that little serious attention has been paid to these questions of faculty hiring and commitment. These days even to raise it—and here I speak from experience—invites criticism that one is intolerant or divisive or narrow or sectarian or unconcerned with academic quality or other labels which carry limited cachet in university circles.[13] Yet the issue must be raised and discussed openly if the atrophy in the distinctive character of Catholic universities is to be arrested and reversed. The question has many different aspects, of course, and I am not in a position to deal with them here at length. Let me address briefly, for illustrative purposes, just two areas which demand attention if a great Catholic university is to be anything but an unfulfilled promise. These are the immediate concern regarding initial recruitment and hiring of faculty and the more long-term concern regarding the provision of a pool of candidates for Catholic universities to draw from in their future hiring.

Despite the occasional public fretting and private hand-wringing by university administrators about the results of current hiring practices, hiring procedures in most Catholic universities differ little from those at secular schools. Advertisements are placed, dossiers are examined, judgments are made about the candidates' research and scholarly prospects, interviews are conducted, limited assessments of teaching ability are reached, and an appointment is made. There is little sustained effort to inform prospective faculty members about what the university is committed to and what is expected of a faculty member in that light. At interviews, the issue of Catholic identity, if raised at all, is likely to be done so defensively—as in, "Oh, Notre Dame's a Catholic university, will that bother you?" My contention is that at many steps along the way the issue must be raised explicitly. For example, in advertising positions, Notre Dame's Catholic identity should be noted and some indication given that the university seeks to employ scholars who support its mission and who can contribute to its distinctive intellectual community; at the interview, the prospective candidate should be asked to discuss how he or she would contribute to the university's mission; the assessment of the candidate's likely contribution to the broad mission of the university should have weight in the final appointment decision.

Such procedures do not exclude faculty appointments for non-Catholics who are willing to respect and in varying ways contribute to the university's mission. (Here I must mention my gratitude to such non-Catholic scholars and colleagues as Alvin Plantinga and George Marsden whose work and witness have influenced my thinking and strengthened my resolve on this question.) In fact, it is likely that given the present intellectual landscape, a great Catholic university will contribute effectively to ecumenism by providing Christian scholars of all traditions and non-Christian scholars an opportunity to study in an environment in which serious moral and religious questions are asked. In this circumstance, there might be an enhanced sense of what unites our traditions and some bridging of what divides them. And, a place like Notre Dame might prove an important place for training a new generation of non-Catholic Christian scholars who might serve in the remaining colleges and universities of their own denominations.

Concern for training the next generation of Catholic scholars and teachers, the candidate pool for the next decade, must be to the fore of the concerns of those who guide Catholic institutions today. Notre Dame should play its part in this endeavor. But the reality is that the vast majority of faculty who will serve in the Catholic universities of the future will be trained in the secular, research universities. Will those trained there be irredeemably branded with disdain for religion and have a narrow concern for the highly specialized professional demands of their particular discipline? Some undoubtedly will, and they should be unlikely candidates for recruitment by Catholic schools. But there are others who see their callings as engineer and artist, as scientist and humanist, as vocation, as their way of being leaven in the world. These must be identified and encouraged. Some interesting new initiatives recently have been undertaken to just this end—the Collegium project, which sponsors summer institutes aimed at recruiting and developing faculty "who can articulate and enrich the spiritual and intellectual life of their campuses"; and the Lilly Fellows Program located at Valparaiso University, which firstly seeks to generate discussion of "Christian understandings of the nature of the academic vocation" and secondly provides postdoctoral fellowships aimed at preparing young scholars for "permanent employment within church-related institutions of higher learning."[14] Worthy and welcome as these two ventures are, they highlight the appalling limits of the efforts of Catholic universities in this area to date.

Much more needs to be done. At a minimum, good Catholic universities should fund postdoctoral programs modeled on the Lilly Fellows Program as a way of identifying and encouraging young Catholic scholars. Notre Dame should go further. It needs to accept fully the responsibility which its prominence in American Catholic higher education places upon it and should handsomely fund an institute charged with grappling with the array of theoretical and practical questions faced by Catholic universities. Sustained and systematic thought and action must replace the ad hoc and limited efforts which occasionally sprout on Catholic campuses. Such an institute—let us christen it the Notre Dame Institute for Catholic Higher Education—might among other things foster reflection and discussion within and beyond the university on significant issues such as the role of theology and its relation to other disciplines in the arts and sciences; initiate and fund research unlocking neglected areas of the Catholic tradition; and organize symposia bringing together intellectuals prepared to wrestle with the Catholic university question. On the practical level, it should be a clearing house both for young Catholic scholars seeking positions and for Catholic colleges and universities seeking to make appointments to their faculties; should encourage able Catholic undergraduates to consider the academic apostolate; and, should track interested Catholic graduate students and provide funding opportunities (dissertation fellowships, research and travel grants) to assist them to excel in their chosen fields. Such an institute might even arrange for training programs and internships for faculty and administrators of Catholic colleges and universities to prepare them better to undertake their important responsibilities.

The matter of faculty hiring is, of course, not a subject easily expressed in felicitous phrasing or beautiful conception, but if it is not addressed effectively and urgently, sublime evocations of the University of Paris in the thirteenth century or formulations of a Catholic university as elegant as Newman's will come to naught. Concerns about the moral development of students, the curriculum, the research agenda, the sacredness of teaching will be moot. It is a matter that must be faced and now. What is needed is the will to act. Without it the "beacon," the "bridge," and the "crossroads" of Father Hesburgh's sturdy vision will be a pipedream supplanted by a one-way street to secularization.

An Exciting Prospect

For some of us who love Notre Dame—both what it is and what it can and must become—hyperbole is a constant danger when we speak and write of it. This having been said, whatever the obstacles that confront us, the prospect for our venture is exhilarating if Notre Dame has the courage to stay on its distinct and professed course. This institution can develop further as a university in the conventional sense of a place of teaching, research, and publication, if its dedicated supporters provide the substantial resources required. But here—and at other Catholic universities—this development must take a more distinct, yet expansive, form. Catholic universities must seek to understand the *whole* of reality. All the world is God's creation and all learning both about God and about the world must be welcomed. The Christian perspective holding to the unity of truth, because it is rooted in God, allows scholars in a Catholic university to seek the truth responsibly as part of their own search for God. And, it holds the prospect of creating a genuine intellectual community linking the sciences, the professions, the humanities, and the arts.

We have a faith that seeks understanding and no area need be ignored, but a Catholic university has a special responsibility to pursue certain areas. Reflection upon and development of what might be termed the Catholic intellectual and artistic tradition is essential.[15] And, by way of example, in the present circumstances where many of the gods of modern thought—postmodernism with its attendant cultural nihilism, Marxism with its terrible consequences, latter-day liberalism with its inability to provide a coherent and grounded conception of good—have failed, the need for Catholic thought is more pressing and has major implications for American and western culture generally.[16] If they fulfill their true vocations, Catholic universities will play their part in contributing to the needed renewal of social and political life of which John Paul II speaks in *Veritas Splendor*.[17] In the current climate, Catholic views on matters such as moral truth, respect for human life, the dignity of persons, concern for the common good, the value of natural law, responsibilities as well as individual rights, the utility of the principle of subsidiarity, the importance of family and community clearly have much to offer.

Catholic universities must manifest a different model of teaching and learning where both the intellectual and moral virtues are witnessed and valued, where questions of ethics and character are not ignored. Those who graduate from these schools should have an informed view of what is good and seek to live a good life—a life in which faith is not sequestered in some private domain. In a Catholic university, neither students nor faculty should separate their religious beliefs from their lives as scientists, engineers, artists, lawyers, psychologists, or philosophers.[18] If we acknowledge the lordship of Jesus Christ and accept Him as "the way and the truth and the life," our lives can hardly be otherwise.

One should not underestimate the difficulty of the challenge that lies before a Catholic university like Notre Dame. Yet the Lord's ringing counsel to "be not afraid" and the recognition that fear and lack of vision are truly the principle obstacles in this venture should call committed women and men forward. Let us be about the work.

Notes

1. Christopher Jencks and David Riesman, *The Academic Revolution* (Garden City, N.Y.: Doubleday, 1968), 405.

2. See George Marsden's *The Soul of the American University* (New York: Oxford University Press, 1994).

3. Peter Steinfels, commencement address, Fordham University, May 22, 1993, as reported in the *New York Times,* May 23, 1993.

4. For a good statement of the strengths in the best secular schools, see Jaroslav Pelikan, *The Idea of the University: A Reexamination* (New Haven: Yale University Press, 1992).

5. See George Marsden, "Christian Schooling: Beyond the Multiversity," *Christian Century,* October 7, 1992, 875.

6. Stephen L. Carter, *The Culture of Disbelief: How American Law and Politics Trivialize Religious Devotion* (New York: Basic Books, 1993).

7. See Richard John Neuhaus, *The Naked Public Square: Religion and Democracy in America* (Grand Rapids, Mich.: Eerdman's, 1984).

8. Michael J. Buckley, "The Catholic University and Its Inherent Promise," *America,* May 29, 1993, 14.

9. Edward A. Malloy, C.S.C., Colloquy for the Year 2000, Final Report, May 7, 1993, in *Notre Dame Report,* June 18, 1993.

10. On this, see Philip Gleason's *Keeping the Faith: American Catholicism Past and Present* (Notre Dame, Ind.: University of Notre Dame Press, 1987); and Gleason's essay "American Catholic Higher Education, 1940–1990: The Ideological Context," in *The Secularization of the Academy,* ed. George M. Marsden and Bradley Longfield (New York: Oxford University Press, 1992).

11. Alasdair MacIntyre, *Three Rival Versions of Moral Enquiry: Encyclopaedia, Genealogy and Tradition* (Notre Dame, Ind.: University of Notre Dame Press, 1990).

12. This formulation relies upon, and is influenced by, the analysis in Burton R. Clark, *The Distinctive College: Antioch, Reed, and Swarthmore* (Chicago: Aldine Publishing Co., 1970), 246–48.

13. In February 1993, I wrote a brief paper, "Constructing a Great Catholic University—Some Specific Proposals," which contained some practical suggestions on hiring and which, to put it mildly, had a mixed reception. I draw on some parts of this paper here.

14. Further information on the Collegium project can be obtained from Thomas Landy, S.J., Director, Collegium, Fairfield University, Fairfield, Conn., 06430. For the Lilly Fellows Program, one might contact Arlin G. Meyer, Program Director, Lilly Fellows Program in the Humanities and the Arts, Valparaiso University, Valparaiso, Ind., 46383.

15. For helpful insights on this matter, see Andrew M. Greeley, "The Catholic Imagination and the Catholic University," *America* 164, no. 10 (March 16, 1991): 285–88.

16. This point cannot be developed here, but see Richard John Neuhaus, *The Catholic Moment: The Paradox of the Church in the Modern World* (San Francisco: Harper and Row, 1987); and the comments of Michael Lacey in "The Backwardness of American Catholicism," *CTSA Proceedings* 46 (1991): 4–5.

17. John Paul II, *The Splendor of Truth*, encyclical letter, August 6, 1993. Note especially the section on "morality and the renewal of social and political life."

18. On this, see Etienne Gilson's celebrated essay, "The Intelligence in the Service of Christ the King," in his *Christianity and Philosophy* (New York and London: Sheed and Ward, 1939), 103–25.

A Baptist View of the Catholic University

Thomas V. Morris

In January of 1981, I visited the University of Notre Dame for the first time. I was on campus for three days as a job candidate going through a whirlwind of interviews, meetings, tours, and meals. Although I am sure I was asked hundreds of questions by faculty, students, staff, and administrators during that visit, I remember to this day only one. During a brief, private visit, the dean of the College of Arts and Letters looked me in the eyes with a kind, but searching, expression and asked, "Do you think that you would be comfortable teaching at a Catholic university?"

As a Southern Baptist born and raised in North Carolina, I had known only three Catholic families in my entire life to that point—one during my elementary school years, one while I was in high school, and one in college. I had never been in a Catholic church and had never before visited a Catholic school. With a fresh Ph.D. in hand, granted jointly by the departments of philosophy and religious studies at Yale, I had become an ecumenically minded, and yet at the same time broadly conservative, Protestant to whom denominational distinctions meant much less than the fundamentals of the faith shared by all traditional Christians. My acquaintance with Catholicism came mostly from my graduate reading at Yale. My knowledge of contemporary Catholic university life could have danced on the head of a pin. And yet I found myself replying to the dean with a hearty and confident "Yes."

I went on to explain that I knew of the high regard that the Catholic church had historically maintained for my discipline of philosophy and particularly for my special interests of philosophical theology and the philosophy of religion. I then went on further to say, with what I now regard as a nearly unbelievably naive youthful presumptuousness, that I wanted to do in my own small way, in our day, some of what I thought St. Thomas Aquinas did in his: I wanted to take the best of contemporary and ancient thought forms and apply them to an understanding of the basic issues in a Christian worldview. So I felt I would be very comfortable in a Catholic university where such endeavors are valued.

After about seven years of teaching at Notre Dame, a student once told me that one of my philosophy courses had been the most thoroughly Catholic course he had taken in his four years here. I was very pleased. And then I was a bit perplexed. How could my class have been the most Catholic in a Catholic university?

Every university exists both for the discovery of new knowledge and for the transmission of the best of human culture and knowledge. It has always been my assumption that a distinctively Catholic university exists for these reasons as well, but that, in addition, it is intended to be predominantly a community of individuals who approach these tasks from the perspective of the historically important and intellectually powerful worldview that forms the foundation of Catholic thought and life—the worldview of traditional Christian theism. I came to Notre Dame assuming that most of the faculty at a Catholic university would be Catholic Christians who valued the intellectual environment that the energies of their faith and religious convictions could help create. But I also saw a very clear role in this sort of institution for a Baptist like me.

In a Catholic university, any sophisticated Christian academic should find a supportive environment for his or her basic intellectual framework. And at such a place, that framework could be freely deployed in academic work in a way that would be not only respected but actively encouraged. I came to Notre Dame because, even though I was not myself a Catholic, I believed that I shared most of the foundational beliefs of Catholicism and that those I did not share I could at least understand and respect. By accepting a faculty position here, I saw myself as making a commitment to being an active and supportive contributor to a certain distinctive sort of educational and scholarly enterprise not identical to that of a state university or private non-religious institution. At a Catholic university, I could develop and teach Christian philosophy. And my student's comment, years into that endeavor, assured me that I was succeeding in the eyes of at least some of those I had come to serve.

But of course, there are people who believe that the phrases *Christian philosophy* and *Catholic university* are, literally speaking, oxymorons, and thus that there can be no genuine enterprise in either case at which to succeed. The idea seems to be that, in the one instance, philosophy is by its very nature an unfettered inquiry, whereas a Christian is by his or her religious commitment tied to an accepted range of doctrine as incontrovertibly true and so cannot consistently engage in the latitude of questioning required for genuine philosophy. Likewise, this general point of view seems to hold that a university is, in principle, a phase of total intellectual openness to truth and, in practice, a forum of conflicting views whose very multiplicity and conversational engagement benefits society, whereas Catholicism is, both in principle and in practice, a closed fortress of predetermined belief allowing very little room for conflict and dissent. The conclusion is then drawn that a Catholic institution can call itself a university; and a Christian can call himself a philosopher: but insofar as religious conviction is a guiding and constraining force in the two cases, neither label can properly apply.

A story is told at my alma mater, the University of North Carolina at Chapel Hill, about the first and most legendary professor of philosophy ever to serve on its faculty. Coming from graduate study at both Yale and Harvard, Horace Williams had been in town only about a day when he learned that he had just one last hurdle to clear in order to secure his teaching position and future at the university. He had been invited to have tea with Cornelia Phillips Spencer, a very southern, but quite formidable, woman who exercised significant influence in the life of the school. The daughter of a professor, sister of two others, and mother-in-law to a fourth, she had multiple, intimate ties to the institution and wanted to see to it that any new faculty member served the legitimate interests and deeply held values of the place. She was a bit suspicious of anyone who had studied philosophy in the North.

As the philosopher approached her house, Mrs. Spencer greeted him from her front porch with a demand that he change the name of the course he proposed to teach and call it not *philosophy* but *Christian philosophy*. He is said to have stood still, thought a moment, and replied, "Mrs. Spencer, I will call my course Christian philosophy if your son-in-law will call his course Christian mathematics." We are told that this guardian of the state's young people gave Williams a penetrating look and then burst out laughing. He had won her over and had made a point frequently to be repeated by advocates of academic freedom within the state universities located in the Bible Belt.

Christian mathematics. Catholic chemistry. Jesuit botany. These labels do sound quite strange. They can even appear comically absurd, as Mrs. Spencer's reaction attested. They certainly seem to play into the hands of critics who sardonically joke that in order to have God the Father, God the Son, and God the Holy Spirit add up to being one God, Christians may indeed require their own mathematics, and that with traditional claims about transubstantiation, Catholics do seem to have their own unique conception of chemistry.

But to Horace Williams, the issue was no joke. He believed that all truth is universal, and thus that no group could ever legitimately claim exclusive ownership over any of it. Christians, Jews, Hindus, Buddhists, and Atheists must deal with one and the same reality. They must acknowledge the same truth in any academic discipline. Neither the laws of logic, the elements of the periodic table, nor the geological strata of the earth will change for special interest groups. Truth is truth. This is why Williams did not want his enterprise to be called *Christian philosophy*. And I suspect that on similar grounds he would have been wary of any institution calling itself a Catholic university, or a Methodist university, if those designations were intended to convey anything more than an historical fact about the founding of the school.

Williams's concern for the truth represented a modern, liberal outlook that for a long time has had a powerful impact on American attitudes toward higher education. But to many present-day critics of religious education and theologically informed research, these concerns can appear a bit quaint. The postmodern spirit, with its relativist, subjectivist, deconstructionist tendencies, seems to have abandoned any traditional quest for truth and to have turned its energies instead in the direction of power. Neither the Catholic church nor the Christian faith, this viewpoint would maintain, should be allowed to have a hegemony of power in the realms of higher education and the new construction of human thought forms, at even a local level. The postmodern problem with a Catholic university, or with Christian philosophy, is a problem primarily of power, not one focused on truth. Ironically, in these times, it is the Catholics, and, more broadly, any Christians whose faith makes a difference to their thinking, who join old Horace Williams in his concern with truth.

A Catholic university should be an institution of higher education and scholarly research that respects and nurtures each of the most fundamental dimensions of human experience, as recognized in its tradition. In following that tradition I have come to believe there to be four such basic dimensions of experience. First, and most obviously in connection with university life, there is the intellectual dimension, the dimension of human experience that aims at truth as its object. Catholics, and Christians more generally, I believe, do not claim exclusive ownership over any domain of truth. But we recognize the concept of truth as being of paramount importance. And we think we have embraced certain significant truths not acknowledged by all people, truths that yield distinctive perspectives on what is commonly seen and that are such as to be able to guide both our scholarly efforts as well as our educational aims.

In line with Horace Williams, whatever his squeamishness over labels, Christians are, I think, committed to a metaphysics that countenances, and indeed insists on, some basic measure of bedrock, objective truth, however much play they may allow to domains of perspectival and antirealist epistemological concerns. Some propositions are just true. And others are false. Human beings may be, and should be, friendly, tolerant, and forgiving. But reality often is not. Not all claims about the world put us equally in touch with truth. Not all are fine to believe, and not all are safe to teach. There are some claims about truth and about reality that a Christian university will not look favorably upon as a proper framework for research and teaching precisely because they conflict with what a Christian worldview recognizes as true. Now, we have to be very cautious and relatively open minded in making these determinations. But unless its Catholicity and its Christianity make some difference in what a university supports, its religious affiliation is no more than a historical relic.

The second fundamental dimension of human experience is the aesthetic dimension, that dimension of our lives which aims at beauty. I believe that a Catholic university should have a perspective on beauty not shared by its secular peer institutions. Notre Dame is a remarkably beautiful place. Visitors have often told me how the physical beauty to be found here conspires in favor of deep philosophical and religious reflection. A Christian believes that the beauty of this world points to a source beyond and greater than itself. In the Catholic tradition, visual, musical, tactile, and even olfactory beauty are seen as very important to the elevation of human beings into the sphere of our proper dwelling. From the perspective of a Christian worldview, there is beauty, and there is ugliness, and an important difference exists between the two. A Catholic university should be a place where aesthetic discernment and appreciation are developed and are woven into an overall, meaningful conception of the full human life.

The third dimension of human experience acknowledged by philosophers in one way or another throughout human history is the moral dimension, which aims at goodness. And this will certainly be a dimension of life to be highlighted at a Catholic university. It has been said that goodness is just truth and beauty in human conduct, and I believe that there is much insight in this judgment. The three dimensions identified so far are distinguishable, but certainly not separable. Beauty is a certain kind of goodness along the aesthetic dimension. And the discovery of truth may often require elements of goodness, along with an eye for beauty, on the part of theorizers in some of the most esoteric domains of intellectual research.

A study of morality and an eye on ethical considerations surrounding every subject matter should be a prominent feature of any university that calls itself Catholic. There is no department where ethical discussion cannot fruitfully arise and inform interactions between colleagues as well as between faculty and students as we grapple with ideas. And no one should receive a degree from a Catholic university without having received some grounding in Christian moral thought relevant to his or her field of study.

The fourth dimension of human experience is the spiritual dimension, which aims at ultimate connectedness and, finally, at God. As there is a spiritual dimension to life, so likewise there certainly should be a spiritual dimension to the life of a Catholic university, and not just in an extracurricular mode. A Catholic university should be a place where the spiritual is not relegated to some private sphere but is discussed, debated, and applied as broadly as possible, intertwining it with other aspects of human life and learning as it is related to matters of the intellectual, aesthetic, and moral dimensions, which it ultimately undergirds. Engaged conversations about spirituality should find a welcome home on a Catholic campus, in classrooms as well as in dormitories and chapels. For on a Catholic, and more generally Christian, worldview, it is the overarching source of guidance for all else.

I believe it is safe to say that, for the most part, our freshmen enter their classrooms with no clue of this. I see some interesting things in my beginning philosophy course, where basic worldview commitments and tendencies easily come to light. I am surprised to find that, year after year, more of our students seem to arrive on campus with bits and pieces of antisupernaturalistic, deterministic, and relativistic assumptions about human beings and our condition, along with no sense of the strength, resiliency, and depth of a traditional theistic view of the world. I see it as one of my jobs to bring the spiritual into view and to show my students how all our foundational views relate to that fundamental dimension of life.

So what is the difference between the Christian scholar, and his or her non-Christian peer, in a particular academic discipline? Well, most obviously, some of their fundamental worldview beliefs will differ, and this may affect to various degrees the way they form beliefs within the domain of their discipline. But even if their properly academic beliefs within such a field as mathematics or chemistry coincide, their attitudes toward that field may diverge, their purposes in scholarship and teaching may differ, and the uses to which they put their discoveries may move down different paths. Now, certainly, a non-Catholic can share with a Catholic academic many of the same intellectual, aesthetic, and moral concerns. And there can also be some spiritual concerns shared in common. So it is possible for the Catholic university, as I envision it, to be a place where a non-Catholic, and a non-Christian, is welcomed, respected, and made to feel comfortable as part of an enterprise mutually entered into. But, as hard as it is for me to say this, it is difficult for me to believe that a person who does not share the fundamental Christian theism of the Catholic could be part of the core, over the long run, of the institution's continuity, given its distinctive identity, an identity that I believe is worth preserving. So, I think, the faculty and administration of a Catholic university should exercise great care in the initial stages of all their hiring decisions, care to act in such a way as to propagate into the future by these decisions the unique strengths and possibilities of such an institution. *Catholic* and *Christian* should be affirmative-action categories for hiring in all facets of university life. And we should be both actively nurturing and aggressively recruiting the scholars of the future who will make the best of the legacy we have. As a non-Catholic, I am glad that there has been at Notre Dame, as at other modern Catholic universities, some flexibility and openness about membership in its community. I hope only that in addition there is some counterbalancing cautious foresight directed at long-term policies about the further development of the university. It would be a shame if a student at Notre Dame ever tells a Baptist professor that his class was the only real Catholic course she had taken in her years of undergraduate study here.

When Horace Williams was eighty-two, and lay dying in his bed in Chapel Hill, his nurse leaned over him and said, "Professor, aren't you going to pray? Do you believe in God?"

The old man, a Methodist trained in divinity at Yale, replied, "That is the only thing I do believe in. My whole life has been a prayer." And this, I think, is the ideal for any Christian professor privileged to be at a Catholic university—that the nature of our community will allow our scholarly and pedagogical lives to be one long prayer.

A Catholic University,
Whatever That May Mean

Marvin R. O'Connell

One sunny August day, more than twenty years ago, I was invited to a meeting in the office of the then provost of the University of Notre Dame. Other attendants included faculty colleagues from various disciplines, along with several senior administrators—ten or twelve people all together. The provost wished to consult us, he said, about the sermon he was preparing to deliver in a few weeks at the festive Mass which marked the formal opening of the academic year. We were all aware that he used this occasion to preach not so much a homily as an annual state-of-the-university address. A special problem had arisen, he said. In the course of the summer the university had rented one of its facilities for a conference sponsored by a pro-abortion group. Predictably, protests from the Right to Life movement, both local and national, had flooded around the base of the Golden Dome. Now the provost asked us to advise him as to whether he should advert to this matter in his sermon, whether indeed he should seize upon the incident as an opportunity to speak to the thorny issue of the university's autonomy and its duty to promote full debate of even the most contentious questions.

The discussion that followed displayed many of the characteristics common to academic conversations; it was diffuse, often obscure, and heavily rhetorical. But, because the participants represented the full length of the ideological spectrum, it did reflect a variety of opinions. Not all the advice the provost received, however, was to the point. "The question is not whether there is life after death," intoned a priest who had never heard a social-work slogan he didn't like. "The question is whether there is life after birth." The provost listened courteously, and everyone had his say, however irrelevant, until, just as the meeting was breaking up, one of the administrators spoke for the first time. "We must always remember," he said solemnly, "that Notre Dame is a Catholic university. Whatever that may mean."

Whatever that may mean. We still have not determined what it means all these years later. Not just for Notre Dame of course but also for the hundreds of colleges and universities across America that continue to employ the descriptive adjective *Catholic*. Or perhaps, more gloomily from my point of view, we have decided that it does not mean very much. A couple of my colleagues—both distinguished and influential academics, both of a generally liberal turn of mind, both priests—have recently opined in my hearing that they were satisfied their institutions had remained Catholic because Catholic liturgies are regularly celebrated there. This sentiment seems to me a sad admission of despair, though my two friends would not consider it so.

Not that I deny the uniquely important Catholic witness provided by the liturgy on campus, of which, a few weeks ago, I received a poignant reminder. I am presently director-in-residence of the Notre Dame undergraduate program in London. On the Saturday after Thanksgiving I offered Mass with our students and American staff in a large, mirrored room borrowed—ironically enough—from the genial owners of the Henry VIII Hotel in Bayswater. It was all in all a memorable and moving experience. There we were, far from home, celebrating together a feast that is especially ours, one that commemorates the singular worth of religious freedom, and observing it with that ancient Eucharistic rite the performance of which, until not so very long ago, was a capital crime in England. The occasion was solemn and reverent but not in the least stuffy, and I have no doubt that we were as a result of it bonded more closely together, even as we proclaimed the death of Jesus until he comes again. (The music the students performed was appropriate and singable, even though I might not have chosen it myself. But then I am sixty-three years old and have an abiding weakness for plainsong and Schubert.)

The liturgy must always and everywhere afford a central focus for Catholic life, since it remains, in Pius X's words, "the indispensable source of the Christian spirit." But liturgical action is a means, not an end, a means of inculcating and strengthening "the Christian spirit." If not rooted in an informed faith and a commitment of the mind and heart, it easily deteriorates into sentimentality or aestheticism. If the worshiping community does not share beliefs and values, or does not understand them, its ritual becomes irrelevant. The Church of England supplies an instructive example. Its liturgy is singularly beautiful, and its houses of worship stand forlornly empty. In the diocese of London, about 2 percent of those who call themselves Anglicans attend services on a given Sunday. Anglicanism remains the state religion—Queen Elizabeth is still Defender of the Faith—but only a handful of its nominal communicants pays any attention to it, not least because of its theological incoherence and overall intellectual bankruptcy. The Church of England stands for nothing and, in the case of not a few of its clergy, believes in nothing. The bishop of Durham, who presides over liturgies in one of the most magnificent gothic cathedrals in Europe, goes out of his way to poke fun at the articles of the ancient Creeds. Recently two vicars formally declared that they were atheists. Neither of them intends, or will be required, to give up his pastorate. "Oh no," one of them said, "I wouldn't do that. I would miss conducting the Sunday service."

How long, I wonder, and how fruitfully, will the liturgy be celebrated on our Catholic campuses as the understanding of it becomes increasingly blurred and compromised? What is worrisome is not only the noisy intrusions of this or that pressure group, each with its alternate Eucharist or its appeal to an ill-conceived ecumenism, which have led to events sometimes silly, sometimes scandalous, always a little bizarre. More alarming is the almost complete absence from our colleges and universities of any sense of the glorious Catholic intellectual tradition, out of which our liturgical expressions have developed. Confusion, ignorance, and chutzpah abound. "Everybody knows," a student in one of my classes told me a year or so ago, "that before Vatican II Catholicism was a peasant religion." One of our university chaplains routinely omitted recitation of the Nicene Creed at Sunday Mass, because, he said, it is divisive. Shades of the bishop of Durham.

It was with a quite wonderful sense of solidarity and good feeling that my students and I, after our Thanksgiving day Mass, sat down together—in the Anne Boleyn Room if you please—to our feast of turkey and all the trimmings. But such emotional satisfaction, worthy as may be, can never substitute for the mind's real appreciation of the sacred action in which we had just participated. "This is eternal life, to *know* thee, the one true God, and Jesus Christ whom thou hast sent." Whatever that may mean. We should hardly be surprised that we cannot figure out how the adjective *Catholic* should apply to our institutions of higher learning. We cannot even agree anymore as to what the nouns *Catholic* and *Catholicism* mean. This is of course the root of all our troubles and the explanation of our failures, of which the academic is only one. We American Catholics have selected a very inauspicious moment to suffer an identity crisis, the very moment indeed when our country and our culture have stood in greatest need of the kind of witness we ought to have been uniquely equipped to offer.

———————

It was George Bernard Shaw, I think, who observed that a *Catholic university* was a contradiction in terms. One must always, of course, consider the source when one quotes even an epigram, and in this instance to do so does not contribute much to its persuasiveness. Shaw was so spectacularly wrong on so many public issues that to expect him to be right on this one is highly presumptuous. In the light of recent events, could there have been any mindset more fatuous than that of a Fabian socialist? The English have a weakness for garrulous people—even expatriate Irishmen—who keep their teeth and hair into old age, and that may help to explain the vogue Shaw managed to enjoy till his death in 1950. Since then at any rate his reputation as a modern sage has vanished like a wisp of smoke on a windy day. Even the plays, once the foundation of his celebrity, no longer excite any interest. Here in London there are fifty or sixty theaters in the West End and its fringes, and during the present season revivals have predominated, revivals by playwrights as various as Terrence Rattigan and Sean O'Casey and Tom Stoppard, to say nothing of Goldsmith and Moliere, of Marlowe and Shakespeare. Not a single play of Shaw's has been produced. Apparently, theatergoers no longer find it chic to see St. Joan of Arc portrayed as a 1914 suffragette.

Yet as we mourn the passing of the Catholic university in the United States—or rather as we mourn its stillbirth—let us give the devil his due. What the too-clever-by-half Mr. Shaw probably meant was something like the following crude syllogism: The Catholic church claims to be the repository of all truth. But a university exists on the assumption that truth, in its manifold and myriad manifestations, remains always to be discovered and refined. Therefore Catholicism and a genuine university experience are radically incompatible. For what value can attach to the hard, relentless, lonely work of research for people who assert that the essential mysteries that confront the human mind have all been settled and placed securely within the covers of the *Baltimore Catechism?*

Certainly this bigoted caricature does not deserve serious attention. But in another, more subtle, sense Shaw's bon mot appears quite unexceptional. If the professional criteria prevailing at Harvard and Stanford and Texas establish the norms to which institutions aspiring to be genuine universities must conform, then a Catholic university is indeed a contradiction in terms. The great fishes that swim in the mainstream of American academe flick away any interloper that would intrude into the waters they regard as their own. And what could be more alien to the contemporary world of savants than an organization that adheres to a body of truths and values that are allegedly rooted in divine revelation? There is nothing unreasonable in that negative reaction; what is unreasonable, and tragic, is that those targeted by the reaction should have cheerfully acquiesced in it.

That Catholic intellectuals have done so is beyond dispute. A massive *traison des clercs* has transpired, a shameless stampede away from those qualities that made Catholic institutions distinctive. As was said of the English bishops at the time of the Reformation, "The fortress is betrayed by them who should have defended it." The ordinary explanation for this flight to the fashionable is that the secular universities possess a transcendent degree of quality. But—if I may press, perhaps rashly, my fish metaphor—this contention amounts pretty much to a red herring. To be sure, the virtues displayed at the institutions like the ones named above should be honored and indeed emulated. At the same time it is quite wrong to romanticize such places. Even prestigious secular campuses hold no monopoly over disinterested scholarship, fastidious respect for the laws of evidence, precision in forms of expression, and dedication to the intellectual development and well-being of students. In fact, some of these attributes—particularly a commitment to excellent undergraduate instruction—are not seldom honored more in the breach than in the observance, usually for the sake of idiosyncratic or even ersatz research.

Nor should the pervasive influence of the market be left out of account. Wealth and prestige walk hand-in-hand through the groves of academe. Harvard and Texas, not Southeastern Mississippi State or Dominiguez Hills, set the parameters whereby the ideal university is defined. Abstract theory contributes less, I think, to such definition than do large endowments and generous legislatures, supplemented almost always by bountiful grants from public and private foundations. Money begets more money and guarantees superior facilities, just as it attracts the most talented faculty and students, the combination of which leads naturally to an enviable record of scholastic achievement.

Could it not be argued that it is precisely the capital sin of envy to which we American Catholic academics have fallen prey? Money, or at any rate the desire for money, has driven too much of our decision making in recent years. To say so is not to deny the requirement of a sound fiscal policy or of strict prudence in the operation of our institutions or indeed of aggressive fund raising. But we have allowed ourselves to roam far beyond such obvious necessities. We wanted our weaker colleges and universities to survive, even when, in the new epoch since the Second World War, a good many of them no longer deserved to do so. We wanted our better institutions to compete as peers of the elite secular universities. These ambitions demanded ever more money, even more, it seemed, than the American Catholic community—the most affluent in two thousand years of history—could supply. Did it not therefore make sense to pattern our schools after those which had tapped into glory by discovering how best to milk the money cow?

And so we started down the slippery slope. Take the celebrated Land O' Lakes manifesto of 1968. This declaration of academic independence, promulgated at the implausible venue of a Wisconsin resort by the heads of notable Catholic institutions of higher learning, had as much to do with satisfying an appetite for public money as it did with affirming any lofty principle. Let me be very clear: I have no quarrel with the assertion made at Land O' Lakes that a university must be able to perform its functions free from outside interference, which, in the case of Catholic schools, includes freedom from intrusion by fussy diocesan chanceries and Vatican bureaus. Nor do I deny that such intrusion by such agencies occurred frequently enough to warrant a formal statement of policy in the name of institutional autonomy and professional integrity. But does it not seem odd that the same educators who legitimately resisted undue encroachment from those who, at least, were members of the household of the faith, should, in the next breath, confess themselves more than ready to accept dictation from government bureaucrats, secular accrediting bodies and honor societies, foundation executives, moguls of business with tax deductible dollars to give away, and, a little later, from race and gender lobbies? Well, maybe consistency is the hobgoblin of small minds. Karl Marx in any event was surely correct about one thing: to understand the unfolding of human affairs, always look first for the economic explanation.

I invoked above the French phrase which translates literally as "the treason of the clerks." I mean *clerks* in a sense broader than merely ordained clergy, though it has been priests and religious who have led the way in bringing us to our present unhappy state. But all we Catholic intellectuals, all we clerks, share responsibility. We all lost our nerve. We all prospered from the financial accommodations entered into by our administrators. We all came to dread the prospect that we might be deemed different from our academic counterparts. If there were unfortunate implications in the Land O' Lakes declaration—opening the door, for instance, to ambitious academic theologians of no particular distinction anxious to style themselves, absurdly, a second magisterium within the church— why did we not repudiate them, or, better, clarify them? In 1968 I held a tenured position in a reputable Catholic college, but I did nothing, except complain in private. My sin of omission was duplicated by thousands of others, anxious as was I to protect personal perquisites, and all the while the erosion was eating away the foundations of our self-esteem as believers who claimed also to be thinkers. We did not, in short, dare to be different, and so we have allowed our colleges and universities to shrink more and more into shadowy imitations of secular institutions. Where your treasure is, there also your heart will be.

―――――――

But we Catholics are different, or, in a manner of speaking, we are nothing. We have a witness to give that possesses an institutional character as surely as it does a personal one. And the circumstances that prevailed in our country after 1945 gave us an opportunity to establish a golden age in Catholic higher education, something worthy of our forebears at Paris and Bologna in the thirteenth century. We let that chance slip away from us, which is why our specific acts of abdication are so chilling. Do not misunderstand me. I am not indulging in phony nostalgia. I do not hanker after the dreary clericalism that governed our colleges as recently as a generation ago, or the facile triumphalism that too often assumed we had definite answers for all the hard questions. I recognize that the tasks taken on formerly by our institutions—primarily training the children of Catholic immigrants and equipping them to enter the great American middle class—have quite properly given way to another set of educational priorities. When I argue that we must at all costs maintain our distinctiveness, I do not thereby champion an exclusivity that not infrequently, in the misnamed good old days, had us talking about serious issues only to ourselves. On the contrary, our very distinctiveness makes possible meaningful conversation with those who disagree with us. But if we Catholic academics deliver ourselves wholly to the secular model, what ground is left upon which to carry on dialogue? What is there to talk about? The trouble is not that American Catholic higher education has changed: "In a higher world it is otherwise," Newman wrote in a famous passage, "but here below to live is to change, and to be perfect is to have changed often." The trouble is how change has been effected, and to what purpose, and with what consequence. And further sobering questions present themselves. Have we, by surrendering our birthright, gained in stature in the eyes of the mandarins of the Ivy League? Do they think better of our schools now? Has there emerged a Catholic Princeton? A *Catholic Princeton;* now there is a contradiction in terms that Bernard Shaw would have chuckled over.

I fancy that little can be done to reverse what has happened, at least for the near future. Now that we have in the name of pluralism become like everybody else, we seem to have confirmed the adage that tragedy evolves into farce. Now, when it is very late in the day, our colleges and universities are beginning to analyze and deliberate about and agonize over the threat to their Catholic character. Whatever that may mean. Of course inquiries of this sort are not farcical in themselves; they have their uses, if only to bring to the fore a situation that for too long has been unacknowledged. But, having obediently invoked for years now the mantra of affirmative action and equal-opportunity employment, having consciously sought to "enrich" our teaching and research faculties by adding to them people who have not the slightest interest in, or understanding of, our intellectual tradition—even in not a few instances people who are hostile to it—and having supinely pandered to every fad and whim favored by the secular academic establishment, it seems rather feckless to expect much to come of such discussions.

On the other hand, since hope springs eternal, let them continue and, if possible, flourish. But let the participants in them exercise enough candor and clarity that no one will be tempted to say, after a spirited exchange, "Whatever that may mean." I shall ask Newman to speak for me: "To separate religion and secular knowledge," he said in one of his Dublin discourses,

> makes of the university a sort of bazaar, or pantechnicon, in which wares of all kinds are heaped together for sale in stalls independent of each other. The majestic vision of the Middle Age, which grew steadily to perfection in the course of centuries, the University of Paris, or Bologna, or Oxford, has almost gone out in the night. A philosophical comprehensiveness, an orderly expansiveness, an elastic constructiveness, men have lost them, and cannot make out why. This is why: because they have lost the idea of unity; because they cut off the head of a living thing, and think it is perfect, all but the head.

The Department of Theology at a Catholic University

THOMAS F. O'MEARA, O.P.

There are over two hundred Catholic universities and colleges in the United States. Catholic higher education had its beginnings in hardship and found its maturity in expansion and success. With little government aid, a growing number of schools emerged and prospered through the dedication and sacrifice of four groups: the founding and guiding faculty (often members of a religious order of women or men), the parents, the alumni, and the students. These schools were not established to offer Catholics catechetical instruction or to isolate them from American society, but to give amid the pursuit of literature or engineering some education in the Catholic faith and to nourish a Christian atmosphere even as they sought to be true colleges and universities.

Up to the 1950s the Catholic identity of these colleges and universities appeared clearly: it was visible in a faculty of priests or sisters, in religious practices, and in classes of neoscholastic philosophy and theology. But the 1960s altered this campus ethos. The educational institutions expanded in size, facilities, and programs, while the ecumenical council, Vatican II, brought to these institutions of Catholic life both an openness to society, churches, and religions, and some diversity in theology. The thought of theologians like John Courtney Murray, Hans Küng, Pierre Teilhard de Chardin, and Karl Rahner replaced what was in most schools a melange of

244 / Thomas F. O'Meara, O.P.

shallow neoscholastic metaphysics and devotions from the nineteenth century. Theology departments, much expanded in size, included as voices of pluralism and ecumenism Catholic laypersons as well as men and women from other religious traditions.

In the 1970s Catholic colleges and universities gave little consideration to the new situation of Catholic identity as it was increasingly being influenced by ecumenism and by the American field of religious studies. But by the 1980s these institutions had begun anew to ask seriously about their relationship to the reality and ethos of Catholicism.

The Question of Catholic Identity

Who is concerned today about Catholic identity in higher education? The members of the sponsoring religious order or diocese are interested in the nature of the school that their community brought into existence. Administrators and board members of the schools grasp more and more the implications of the issue and its recent metamorphoses. The staffs of the college or university dealing with public relations, fund raising, and recruiting have known for some years that, contrary to what the prior decade expected, Catholic identity is publicly appreciated and highly marketable. The issue remains important. Will a school be a competitive American college or university with little connection to past traditions? Will a school follow the path of extensive or total separation from church affiliation, the path many Protestant schools had taken? Is not a religious presence in an American university contradictory? Is not even the consideration of faith or church offensive to modern academics? Seeking the identity of a school is like pursuing the identity of an individual. Purpose nourishes identity. The goal of a Catholic college and university is of great significance, for as medieval theologians liked to say, "The goal is the cause of everything else."

The role of religious and Catholic thought will be different in faculties of science or business, in graduate schools of law and medicine, or in the humanities. In each, however, Catholic origins and ethos should not be viewed as limiting or as an embarrassment to the school. The argument can be made that a modern, Anglo-Saxon secularism is much more limiting. The arts and letters, of course, mirror implicitly faith and grace (whatever these might be called) amid personality and society. Literature and imagination touch upon theologies, because great fiction describes a triad pervading all of the humanities: personality, sin, and grace—but this triad has found different elucidations. There is something odd when students study only recent literature in which moral questions or figures caught in the dialectic of violence (sin) and question (grace) are absent, or when political science and law presume that contemporary men and women have throughout the world long lost interest in religion.

In this essay I look at this issue from the perspective of a department of theology, from an understanding of theology as a thinking about being a Catholic today and as a correlation of Christian revelation to contemporary life. This does not imply that the development of religious identity occurs only in theology courses—to relegate the Catholic presence at the university or college to any one department can begin the removal of the Catholic ethos from the campus—but that theology is a catalyst and a reflection of the university's atmosphere and goals.

The theology department has an obvious, special interest in Catholic identity. But the deepest and broadest expressions of the Catholic interpretation of life and Christianity touch other departments and affect the administration of the university. Parents, students, and donors expect a Catholic presence with its characteristic interest in the visible and the tangible. An awareness by university leaders and alumni of the deeper issues of the Catholic faith and mentality in this period after the ecumenical council is important and is furthered by theology.

The struggle just to ask these questions alerts us to how the ethos of the Enlightenment dominates American academia and how politically awkward this topic is. American intellectual life has repeatedly expected faith, church, and religion to disappear. Largely blind to the contemporary prominence of religion in American life, the secular university does not look favorably on the strengthening of the presence of any faith or religious community. American universities can teach the history of Spain without alluding to mysticism and pursue art history without knowing much of Franciscans or Jesuits who influenced certain styles of art. Most of the universities founded by Protestant churches have not retained their earlier church identity, and part of this process has been to relegate church and faith to divinity schools with ministerial and doctoral programs and then to keep those schools largely removed from the life of the university, and in some nondenominational schools to hold them apart from the life of the church and society. There still remain a number of fine schools sponsored by individual Protestant churches, and the following issues can be transposed into their situation: namely, How would a Reformation heritage be preserved in a school? In the last analysis, a search for identity, great or small, is in some way a struggle of life and death.

The Search for Catholic Identity

Where is Catholic identity to be found? One response might be that it lies in religious externals. The university is Catholic because there is a church on the campus or crucifixes in the classrooms, or because the name of the university has religious associations, e.g., Aquinas, Loyola, or because priest-administrators wear clerical dress. Images and symbols are important, but ultimately they look to theology for their meaning and interpretation. Or, is a university Catholic because the liturgy is present? The sacraments of baptism, Eucharist, and marriage, and the various liturgies and quasi-liturgies during the school year, are at the heart of Catholic life. Liturgy realizes and symbolizes community and faith, and campus ministry serves the deeper facets of Catholic identity—but these need theological knowledge and reflection. Social action might be selected to give Catholic identity—a school serves the poor, opposes abortion, or advocates women's rights—but these causes are themselves grounded in an understanding of what is Christianity. Retreats, liturgy, personal counseling, and social activism—all bestow Catholic identity, but these lie partly outside of the educational purpose and business of the university, and they depend upon an intellectual interpretation of Christian revelation in today's world. Evidently, Catholic identity must be anchored in something more than religious practices and symbols.

Surveys tell us that students, parents, and alumni (from a variety of religious traditions) are deeply interested in Catholic schools' furthering a religious perspective. The parents of the students and the alumni of the school expect some reality to stand behind the rhetoric attached to a Catholic school. Where do the ground, the ideas, the impetus of the Catholic spirit come from if not from Catholicism's self-interpretation over many centuries and in many cultures, from its theology and theologies?

Thinking Theologically about Catholic Presence

To discuss "Catholic identity," some in the school's faculty and administration need to be able to articulate the fundamental theology and ethos of Catholic Christianity. Today, one can meet a few who think they know immediately what Catholicism is, but they are Catholics uneducated in history and theology, fundamentalist Protestants, or recent converts. Still they are absolutely certain of what constitutes Catholic life: e.g., papal documents, medieval phrases, devotions from the nineteenth century. Not long ago, a Catholic lay president of a middle-sized Catholic college longed for priest faculty members to wear clerical dress but hired agnostics as deans and fundamentalists as teachers. Administrators have made disastrous commitments in hiring people who were enthusiastic about Jesus or Aristotle but whose worldview was vigorously opposed to the Catholic perspective on humanity and divine presence. Catholicism is rich and multilayered, and to understand it one cannot stay on the colorful surface.

Catholicism is ultimately a way of seeing self and world. To be a Catholic is a way of being human as well as a way of being a Christian. Richard McBrien writes that "Catholicism is an understanding and affirmation of human existence before it is a corporate conviction about the pope, or the seven sacraments, or even about Jesus Christ." The Catholic mind and life are drawn from sacramentality and mediation, community, and a family of traditions. The sacramental vision finds God in and through things; the visible, the tangible, the finite, the historical bear the divine presence. Mediation extends sacramentality. Not only human beings and their communities but also word and matter, action and liturgy signify and cause grace. Human nature is not always ugly, decrepit, or at war with God's grace. Catholicism is an active, symbol-making church, and the church community explains the prominence of local churches, different ministries, liturgies in a hospital room or a cathedral, the contours of the sacramental in architecture or social action. To the surprise of many, Catholicism is not particularly monoform or authoritarian but is composed of many groups and movements: different religious orders, an international panoply of theological schools, many liturgies and ethnic devotions. These characteristics explain the perduring ethnic character of Catholicism—the extended family of the church worldwide, and the ability to adjust to new cultures.

Some religious orders who founded a college or a university have faced this issue of identity by emphasizing their particular charism and spirituality. Institutes established for this purpose make a contribution, but it is one which is introductory and supportive. The idea of extending the Franciscan charism and theological approach to the entire faculty (who will more and more direct the school) is laudatory, but this solution can easily avoid the issue of the Catholic worldview and communal ethos. There can be less opposition to discussing, for instance, "Jesuit presence" than there is to facing "Catholic identity"—perhaps because many or most administrators and faculty will not be deeply touched by the charism or spirituality of Ignatius. Papers at a symposium on spirituality or values in literature only explore what eventually policies must protect. A school must show that it can explain accurately and maturely the Catholic realization of Christianity as well as explaining the spirituality of a group within the church.

The Department Teaching Theology

Since the department of theology is such an important factor and force in the articulation of identity, its teachers and programs should not be mainly secularist, fundamentalist, or pan-Christian. This department should be adequate in size and quality—these are visible signs of commitment to the religious identity of the school. In expressing the Catholic identity, the theology department is involved neither in advanced catechesis nor in theories of religious epistemology but in the expression of past and present theological viewpoints on, for instance, God's presence or social ethics. Its first audience is the students who cannot be reached apart from their life, their society, and their faith and church. The intellectual interests of the teachers should not be completely indifferent to the real sociology and geography of religion in America: the faculty's specializations should usually not be hobbies in the field of religion, something of interest only to a small number of professionals in religious studies. When considering teaching it is important to imagine the students as they are and perhaps to recall Jesus' metaphor of not giving people stones when they need bread.

What is the goal of the undergraduate courses in the theology department? There is a difference between levels in university teaching, but the same topic can be treated at different levels. Theology is not primarily about translations of Semitic texts or post-Cartesian philosophies of religion; theology explains Christian faith in light of contemporary issues and ways of thinking. As new generations of students arrive, a theology department must ask about its courses and its faculty. Born after Vatican II, today's students have neither the problems of the preconciliar church nor the interests of the 1960s. The purpose of the department is to teach something of value to the students in the classes, and no research or theory is so valuable as to preclude engaging teaching. For undergraduates, a theology department should provide courses in the living interpretation of Christianity. The Catholic teachers need to represent the pluralism present in today's church, and they need to be able to express, from the historical and ecclesial perspectives, how Catholicism can include a certain diversity within its strong orientation to doctrine. To teach theology today is to teach it within the encounter of theological times (the end of the Catholic baroque, the end of liberal Protestantism), and to teach theology is to teach it to students who have little interest in either a dry scholasticism or an agitated string of new trends. Theology is more than recent intellectual theories, for it has a broad panoply of content and a long history; it is more than history, for vitality means attraction, interest, contemporary application. While every course pays attention implicitly and explicitly to methodology, only doctoral studies can begin to justify a course solely concerned with methodologies and hermeneutics. In general, American academia shies away from content and major themes, and it might be that the too-prevalent interest in methodologies and texts signals the end of the culture of the self in late modernity, lost in the forms and signs of its own mediocrity. Far from being naive or exemplifying seminary tracts or advanced catechetics, some courses should be about the great areas of the gospel, about the main themes of revelation and faith. The students will have few opportunities to study the Christian faith, and the opportunity they have should not be spent mainly in terms of philosophical issues, abstractions, and linguistic theories while avoiding the person of Jesus Christ, the meaning of salvation, the church, marriage. Theology takes a major (but hardly completely original) theme and challenges it with the important, pertinent issues of today; at the same time it shows how our theological attitudes and solutions have historical roots. An undergraduate course can be one in exegesis, ethics, systematic theology, etc., but each will in their overall development pay some attention to other areas of theology, that is, to the historical and biblical sources of a topic. Young students are not specialists. A department of theology must have the resources to explain somewhat the major periods of western Christianity, the major areas of systematic and moral theology from the Catholic perspective, and to offer some courses in areas of particular interest to Catholics: spirituality, liturgy, social ethics, ecclesiology, bio-medical ethics.

At the beginning of a course on the reign of God and human personality, I ask students fulfilling their second required theology course to list an issue in religion that they (and perhaps too the media) think important today. They never list the need to demythologize the New Testament, the reduction of revelation and grace to the transcendental psychology of the apostles, marginal Egyptian sects, a comparison of theological methods, ecumenism, or reconciling God with physics. The topics most chosen are biomedical issues; the ordination of women and married men; an effective theology of peace; the spiritual life; the need for believers to bring their faith into social issues, church, and politics; the humanity of Christ; the relationship of Christianity to the world religions. Students—not all, but many—are interested in theology, and of course they are interested first in their own traditions upon which any wider interests must build.

Three basic models of departments have been competing over the past thirty years for attention in Catholic schools (a department's identity is not given only its present name, e.g., *Religious Studies* or *Theology*, although names are important). The first model is that of a department of religious studies at a state-funded school. This is fashioned by the ethos of liberal Protestantism and sustained by the

American separation of church and state. Departments of religious studies exist almost exclusively in the United States (amid several thousand departments of theology in seminaries, colleges, universities) and were set up, largely in the 1950s and 1960s, to bring some teaching of religion to the expanding world of secular state universities. Surveys of beliefs and rituals in the religions of humanity joined to current theories in the theory of religion produce courses detached from the faith, church, and religious life of the student. A great deal of American religious studies tends to avoid the areas of church, Jesus Christ, spirituality, and liturgy and to offer alternatives to the history, reality, and content of revelation. But a department of religious studies imposes severe limits upon what is studied as it remains within a few centuries and a few countries; one misses there anything before 1500, Trinity or liturgy, monasticism, icons. The reduction of theology to a detached phenomenology of someone else's religious practices and methods is an impoverished approach for undergraduates and sometimes silently presupposes that anything in religion is worth learning except Christianity. Recent surveys of religious studies in state schools have noted a lack of clarity in what is being undertaken, a lack of interest from administration and from faculty in other fields, a desire among students for courses more directed to their life, and an absence of support from churches and synagogues. (I suspect that students are attracted to the courses not through but despite their detached view of the world of faith, and because they are the only available "theology.") The past year has seen some departments closing and that trend will continue. A replacement twenty years ago of *theology* with *religious studies* as a sign of openness can now be seen as problematic.

The second model might be called *ecumenical* in that it offers a spectrum of Judeo-Christian courses. Students do need to be exposed to other theologies. They also need to have access in some areas (liturgy and spirituality) to eastern Orthodox theologies, past and present. Many of the lessons of the Reformation were learned by Catholicism after Vatican II, and ecumenism has for fifteen years been on a plateau (partly because of its success) and today generates little interest. Sometimes this ecumenism can mean not a comparison of different Christian perspectives but a melange of liberal Protestantism and modern philosophy: many courses on

Schleiermacher or on post-Kantian, more or less Bultmannian directions, but almost no courses on Christ, the Eucharist, spirituality, social ethics, the eastern churches. Catholic institutions cannot be mainly or essentially ecumenical: there is no ecumenical church or one ecumenical theology (nondenominationalism has few followers today). Catholicism has its own ethos very much drawn from Thomas Aquinas, reexpressed in John of the Cross or Ignatius Loyola, evident in Karl Rahner, and present in countless theological and communal traditions.

The accepted principle that there should be Protestant members of the department cannot presume that Catholicism has no differences from certain basic Protestant theologies and mindsets. First, Catholic conservatism in dogma renders it quite different from the recent century and a half of liberal Protestantism; second, Catholicism is in many ways the polar opposite of Protestant fundamentalisms (Catholicism is plagued with its own fundamentalism); third, there are basic orientations of the Protestant mind which are quite different from Catholicism (and often of little interest to Catholics): a view of God as transcendent or hostile, a negative anthropology, little interest in liturgy and spirituality, a timeless view of the Bible— differences which in the last analysis reflect different views of nature and grace. From members of the Jewish tradition and from other great religions, there is much to be learned. Here a school should seek out for faculty members those who have proved ecumenical experience, who have some positive interests in Catholicism as it exists today, and who can lead the various audiences on the campus to a positive and enriching knowledge of other faiths and traditions.

The third model is contemporary Catholic. It should be pluralistic and global because postconciliar Catholicism is seeking to be such. Adequately ecumenical, it should not pursue the fundamentalisms of the Middle Ages or of today. It should offer the rich traditions (there is no such thing as *the* tradition in Catholicism) of western and eastern Christianity. The Catholic sacramental perspective should be recognized, and some courses (joining gospel and philosophy, theories and problems) should teach liturgy, church, spirituality, or ethics. Teachers in a theology department which wants to have a chance of interesting students cannot spend their entire time in transitory theories about epistemology, in ahistorical denunciations of past cultures, or in fantastic revisions of the present, while in daily life religion is arousing new sects and igniting military conflicts, facing difficult issues of genetic research, and pondering the search for the mystical. Today's teachers should be aware of the epochal shifts which have occurred in Catholic life and understand the recent history of Catholic thinking and life as well as its more distant sources in the worlds of the nineteenth century, the baroque, the Middle Ages, and earlier. College students should have the opportunity to learn something about their own faith at a mature level before being exposed to facts and theories about other religions. The dialogue between Christianity and the world religions is of the utmost importance but that would not be the excuse for a Catholic university to offer more courses in Iranian religion than in Christology.

The Catholic university can no longer presume that all who seek to join its teachers understand Catholicism well or at all. People seek positions, and jobs can be hard to find. Those coming from the world of a secular university may expect (and hope) that the anachronism of a university at all involved with religion will fade away politely. Protestants often presume that postconciliar liberal Catholicism resembles liberal Protestantism, but Catholic liberalism has to do with forms and movements rather than with faith and dogmas. Fundamentalist Protestants have shown enthusiasm for Catholic institutions, but, while they admire the Catholic respect for the literal teaching of the gospel, they do not always understand (or they reject) the deeper Catholic realities which touch on nature and grace. Catholic schools, for faculty and students, have become something of a refuge for religiously minded people of other churches and faiths, but then they may fail to see the paradox that it is precisely the affirmed Catholic teaching and ethos which sustains whatever has attracted them.

We have arrived again at the what it means to be a Catholic, at the deep mentality and ethos of worldwide Catholicism, at theology. Outsiders presume it lies somewhere in a collection of church dogmas; secularists are quite content to leave it in a church or a grotto far from their offices. But in fact the reality of Catholicism—not at all monoform or particularly authoritarian but much more diverse than modernity—permeates the entirety of Catholic life. So the reconsideration of Catholic identity is very much a theological issue: it means here the thinking and the life of the worldwide Catholic church, its many schools, its traditions, its involvement in countries as different as Brazil and Sri Lanka.

Ethos and World

Catholicism is not only a church and a creed but is very much an ethos. As we have seen, its institutions and interpretations build a family of theologies and traditions. Catholics absorb implicitly their world, and this world comes not only through churches and books but through language and rituals or all sorts of familial and communal celebrations. Catholicism as ethos explains why a Catholic university needs to have a number of Catholics active within it, for those raised consciously and subliminally in this world can express it well.

This ethos also indicates why a healthy theology department does not disdain the nonacademic side of the university. Theology does not hide from the personal and spiritual life of the students, from their liturgies and their politics. Education comes through teachers, and to be a teacher in theology has various communicative as well as intellectual dimensions. Faith and religion are not purely abstract topics but involve experience, personality, community. If the teacher has no experience of the students' faith world or sees no connections between religion and much-publicized ethical issues, the young hearers will be puzzled and bored. Experience—whether of medical decisions or parish liturgical action or service on a parish council—is an important part of religion and consequently of teaching about religion. It should not be fully absent from the Catholic university. Catholic theology departments need to have a few people who can explain recent books about Christ and social ethics but who also have experienced the society with its health care centers and prisons, and who have participated in the church with its parishes and schools. A combination of experience and intellectual presentation marks the best teachers and creates a dynamic and personal atmosphere for the school, while a detached seminar devoid of personal experience or interest in society and church is moribund.

Just as it does not exist apart from the world of its students, a healthy theology department does not exist apart from the wider world. Catholics expect faith and theology to move within family life, ethnic groups, and political movements. Sadly, this very involvement in ethos and world can become a reason why secular institutions question such departments of theology. Doesn't life compromise intellectual rigor? But it would be a mistake, getting in line with the secularizing and ephemeral trends of much of American intellectual life, to withdraw from these worlds. The courses of a theology department should display some of the sparks which keep religion important among people outside of academia, and the faculty should find that teaching theology is less the mustering of recent experts' transcendent and transcendental diminishment of religion than the disclosure of insight into what is unseen but nonetheless most real. Theology concerns not only vision but realization and should include the American church in its diversity, the Hispanic churches not only in Central and Latin America but in the United States, emerging African forms of Christianity, and the world of active church life from Prague to Kiev. The future of Christianity—whether in Los Angeles, Lagos, or Kiev—will not be fashioned by post-Enlightenment epistemologies, and it is a mistake to exchange the opportunity for a global perspective for the enterprise of American academia.

These considerations of theology or religious studies at a Catholic college or university might be attacked as unecumenical, provincial, immature, confessional. Certainly to consider Catholic identity in higher education is, within the confines of American society, to embark upon something of a reversal: it turns from mental structures to content, from books to life, from detached surveys to engaged teaching.

One of the paradoxes of life at a Catholic university is that the very department, theology, which would seem to have the least opportunity to gain a public audience in America can find wide clienteles, can have access to the media. Church authorities, ethical discussions, religious movements generate media attention in ways not active in other areas of the humanities. If Catholic theologians wish to go out into society, there are waiting and interested audiences.

Cultures changing, churches ending and expanding, the end of modernity, a desired union of life and faith, the passage of religion beyond theories to liturgies, the sacramental extended into the pedagogy of media—these big themes bring us to a conclusion. There are, of course, powerful forces working against the role of theology in Catholic institutions. Theology generates no revenue; Vatican and episcopal offices focus control rather than substance; the secular intellectual establishment distracts from tradition and content by pursuing the avant garde of empty issues. But one can hope that neither the normalcy of media-encouraged secularism or the repetition of modern theories about religion will put to sleep what great faith and hope have fashioned. Catholic schools, large and small, are involved in more than a new affirmation of Catholic vision: they engage in an enterprise which is both attentive to the true breadth of human religion and is countercultural in its rejection of the abstract formalism of the study of the religiously human. Having been awakened to the passage of time in the decades since the 1960s, the schools seem determined to support the ethos and teaching of the unseen realities which faith, community, and liturgy accept.

The Idea of a Catholic University:
A Personal Perspective

Timothy O'Meara

Each August when preparing my homily for the Mass inaugurating the academic year at Notre Dame, I am driven to two things: to think through anew the very idea of a Catholic university; and to find inspiration for the year ahead in the readings of the Sunday. For me the task has always been very rewarding, both spiritually and intellectually. I have found that even the most obscure readings can be mined for profound reflections on the special circumstances in the university community at the time.

The opening Mass is the Mass of the Holy Spirit, the Spirit of Wisdom, and celebrates the essence of a Catholic university—an intellectual life, a spiritual life, and an ideal of integrating the two. Faith seeking understanding is, in fact, characteristic of the Catholic tradition. It goes back to Job arguing with God about his lot; to the monastic tradition of the Middle Ages; to *fides quaerens intellectum* of St. Anselm; to the founding of the first universities in Salerno, Bologna, and Paris; to Thomas Aquinas and his rediscovery of Aristotle; to John Henry Newman and his idea of a university; and to the founding and flourishing of Catholic colleges and universities in our own land. In fact, it is a constant thread in our relationship with God.

Faith seeking understanding is also portrayed artistically in the panoramic mural of the Hesburgh Library at Notre Dame and the groups of individuals it depicts—the apostles and early Christians with Christ at the center, the Hebrew prophets, ancient classical cultures, the eastern world, the medieval era, Byzantium, the Renaissance, and the age of science and exploration. In the university church, Sacred Heart Basilica, we are also surrounded with images of saints and scholars of all ages: Catherine of Alexandria, teacher and philosopher of the fourth century; Cecilia, patroness of musicians; Teresa of Avila of the sixteenth century, intellectual, theologian, reformer, and doctor of the church.

Insofar as men and women of all faiths dedicate themselves to seeking the truth, their work becomes a holy thing. This is true in a special way of the intellectual life, be that in plumbing the depths of the human soul through psychiatry, or in reflecting on the human condition through literature, or in exploring the breadth and depth of the universe through science. And it applies to us in a university where, through our teaching, writing, artistic achievement, research, and invention, we participate in discovering God's grand design and in initiating the next generation into the ongoing dialogue.

All these signs and symbols represent why I believe that there is a fundamental rapport between the spiritual and intellectual life and, by extension, an underlying principle for the very idea of a university that is Catholic. This belief has been fostered for me not by a process of pure reasoning but through a lifetime of reflection on experiences in the church, in the academy, and in the home.

I grew up in Cape Town on the second story of the family bakery. My two brothers and I were fortunate to have been raised in a large family setting which included our grandmother and all sorts of cousins, uncles, and aunts. My father was Irish, a businessman, a person of integrity with a sense of humor and a great interest in people. My mother was of Italian descent, liberated without being combative, deeply spiritual with a slight air of the mystic. South Africa at that time was politically dominated by certain kinds of condescending colonial English and by Calvinist Afrikaners who referred to Catholics as *die Roomse gevaar*—the Roman danger. We were a minority within a minority, but I certainly did not look upon myself that way at any time. We lived in a mixed neighborhood.

On the second floor of the bakery's garage was a large hall which we rented out as a black Christian church. Our house was always full of people: Italians, Irish, Cape Coloureds, Xhosas, English, Afrikaners, Portuguese, and Indians; Catholics, Protestants, Jews, and Mohammedans; bakers, plumbers, bookkeepers, carpenters, police, doctors, servants, lawyers, and priests. Everyone was welcome: many came—some to stay, a few to die. If we objected to the traffic, my mother would simply say, "Then I don't understand what is meant by being a Christian." In this rich environment, filled with contradictions and polarities, the family gave us a great stability and intrinsic belief in our Catholic faith.

My school days go back to the Loretto Convent, the Irish Christian Brothers, and the University of Cape Town. My total theological training started with the penny catechism; then the sixpenny catechism; then the New Testament, almost to the point of knowing it by heart; followed by *Fortifying Youth,* a book published by the Irish Christian Brothers; and finally two massive volumes of Dr. Rumble's *Radio Replies.* I spent a good deal of my youth thinking about doctrinal and moral questions, often trying to analyze them in a mathematical sort of way. Instinctively I believed that all of theology was already known. Somebody somewhere really understood it all. Perhaps Father Gavan Duffy did—that awesome figure, the Catholic chaplain at the University of Cape Town and the only Jesuit I ever saw in South Africa.

There were practically no Catholics at the University of Cape Town and, subsequently for that matter, in the graduate school at Princeton. Whenever we were together we would find ourselves discussing questions of faith, proofs of the existence of God, the Galileo problem, the matter of evolution, the validity of holy orders in the Roman tradition versus the Anglican one. Social concerns were really nonexistent—to be sure, there should be equality among the races, but that was not our immediate concern. The arguments against abortion were simple, clear, and acknowledged by all. The empowerment of the laity, the ordination of women, the idea of married priests were concepts so inconceivable that they were not even raised for discussion. I found the arguments against contraception utterly perplexing (and still do). Nevertheless, I assumed that somebody somewhere would be able to explain them to me in due course. Although infallibility was clearly and narrowly defined, there was always the subconscious assumption of what I might call pseudo-infallibility, namely, that the kinds of questions we were discussing could always be answered by a representative of the institutional church. To make the point, let me recall that while a graduate student at Princeton, I decided to see America by motorcycle and on my own. The problem of Galileo was on my mind when I left New Jersey, and by the time I got to Kansas I was so obsessed with it that I finally decided to drop in on the pastor of a local Catholic church in a small town, fully expecting that my questions would be resolved. His reaction to my knock on the door was that he was tired and resting and he suggested that I ride on to the church in the next town. Prophetic? Perhaps the wise pastor was giving me a more pertinent direction than I could grasp at the time.

In those days we were engaged not only in personal probing of this sort but also in the art of polemics in religion, as two incidents in particular illustrate. The first occurred when I was a university student in Cape Town. An ad in the *Cape Times* announced a lecture by a Protestant minister entitled "The Immaculate Conception: Fact or Fiction." A few of us at the university, no doubt fortified by Dr. Rumble, decided to attend the lecture and challenge the speaker. We did in fact disrupt the meeting, we were then invited to dinner by the minister, and we subsequently became friends. The second experience occurred when I was a graduate student at Princeton. A small group of us regularly attended daily Mass at the Aquinas Center. Among us were three luminaries: Marston Morse, a distinguished mathematician at the Institute for Advanced Study; Jacques Maritain, the Thomistic philosopher at the university; and Hugh Taylor, the dean of the graduate school. We were all on very good terms with each other and with the Catholic chaplain, Hugh Halton— a Dominican priest and a brilliant polemicist. After I completed my Ph.D., my wife Jean and I went to New Zealand for a period of three years. When I returned to the faculty at Princeton we found the Catholic community there in utter turmoil. A constant stream of polemics was being aimed by Hugh Halton at the university and its president on issues involving Catholicism and Catholics at the university. This lead to a shunning of Marston Morse, Jacques Maritain, and Hugh Taylor, who were denounced from the pulpit as fellow travelers of the university. For all too long Halton had the support of the bishop and also of his order. Eventually he was removed from his position. Subsequently he left the priesthood.

These incidents and others have left their mark on me. Quite specifically, they have reinforced in my mind the fact that, for all its contradictions and polarities, a Catholic university must be inclusive rather than exclusive, and the underlying rhetoric must be inspirational, not strident or polemical.

———————

For whatever reasons, my interest in mathematics was inseparable from my interest in religion. For years I had instinctive beliefs that mathematics was known once and for all, probably discovered by Euclid or Pythagoras. I still have vivid memories of learning algebra and geometry from the Christian Brothers. I can still see in my mind's eye the page in my geometry book with the proof of Pythagoras's theorem. I had an insatiable appetite for solving mathematical problems, even to the point of doing them for fun during my summer vacations. After graduating from the University of Cape Town, I started doctoral studies at Princeton. During my student days I lived at the Graduate College, mixing with doctoral students from all disciplines and from all parts of the world. In retrospect I think that experience was as valuable as, if not more valuable than, the mathematical training which I received at the university. (Parenthetically let me say that I cannot recall a single graduate student or professor in mathematics at Princeton who was a Catholic.) It was not until my second year as a doctoral student that I began to understand that mathematics was an ever-expanding universe. My thesis advisor at Princeton was Emil Artin, one of the great algebraists of the century. Unfortunately, or perhaps fortunately, he offered me no advice in the selection of a thesis topic. I think it was a fluke that I got started at all. But once I did, a whole new world opened up, to which I would devote a vast amount of time and energy for over thirty years. In the 1950s and 1960s and even the 1970s I had a view of mathematical truth which might be called absolutist, in the sense that I viewed mathematics as the only branch of knowledge in which you could be absolutely sure of what you were talking about. Not even Jean could knock that out of me. It was not until I became provost that I realized that there were areas of life in which strict adherence to pure logical thinking could prove disastrous.

I am not going to write about my specific research except to say that it is in areas intersecting with modern algebra and the theory of numbers. On the broad motivational side, however, I have been fascinated with the mysterious interplay between good mathematics and reality. Consider, for example, the lines, triangles, squares, and circles of Euclid. These are examples of forms that occur to us through our experience in nature. People—mathematicians—then study relationships among all sorts of these forms in increasing degrees of abstraction based only on the intrinsic harmony which is found in the relationships that unfold. Centuries later, some of the relationships derived in a world of total abstraction, in hyperspace, as it were, come back to earth and allow us to explain nature or even to change it. There is an intrinsic harmony then between mathematical forms, nature, and the mind. That is what I find fascinating. That is what I find mysterious. Take yourself back in time and imagine the mathematics of the Babylonians, leading to the discovery of algebra by the Arabs in the Middle Ages, ultimately providing Newton with a framework for the calculus and his force of gravitation which finally explained what held the heavens in their place. To take another example, who could have believed that mathematical logic, as abstract as abstract can be, would unlock the door to an instrument as revolutionary to our society as the computer? So far as I am concerned if these are not visible signs of the hand of God at work then I would like to know what is.

———————

Jean and I came to Notre Dame in 1962 because we liked the emphasis on the spiritual and the intellectual, because of Notre Dame's potential as a great university, because of our cultural identity with Notre Dame, and because of the persuasiveness of Father Hesburgh, Marston Morse, and individuals in the mathematics department at Notre Dame. This was at the time of the Second Vatican Council. Little did we realize what impact the work of the council would have on the growth and development of the university and on our role in shaping its future, not just academically but in all its dimensions. I was a distant observer of the Second Vatican Council during the 1960s, occasionally wide-eyed at some of the developments, but always protected in my remote mathematical world. Not until the 1970s did I begin to appreciate the real questions that we as a Catholic people had to come to grips with—the empowerment of the laity, the role of women in the church, questions of human sexuality. For the first time I realized what I had already realized twenty years earlier about mathematics; theology, too, was in a process of growth and development. I attribute my growth to various factors—an increased awareness of all these changes in our society, in the church, and especially at Notre Dame; vigorous discussions at the dinner table with our children (four daughters and one son) who were now in their teens; and the invaluable experience of serving as provost under Father Hesburgh, my greatest teacher from whom I gained a sense of vision of the church and of the university.

In reflecting on my experiences as a scholar, as a provost, and as a Catholic, I have come to think that there are these important areas for growth and development among Catholic universities today. First, I believe that it is essential that we take our place among the great and influential universities of our country. From their very inception, Catholic universities in the United States have been tied to the aspirations of American Catholics generally. During the last century and the first half of this century these have been the aspirations of an immigrant people. Now as these aspirations are changing, we must be responsive to new challenges for leadership at a higher level of academe. We must become increasingly influential in our society on the one hand and in the church on the other, through highly creative contributions to the arts and sciences, technology, the professions, and public service. We have a special responsibility to encourage increased participation of Catholics in the intellectual life. For all our advances we still have to ask the rhetorical question posed by John Tracy Ellis in the 1950s: "Where are the Catholic intellectuals?" We must emphasize the fact that the quest for knowledge is part of our search for God and therefore a natural source for sanctifying our lives.

In today's secular society it is at last possible for scientists and people of faith to converse in a civilized way. Unfortunately this is often accomplished by a sort of protocol which keeps science and religion in separate compartments. This has certainly been my own observation from my days as a graduate student at Princeton to the present time. But in a Catholic university we have a special challenge to make sure that the door between the life of the mind and the life of the spirit is kept wide open. In our tradition of faith seeking understanding it is essential that we be engaged in, and wholeheartedly committed to, the creative process. We cannot simply be reactionary bystanders or critical commentators. We must reverse a cultural condition in our church where caution squelches intellectual curiosity. These are matters at the very heart of our existence as Catholic academic communities. Ideally, such growth needs not only the tolerance but also the enthusiastic encouragement of the institutional church. There will always be tensions between democracy and authority, between teaching and research, between conserving and growing. How we resolve these polarities in our own universities will determine whether we are reactive to society or progressive within it and the extent to which our students and our ideas will influence American and Catholic culture in the twenty-first century.

Our second and more difficult problem, one with which we shall always have to grapple, is how, in a pluralistic society such as ours, we can be ecumenical in spirit while maintaining a predominant presence on the faculty of individuals dedicated to, and excited about, furthering the growth of our institutions as Catholic universities. Without that presence it will simply be a matter of time before our Catholic universities follow the rest of American higher education on the road to secularization. I have no doubt that the surest way to maintain our Catholic identity is through a partnership between our founding religious orders and the laity. In the early American church, laypeople were loyal contributors, passive and defensive, but not partners. Now, thanks in large measure to generations of missionaries and religious, we have a well-educated Catholic population. But since the time of the Second Vatican Council, vocations to the priesthood and religious life have decreased sharply. In some religiously founded colleges their presence has all but disappeared. Whether or not this trend continues, the working hypothesis must be that it will. Already a few Catholic universities are being founded almost entirely through strong lay initiatives. The role of the laity is constantly changing from dependency to shared responsibility, a shared responsibility which embraces women as well as men, theologians as well as scientists, and Catholics of a variety of views as well as individuals of other beliefs.

This third area of growth for Catholic universities, shared responsibility, is indeed crucial. Its potential derives, obviously, from the sheer number and expertise of the laity, and more importantly, from a straightforward, independent, American way of questioning things and looking at the world. But shared responsibility requires active involvement as well as shared consequences. It depends on individuals, not systems. It relies not on structures and rules but on the deep inner conviction of those who clearly see the intersection of spiritual and intellectual values as important and valid. In the Catholic university, this shared responsibility is marked by generosity of spirit, it respects the academic freedom of each individual, and it welcomes a variety of views and their differing modes of expression. It demands that all of us committed to this academic enterprise, lay and ordained, women and men, Catholics and people of all faiths, must focus not only on our teaching and engaging in research but also on our sustaining and deepening the religious character of our university communities as well as providing for their evolution and continuation.

Fully conscious of the creative polarities these aspirations necessarily involve, I am more convinced than ever that our goals are well worth achieving. Indeed we *must* succeed so that the great heritage of faith seeking understanding continues to enliven and enlarge the intellectual life of the world. Confident of the Holy Spirit's presence among us, we can strive ever onward toward this vibrant vision of the genuine Catholic university, great in every sense of the word.

Note

The lecture I gave upon receiving the University of Dayton's Marianist award ("A Pilgrim's Progress in a Catholic University," University of Dayton, 1988), is one of several sources for this essay; others include the homilies I have delivered at the opening Mass each academic year and, above all, my continuing study and thought in this area.

On Christian Scholarship

Alvin Plantinga

How does the vocation of a Catholic or Christian university as Christian bear on its vocation as a university? This is a question of impressive difficulty. The question is so difficult in part because there is no developed and recognized specialty or discipline here. If education is a discipline, it does not have a subdiscipline or specialty called "how to be a Christian university." There are not any experts on the subject (certainly I am not one). There is not much by way of tradition to appeal to: there is the example of the great medieval universities, but our problems were not theirs. Unlike them, we live in a society that has been becoming increasingly secularized for the last couple of hundred years or more. To find a parallel to our situation, we have to go back to the time of the church fathers. Furthermore, the question is relatively recent: it is only during the last seventy-five or one hundred years that universities and colleges have become secularized and much more recently that the Christian community has started to become aware of the nature and proportions of that secularization.[1] This question is therefore of great importance, of great difficulty, and such that it does not fall within anyone's specialty; it is also potentially divisive. That is perhaps reason for shying away from it, for letting sleeping dogs lie. But this particular sleeping dog cannot be let lie; too much is at stake. No question that confronts or will confront the University of Notre Dame during the next century is of comparable importance.

Furthermore, the question comes in many parts. There is the religious life of the students and of the faculty; there is the question of how other universities have become secularized, precisely what secularization consists in, to what extent it is a good thing, what our relationship to such universities should be, what we can learn from them, where we must be different from them, what our distinctiveness should consist in, what stake the Christian community has in this secularization, and so on. We must think about graduate education as well as undergraduate education; we must think about the need for the kind of conversation mentioned by Craig Lent—both about the need for such a conversation, and about the appropriate topics; we must think about curricula; we must think about how all this bears on hiring policies; we must think about these things and a thousand others.

I want to consider just one question out of this vast horde of questions: How should a Christian university and how should the Christian intellectual community think about scholarship and science? Should the kind of scholarship and science that go on at a Catholic university differ from the sort that goes on elsewhere? If so, in what way? I want to present one sort of view—not, of course, with the thought that this is the whole and unvarnished truth but as a contribution to our conversation.

The Augustinian Struggle

Christian thinkers going back at least to Augustine have seen human history as involving a sort of contest, or battle, or struggle between two implacably opposed spiritual forces. Augustine spoke of the City of God and the Earthly City or City of the World: the *civitas dei* and the *civitas mundi*.[2] The former is dedicated, in principle, to God and to his will and to his glory. The latter is dedicated to something wholly different. Augustine, I think, is right, but I want to develop his insights in my own way.[3] Indeed, we *must* do this in our own way and from our own historical perspective. The precise relationship between the City of God and the Earthly City constantly changes; the form the Earthly City itself takes constantly changes; an account of the fundamental loyalties and commitments of the Earthly City that was correct in Augustine's day, now some fifteen centuries ago, does not directly apply now.

Augustine was right; and the contemporary western intellectual world, like the world of his times, is a battleground or arena in which rages a battle for our souls. This battle, I believe, is a three-way contest. There are three main contestants, in the contemporary western intellectual world, and I want to try to characterize them. Of course an undertaking like this is at best fraught with peril (and at worst arrogantly presumptuous); the contemporary western world is a vast and amorphous affair, including an enormous variety of people, in an enormous variety of places, with enormously different cultural backgrounds and traditions. We all know how hard it is to get a real sense of the intellectual climate of a past era—the Enlightenment, say, or thirteenth-century Europe, or nineteenth-century America. It is clearly much more difficult to come to a solid understanding of one's own time. For these general reasons, real trepidation is very much in order.

As I see it, therefore, there are at present three main competitors vying for spiritual supremacy: three fundamental perspectives or ways of thinking about what the world is like, what we ourselves are like, what is most important about the world, what our place in it is, and what we must do to live the good life.

The first of these perspectives is Christianity, or Christian theism, or Judeo-Christian theism; here I shall say little about that. I do want to remind you, however, that this theistic perspective has been very much on the defensive (at least in the west) ever since the Enlightenment.

In addition to the theistic perspective, then, there are fundamentally two others. Both of them have been with us since the ancient world, but each has received much more powerful expression in modern times. According to the second picture, there is no God, and we human beings are insignificant parts of a giant cosmic machine that proceeds in majestic indifference to us, our hopes and aspirations, our needs and desires, our sense of fairness or fittingness. This picture receives eloquent, if florid, expression in Bertrand Russell's "A Free Man's Worship"; it goes back to Epicurus, Democritus, and others in the ancient world. Call it *perennial naturalism*. (It is the perspective of Carl Sagan, with his portentous incantation "The cosmos is all there is, or has been, or will be.") According to the third perspective, on the other hand, it is we ourselves—we human beings—who are responsible for the basic structure of the world. This notion goes back to Protagoras, in the ancient world, with his claim that man is the measure of all things; it finds enormously more powerful expression in modern times in Immanuel Kant's *Critique of Pure Reason.* Call it *creative antirealism.* These two perspectives or pictures are very different indeed; I shall say something about each.

PERENNIAL NATURALISM

Perennial naturalism (*naturalism* for short), as I say, goes back to the ancient world; naturalism is also to be found in somewhat muted form in the medieval world (among some of the Averroists, for example). But it was left to modernity and to contemporary times to display the most complete and thorough manifestations of this perspective. The Enlightenment encyclopedists and Baron D'Holbach are early modern exponents of this picture; among our contemporaries and near contemporaries there are John Dewey, Willard van Orman Quine, Bertrand Russell, an astounding number of liberal theologians, and a host of others in and out of academia. It is especially popular among those who nail their banners to the mast of science. From this perspective, there is no God, and human beings are properly seen as parts of nature. The way to understand what is most distinctive about us, our ability to love, to act, to think, to use language; our humor and playacting; our art, philosophy, literature, history; our morality; our religion; our tendency to enlist in sometimes unlikely causes and devote our lives to them—the fundamental way to understand all this is in terms of our community with (nonhuman) nature. We are best seen as parts of nature and are to be understood in terms of our place in the natural world.[4]

The form this perspective takes in our own day is broadly evolutionary: we are to try to understand basic human phenomena by way of their origin in random genetic mutation, or some other source of variability, and their perpetuation by way of natural selection. Consider sociobiological explanations of love, for example: love between men and women, between parents and children, love for one's friends, of one's students, love of church, college, country—love in all its diverse manifestations and infinite variety. Taken thus broadly, love is a most significant human phenomenon and an enormously powerful force in our lives. And how are we to think of love on the sort of evolutionary account in question? Well, the basic idea is that love arose, ultimately and originally, by way of some source of genetic variability (random genetic mutation, maybe); it persisted via natural selection because it has or had survival value. Male and female human beings, like male and female hippopotami, get together to have children (colts) and stay together to raise them; this has survival value. Once we see that point, we understand that sort of love and see its basic significance; and the same goes for the other varieties and manifestations of love. And that, fundamentally, is what there is to say about love.

From a theistic or Christian perspective, of course, this is hopelessly inadequate. The fact is, love reflects the basic structure and nature of the universe; for God himself, the first being of the universe, is love, and we love because he has created us in his image.

From the naturalistic perspective, furthermore, what goes for love goes for those other distinctively human phenomena: art, literature, music; play and humor; science, philosophy, and mathematics; our tendency to see the world from a religious perspective, our inclinations towards morality, and so on. All these things are to be understood in terms of our community with nonhuman nature. All of these are to be seen as arising, finally, by way of the mechanisms driving evolution and are to be understood in terms of their place in evolutionary history, in terms of their contribution to present or past fitness.

Perennial naturalism has made enormous inroads into western culture; indeed, Oxford philosopher John Lucas thinks that it is the contemporary orthodoxy. In support of Lucas's claim, we might note, as I mentioned above, the astonishing fact that perennial naturalism has a considerable following among allegedly Christian theologians. Thus Harvard theologian Gordon Kaufman suggests that in this modern nuclear age, we can no longer think of God as the transcendent creator of the heavens and the earth; we must think of God instead, says Kaufman, as "the historical evolutionary force that has brought us all into being."[5] (Perhaps one may be pardoned for wondering what the nuclear age has to do with whether God is the transcendent creator or just a historical evolutionary force; we can imagine an earlier village skeptic making a similar remark about, say, the invention of the steam engine, or perhaps the long bow, or the catapult, or the wheel.)

Perennial naturalism is particularly popular among those—scientists or others—who take a high view of modern science. Perennial naturalism also constantly influences and, as I see it, corrupts Christian thinking. Christians who think about science, for example, sometimes say that science cannot take any account of God in giving its explanations; science is necessarily restricted, both in its subject matter and in its explanations and accounts, to the natural world. But why think a thing like that? Of course the claim might be merely verbal: "the word *science*," it might be said, "is to be defined as an empirical and experimental account of the natural world that is restricted, both in its subject matter and its conclusions, to the natural world." But then the question would be: Should Christians engage in science? Or, more exactly, in trying to understand ourselves and our world should they engage *only* in science, so defined? Why should they not instead or in addition engage in a parallel explanatory activity that takes account of *all* that we know, including such facts as that human beings were created by the Lord in his image, that they have fallen into sin, and the like? Presumably these truths will be important with respect to empirical studies of humanity, in thinking, for example, about aggression, altruism, and other topics studied in the human sciences.

It is hard to overestimate the dominance and influence of perennial naturalism in our universities. Yet Lucas errs in promoting it to the status of the contemporary orthodoxy, although it is indeed orthodoxy among those who put their trust in science. But there is another basic way of looking at the world that is, I think, nearly as influential—and just as antithetical to Christianity. Perennial naturalism gets fierce competition from creative antirealism.

CREATIVE ANTIREALISM

Here the fundamental idea—in sharp contrast to naturalism—is that we human beings, in some deep and important way, are *ourselves* responsible for the structure and nature of the world; it is *we*, fundamentally, who are the architects of the universe. This view received magnificent, if obscure, expression in Immanuel Kant's *Critique of Pure Reason.* Kant did not deny, of course, that there really are such things as mountains, horses, planets, and stars. Instead, his characteristic claim is that their existence and their fundamental structure have been conferred upon them by the conceptual activity of persons—not by the conceptual activity of a personal God, but by *our* conceptual activity, the conceptual activity of us human beings. According to this view, the whole world of experience—the world of trees and planets and dinosaurs and stars—receives its basic structure from the constituting activity of mind. Such fundamental structures of the world as those of space and time, object and property, number, truth and falsehood, possibility and necessity, and even existence and nonexistence—these are not to be found in the world as such (do not characterize those *Dinge an sich*) but are somehow constituted by our own mental or conceptual activity. They are contributions from our side; they are not to be found in the things in themselves. We impose them on the world; we do not discover them there. Were there no persons like ourselves engaging in conceptual, noetic activities, there would be nothing in space and time, nothing displaying object-property structure, nothing that is true or false, possible or impossible, no kinds of things coming in a certain number.

We might think it impossible that the things we know—houses and horses, cabbages and kings, planets and stars—should be there at all but fail to be in space-time, fail to display object-property structure, and fail to conform to the category of existence; indeed, we may think it impossible that there be a thing of any sort that does not have properties and does not exist. If so, then Kant's view implies that there would be nothing at all if it were not for the creative structuring activity of persons like us. Of course I do not say Kant clearly *drew* this conclusion; indeed, he may have obscurely drawn the opposite conclusion: that is part of his charm. But the fundamental thrust of Kant's self-styled Copernican revolution is that the things in the world owe their basic structure and perhaps their very existence to the noetic activity of our minds. Or perhaps I should say not *minds* but *mind*; for whether, on Kant's view, there is just one transcendental ego or several is, of course, a vexed question, as are most questions of Kantian exegesis. Indeed, this question is more than vexed; given Kant's view that quantity, number, is a human category imposed on the world, there is presumably no number n, finite or infinite, such that the answer to the question "How many of those transcendental egos are there?" is n.[6]

Until you feel the grip of this sort of way of looking at things, it can seem a bit presumptuous, not to say preposterous. Did we structure or create the heavens and the earth? Some of us think there were animals—dinosaurs, let's say—roaming the earth before human beings had so much as put in an appearance; how could it be that those dinosaurs owed their structure to our noetic activity? What did we do to give them the structure they enjoyed? And what about all those stars and planets we have never so much as heard of: how have we managed to structure them? When did we do all this? Did we structure ourselves in this way too? And if the way things are is thus up to us and our structuring activity, why do we not improve things a bit?

Creative antirealism can seem a bit hard to swallow; nevertheless it is widely accepted and an astonishingly important force in the contemporary western intellectual world. Vast stretches of contemporary continental philosophy, for example, are antirealist. There is existentialism, according to which, at least in its Sartrian varieties, each of us structures or creates the world by way of her own decisions. There is also contemporary Heideggerian hermeneutical philosophy of various stripes; there is contemporary French philosophy, much of which beggars description but, insofar as anything at all is clear about it, is clearly antirealist. In Anglo-American philosophy, there is the creative antirealism of Nelson Goodman and at least one stage of Hilary Putnam; there is the reflection of continental antirealism in such American philosophers as Richard Rorty; and perhaps most important, there is the linguistic antirealism of Wittgenstein and his many followers. It is characteristic of all of these to hold that we human beings are somehow responsible for the way the world is—by way of our linguistic or more broadly symbolic activity, or by way of our decisions, or in some other way. And of course creative antirealism is not limited to philosophy; it has made deep inroads in many areas of the humanities and even into law.[7]

Like perennial naturalism, creative antirealism is to be found even in theology, which is heavily under the influence of Kant. Indeed, it is a bit naive to say that it is found *even* in theology; in the sort of theology that, according to its exponents, is the most up to date and *au courant*, these notions run absolutely riot. Creative antirealism is developed (if I may speak loosely) in theological fashion in Don

Cupitt's book *Creation out of Nothing*. The blurb on the back of the book nicely sums up its main claim:

> The consequence of all this is that divine and human creativity come to be seen as coinciding in the present moment. The creation of the world happens all of the time, in and through us, as language surges up within us and pours out of us to form and reform the world of experience. Reality . . . is effected by language . . . .

This is said to be "a philosophy of religion for the future" and "a genuine alternative to pietism and fundamentalism" (as well, we might add, as to any other form of Christianity). The same view has made its way into physics or at least the philosophy of physics. It is said that there is no reality until we make the requisite observations; there is no such thing as reality in itself and unobserved, or if there is, it is nothing at all like anything we can make sense of. In ethics, this view takes the form of the idea that no moral law can be binding on me unless I myself (or perhaps my society) issue or set that law.

Perennial naturalism and creative antirealism are related in an interesting manner: the first vastly underestimates the place of human beings in the universe, and the second vastly overestimates it. According to the first, human beings are essentially no more than complicated machines, with no real creativity; in an important sense we cannot really act at all, any more than can a spark plug, or coffee grinder, or a tractor. We are not ourselves the origin of any causal chains. According to the second, by contrast, we human beings, insofar as we confer its basic structure upon the world, really take the place of God. What there is and what it is like is really up to us and a result of our activity.

RELATIVISM

In addition to theism, then, the two basic pictures or perspectives at present and in the west, as I see it, are naturalism and creative antirealism. But here I must call attention to a couple of important complications. First, I say that on these antirealist views, it is we, we the speakers of language, or the users of symbols, or the thinkers of categorizing thoughts, or the makers of basic decisions, who are responsible for the fundamental lineaments of reality; in the words of Protagoras, "Man is the measure of all things." But often a rather different moral is drawn from some of the same considerations. Suppose you think our world is somehow created or structured by human beings. You may then note that human beings apparently do not all construct the same worlds. Your *Lebenswelt* may be quite different from mine; Jerry Falwell, Carl Sagan, and Richard Rorty do not seem to inhabit the same *Lebenswelt* at all; they think very differently about the world; which one, then (if any), represents the world as it really is, i.e., as we have really constructed it?

Here it is an easy step to another characteristically contemporary thought: the thought that there simply is not any such thing as *the* way the world is, no such thing as objective truth, or a way the world is that is the same for all of us. Rather, there is my version of reality, the way I have somehow structured things, and your version, and many other versions: and what is true in one version need not be true in another. As Marlowe's Dr. Faustus says, "Man is the measure of all things; I am a man; therefore I am the measure of all things."[8] But then there is not any such thing as truth *simpliciter*. There is no such thing as *the* way the world is; there are instead many different versions, perhaps as many different versions as there are persons; and each at bottom is as acceptable as any other. (From a Christian perspective, part of what is involved here, of course, is the age-old drive on the part of fallen humankind for autonomy and independence: autonomy and independence, among other things, with respect to the demands of God.) Thus a proposition really could be, as some of our students are fond of saying, true for me but false for you. Perhaps you have always thought of this notion as a peculiarly sophomoric confusion; but in fact it fits well with this formidable and important, if lamentable, way of thinking. The whole idea of an objective truth, the same for all of us, on this view, is an illusion, or a bourgeois plot, or a sexist imposition, or a silly mistake. Thus does antirealism breed relativism. And this relativism is perhaps the most prominent form, nowadays, of creative antirealism.

In some ways this seems quite a comedown from the view that there is indeed a way the world is, and its being that way is owing to our activity. Still, there is a deep connection: on each view, whatever there is by way of truth is of our own making. The same ambiguity is to be found in Protagoras himself. "Man is the measure of all things": we can take this as the thought that there is a certain way the world is, and it is that way because of what we human beings— all human beings—do, or we can take it as the idea that each of some more limited group of persons—perhaps even each individual person—is the measure of all things. Then there would be no one way everything is, but only different versions for different individuals. This form of creative antirealism, like the previous ones, suffers, I think, from deep problems with self-referential incoherence; but I do not here have the time to explain why I think so.

A second complication: Alasdair MacIntyre pointed out (personal communication) that my account here omits a very important cadre of contemporary academics and intellectuals. There are many intellectuals who think of themselves as having no firm commitments at all; they float free of all commitment and intellectual allegiance. Not only do they not display commitment; they disdain commitment as naive or ill informed, a failure to understand, a foolish failure to see something obvious and important. So, said MacIntyre, they are not committed either to the perennial naturalism of which I spoke, or to one or another form of antirealism; they are not committed to anything at all. But they are nonetheless a most important part of the contemporary picture.

This is both true and important. MacIntyre is quite right; the attitude he describes is indeed common among intellectuals and in academia. As a matter of fact, there is a deep connection between antirealism and relativism, on the one hand, and this intellectual *anomie* on the other. Maybe it goes as follows. The dialectic begins with some version of Kantian antirealism: the fundamental lineaments of the world are due to us and our structuring activity and are not part of the *Dinge an sich*. The next step is relativism: it is noted that different people hold very different views as to what the world is like; the result is the notion that there is not any *one* way things are like (a way which is due somehow to our noetic activity) but a whole host of different *versions* (as Nelson Goodman calls them), perhaps as many as there are persons. On this view there is not any such thing as a proposition's being true *simpliciter*: what there is, is a proposition's being true *in a version* or *from a perspective*. (And so what is true for me might not be true for you.)

To see this point, however, is, in a way, to see through any sort of commitment with respect to intellectual life. Commitment goes with the idea that there really is such a thing as truth; to be committed to something is to hold that it is true, not just in some version, but *simpliciter* or absolutely—i.e., not merely true with respect to some other discourse or version, or with respect to what one or another group of human beings think or do. To be committed to something is to think it is *true*, not just true relative to what someone believes. But once you see (as you think) that there is not any such thing as truth as such, then you are likely to think you also see the futility, the foolishness, the pitiable self-deluded nature of intellectual commitment. You will then think the only path of wisdom is that of the roaming, free-floating intellectual who has seen through the pretensions or naivete of those who do make serious intellectual and moral commitments. (And you may indeed go so far as to join Richard Rorty in thinking such people insane—in which case, presumably, they ought not to be allowed to vote or take full part in the liberal society and perhaps should be confined to its gulags pending recovery from the seizure.) As MacIntyre observes, this lack of commitment, this seeing through the pitiful self-delusion of commitment, is rampant in academia; it is, I think, close to the beating heart (or perhaps the central mushy core) of contemporary deconstruction.

So we have, as I said, three major perspectives, three wholly different and deeply opposed perspectives: Christian theism, perennial naturalism, and creative antirealism with its progeny of relativism and anticommitment. But of course what we also have, as William James said in a different connection, is a blooming, buzzing confusion. The above description is only a first approximation, accurate only within an order or two of magnitude; much fine tuning is necessary. These perspectives flow together and mingle in a thousand different ways. Each calls out a sort of reaction to itself; there can very well be a sort of dialectic or development within a given paradigm or way of thinking; there are of course channels of influence flowing between them. These three main perspectives or total ways of looking at humankind and the world can be found in every conceivable and inconceivable sort of combination and mixture. There are many crosscurrents and eddies and half-submerged islands; people think and act in accordance with these basic ways of looking at things without being at all clearly aware of them, having at best a sort of dim apprehension of them. Thus, for example, those who adopt skeptical, ironic, detached anticommitment with respect to the great questions, do not all themselves do so out of the motivation I suggest as to what really underlies it—i.e., that "seeing through" the more committed stances. It can be or start as simple imitation of one's elders and betters; this is the cool way to think, or the way the second-year graduate students think, or the way my teachers or the people at Harvard think. Our ways of thinking are as much arrived at by imitation of those we admire as by reasoned reflection.

As we saw above, ironically enough, both perennial naturalism and creative antirealism (with its progeny of relativism and anticommitment) find contemporary expression in allegedly Christian theology. These ways of thinking are touted as the truly up-to-date and with-it way to look at these matters, and as the up-to-date way of being a Christian. It is indeed a common human characteristic to claim that now, finally, we have achieved the truth (or the correct attitude to take, given that there is no truth) denied our parents. But here there is another sort of irony: these positions go back, clearly enough, all the way to the ancient world; as a matter of fact they antedate classical Christianity. What is new and with-it about them is only the attempt to palm them off as developments or forms— indeed, the intellectually most viable forms—of *Christianity*. This is new and with-it, all right, but it is also preposterous. It is about as sensible as trying to palm off, say, the Nicene Creed or the Heidelberg Catechism as the newest and most with-it way of being an atheist.

I trust it is unnecessary to point out that these ways of thinking are not just alternatives to Christianity; they run profoundly counter to it. From a Christian perspective the naturalist is, of course, deeply mistaken in rejecting or ignoring God. That is bad enough; but in so doing he also cuts himself off from the possibility of properly understanding ourselves and the world. And as for creative antirealism, the idea that it is really we human beings who have made or structured the world is, from a Christian perspective, less heroically Promethean than laughably Quixotic; and the idea that there is no truth, no way things are, is no less absurd from a Christian perspective. These ways of thinking, then, are predominant, pervasive, and deeply ingrained in our culture; they are also deeply antagonistic to a Christian way of looking at the world. And the sad truth is that these ways of thinking, at the moment, have the upper hand in our universities and in intellectual culture generally.

Are Science and Scholarship Neutral?

The first thing to see is that the answer is No; science and scholarship are not neutral with respect to this struggle for our souls. It is not as if the main areas of scholarship are neutral with respect to this struggle, with religious or spiritual disagreement rearing its ugly head only when it comes, say, to religion itself. The facts are very different: the world of scholarship is intimately involved in the battle between these opposing views; contemporary scholarship is rife with projects, doctrines, and research programs that reflect one or another of these ways of thinking. At present, the sad fact is that very many of these projects reflect the fundamentally non-Christian ways of thinking I have been mentioning. There are hundreds of examples: I shall give just a few, and each of you can add your own.

First, creative antirealism, with its accompanying entourage of relativism and anticommitment, is a dominating force in the humanities. Contemporary philosophy, for example, is overrun with varieties of relativism and antirealism. One widely popular version of relativism is Richard Rorty's notion that truth is what my peers will let me get away with saying. On this view, what is true for me, naturally enough, might be false for you; my peers might let me get away with saying something that your peers will not let you get away with saying: for we may have different peers. (And even if we had the same peers, there is no reason why they would be obliged to let you and me get away with saying the same things.) Although this view is extremely influential and very much *au courant* and up-to-date, it has consequences that are, to put it mildly, peculiar. For example, most of us think the Chinese authorities did something monstrous in murdering those hundreds of young people in Tienanmen Square; they then compounded their wickedness by denying that they had done it. On Rorty's view, however, this is perhaps an uncharitable misunderstanding. What the authorities were really doing, in denying that they had murdered those students, was something wholly praiseworthy: they were trying to bring it about that the alleged massacre never happened. For they were trying to see to it that their peers would let them get away with saying that the massacre never happened; if they were successful, then (on the Rortian view) it would have been *true* that it never happened, in which case, of course, it would never have happened. So in denying that they did this horrifying thing, they were trying to make it true that it had never happened; and who can fault them for that? The same goes for those contemporary neo-Nazis who claim that there was no holocaust; from a Rortian perspective, they are only trying to see to it that such an appalling event never happened: why should we hold *that* against them? Instead of blaming them, we should cheer them on.

This way of thinking has real possibilities for dealing with poverty and disease: if only we let each other get away with saying that there is not any poverty and disease—no cancer or AIDS, let's say—then it would be true that there is not any; and if it were true that there is not any, then of course there would not be any. That seems vastly cheaper and less cumbersome than the conventional methods of fighting poverty and disease. At a more personal level, if you have done something wrong, it is not too late: lie about it, thus bringing it about that your peers will let you get away with saying that you did not do it; then it will be true both that you did not do it, and, as an added bonus, that you did not even lie about it. One hopes Rorty is just joshing the rest of us. (But he isn't.)

As you would expect, there are very many examples of this sort in philosophy. But the main point to see here is that this is not just a problem for philosophers and maybe theologians: examples of these kinds can be found across most of the intellectual and disciplinary spectrum, and I shall give some examples from other fields. Here, of course, I run a risk; I am reasonably well acquainted with philosophy (and even that is less than wholly uncontroversial among my colleagues), but I am venturing out on an interdisciplinary limb in mentioning examples from other fields. Still, it needs to be done. So my second example is presented by structuralism, poststructuralism, and deconstructionism in literary studies. All of these, at bottom, pay homage to the notion that we human beings are the source of truth, the source of the way the world is, if indeed there is any such thing as truth or the way the world is. Sometimes this is explicit and clear, as in Roland Barthes:

Once the Author is removed, the claim to decipher a text becomes quite futile. To give a text an Author is to impose a limit on that text, to furnish it with a final signified, to close the writing. . . . In precisely this way literature (it would be better from now on to say *writing*) by refusing to assign a secret, an ultimate meaning, to the text (and to the world as text) liberates what may be called an antitheological activity, an activity that is truly revolutionary since to refuse to fix meaning is, in the end, to refuse God and his hypostases—reason, science, law.[9]

The move from structuralism to poststructuralism and deconstruction, furthermore, nicely recapitulates the move from Kantian antirealism to relativism. According to the structuralist, we human beings constitute and structure the world by language, and do so communally; there are deep common structures involved in us all by which we structure our world. The poststructuralists and deconstructionists, noting in their incisive way that different people structure the world differently, insist that there are not any such common structures; it is every woman for herself; each of us structures her own world her own way. Put thus baldly and held up to the clear light of day, these views may seem to be hard to take seriously. But the fact is they can be deeply seductive: for first, they ordinarily aren't put clearly and usually are not held up to the clear light of day; and second, they come in versions—Wittgensteinian antirealism, for example—that are vastly more subtle and thus vastly more enticing.

A third example is from science more narrowly so called. Consider the Grand Evolutionary Myth (GEM). According to this story, organic life somehow arose from nonliving matter by way of purely natural means and by virtue of the workings of the fundamental regularities of physics and chemistry. Once life began, all the vast profusion of contemporary flora and fauna arose from those early ancestors by way of common descent. The enormous contemporary variety of life arose through such processes as natural selection operating on such sources of genetic variability as random genetic mutation, genetic drift, and the like. I call this story a myth not because I do not believe it (although I do not believe it) but because it plays a certain kind of quasi-religious role in contemporary culture: it is a shared way of understanding ourselves at the deep level of religion, a deep interpretation of ourselves to ourselves, a way of telling us why we are here, where we come from, and where we are going.

Now it is certainly possible—epistemically possible,[10] anyway—that GEM is true; God could have done things in this way. Certain parts of this story, however, are to say the least epistemically shaky. For example, we hardly have so much as decent hints as to how life could have arisen from inorganic matter just by way of the regularities known to physics and chemistry.[11] (Darwin found this question deeply troubling; at present the problem is vastly more difficult than it was in Darwin's day, now that some of the stunning complexity of even the simplest forms of life has been revealed.) No doubt God could have done things that way if he had chosen to; but at present it looks as if he did not choose to.

So suppose we separate off this thesis about the origin of life. Suppose we use the term *evolution* to denote the weaker claim that all contemporary forms of life are genealogically related. According to this claim, you and the flowers in your garden share common ancestors, though we may have to go back quite a ways to find them. (So perhaps herbicide is a sort of fratricide.) Many contemporary experts and spokespersons—Francisco Ayala, Richard Dawkins, Stephen Gould, William Provine, and Philip Spieth, for example—unite in declaring that evolution is no mere theory, but established fact. According to them, this story is not just a virtual certainty but a real certainty.[12] This is as solid and firmly established, they say, as that the earth is round and revolves around the sun. (All of those I mentioned explicitly make the comparison with that astronomical fact.) Not only is it declared to be wholly certain; if you venture to suggest that it is not absolutely certain, if you raise doubts or call it into question, or are less than certain about it, you are likely to be howled down; you will probably be declared an ignorant fundamentalist obscurantist or worse. In fact this is not merely probable; you have already been so-called: in a recent review in the *New York Times*, Richard Dawkins, an Oxford biologist of impeccable credentials, claims that "It is absolutely safe to say that if you meet someone who claims not to believe in evolution, that person is ignorant, stupid or insane (or wicked, but I'd rather not consider that)." (Dawkins indulgently adds that "You are probably not stupid, insane or wicked, and ignorance is not a crime . . . .")

Now what is the source of these strident declarations of certainty, these animadversions on the character, intelligence, or sanity of those who think otherwise? Given the spotty character of the evidence—for example, a fossil record displaying sudden appearance and subsequent stasis and few if any genuine examples of macroevolution—these claims of certainty seem at best wildly excessive. From a Christian perspective, evolution is not remotely as certain as all that. Take as evidence what the Christian knows as a Christian together with the scientific evidence—the fossil evidence, the experimental evidence, and the like: it is at best absurd exaggeration to say that, relative to that evidence, evolution is as certain as that the earth is round. The theist knows that God created the heavens and the earth and all that they contain; she knows, therefore, that in one way or another God has created all the vast diversity of contemporary plant and animal life. But of course she is not thereby committed to any particular way in which God did this. He could have done it by broadly evolutionary means; but on the other hand he could have done it in some totally different way. For example, he could have done it by directly creating certain kinds of creatures—human beings, or bacteria, or for that matter sparrows and houseflies—as many Christians over the centuries have thought. Alternatively, he could have done it the way Augustine suggests: by implanting seeds, potentialities of various kinds in the world, so that the various kinds of creatures would later arise, although not by way of genealogical interrelatedness. Both of these suggestions are incompatible with the evolutionary story. And given theism and the evidence, it is absurd to say that evolution (understood as above) is a rock-ribbed certainty, so that only a fool or a knave could reject it.

So why that insistence on certainty and the refusal to tolerate any dissent? The answer can be seen, I think, when we realize that what you properly think about these claims of certainty depends in part on how you think about theism. If you reject theism in favor of naturalism, this evolutionary story is the only visible answer to the question Where did all this enormous variety of flora and fauna come from? Even if the fossil record is at best spotty and at worst disconfirming, even if there are anomalies of other sorts, this story is the only answer on offer (from a naturalistic perspective) to these questions; so objections will not be brooked.

A Christian, therefore, has a certain freedom denied her naturalist counterpart: she can follow the evidence[13] where it leads. If it seems to suggest that God did something special in creating human beings (in such a way that they are not genealogically related to the rest of creation),[14] or reptiles, or whatever, then there is nothing to prevent her from believing that God did just that. From a naturalistic perspective, on the other hand, evolution is vastly more likely and has vastly more to be said for it. First, there is the evaluation of the scientific evidence itself: some of this evidence is much stronger taken within a naturalistic context than taken within a theistic context. For example, *given* that life arose by chance, without direction by God, the fact that all living creatures employ the same genetic code strongly suggests a common origin for all living creatures. Again, given the enormous difficulty of seeing how life could have arisen even once by natural, nonteleological means, it is vastly unlikely that it arose in that way more than once; but if it arose only once, then the thesis of common ancestry follows.

But second, from a naturalistic perspective evolution is the only game in town. It is the only available answer to the questions How did it all happen? How did all of these forms of life get here? Where did this vast profusion of life come from? And what accounts for the apparent design (Hume's "nice adjustment of means to ends") to be found throughout all of living nature? A Christian has an easy answer to those questions: The Lord has created life in all its forms, and they got here by way of his creative activity; and as for the appearance of design, that is only to be expected, since living creatures are, in fact, designed. But the naturalist has a vastly more difficult row to hoe. How did life get started and how did it come to assume its present multifarious forms? It is monumentally implausible to think these forms just popped into existence; that goes contrary to all our experience. So how did it happen? The evolutionary story gives the answer. Somehow life arose from nonliving matter by way of purely natural means, without the direction of God or anyone else; and once life started, all the vast profusion of contemporary plant and animal life arose from those early ancestors by way of common descent, driven by random variation and natural selection. Richard Dawkins once made a telling remark to A. J. Ayer at one of those candle-lit, elegant, and bibulous Oxford dinners: "Although atheism might have been logically tenable before Darwin", said he, "Darwin made it possible to be an intellectually fulfilled atheist."[15] And here Dawkins seems to me to be quite correct. I do not mean to endorse his claim that it is possible to be an intellectually fulfilled atheist; I myself believe that claim to be false. The point about evolution, however, is that it is a plausible effort to remove one of the major embarrassments for the atheist. Evolution is an essential part of any reasonably complete naturalistic way of thinking; it plugs a very large gap in such ways of thinking; hence the pious devotion to it, the suggestions that doubts about it should not be aired in public, and the venom and abuse with which dissent is greeted. In contemporary academia, evolution has become an idol of the tribe; it serves as a shibboleth, a litmus test distinguishing the benighted fundamentalist goats from the enlightened and properly acculturated sheep. It plays that mythic role.

The point here can be put like this: the probability of the whole grand evolutionary story is quite different for the theist than for the naturalist. The probability of this story with respect to the evidence, together with the views a theist typically holds, is much lower than its probability with respect to evidence together with the views the naturalist typically holds. So the way in which evolution is not religiously neutral is not that it is incompatible with Christian teaching; it is rather that it is much more probable with respect to naturalism and the evidence than it is with respect to theism and that evidence. And my point: the Christian community must recognize that there is vastly more to the role played by evolution in contemporary academia than a sort of straightforward science which has the same credentials viewed from any perspective.

A third example from the same area but with a different twist: prominent writers on evolution—for example, Dawkins, Futuyma, Gould, Provine, and Simpson—unite in declaring that evolutionary biology shows that human beings are the result of chance processes and hence have not been designed, by God or anyone else. Thus Simpson:

> Although many details remain to be worked out, it is already evident that all the objective phenomena of the history of life can be explained by purely naturalistic or, in a proper sense of the sometimes abused word, materialistic factors. They are readily explicable on the basis of differential reproduction in populations (the main factor in the modern conception of natural selection) and of the mainly random inter-

play of the known processes of heredity. . . . Man is the result of a purposeless and natural process that did not have him in mind.[16]

These prominent scientists unite in declaring that modern evolutionary thought has shown or given us reason to believe that human beings are in an important way merely accidental; there was not any plan, any foresight, any mind, any mind's eye involved in their coming into being. But of course no Christian theist could take that seriously for a moment. Human beings have been created, and created in the image of God. No doubt God could have created us via evolutionary processes; if he did it that way, however, then he must have guided, orchestrated, directed the processes by which he brought about his designs. We might say, of course, that strictly speaking, when these people make these declarations, they are not speaking as scientists and are not doing science. Perhaps so, perhaps not (it has become increasingly difficult to draw a line between science and other activities); in either case we have deep involvement of the science in question with the spiritual struggle Augustine points out; in either case that involvement must be noted and dealt with by the Christian intellectual community, and in particular by the part of the Christian intellectual community involved in the science in question

Another example. Herbert Simon won a Nobel Prize in economics but is currently professor of computer studies and psychology at Carnegie-Mellon. In a recent article, "A Mechanism for Social Selection and Successful Altruism,"[17] he addresses the topic of altruism: Why, he asks, do people like Mother Teresa, or the Scottish missionary Eric Liddel, or the Little Sisters of the Poor, or the Jesuit missionaries of the seventeenth century, or the Methodist missionaries of the nineteenth—why do these people do the things that they do? Why do they devote their time, and energy, and indeed their entire lives to the welfare of other people? Of course it is not only the great saints of the world who display this impulse; most of us do so to one degree or another. Many of us give money to help feed and clothe people we have never met; we support missionaries in foreign countries; we try, perhaps in feckless and fumbling ways, to do what we can to help the widow and orphan.

Now how, says Simon, can we account for this kind of behavior? The rational way to behave, he says, is to act or try to act in such a way as to increase one's personal fitness, i.e., to act so as to increase the probability that one's genes will be widely disseminated in the next and subsequent generation, thus doing well in the evolutionary derby.[18] (A paradigm of rational behavior, conceived Simon's way, was reported in the *South Bend Tribune* of December 21, 1991, dateline Alexandria, Va.: "Cecil B. Jacobson, an infertility specialist, was accused of using his own sperm to impregnate his patients; he may have fathered as many as seventy-five children, a prosecutor said Friday.") Unlike Jacobson, however, such people as Mother Teresa and Thomas Aquinas cheerfully ignore the short- or long-term fate of their genes; what is the explanation of this bizarre behavior? The answer, says Simon, lies in two mechanisms: "docility" and "bounded rationality":

> Docile persons tend to learn and believe what they perceive others in the society want them to learn and believe. Thus the content of what is learned will not be fully screened for its contribution to personal fitness. (P. 1666)

> Because of bounded rationality, the docile individual will often be unable to distinguish socially prescribed behavior that contributes to fitness from altruistic behavior [i. e., socially prescribed behavior that does not contribute to fitness]. In fact, docility will reduce the inclination to evaluate independently the contributions of behavior to fitness . . . . By virtue of bounded rationality, the docile person cannot acquire the personally advantageous learning that provides the increment, d, of fitness without acquiring also the altruistic behaviors that cost the decrement, c. (P. 1667)

The idea is that a Mother Teresa or a Thomas Aquinas displays "bounded rationality"; they are unable to distinguish socially prescribed behavior that contributes to fitness from altruistic behavior (socially prescribed behavior which does not). As a result they fail to acquire the personally advantageous learning that provides that increment d of fitness without, sadly enough, suffering that decrement c exacted by altruistic behavior. They acquiesce unthinkingly in what society tells them is the right way to behave; and they do not quite have the smarts needed to make their own independent evaluation of the likely bearing of such behavior on the fate of their genes. If they did make such an independent evaluation (and were rational enough to avoid silly mistakes) they would presumably see that this sort of behavior does not contribute to personal fitness, drop it like a hot potato, and get right to work on their expected number of progeny.

Clearly no Christian could accept this account as even a beginning of a viable explanation of the altruistic behavior of the Mother Teresas of this world. From a Christian perspective, this does not even miss the mark; it is not close enough to be a miss. Behaving as Mother Teresa does is not a display of "bounded rationality"—as if, if she thought through the matter with greater clarity and penetration, she would cease this kind of behavior and instead turn her attention to her expected number of progeny. Her behavior displays a Christ-like spirit; she is reflecting in her limited human way the magnificent splendor of Christ's sacrificial action in the atonement. (No doubt she is also laying up treasure in heaven.) Indeed, is there anything a human being can do that is more rational than what she does? From a Christian perspective, the idea that her behavior is irrational (and so irrational that it needs to be explained in terms of such mechanisms as unusual docility and limited rationality!) is hard to take seriously. First, from that perspective, behavior of the sort engaged in by Mother Teresa is anything but a manifestation of "limited rationality." On the contrary: her behavior is vastly more rational than that of someone who, like Cecil Jacobson, devotes his best efforts to seeing to it that his genes are represented *in excelsis* in the next and subsequent generations. And second, the account of rationality—that an action is rational for me if and only if it increases my fitness—is also incompatible with Christian teaching.

Again, someone might say that the sort of thing represented by Simon's article is not really science; but can we sensibly make that claim in these post-Kuhnian days? It gets called *science* by scientists and others; it gets grants from the National Science Foundation; it involves experiments, mathematical models, and the attention, customary in science, to the fit between model and data; it is written in that stiff, impersonal style common to scientific writing; can we sensibly say, then, that it really is not science?

So here we have some examples: each is an example showing that scientific theory and scholarly effort are often not, in the specified ways, religiously or metaphysically neutral. There will of course be many more (and they will be much more obvious and abundant in the humanities and human sciences than in physics and chemistry). Consider, for example, contemporary cognitive science: the area including cognitive psychology, artificial intelligence, and philosophy of mind. This is a whole congeries of research projects (or perhaps one vast research project with many subprojects) dedicated to the attempt to give a naturalistic account of the phenomena of mind: such mental phenomena as consciousness, desire, belief, intentionality, and the like. These research projects have turned up much that is fascinating and useful and informative. But the fundamental quest—the effort to give naturalistic accounts of mental phenomena—is at least questionable from a theistic perspective; the theist will not, of course, feel the need of a naturalistic account of mind. Or consider Jean Piaget (that great Swiss psychologist) and his claim that a seven-year-old child whose cognitive faculties are functioning properly will believe that everything in the universe has a purpose in some grand overarching plan or design; a mature person whose faculties are functioning properly, however, will learn to "think scientifically" and realize that everything has either a natural cause or happens by chance.[19] Or consider the fine-tuning considerations in cosmology: one reason sometimes given for moving to a many universes perspective is that if we do not, we shall be stuck with cosmic coincidence pointing in the direction of intelligent design. Or consider biblical scholarship, surely an area where one would not expect issues of this sort to rear their ugly heads. That expectation, sadly enough, is disappointed. Many Scripture scholars tell us that a properly pursued project in this area must conform to certain standards of *objectivity*; this means that in pursuing such projects, the scholar must bracket or set aside any theological assumption—for example, the traditional Christian idea that the Bible has special divine authority, or is a revelation to humankind from the Lord. Thus, for example, John Collins, recently of Notre Dame: "Critical method is incompatible with confessional faith insofar as the latter requires us to accept specific conclusions on dogmatic grounds."[20] Many more examples could be given—from psychology, sociology of religion, economics—across the length and breadth of the academic disciplines. Scholarship and science are not neutral but are deeply involved in the struggle between Christian theism, perennial naturalism, and creative antirealism. And the unhappy fact is that at present (and in our part of the world) the latter two are in the ascendency. Christian theism has perhaps made some small steps forward in recent years; but it is surely the minority opinion among our colleagues in western universities.

What Should Christians Do?

What must Christians do about this unhappy fact; how ought they to react to it? In many ways, no doubt; but I want to call brief attention to one of these ways. Christians, and especially Christian academics, must become very serious about Christian scholarship. Two kinds in particular are needed. First, we need consciousness raising, Christian cultural criticism. The Christian community as a whole must be aware of the facts I was arguing for above; it must be attuned to them, sensitive to them. We must see that intellectual culture is indeed involved in this contest for basic human allegiance, and that this conflict penetrates deeply into intellectual culture. It is not enough to make the occasional ceremonial reference (at opening convocations, perhaps) to Christian or Catholic intellectual life. We must really understand that there is a battle here, and we must know who and what the main contestants are and how this contest pervades the various scholarly disciplines. These perspectives are seductive; they are widespread; they are the majority views in the universities and in intellectual culture generally in the west. We live in a world dominated by them; we imbibe them with our mother's milk; it is easy to embrace them and their projects in a sort of unthoughtful, un-self-conscious way, just because they do dominate our intellectual culture. But these perspectives are also deeply inimical to Christianity; these ways of thinking distort our views of ourselves and the world. To the degree that we are not aware of them and do not understand their allegiances, they make for confusion and for lack of intellectual and spiritual wholeness and integrity among us Christians. Christians of all sorts, Catholic, Protestant, and Orthodox, must be aware of these things. Indeed, believers in God of all sorts—Christians, Jews, Muslims, and others—must be aware of these things.

And second, we need *Augustinian scholarship;* we must work at the various areas of science and scholarship in a way that is appropriate from a Christian or more broadly theistic point of view. We should not assume, automatically, that it is appropriate for Christians to work at the disciplines in the same way as the rest of the academic world. Take a given area of scholarship: philosophy, let's say, or history, or psychology, or anthropology, or economics, or sociology; in working at these areas, should we not take for granted the Christian answer to the large questions about God and creation and then go on from that perspective to address the narrower questions of that discipline? Or is that somehow illicit or ill advised? Put it another way: To what sort of premises can we properly appeal in working out the answers to the questions raised in a given area of scholarly or scientific inquiry? Can we properly appeal to what we know as Christians? In psychology (which I mention because it is an area in which I am unencumbered by a knowledge of the relevant facts): Must the Christian community accept the basic structure and presuppositions of the contemporary practice of that discipline in trying to come to an understanding of its subject matter? Must Christian psychologists appeal only to premises accepted by all parties to the discussion, whether Christian or not? I should think not. Why should we limit and handicap ourselves in this way?

Consider love, once more, love in all its multitudinous manifestations. When a Christian psychologist addresses this phenomenon, can she properly take into account what she knows as a Christian—that, for example, we are created in God's image, that God himself *is* love, that our loving is something like a reflection of his? Or how shall we understand the sense of beauty we human beings share? We exult in those marvelous, golden, luminous days of autumn or in the glorious beauty of the mountains; Kathleen Battle or a Mozart concerto can bring tears to our eyes. How shall we think about this sensitivity to beauty on our part? How shall we understand this phenomenon? No doubt some will tell us that it arose, somehow, by way of genetic mutation; its significance is to be seen in the fact that it turned out, somehow, to be adaptive, to contribute to fitness, or to be somehow connected with something that was adaptive. But if we take for granted a Christian explanatory background, we might come up with an entirely different view. What we need here is scholarship that takes account of all that we know and thus takes account of what we know as Christians. The same holds for a Christian psychologist attempting to understand aggression and hate in all their forms: she should take account of the reality of sin.

Indeed, the same holds for a thousand different topics and concerns. If we need to understand love, or knowledge, or aggression, or our sense of beauty, or humor, or our moral sense, or our origins, or a thousand other things—if it is important to our intellectual and spiritual health to understand these things, then what we must do, obviously enough, is use all that we know, not just some limited segment of it. Why should we be buffaloed (or cowed) into trying to understand these things from a naturalistic perspective? So the central argument here is simplicity itself: as Christians we need and want answers to the sorts of questions that arise in the theoretical and interpretative disciplines; in an enormous number of such cases, what we know as Christians is crucially relevant to coming to a proper understanding; therefore we Christians should pursue these disciplines from a specifically Christian perspective.

By way of conclusion, then: contemporary scholarship is an arena in which a fundamentally religious conflict is being played out: the struggle is between a theistic perspective, on the one hand, and perennial naturalism and creative antirealism (along with the relativism and anticommitment it spawns) on the other. These last dominate contemporary scholarship; furthermore, they are deeply opposed to the Christian perspective. What the Christian and theistic community needs, therefore, is, first, Christian cultural criticism and, second, Christian scholarship. One of the principal tasks of a Catholic or Christian university, therefore, is the pursuit of Christian cultural criticism and Christian scholarship.

Notes

1. See, for example, George Marsden's contribution to this volume, "What Can Catholic Universities Learn from Protestant Examples?"

2. See in particular Augustine, *The City of God,* book 14, chap. 28.

3. My way of developing them has been influenced by the Dutch Augustinian tradition associated in particular with the work of Abraham Kuyper (the last prime minister who was also a really first-rate theologian). See his *Calvinism: Six Stone Foundation Lectures* (Grand Rapids: Eerdmans, 1943); and his *Encyclopedia of Sacred Theology* (New York: Charles Scribner's Sons, 1898), especially 59–181.

4. See J. J. C. Smart, *Our Place in the Universe* (Oxford: Blackwell, 1989), for a simple and clear statement of a naturalistic view.

5. Gordon Kaufman, *Theology for a Nuclear Age* (Manchester: Manchester University Press, 1985), 43.

6. Here I assume the so-called two-world interpretation of Kant's transcendental idealism; this has traditionally been the dominant interpretation of Kant's thought. More recently, many Kant scholars have tended to a one-world interpretation. I am inclined to think the two-world interpretation is the better; but whatever Kant himself thought, it is the two-world version that has been historically most influential.

7. See Phillip Johnson's "Nihilism and the End of Law," *First Things,* March 1993.

8. Quoted in David Lyle Jeffrey, "*Caveat Lector*: Structuralism, Deconstructionism, and Ideology,"*Christian Scholar's Review,* June 1988.

9. Roland Barthes, *Image-Music Text,* trans. Stephen Heath (New York: Hill and Wang, 1977), 147.

10. Here I leave to one side the teachings of early Genesis, since I am not sure just how those teachings bear on the issue at hand. See my "When Faith and Reason Clash," 21; and "Evolution, Neutrality, and Antecedent Probability," 94; *Christian Scholar's Review,* September 1991.

11. In the 1960s Harold Urey showed that amino acids could arise under what may have been the conditions of earth before life; this generated a sizable, but temporary, burst of dithyrambic optimism. The optimism dissipated when the enormous distance between amino acids and the simplest forms of life sank in and when there was little or no progress in showing how that distance could have been traversed.

12. Evolution, says Francisco J. Ayala, is as certain as "the roundness of the earth, the motions of the planets, and the molecular constitution of matter" ("The Theory of Evolution: Recent Successes and Challenges," in *Evolution and Creation,* ed. Ernan McMullin [Notre Dame: University of Notre Dame Press, 1985], 60). According to Stephen J. Gould, evolution is an established fact, not a mere theory; and no sensible person who was acquainted with the evidence could demur ("Evolution as Fact and Theory," in *Hen's Teeth and Horse's Toes* [New York: W. W. Norton, 1980], 254–55). According to Richard Dawkins, the theory of evolution is as certainly true as that the earth goes around the sun. This astronomical comparison apparently suggests itself to many; in "Evolutionary Biology and the Study of Human Nature" (presented at a Consultation on Cosmology and Theology Sponsored by the Presbyterian (U.S.A.) Church in December 1987), Philip Spieth claims that "a century and a quarter after the publication of *The Origin of Species,* biologists can say with confidence that universal genealogical relatedness is a conclusion of science that is as

firmly established as the revolution of the earth about the sun." And Michael Ruse adds his nuanced and modulated view that "evolution is Fact, Fact, Fact!"

13. And of course part of the evidence, for a Christian, will be the biblical evidence. I myself think that the biblical evidence for a special creation of human beings is fairly strong.

14. Of course it is possible both that God both did something special in creating human beings *and* that they are genealogically related to the rest of the living world.

15. Richard Dawkins, *The Blind Watchmaker* (New York: W. W. Norton, 1986), 6–7.

16. George Gaylord Simpson, *The Meaning of Evolution,* rev. ed. (1967), 344–45.

17. Herbert Simon, "A Mechanism for Social Selection and Successful Altruism," *Science* 250 (December 1990): 1665 ff.

18. More simply, says Simon, "Fitness simply means expected number of progeny" ("Mechanisms," 1665). That this is the rational way to conduct one's life is somehow seen as a consequence of evolutionary theory. But even if evolutionary theory is in fact true, does this alleged consequence really follow? Perhaps my having lots of progeny is in some way best for my genes; but why should I be especially interested in that? Couldn't I sensibly be concerned with *my* welfare, not theirs?

19. Jean Piaget, *The Child's Conception of Physical Causality* (London: Kegan Paul, 1930).

20. See John Collins, "Is Critical Biblical Theology Possible?" in *The Hebrew Bible and Its Interpreters*, ed. William Henry Propp, Baruch Halpern, and David Freedman (Winona Lake, Ind.: Eisenbrauns, 1990), 1 ff.

Thirty-two Years at Notre Dame

MORRIS POLLARD

In August of 1961, my family and I came to Notre Dame with mixed feelings of concern and optimism. I had resigned from the University of Texas where I was a tenured professor and was moving to this university as an untenured professor of biology, since tenure for newcomers was deferred for one year. I was moving from twenty years in Texas with its more moderate weather than could be expected in northern Indiana. I was moving from a secular university with huge resources to a Church-related university. I was concerned about real and hypothetical problems related to this move. The fact that I have been at Notre Dame for thirty-two years will indicate that my anxieties were for the most part unfounded.

My first winter was tough. I had forgotten the hard winters growing up in my youth on a dairy farm in upper New York State. In South Bend I was reluctant to drive my car from home to the university if there was a thin cover of snow on the road. It was occasionally necessary to chop ice from the tires in order to free them from the pavement. The challenges of winter were learning experiences for me and my family. However, the excitement of the spring awakening from the slumber of winter and the flamboyant colors of the fall foliage compensated for the discomforts of winter. Now, I drive in all extremes of weather and consider the problems normal.

I was given tenure on schedule. The excitement of participating in the germfree program which was initiated at Notre Dame by Professor Arthur Reyniers and associates was difficult to control, since this discipline opened doors to many biomedical projects which could not be implemented otherwise; and we were impatient to get started. This was the LOBUND program, an acronym for Laboratory of Bacteriology University of Notre Dame. The technology was ready for examples to determine if viruses were universal causes of cancer, if bone marrow transplantation would be a practical procedure for prevention and treatment of leukemia and Hodgkin's disease, if aspirin-like drugs had a role in preventing colon cancer, if prostate cancer could be prevented, and if metastatic spread of cancer cells could be prevented. The results were positive. Realistically, while these projects required the use of germfree animals in sufficient numbers, Lobund's multidisciplinary support staff had an essential role in the results. I would have failed without the dedicated staff of experts: they included Philip Trexler, Bernard Teah, Bernard Wostmann, Morris Wagner, Julian Pleasants, Erwin Zelmer, and many others. The collaborative efforts of Phyllis Luckert, for over thirty years, were very important to the implementation of my research projects. In general, it was, and is, a very good and exciting experience in which the university administration has been very supportive and encouraging.

When I arrived here, the Lobund Institute (as it was known) was part of the Department of Biology. The highly visible and active research and development program in Lobund had attracted considerable funding from national organizations, which permitted a reduced teaching load for the Lobund-affiliated faculty members. It was thus understandable that some members of the department were envious and actually antagonistic to the entire Lobund operation. In response to such a "problem," the university created a graduate-level Department of Microbiology with responsibilities for teaching and research. I served as chair of the new department from 1966 to 1981. After I was awarded emeritus status, the microbiology department was absorbed into the newly designated Department of Biological Sciences. Meanwhile, the Reyniers Germfree Life Building had been expanded to accommodate the growing germfree research and a new building for research laboratories was constructed with funds from the National Science Foundation and from the university. Visiting scientists came to Notre Dame from all over the world to learn and to use the germfree technology which had been developed here. As an emeritus professor, I was obliged to retire under the existing rules. However, as director of a university institute, I was permitted to continue working full time, and this was helped by the establishment by the Coleman Foundation of Chicago of an endowed professorship in cancer research for the director of the laboratory.

The scientific program was a source of great satisfaction to me and to my colleagues. But what was the social and academic environment which my family and I experienced? It was clear to me that Notre Dame was an important educational center with roots in Catholic doctrine. However, it was different from its counterparts in Europe which, to great extent, lost their original religious character. Notre Dame is a Catholic university which reflects the diversity of New World thought in that I found here faculty members, staff, and students who were Catholic, Protestant, Hindu, Moslem, and Jewish. People came to Notre Dame from North and South America, Europe, Asia, and Africa. I had entered a multicultural university which was both comfortable and exciting without losing sight of its Catholic character.

Many events influenced my sense of being a part of this university. Some I mention here:

1. Soon after my arrival on campus, I was told of a nasty verbal attack on a Jewish student by his roommates who told him that he was not wanted at Notre Dame and that he should leave. He left prior to the Christmas holiday. When Father Hesburgh heard of this, he asked the roommates if that event were true, and they admitted their guilt. They were expelled from the university; however, if they wished to return to school after the holiday, Father Hesburgh advised that they should bring the Jewish student with them—which they did. That lesson on tolerance and forgiveness will not be forgotten by those students, or by me.

2. After getting settled at Notre Dame, I was visited by Gustav Stern, a long-time friend, an art collector, the president of the Hartz Mountain Corporation in New York City. After visiting the art gallery in O'Shaughnessy Hall, Stern determined that Notre Dame needed help; and he transferred, on long-term loan, paintings by eighteen important impressionists plus two world-class paintings: *Le Miroir* by Picasso and *Le Grand Cirque* by Marc Chagall. Then Stern

asked if he could invite his friend Marc Chagall to visit our campus for conferences with students and staff. Chagall was awarded an honorary degree, and I was elected to translate his comments from French to English, an assignment for which I was moderately prepared. After receiving the honorary degree, Chagall revealed the European view of a Catholic university by asking me if his friends would think that he had converted. Chagall's visit was a significant transition in the development of the art center on this campus. The collection of paintings provided by Stern contributed indirectly to the construction of the Snite Museum. His paintings were stored in the basement vault due to lack of space in the old gallery. I was told that Mr. Snite was upset that our students were deprived of the benefits of the Stern collection and other paintings, and that this influenced his gift to the university for construction of the museum. During the years, it has been a joy to be associated with Father Anthony Lauck and Dean Porter. *The Grand Cirque* has been a major exhibit here for twenty-nine years.

Because of these events, some of our art faculty had the mistaken impression that I was an art connoisseur. I eventually revealed my limited knowledge by announcing that an abstract painting under consideration for purchase must have been the product of an amateur, not knowing that the artist was standing behind. My reputation as an art connoisseur was demolished.

3. I had a minor role as a volunteer in fund raising for the university. It involved discussions of our cancer programs and other activities on campus with alumni who were flown here over weekends by the Flying Tiger organization. The subjects of leukemia, colon cancer, and prostate cancer were subjects of personal interest to our visitors. During one luncheon session, an alumnus asked me if I was Catholic. When I told him that I was Jewish, he responded, "Why are you working so hard for this university?" This caught me by surprise. I answered, "This is a great university and if you provide support, it would be even greater." He contributed generously, with a twinkle in his eye. Evidently, the program had been successful. The pride of our alumni and friends in Notre Dame was contagious. In this respect my personal commitment to Notre Dame was and is consistent with my role as a faculty member, and I am sure that others feel the same way.

4. Notre Dame was a school for men, although my first graduate

student here was Sister Elizabeth Anne Sueltenfuss, now president of Our Lady of the Lake University in San Antonio. In casual conversation with the dean of the graduate school, I was told that any woman who applied for admission to the graduate school to study a subject not available elsewhere would be admitted. A woman with a very high academic record from the University of Chicago applied for a job, then for admission, in order to study germfree technology, a subject not available anywhere but here. She was admitted with the statement by the dean that this was bad for the university. Dr. Jeannine Majde completed the program and is now one of the leaders in the U.S. Office of Naval Research. Thereafter, many women registered and completed the curricula in the graduate school, with credit to the university. It was the right action.

5. I was the first exchange professor from Notre Dame to the Katholieke Universiteit Leuven, in Belgium. We were welcomed most graciously by the rector, Pietr de Somer, a long-time friend who knew that I was Jewish. At a banquet in his home, he introduced me to his administrators with the following statement: "I welcome the first exchange professor from the most prestigious Catholic university in America to the oldest Catholic university in Europe. That Morris Pollard was sent here is most appropriate." That visit was kind, gentle, instructive, comfortable, and soothing to the soul. That was a unique privilege given to me by Notre Dame.

6. About ten years ago, a friend of mine and of Notre Dame, Alfred Roach, chairman of the board of Telecommunications Industries, Inc., came to me with a proposal. He wanted to bring a new discipline (biotechnology) to this campus through a joint venture with Notre Dame. He offered $250,000 for that purpose; and not knowing what I know now, I thought it worth considering. We consulted with Father Hesburgh who was fascinated by that idea; and after consultation with members of the administration, a joint venture was drawn up whereby Notre Dame would share the earnings from that program. Thus, American Biogenetic Sciences, Inc. (ABSI), with quarters in the Reyniers Building, started with recruited scientists and technicians and Emeritus Professor Julian Pleasants. A new colony of germfree mice, maintained on an antigen-free diet, was developed. They produced unique monoclonal antibodies which were used to detect blood clots in the lungs, heart, and peripheral blood vessels in the remarkably short

time of thirty minutes. Antibodies were produced by the germfree mice which would predict a heart attack, and others which could diagnose an ongoing heart attack. All of these agents are now under clinical test at Johns Hopkins Hospital and at Yale Medical School. Also, a new, effective biosynthetic vaccine for infectious hepatitis was developed, which has been licensed for commercial development to the Medeva Company in England. Eventually Mr. Roach's contribution to the joint venture was $4.5 million. When the products of the joint venture have been commercialized through licensing to industrial companies, they should bring considerable income to Notre Dame. ABSI has now gone public and is in the process of constructing a new laboratory building in the Center for Senior Living, a research park near this campus. It has a solid future which will be remembered as a unique project at Notre Dame.

7. Now I will write of a more personal matter. From my early days here, I was witness not only to the responses of the "Notre Dame Family" to the joys of colleagues but also, more significantly, to their tragedies, as exemplified by a young Indian scientist who lost his wife through cancer. A delegation of faculty wives took care of his children and the running of the household until he recovered from that shocking experience. A faculty member suffered a stroke in Florida: the university brought him home by private jet. Students were killed in an accident: members of the faculty visited the homes of the students to console their families. An employee needed an immediate blood transfusion: blood donors came from all segments of the Notre Dame family. When tragedy strikes, this family does respond.

Our son, Jonathan, was arrested and sentenced to life in prison for transmitting classified information to Israel regarding the development of chemical weapons in Iraq which were aimed at Israel, and later at our troops in the Gulf War. His action was legally wrong, but it was interpreted by some as morally right. We received letters from 150 members of our faculty in which they expressed concern and support for our well-being. Father Hesburgh embraced me with expressions of strength and confidence and promised to help whenever and wherever possible. He has helped substantially. Father Hesburgh is a role model for me and for many others on campus. He is a person of vision for whom I have great respect and pride. It was a frequent experience while walking on campus to feel an arm over my shoulder and hear the words, "We are praying for him." We continue to receive words of hope from faculty and staff, from post office clerks, from the waitresses in Morris Inn, the security personnel, and grounds people. Two faculty members in the Law School (Charles Rice and Joseph Bauer) initiated an eloquent *amicus curiae* in preparation for the brief to the court of appeals, which stated that "our government does not have the right to promise what it knows it will not deliver." I doubt that we would have retained our sanity over this troubling experience if we had been elsewhere. If support from the Notre Dame family means anything, we have received a full measure of attention and love for which we cannot find the words to express our feelings adequately. Can the extent of our commitment to Notre Dame be understood from this?

When people ask if I am part of the Notre Dame community, I am happy to say, "Yes." I am part of the community, without compromising my Jewish heritage. This is a unique situation. I feel more content and at home as a Jew at Notre Dame than in the secular University of Texas.

I have written here some sketches of my experiences during thirty-two years at Notre Dame. I have been here for half of my scientific career, and whatever I have done I identify with Notre Dame history. I hope that my words express adequately my pleasure in being part of this place. We find here that love, friendship, tolerance, and understanding involve hands that are extended to ours and ours to theirs. Many of us are impressed by the Notre Dame mystique, and a few of us strive to be part of it.

I endorse the words of Rabbi David Rosen, who during his years as Chief Rabbi of Ireland first became aware of the warmth, depth, and beauty of traditional Catholicism. For my family and me, those sentiments apply to Notre Dame—a very special place.

Catholic Universities and the New Pluralism

ROBERT E. RODES, JR.

Catholic universities naturally have to be understood in the light of their place in the ongoing dialogue between the church and the world whose redemption the church proclaims and strives to implement. And to understand that dialogue, we must have some understanding of the world as we encounter it in particular times and places. The world in which the Catholic universities of today were founded is the one that grew up after the fratricidal battles brought on by the Reformation and the breakup of the medieval synthesis had petered out into weariness and stalemate.

I will call that world *Grotian,* after the scholar who did the most to lay its intellectual foundations on the ruins of the former synthesis. Huig de Groot (1583–1645), a Dutchman, better known by his Latin name, Hugo Grotius, is recognized as the father of modern international law, because he developed a way for nation-states to live together despite their religious differences. Whether because of his influence or because other people were thinking along similar lines, his approach to differences between nations became the model for dealing with differences between groups within particular nations.

What Grotius did was seek out and articulate common ground. He found such ground in the classical heritage that both Catholic and Protestant scholars were in the process of recovering and assimilat-

305

ing, in the philosophical principles of natural law, and in those Christian values that both Catholics and Protestants retained. This common ground was not enough to provide the religious and political unity for which Grotius continued to hope. But it was enough to form the basis for an orderly pluralist society and a coherent pluralist intellectual life—that is, for what we have called western civilization ever since.

In the Grotian world, there is a common core of generally accepted principles, values, and methodologies. Within this common core, particular factions, whether religious, philosophical, or political, are set apart by specific distinguishing characteristics—Quakers will not take oaths or fight wars; Jews keep their shops closed on Saturdays; Methodists oppose drinking. The core forms the basis for a modus vivendi in which the distinguishing characteristics of the different constituencies are known and allowed for with a minimum of friction. This pattern of common core and specific distinguishing characteristics not only accommodated Catholics and Protestants after the Reformation; it incorporated without serious disruption most of the new intellectual movements set in motion by the Enlightenment in the eighteenth century and the expansion of science in the nineteenth.

Until quite recently, the common American version of a pluralist society accorded fully with this Grotian pattern. When Tocqueville said in 1840 that American clergymen do not go against public opinion unless the tenets of their faith require them to do so; when Herberg said in 1955 that being Protestant, being Catholic, and being Jewish are commonly regarded as alternative ways of being American; when Murray argued in 1960 that being a secular humanist should be regarded as a fourth way: all were invoking a broad pluralist consensus whose adherents differed from one another only with regard to specific distinguishing characteristics.

Until the upheavals of the 1960s, American Catholic universities were as firmly Grotian as the society around them. The most important distinguishing marks related to personal conduct. Few campuses were as permissive then as most are now, but Catholic campuses were generally less permissive than others. Mass attendance was often required, or at least heavily encouraged. On the academic side, there were requirements in theology (*religion,* as it was then called) and philosophy that other universities did not impose. There were also certain Catholic buttons that were pressed from time to time in certain departments (in my field, law, they were abortion, birth control, divorce, pornography, and the status of parochial schools). Otherwise, Catholic universities were doing and teaching about the same things as other American universities.

I am not sure when the academic upgrading of Catholic universities became a major agenda item; it was in full swing when I first came to Notre Dame in 1956. The aspiration was commonly stated in Grotian terms: a great Catholic university must first be a great university. It must do greatly what all universities do, and must still possess the distinguishing characteristics that make it Catholic. As the implementation progressed, the distinguishing characteristics were affected as well. Student life, liturgy, philosophy, theology, and other concerns specific to particular departments were all drastically altered. But the articulation in terms of common core and specific distinctions remained. When we ask today how a great university can preserve its Catholic character, we are still putting the question in Grotian terms.

I believe it is time to find a new way of putting it. With the expansion of pluralism in recent decades, we have finally reached a point where the Grotian approach is no longer viable. The common core has become by now too attenuated, too secularized, and too trivial to define the relations among the different constituencies in society. Catholics today are challenged not merely on discrete points of doctrine or practice but on what is most fundamental to a Christian vision of human beings and their affairs. Business executives are adopting technologies and capital shifts that displace workers and give them only bread and circuses in return. Serious economists are telling us that we must put up with the poverty and marginalization of some segments of our people so that the rest may prosper. Social commentators tell us that we have either no right or no power to prevent the erosion of the family or the trivialization of sex. Critics applaud the extrusion of significance from literature and of beauty from the arts. With all these forces at work around us, we now have to think of reaching across differences rather than resting on common ground.

In meeting the challenge before us, we cannot expect to take our lead from the pluralist academic enterprise around us, because by and large that enterprise has no lead to give us. Too often, its commitment to generous tolerance in support of free inquiry has been deflected into mindless eclecticism in support of no inquiry at all. The intellectual waifs and strays that it keeps letting in out of the cold keep making bids to take possession of the house. As a group, those in control of the enterprise cannot lead an intellectual journey because they cannot agree on the starting point or the destination and are suspicious of anyone who displays too much conviction regarding either. They cannot lead a pursuit of truth because they are not sure there is any truth to pursue, and they tend to marginalize anyone who claims to have caught up with some. I do not mean by this to belittle the importance of the pluralist universities in which our colleagues serve. These institutions have portions of a proud tradition still in place, and great ideas and noble causes continue to find shelter on their campuses. We can admire them, support them, work with them, and learn from them. But we cannot allow them to set our agenda for us.

Nor, indeed, can we let them set the agenda for society in general. We are called as Christians not merely to survive in the world but to help redeem it. Whatever is redemptive in our intellectual heritage we must hold and proclaim whether or not it is specifically Christian, and whether or not our colleagues elsewhere support it. Even if a time should come like that envisaged by Chesterton in *The Ballad of the White Horse* when only Christians guard even heathen things, guarding them would still be a part of our calling.

The redemptive task of Catholics in a world no longer dominated by a Grotian core was set forth with prescience by the Second Vatican Council in *Gaudium et Spes*, its Pastoral Constitution on the Church in the Modern World. That document makes three points that seem to me crucial for the orientation of today's Catholic universities:

1. Human beings, Christian and non-Christian alike, are embarked on a common spiritual journey to which the church stands witness. At the consummation of history, everything good in human experience will find its place in the kingdom of God. That kingdom is "already present in mystery," and the church is to express it to the world (nos. 1, 39).
2. In the political and social order, the church is a sign and a safeguard of the transcendence of the human person. In every state of

society, therefore, Christians are called to challenge the forces by which that transcendence is belied (no. 76). In more recent documents, this calling has been articulated in terms of a *preferential option for the poor,* a term that assigns priority of concern to the victims of economic deprivation but that can be extended by analogy to other people whose circumstances place them at the margins of society.

3. To fulfill their calling effectively, the church and individual Christians are to study the world carefully (nos. 43, 44) and to read the signs of the times (no. 4).

The role of Catholic universities in implementing these principles seems fairly clear. We are to teach our students to participate fully in the world around them and to make their participation a sign and safeguard of human transcendence. We are to show them how to recognize conditions that drive people to the margins of society and do whatever they can to make them better. Our scholarship is to bear the same witness as our teaching. To support it, we are to study the world, deploying for the purpose the best methodologies our several disciplines afford.

The task will require of us courage and cheerful trust as well as learning and skill. Some of the investigations it calls for will yield answers we would prefer not to hear. We will find that the most serious challenges to human transcendence that we encounter are intrinsic to a complex and cohesive world order in which we ourselves are inextricably complicit. We are living in comfort and prosperity on the flip side of other people's misery and degradation. The economic, social, political, and cultural structures that fund our research, publish our books and papers, put us up in nice hotels while we read them to each other, and provide our graduates with interesting and remunerative jobs are the same ones that imprison our poor people in a world of hamburger flipping, teenage pregnancy, drive-by shootings, and crack, and inveigle many of our rich people into a world of gilded banality punctuated by alcoholism and casual sex.

For all its breadth and sophistication, our academic enterprise can show us no way out of this situation. It is easy, therefore, and all too comfortable when we are confronted with it, to respond by pinning exaggerated hopes on minor improvements, by retreating into enclosed academic gardens that we can tend without engaging the larger issues, or by adopting a jejeune nihilism and calling it reality. We need to do better than that. Our calling is to further the kingdom of God, and we are assured of the final consummation of our efforts to do so. Because the kingdom is now present in mystery, the work of furthering it is mysterious work. We cannot limit our aspirations to what our methodologies tell us is possible. If the church is to be a sign and safeguard of transcendence, then when we cannot be a safeguard, we must still be a sign.

This is an eschatological vision. The church's mission in the present world is one of service, with particular focus on serving people at the margins of society, victims of poverty and oppression, people whose transcendence is belied by their condition, i.e., with a preferential option for the poor. The mission of the Catholic university is to provide an intellectual foundation for the mission of the church. Short of the final consummation of history, we cannot be sure where this will lead us. But it seems likely that it will eventually bring down many of the economic, social, and cultural structures on which we now depend for the abundant material and psychic rewards of the academic life. The price may not be exacted of us today or tomorrow, but if we are to do our job with honesty and commitment, we must be prepared to pay it.

At this point we encounter the hard practical questions. What do our theories tell us about hiring, promotions, admissions, funding of research? These are the questions whose answers will determine whether we are true to our calling, whether we live up to our rhetoric, and whether we deal honestly and respectfully with all the different constituencies, Catholic and non-Catholic, that are affected by what we do. Most such questions will be different for different disciplines. A few, though, will be applicable across the board:

1. Do we support our Catholic character by filling faculty positions with Catholics regardless of the direction taken by their teaching and scholarship, or do we look for people of whatever persuasion whose teaching and scholarship support the transcendence of the human person and the intellectual mission of the church?

2. In addition to imparting the usual academic skills to our students, we encourage them to be honest, loyal, decent, docile, and well spoken. They are therefore a good deal in demand in the business world. Do we encourage them to look critically from the vantage

points provided them, see what effect their employers and associates are having at the margins of society, and ameliorate that effect as far as they can?

3. In our tenure and promotion decisions, do we support the kind of intellectual enterprise we profess to desire, or do we rely on forms of peer review that look only at a candidate's achievements within some hermetic field of inquiry that excludes important aspects of the human and the real?

4. Do our teaching and research priorities reflect a preferential option for the poor, a concern for the margins of society? Or do we go with the courses that impress the biggest employers and the most important graduate schools, and with the research topics that attract support from the wealthiest foundations and publication in the most prestigious journals? Do we encourage dependence on outside funding to the point of letting outsiders control our research agendas? To the point of exercising a preferential option for the rich?

What we have to worry about with all these questions is not so much deliberate selling out as hanging onto Grotian approaches that no longer work. As long as we had a distinct list of things that set us apart, we could participate comfortably in the mainstream and follow its leaders regarding anything that did not appear on the list. But the lines of distinction are now very different. Our call to support transcendence and to pay special attention to the people at the margins of society does not set us apart from non-Catholics as such—far from it. But it does set us apart from much that is being done by those who run our society. We have accordingly both a new problem and a new opportunity. A new problem because we no longer have an extensive and well-defined set of concerns on which we can safely follow the mainstream. A new opportunity because if we are faithful to our calling, we will not have to follow the mainstream. We can lead.

What Is Catholic about a
Catholic University?

Timothy R. Scully, C.S.C.

Though I have been involved in one way or another with Catholic education most of my life, what has struck me about my experience with Catholic higher education since joining the Notre Dame
faculty in 1989 has been the considerable degree of confusion surrounding the idea and purpose of a contemporary Catholic university. At first, I found this confusion quite troubling, even somewhat
threatening. After all, as a member of Notre Dame's founding religious community, the Congregation of Holy Cross, I felt I owed it to
my colleagues and friends to offer cogent and persuasive responses
to tough-minded questions about the specifically intellectual implications of our faith. Yet, when I gave serious thought, for example,
to the intellectual difference my Catholic convictions make for the
pursuit of truth in the many different fields and disciplines that
make up a university community, I would inevitably find myself
engaged in a delicate exercise of balancing multiple and competing
ideas and images.

Puzzling through different aspects of these questions, I thus discovered the multiple dimensions of the problem to be at once exciting and frustrating. I took considerable solace in the fact that some
of my most distinguished and thoughtful colleagues were thinking
and worrying about the same problems. I was greatly comforted, for

313

instance, to find the likes of Alasdair MacIntyre and Alvin Plantinga in the philosophy department each wrestling in his research and writing with the relationship between faith and what we call knowledge. If MacIntyre, Plantinga, and many other worthy colleagues had not yet succeeded in dissecting this problem, I thought, then my own struggle to achieve a more clear-cut and forceful vision of the Catholic university was perhaps understandable. In fact, it was the discovery of these common questions among a number of us that led to the formation at Notre Dame of the "Conversation on the Catholic Character," an open group of scores of faculty members drawn from all five colleges of the university who have gathered regularly at Notre Dame since the fall of 1992 to deepen our collective understanding of the challenges posed by a Catholic university.

Drawing on insights gained from this ongoing conversation, I seek in this brief essay to explore several dimensions of what might be implied by the qualifier *Catholic* when we speak of a *Catholic university.* I wish to focus on only one side of this dual reality, on the term *Catholic,* because one of the greatest frustrations I have experienced in conversations surrounding the Catholic university stems from implicitly divergent, and sometimes incompatible, underlying ecclesiologies implicit in the debate. My assumption here is that most everyone who forms part of the university community, faculty and students, alumni and staff, be they Catholic or not, all bring to their involvements within the university guiding images about the church that shape relationships and expectations in the university. These provide cognitive maps for navigating transactions within the university community. Though often unarticulated, these images of the church, forged over a lifetime of (both positive and negative) experiences, lend powerful form, color, and texture to how members of the university community view and interpret their experiences and involvements. Different images of the church, of what the church is, and of what the church ought to be, shape our understanding and give meaning to the activities which we have undertaken. When these implicit images are violated in our experience, a feeling of betrayal can result.

My claim is that when we engage in discussion, and sometimes argument, about Notre Dame as a Catholic university, we invariably bring to the conversation competing and dearly held operative ecclesiologies. Drawing out differences in underlying assumptions about the church will not necessarily bring about agreement regarding the nature and purpose of the Catholic university, but it might help us better understand why we disagree, and where. Fewer ships passing in the night; alas, perhaps more in broad daylight.

I shall elucidate three approaches to the church that I find operative in discussions about the contemporary Catholic university as servant to the church and the world; as a community of witness; and in terms of the university's relationship to the institutional church.[1] A brief overview of these three approaches, or images, will, I hope, point out differences that are consequential for our understanding of the nature and mission of the Catholic university. I do not seek to persuade that the three perspectives are either the only ones or somehow the correct ones. Quite the contrary. A central goal of this exercise is to suggest that no single perspective can exhaust the mystery of the church.

I wish to argue that, if we are to gain a fuller understanding of the proper vocation of a Catholic university, we must learn to work simultaneously with several different ecclesial dimensions. For, in the end, a most distinctive feature of the Catholic university may be the way multiple and competing dimensions of the mystery of the church are embodied. Whether we like it or not (and I suspect some may not like it at all), the challenge of building a Catholic university is an extremely complex and interactive process which involves something of a juggling act. Those collaborating in the exercise must learn to handle simultaneously multiple and competing ideas and images and still retain the ability to function.[2] Indeed, to flourish.

A Catholic university is nothing if it is not the fruit of the continuous work of the Holy Spirit in the lives of those who constitute it. Ultimately, those whom the Spirit calls to pursue this work will freely explore the multiple dimensions of what it means to build a Catholic university ever in pursuit of fuller and more complete knowledge. We have never to fear our differences; the plurality of backgrounds, experiences, and perspectives we bring enrich our efforts. The very nature of the questions that drive our enterprise suggests that a plurality of underlying ecclesiologies and views is, in fact, a precondition for a Catholic university.

The Catholic University at the Service
of the Church and the World

How we each come to appropriate a given set of ecclesiologies as our own is a lifelong process framed in mystery. It is a consequence of intensely personal—sometimes painful, sometimes joyful—cumulative experiences of the church and the world and, even more importantly, of how we have experienced the presence of the risen Lord in our lives. What we experience in a Catholic university is very much related to our own life journeys. My own path, mediated by the contemporary experience of the Congregation of Holy Cross, has led me to see and experience the Lord as servant. Consequently, one important dimension of my own operative ecclesiology focuses on the invitation to discipleship in the context of a Catholic university as an invitation to service to the church and the world.

Again, let me emphasize that I do not wish to make a case for the superiority of an approach that focuses on Christian service over, let us say, the sacramental work of the church. Or the church's obligation to preach the gospel faithfully. Nor do I wish to claim that working for justice and peace, or a values-centered education per se, is what makes Catholic higher education distinctive. In fact, this dimension of the identity and mission of the Catholic university is held most easily in common with our more secular counterparts in American higher education. Indeed, in part because of this, some of the tensions implicit in building a Catholic university are perhaps more easily conciliated by this approach. I am only suggesting that the way grace has entered my own life, and the life of the Congregation of Holy Cross, over the past several decades has led me to view a vocation to service as lying at the heart of the call to discipleship. Therefore, from this perspective, a crucially important dimension of a Catholic university calls forcefully for a commitment to service to the church and society.

Allow me to share a bit of personal history. I learned to be a priest of Holy Cross in a privileged context. After completing my graduate studies in theology in 1979, I was sent to live and work for four years in the apostolates of the congregation in Santiago, Chile. The Chile of General Pinochet. It was a time when the Catholic church in Chile, and the Congregation of Holy Cross, had to redefine itself and its mission continually in the face of systematic violations of human rights by a military regime. Over the course of the regime's seventeen-year history, the church became the only institution willing or able to stand up consistently and unambiguously for the intrinsic dignity of the human person. It did so with courage and strength, and during these years my love for the church deepened. This church became a church of solidarity. During my years in Santiago, the central parable of the gospel ethic, the story of the Good Samaritan, wherein Jesus gave fresh meaning to the commandment to love, took on meaning in a way that I had never before experienced. The boundaries of membership of the church seemed to matter less than a shared belief in human dignity and a commitment to join efforts on behalf of those who suffered. The central motifs of Christian existence, the reality of the cross and the power of the resurrection, took fresh form.

The Congregation of Holy Cross, taking its inspiration from Scripture and church teaching, as well as from its own pastoral experience, has called for all of our work "to reach out to the afflicted and in a preferential way to the poor and the oppressed."[3] Those of us who work as "educators in the faith" in the apostolate of Catholic higher education seek to contribute to the reign of God—a reign of justice, communion, and peace—by dedicating our lives to a search for truth about the world and the place of the human person within the world. As educators we seek to communicate that truth to others. Sometimes, both as individuals and as a religious community, we fail to live up to the ideals we profess. This can lead to cynicism about the congregation and doubts about our sincerity. But we cannot allow our failures to proscribe our purpose. We seek to live in such a way as to educate young people to bear the burden of truthfulness in a world of ambiguity and hypocrisy.[4]

The Catholic university seeks to be of service to the church. Thus, it is sometimes said that the Catholic university is a place "where the church does its thinking." The church has charged the university to educate members of the Catholic community in the values and traditions of the faith. The Catholic university seeks to develop critical intelligence among (though not exclusively among) its own members. Because of the nature of its own mission, the church must develop members within the Catholic community who are unafraid to search for the truth. It seeks to develop people who, with Saint Thomas Aquinas, live by the claim that "all truth, whoever utters it, is from the Holy Spirit."[5]

But the Catholic university does not seek only to serve the needs of the Catholic community. According to this diaconal ecclesiology, the Catholic university regards the world as an appropriate locus of both anthropological and theological reflection and action. It takes, for example, the plight of the roughly two-thirds of the world's population that lives in conditions of poverty and oppression as a relevant datum for the type of education it seeks to offer. The Catholic university promotes a critical understanding of the world, aiming to challenge all that dehumanizes God's children.

Though this mission of service to the world is surely shared by many universities, the vocation of the Catholic university is grounded philosophically and theologically in a distinctive and compelling way. As the bishops have put it, "Action on behalf of justice and participation in the transformation of the world fully appears to us as a constitutive dimension of the preaching of the Gospel, or, in other words, of the church's mission for the redemption of the human race and its liberation from every oppressive situation."[6] At Notre Dame, we seek to deepen our understanding of the human condition both in the classroom and outside of it, and to develop "a disciplined sensibility to oppression, poverty, and alienation."[7] We do so not just in the hope of better understanding the world but also striving to enable our students and ourselves to develop the creativity and imagination to envision new ways to transform it.

I do not wish to assert that the mission of the Catholic university is coterminous with the mission of the church. The Catholic university qua university is not in the business of holding out salvation. But it is ultimately in service to the kingdom that the Catholic university develops people of critical intelligence and in so doing participates in the evangelizing mission of the church.

If it is true that universities differ "according to the questions to which they give priority and the knowledge they think most worth having,"[8] then the teaching and research of Catholic universities will be characterized by questions that get at the heart of the contemporary human condition. This implies that Catholic universities will risk to be different. Let me emphasize: not different in terms of the professional exigencies characteristic of each discipline. Here, we must strive for excellence. But rather, different in terms of the questions we are willing to ask and the resources we are willing to place at the service of their unbridled pursuit.

The mission of service to the world is, above all, service to the truth. Constitutive to this mission, the Catholic university seeks to deepen our understanding of the tools God gave humankind to be responsible stewards of all creation. Scientific invention and discovery, artistic creativity, advances in the humanities are all essential activities to the vocation of service of the Catholic university. The university is Catholic precisely because it "provides a forum where through free inquiry and open discussion the various lines of Catholic thought may intersect with all the forms of knowledge found in the arts, sciences, professions, and every other area of human scholarship and creativity."[9]

The Catholic university has a special vocation, grounded in faith, to develop the kind of critical intelligence necessary for effective service to the world. In imitation of Jesus, the "man for others," the Catholic university seeks to be an intellectual "community for others." Like any institution in this world, the Catholic university is a place of sin as well as grace, and its members will not always pursue this vocation for service with integrity. Even so, to aim for anything less than full integrity in this mission would be to fail the test of faith.

The Catholic University as a Community of Witness

The Catholic university as a community of witness places Christ at the center of the university. The university thus consists of a fellowship of disciples, many of whom, to use the words of John Paul II, "in very different ways—at times very consciously and consistently, at other times not very consciously or very consistently—are following Christ."[10] An advantage of this viewpoint is that disciples are, by definition, still learning, continually struggling to understand life's most puzzling mysteries. No one is anything but a follower and a learner in relation to Jesus. Disciples are companions on the journey who have not yet arrived. Discipleship is a dynamic, while at the same time slightly precarious, relationship. Thus, the Catholic university should be understood as a process of continually striving to become rather than a condition which is achieved.

The university as community of disciples suggests that, beyond our expertise in each area of specialized competence, the quality of our teaching will depend upon the quality and depth of our lives, of our own discipleship. To be good educators, we must become attentive students of the Lord. As educators, we find ourselves called to be witnesses of "something which has existed since the beginning, that we have heard, and we have seen with our own eyes; that we have looked upon and touched with our hands, the Word, who is life" (John 1:1). In the classroom, in the laboratory, in the studio, in the residence halls, on the playing fields, we give witness in multiple and diverse ways, both implicitly and explicitly, that we have been loved by God and seek to love in return.

By the quality and character of our lives dedicated to a search for truth, the Catholic university seeks to collaborate in the church's larger mission of the evangelization of culture. Vitalized by the Holy Spirit, we come together in the hope of being transformed, knowing that alone, our efforts will fall far short. While we strive to move minds by the quality of our research and teaching, we will only move hearts and change lives if we have seen Jesus, are filled with his presence, and reflect that presence in our own lives. Our students look behind our words to our person, behind what we say to who we are. They learn from our expressions, our gestures, from our inmost being whether or not we take joy in human living: in the life of the mind, in the Eucharist, in our lives. Indeed, our students peer within us to see if we take joy in them![11]

If education is to evangelize, then we would do well to recall the words of Paul VI, in *Evangelii Nunciandi,* who reminds us over and over again of the primary importance of the character of our witness, personal and collective:

> Above all the Gospel must be proclaimed by witness. Take a Christian, or a handful of Christians who, in the midst of their own community, show their capacity for understanding and acceptance, their sharing of life and destiny with other people, their solidarity with the efforts of all for whatever is noble and good. Let us suppose that, in addition, they radiate in an altogether simple and unaffected way their faith in values that go beyond current values, and their hope in something that is not seen, that one would not dare to imagine. Through this wordless

witness these Christians stir up irresistible questions in the hearts of all those who see how they live: Why are they like this? Why do they live in this way? What or who is it that inspires them? Why are they in our midst? Such a witness is already a silent proclamation of the Good News and a very powerful and effective one.[12]

In the end, the common wisdom may hold considerable truth: In educating the heart, "Actions speak louder than words."

The Word, powerfully and effectively proclaimed, cannot be absent from the Catholic university. "By its very nature," as *Ex Corde Ecclesiae* notes, "each Catholic university makes an important contribution to the church's work of evangelization."[13] Yet, the invitation to evangelize presents an important challenge to the university community. Whereas the source of our life, our hope, and our inspiration never changes, the concrete cultural circumstances in which our universities find themselves are constantly in flux. In fact, nothing could be more characteristic of our contemporary world than the unprecedented pace of change at every level of culture. The "disrythmia" between the unchanging gospel of Jesus Christ and the dynamism of human culture forces a question: How does the university embody powerfully and effectively the Good News of the Lord in a changing cultural context? More specifically, How is the gospel best proclaimed in the multicultural reality of higher education in the United States in the late twentieth century?

This is a pressing question for those of us in the Congregation of Holy Cross, as well as all who are involved in Catholic education. In my two decades as a Holy Cross religious, I have been blessed to spend time with Holy Cross educators: priests, brothers, and sisters, in the *barriadas* of Lima and Santiago, in the inner cities of Chicago and New York, in the suburbs of San Francisco and Washington, D.C., on the plains of northern Indiana, and on the dusty streets of Nairobi and Kampala. Despite the many changes in context, one feature of the Holy Cross presence always draws my attention: the degree to which Holy Cross is absorbed into the culture of the local church. The ease or affinity of the congregation with cultures is both a gift and a temptation for the evangelizing mission of Holy Cross education.

Holy Cross higher education, like that at the university of Notre Dame, always takes place in the context of a strong sense of community. The power and effectiveness of the residential model of education at Notre Dame is part of the distinctive genius of the place. The life of the mind, the body, and the spirit are nurtured in a uniquely and powerfully integrated way. Faculty, administrators, and hall staff are available to students. Students often find educators easy and appealing to be with. This is as it should be.

But, and here I wish to refer most especially to the role of the Congregation of Holy Cross in the university, in the United States the predominant secular culture is as powerful as it is seductive. Such is the case that, in the closing years of the twentieth century, some speak of the death (or, at least, nonviability) of alternative cultures and ways of life. Oddly, the church in the modern world probably does best when it is in open opposition to the prevailing culture. Yet, secular culture in the United States offers little open opposition to the gospel. It becomes easy to ignore the various ways in which we have become uncritically assimilated into the culture that predominates in the United States. And, to the extent that we as Catholic educators have become assimilated into the predominant culture, our teaching also tends to bring our students unquestioningly into the mainstream.

A key challenge for contemporary Catholic universities, and especially for the religious communities that seek to inspire them, rests in the ways we articulate the relationship between the gospel and the prevailing culture too often characterized by utilitarian and individualistic values.[14] While I do not advocate here a version of Niebuhr's "Christ against Culture,"[15] I do wish to argue on behalf of a hermeneutic of skepticism, and perhaps even of suspicion, with regard to the often unchallenged premises of late twentieth-century American culture. Our task is tricky, but not impossible: in the United States, we must seek to insert ourselves in the predominant culture in order to transform it, while at the same time insuring that we—and our students—do not simply become uncritical parts of it.

The Catholic University and the Institutional Church

For many, the most troublesome dimension of a Catholic university lies in the nature of the commitments between the university and the institutional church. In fact, it is probably a derivative of this dimension of the Catholic university that once provoked George Bernard Shaw to remark that *Catholic university* is an oxymoron. If the essence of a university is a community of learners who spend their lives freely in a search for knowing the truth more fully, then any qualification of that search by ecclesial commitments would seem to threaten the whole enterprise.

The many extraordinary declarations issued by Vatican II notwithstanding, one prevailing image of the Catholic church among most scholars in contemporary America is of a highly structured institution: formalistic, hierarchical, and dogmatic. There are, of course, many Catholics involved in higher education who also hold a predominantly institutional view of the church. According to this view, the church is like any other organization, with a constitution, a set of rules, a governing (decidedly male) body, and a set of members who accept these rules as binding. The boundaries of the church are clear, and tests for membership follow clearly delineated juridical norms. Baptized Catholics who have not otherwise been disqualified can check the Catholic box on university personnel forms with impunity. Pure numbers matter according to this ecclesial view, and a key indicator for progress toward (or decline of) a Catholic university becomes the percentage of different university members who check the box. The presumption is that the greater the percentage of the faculty who can claim formal membership in the Catholic community, the better off we are as a Catholic university. Unfortunately, there is sometimes little in the assessment of the real contribution of nominal Catholics that goes beyond these purely formal criteria.

Catholic proponents of a predominantly institutional model possess an enviable degree of conceptual clarity when it comes to understanding things Catholic. Indeed, clarity is one of the great strengths of this approach. In terms of curriculum, proponents sometimes sound as though the single, integrated worldview espoused by Thomist revivalists were as current today as it was when Thomism was successfully resurrected in the late nineteenth century. And though it is possible that a new synthesis analogous to the intellectual unity provided by Thomism might come to the rescue of the contemporary undergraduate curriculum, a convincing synthesis has thus far proved elusive.

Though the Catholic university is not coterminous with the church, if it is to be Catholic in any meaningful way it must have some visible ties to the institutional church. An important source of controversy in the contemporary university remains the nature of the relationship between the Catholic university and the local bishop. The general feeling in the academy today is that any intrusion at all of an external body to the community of scholars that makes up the essence of the university, and especially involving the church hierarchy, is improper and illegitimate. Thus, though the Vatican's recent Apostolic Constitution on Catholic Universities, *Ex Corde Ecclesiae*, and especially the proposed ordinances that followed, were viewed by some as an opportunity to reinforce the Catholic character of the university, most viewed the efforts of the church hierarchy (especially the proposed ordinances) as an egregious trespass of the fundamental lines of academic freedom.

What is the appropriate relationship between the Catholic university and the magisterium (the teaching authority) of the Roman Catholic church? One American response to this question was articulated by the International Federation of Catholic Universities in 1967. These church and university leaders argued that in order to function as a university, to pursue excellence in teaching and research, "the Catholic university must have a true autonomy and academic freedom in the face of authority of whatever kind, clerical or lay, external to the academic community itself." The deep, and growing, involvements of government, business, and philanthropic organizations in the life of both private and public universities during this period were either ignored by Catholic university administrators at the time, or somehow seen to be more legitimate, especially given the fact that other universities seemed to take such involvements for granted. Parallel involvements by the magisterium, even if, for example, restricted to recognizing or accrediting the contents of theology as Catholic or not, were viewed as an unacceptable violation of the university's academic freedom. In so many words, the administrators of Catholic universities told the hierarchy in the wake of Vatican II, "trust us." This soon became the predominant, if not the only, legitimate position regarding the relationship between the Catholic university and the formal teaching authority of the church. In fact, the almost unanimous negative response of administrators of major Catholic universities to the most recent efforts of the Catholic hierarchy to gain some leverage over the Catholic character of colleges and universities claiming to be Catholic was framed in precisely the same language as over twenty-five years ago.

Not surprisingly, almost any discussion of the institutional dimension of the Catholic university inevitably includes some reference to structures of governance within the university. In these discussions, it is common to hear complaints in some quarters about the excessively hierarchical conception of authority in the Catholic tradition. Heard less often is the argument from institutionalists, who claim that the only real hope for continued fidelity to the university's Catholic roots is a reassertion of clerical power at the top. This struggle over appropriate structures of governance, of course, only reinforces in Catholic universities the ubiquitous cleavage in higher education between administrators and faculty.

In sum, any discussion of the university as Catholic must consider the institutional dimension of its commitments, without allowing mere formalism to predominate. As *Ex Corde Ecclesiae* rightly asserts, any university that claims to call itself Catholic "must be linked with the church either by a formal, constitutive and statutory bond or by reason of an institutional commitment made by those responsible for it."[16] This provision ought not violate in any substantive way the academic freedom essential for the full and unobstructed pursuit of scholarship and teaching. At the same time, bishops have a duty and responsibility to protect and defend doctrinal orthodoxy for the Catholic community. Though different ecclesial starting points will yield quite different positions regarding the types of institutional arrangements that best express the relationship between the university and the teaching authority of the church, heightened attentiveness to the operative approaches to the church underlying this relationship may enable us to articulate this relationship more honestly and usefully.

I have argued that the members of the many different constituencies of a Catholic university each bring to their involvements diverse, and often competing, operative ecclesiologies. By exploring alternative dimensions of what might be meant by *Catholic*, I have attempted to bring into view several different images that shape preconceptions of what the Catholic university ought to be about. If the church, and indeed the Lord, is understood primarily as servant, then the Catholic university has a mandate to place its gifts of the intellect at the active service of the reign of God. When the guiding ecclesial image shifts to community, then the sign of the Catholic university becomes a witness to the truth in the world. Finally, any university that claims to be Catholic must articulate an appropriate and ongoing relationship with the teaching authority of the church. The Catholic university provides an institutional context in which we can openly wrestle with these competing views and perspectives.

I have made no attempt in this essay to be exhaustive in my treatment of competing views of the church. I have briefly elaborated three possible approaches; many other possibilities exist. My central argument is that inattention to the different presuppositions we bring to our involvements at a Catholic university can lead to frustrating, and even painful, misunderstandings. Though sharp differences will undoubtedly persist, if our future efforts to build a Catholic university are characterized by a deeper awareness and appreciation of our respective viewpoints, the chances for understanding are greatly enhanced.

The particular ways in which a university such as Notre Dame will be Catholic in the future will depend upon many more factors than can be addressed here. In closing, I wish to stress the importance of just one: the vision and determination of those who together make up the Notre Dame community. There exists no unseen force in the world, not even the much-celebrated (and, according to some, inexorable) power of secularization, that can thwart the active and determined collaboration of members of the Notre Dame community to cooperate energetically with the Spirit to realize Father Sorin's dream for Notre Dame: a university at once profoundly Catholic and unsurpassed in scholarship. To this task we consecrate our lives.

Notes

1. I have found Avery Dulles's work on ecclesiology to be most helpful in my own understanding of debates about the contemporary church. I am especially indebted to Dulles for two works that I rely upon here. See *Models of the Church* (New York: Doubleday, 1978); and *A Church to Believe In: Discipleship and the Dynamics of Freedom* (New York: Crossroad, 1982).

2. F. Scott Fitzgerald once noted that "the test of a first rate intelligence is the ability to hold two opposed ideas in the mind at the same time, and still

retain the ability to function." Though not opposed, multiple and competing ecclesiologies suggest the relevance of his remark.

3. Taken from Congregation of Holy Cross, *Proceedings of the 1992 General Chapter*, 29. I am grateful to Father Thomas Smith, C.S.C., for his penetrating insights into the educational mission of the Congregation of Holy Cross. I found especially inspiring and useful his contribution to the sesquicentennial celebration of Holy Cross education in the United States entitled, "Bread and Truth Must Make the Rounds," delivered at Moreau Seminary, September 19, 1992.

4. For this phrase, I am indebted to Stanley Hauerwas, *Christian Existence Today: Essays on Church, World, and Living in Between* (Durham, N.C.: Labyrinth Press, 1988), 233.

5. Cited from Dulles, *A Church to Believe In*, 168. St. Thomas attributed this statement to St. Ambrose.

6. Synod of Catholic Bishops, *Justice in the World*, 1971, cited from Dulles, *A Church to Believe In*, 168.

7. University of Notre Dame, Mission Statement, Colloquy for the Year 2000, May 7, 1993.

8. Father Michael Buckley, S.J., "A Collegiate Conversation," *America* 169, no. 6 (September 11, 1993): 22.

9. University of Notre Dame, Mission Statement, Colloquy for the Year 2000, May 7, 1993.

10. John Paul II, *Redemptor hominis* (Washington, D.C.: U.S. Catholic Conference, 1979), no. 21, 89–90.

11. For the importance of the power of witness in Christian education, I am indebted to Walter Burghart, S.J., *Sir, We Wish to See Jesus: Homilies from a Hilltop* (New York: Paulist Press, 1982), 181–85.

12. Paul VI, *Evangelii Nunciandi* (Washington, D.C.: United States Catholic Conference, 1976), 17.

13. John Paul II, *Ex Corde Ecclesiae*, in *Origins*, C.N.S. Documentary Services, 20, no. 17 (October 4, 1990): 273.

14. For a compelling critique of contemporary liberal culture, see Charles Taylor, *The Ethics of Authenticity* (Cambridge, Mass.: Harvard University Press), 1992.

15. I am referring here to the work of H. Richard Niebuhr, *Christ and Culture* (New York: Harper and Row, 1951). It should be clear from the text that I advocate an ecclesiology more consistent with Niebuhr's "Christ Transforming Culture."

16. John Paul II, *Ex Corde Ecclesiae*, in *Origins*, C.N.S. Documentary Services, 20, no. 17 (October 4, 1990): 274.

Professional Education in a Catholic University

LEE A. TAVIS

This essay is directed to the professional components of the Catholic university such as engineering, law, medicine, or business. Professional schools share the research and teaching goals of the university. They are assigned the responsibility to enhance our understanding through expanding the frontiers of knowledge and to share that knowledge with students who are enriched by and, in their turn, push the frontiers. Professional schools carry an added responsibility to the practice of the profession. The profession encourages a focus for academic research and teaching. The requirement of practice guides the relationship between research frontiers and application, where the goal of research is to enhance practice.

In a university such as Notre Dame, the professional schools are thus counseled by Catholic, university, and profession. All three are reflected in research and teaching. In a Catholic university, the professional school faculty must be identified by its involvement in the moral as well as the technical aspects of their profession. In research, moral issues will help to drive the selection of areas for inquiry and analytical approach. In teaching, the research-enhanced insights will enrich the preparation of the students for the practice of their profession.

As reported daily in the press, the professions are not lacking in moral issues. In my field of international financial management, these issues range from the unethical behavior of managers, to the imbalance of development across the world. Immoral managers serve their own misguided self-interests at the expense of their firm and of others outside the enterprise. Even when managers serve the best economic interests of their firms, however, the results of their decisions, the consequences of corporate behavior, may impinge on the well-being of some segment of society. These could include maximizing today's economic returns through environmental degradation to be paid for by future generations, or in decisions that serve the needs of the powerful constituents in the developed countries at the expense of the poorly represented constituents in the developing countries. As these kinds of economically focused, power-based decisions collectively drive the economic/financial system, we are faced with the injustice of global resource allocation.

These moral issues in the business profession provide opportunities along with challenges and risks for the faculty of a Catholic university. Catholic social teaching offers guidance in addressing these individual, corporate, and systemic concerns. As a living, continually renewing tradition, it provides a viewpoint from which to assess the issues, a structure for analysis, and a challenge for action.

This essay explores what it means to be Catholic as well as university in business education. The tensions and the potential synergy will be addressed in terms of faculty research, teaching, and outreach to the profession.

Research

If a business school faculty is to be Catholic, its research must expand our understanding of moral issues that arise in business and enhance our ability to deal with them. For the individual faculty member, there is a tension in research between success as Catholic and success as university. This tension can readily lead to research into moral issues characterized as *research for tenured faculty only*. The analysis of moral issues is necessarily interdisciplinary; it deals with current, critical issues where research must stay close to practice; it involves individual human behavior rather than abstracted models.

The analysis of moral issues in business violates the unfortunately impermeable boundaries of our academic disciplines. As these issues pervade the practice, they draw the analysts into disciplines beyond their technical expertise where they can readily find themselves on thin ice far from shore. Pursuing issues across interdisciplinary boundaries violates the standard counsel of technical dissertation advisors to their students: The key to tenure is to keep your research interests narrowly defined so you are a true expert in a specific topic where anyone writing in that area must refer to your work. Integrating the insight from other disciplines is left until after tenure. For young scholars, a solid grounding in their own discipline before venturing into others is more appropriate and less risky.

The study of business morality, referred to as business ethics, is practice oriented. The moral issues arise from practice at the individual, the organizational, and the systemic levels. They are addressed by managers pursuing their own value judgments within the constraints on the enterprise, its organizational structure, and its ethos. Business ethics cannot be isolated from the manager. Thus, the limits on the spread between research frontiers and practice that bound all professional analysis are even more constraining in the study of moral issues. Take, for example, the study of security investments where the market has been separated from the individual market participant. This abstraction with its large data bases and computerized analyses has led to great insight into how markets operate. There are few moral issues that can be abstracted to this extent. Esoteric abstraction used to gain the elegance of simplicity in conceptual or mathematical models, while intellectually inviting and academically rewarding, can quickly lead to irrelevance for the practitioner.

Catholic social teaching calls for attention to the individuality of the corporate stakeholders who are affected by the activities of the corporation. In the study of the global economic/financial system, for example, technical analysis has led to significant improvements in efficiency. Catholic social teaching requires a focus on the unevenness of the benefits associated with enhanced productivity where some people gain disproportionally while others slide further behind. The centrality of human dignity in Catholic social teaching insists that both the individual and, particularly, the poor be represented in any consideration of global resource allocation. In this context, a study of the global textile markets, for example, would include considerations of the working conditions under which the garments were sewn as a critical component of the analysis. As one whose early academic career was based on mathematical planning models for multinational corporations, I can attest to the challenge of including the poor in the analysis and in encouraging their participation.

As a reflection of its interdisciplinary nature, its practice orientation, and its attention to human dignity, research into the moral issues of business tends not to publish well in the leading academic journals, in spite of their interest to the practitioner. That kind of research is often considered to be "too soft." With acceptance rates well under 10 percent, editors drift to the elegant models and frontier research of the journals specific discipline. Beyond that, technical journals target to the enhancement of global productivity more than the quality of life for those on the fringes of that system. The kind of technical research recognized as a contribution to allocative efficiency generally leads to easier publication and broader recognition.

Since published research is, and will continue to be, a necessary condition for the success of academy members, the tension between contribution to the technical and to the ethical practice of management must be a pivotal concern for the Catholic university. Still, the concern is one of balance not of absolutes. A portfolio effect is always present. Faculty are a diverse lot. At any time some members of the faculty will be focusing on moral issues in the profession, even in universities where this kind of research is not encouraged. The Catholic university strives for a larger share of its portfolio devoted to moral issues while maintaining space for faculty diversity in research. There is room for technical research, for business ethics, and for the counsel of Catholic social teaching. The key is to find a balanced way to nurture the study of moral issues advised by Catholic social teaching in a manner that enhances and is enriched by technical research. There are potential synergies here.

Teaching

In teaching, the balance among objectives and, thus, between professional, Catholic, and university varies with the level of study.

At the undergraduate level, the goal is basic education with an exposure to professional studies. Undergraduate business curricula should draw heavily on other educational components of the university. At Notre Dame, undergraduate students take half of their courses outside the College of Business. When that learning is Catholic, when it includes theology and philosophy, the business student is enhanced by the Catholic university. Within the College of Business, courses draw on other basic disciplines. It must be recognized that the study of business is interdisciplinary. Its base is in economics, mathematics, psychology, and political science, with a more recent inclusion of the humanities. Indeed, business is a successful example of interdisciplinary study. Inclusion of the Catholic tradition in these basic disciplines thus contributes to the study of business and, in turn, benefits from the interdisciplinary nature of the business curriculum.

The business faculty of a Catholic university has a major teaching advantage over their secular colleagues. Students who are attracted to the Catholic university understand the importance of morality in their lives and in society. They understand that ethical considerations are appropriate in professional as well as in personal decisions. Our role is to help them understand the evident moral dimension in all business decisions, to incorporate these considerations as they interact with the more measurable economic and organizational variables, and to articulate the organic whole to other members of their profession.

The professional component of teaching is central in the masters of business administration. Here the goal is to build upon a student's basic undergraduate education as it applies to the practice of management—to add the professional dimension to a basic education in the arts or sciences. Business ethics should be a major component of a Catholic university's M.B.A. program. It must be an integrated component of the whole curriculum as well as a separate topic of study. It is not enough for students to understand how to apply ethical reasoning, they must recognize the moral dimension of every business decision. The real concern in the practice of management is the manager who simply does not see the moral component of the decisions he or she is called to make. As with any Catholic professional education, ethics must be in addition to, not in place of, other learning. At Notre Dame, we do well in teaching moral reasoning, but less well in integrating the ethical dimension into decision models.

At the doctoral level, research issues dominate. As noted, this is where the greatest tension between Catholic and university is to be encountered. Notre Dame Ph.D. graduates must be technically qualified for research and teaching positions at the best universities in the country if we are to contribute to the advancement of learning. Notre Dame Ph.D.'s must be more. They must understand the ethical dimension of their research area if they are to change the way other universities view their contribution to the academy and the business profession. The demands on our doctoral graduates are greater than on those from other universities.

Direct Involvement with Professional Practice

Many professional school faculty take it as an extension of their research and teaching contributions to be directly involved with the practice of the profession. Those concerned with moral issues often feel a sense of urgency that draws them into this direct involvement. While research surely influences the profession, there is always the gap between research and practice. Teaching awaits the professional contribution of the students as they lever their newfound technical and ethical analytic skills and values through the allocation of corporate resources.

There are numerous formats for this direct interaction. One approach has, in my view, been effective.

The Program on Multinational Managers and Developing Country Concerns grew out of a discussion (debate) with a theologian (Father Donald McNeill) and a political scientist (David Leege) in 1977. We were, all three of us, concerned about the persistence of poverty in the poor countries of Africa, Asia, and Latin America. We all recognized that the global economic financial system was a major factor in the imbalance of global well-being. We disagreed about the positive and negative involvement of multinational corporations in the process of development. A greater number of informed voices was needed to extend this discussion.

Our first step was fortuitous. Based on our concerns, not conclusions, we drew together a group of observers with diverse experience, capabilities, and world views concerning multinational corporations and Third World development. Our first two-day workshop succeeded in drawing faculty from across the university to a focus on this critical issue—ten members from theology, philosophy, economics, government, and anthropology, as well as business disciplines. They were joined by twenty-three multinational managers with responsibility for some dimension of their corporate activities in the Third World. Completing the seminar were ten missionaries, activists, and officials from governmental and international agencies.

The group stormed, but then formed. One academic colleague actually became nauseated over the confrontations in the initial debate. After two days, however, participants began to know each other as individuals rather than as representatives of some alien force, and trust grew. We then understood what Father Hesburgh meant when he opened the workshop with a statement on the appropriateness of Notre Dame as the site for this work: "Universities are, by nature, mediators. Just as the priest mediates between the two great extremes, finite and infinite, in universities truth emerges through the nurturing of ideas, the interpretation of opinions, and the interplay of opinions and thoughts that may go in quite opposite directions."

The process has evolved since that first meeting to one of identifying specific issues concerning multinational involvement in Third World development; forming diverse study groups of concerned participants with experience in that particular topic; structuring a four-phase process of assembling the group for an initial debate over the issue, fielding a research team to collect evidence on some specific case, reassembling the participants to assess the evidence in a second workshop, and sharing the findings through publication of the various papers, research evidence, and most importantly, the workshop discussions. To date we have dealt with topics such as the influence of multinational corporations in Third World societies and how their role is worked out in conjunction with host governments, the potential contribution of multinationals to rekindling development within the constraints of the global debt crisis, the contribution of pharmaceuticals to health in developing countries as analyzed in the context of Third World traditional medicine as well as First World scientific health systems, and the management of within-country linkages to microentrepreneurs in informal sectors. Four volumes are in print with a fifth, summary volume, in manuscript.

Through this process we have come to understand the power of informed people learning from one another. Academics have found how out-of-touch their conceptual structures can be with the reality of the multinational corporate decision environment. Managers have learned to assess the full effect of their decisions as the impact works its way through their local constituents, to families, local communities, and further through the national to the international system. Missionaries have learned how the specific corporate unit with which they interact is part of a complex organization that, while often willing to respond to local needs, seldom knows how. I have learned the importance and the possibility of including the individual poor person into my work on multinational corporate decision models.

How much of this seminar is university and how much is Catholic?

The Catholic component is more clear than university. The topic is Catholic. The moral need is to alleviate the persistent poverty in the Third World and the injustice of global resource allocations. It extends the sense of the Notre Dame mission statement from students to the practice of management: "The University seeks to cultivate in its students not only an appreciation for the great achievements of human beings but also a disciplined sensibility to the poverty, injustice, and oppression that burden the lives of so many. The aim is to create a sense of human solidarity and concern for the common good that will bear fruit as learning becomes service to justice."

The program's approach is Catholic. We attempt to interpret Catholic social teaching as it applies to decisions made by corporate management within the economic and political reality of the global system. The morally aware manager is supporting the unmet needs of local peoples in these countries. The corporate constituents such as local employees and suppliers, their families and communities are poor in part because they are not adequately represented to the firm. To enhance their well-being, however, involves giving them voice and leaning against the power of the international marketplace and the demands of other powerful constituents in the home country such as investors and organized labor. Complicating our discussions is the fact that the corporation whose resources are being allocated by the morally aware manager is a secular organization, and the vast majority of the poor being represented to the firm are not Catholic. The seminar process is also Catholic—the bottom-up principle of subsidiarity.

The professional contribution is clear. The causes of poverty and injustice are analyzed as a means of evaluating corporate strategic planning information and control systems as they enhance or diminish the quality of life among the poor. We are making a difference. For example, as a result of our study group on "Multinational Managers and Host Government Interactions," two participating corporations changed their policies on interacting with host governments. Our publications are being widely read.

As for university, a program of this nature is appropriate in that a university forum stresses free, open interactions. The university faculty brings a conceptual dimension to the issue which helps in expanding the vision of corporate decision makers. The standard notions of university research and teaching, however, are redefined in this program. The field research is limited to the collection of data which the participants in the study group will trust. Interpretation of the data and conclusions are left to the participants in the follow-up workshop. All participants share in teaching and learning.

There are risks for supporters and participants in this kind of a program. Corporations contribute funds and their name to discussions and publications on controversial issues over which they have no control. Participants are invited to respond as individuals not as representatives of their institutions. They do so freely, sometimes to the consternation of their colleagues and seniors. For faculty participants the risk is the commitment of time to a program with little promise of near-term reward. They are drawn into the broad moral issues with many dimensions unfamiliar to them and know their time commitment does not speak loudly as a contribution to their academic field. Fellow faculty see participants as diverting precious research time away from work with colleagues and mentoring in technical research. These risks reflect the Catholic versus university research tensions. Still, over the long term, participating faculty are enriched by new and exciting ways of looking at our world. We come to understand that the economic optimization we study and teach, while enhancing productivity and serving society, can lead to agony for some people who are exploited or marginalized.

That Notre Dame has undertaken this program reflects the university's commitment to Catholic values. The most active participants are Notre Dame alumni (John Caron, Jack Mullen, and others). The university administration has endorsed and supported the successful solicitation of funds from the Rockefeller Foundation and twenty-nine multinational corporations. (Participants and corporate supporters are listed in each published volume.)

These observations are drawn from my own experience as a member of the academy for the past twenty-five years at Stanford, Indiana, Texas, and Notre Dame. Although this reflection covers but a small slice of the centuries-old and centuries-future issue of Catholic and university, the tension in professional education between the two and the potential for synergy will continue to affect the individual member of the faculty and thus the university. We know how to be university but need to define and work at what it is to be Catholic in a way that enhances both. The existence of global academic professions and the ability of faculty to move from one university to another assure the continuation of quality university research and teaching. Ours is a greater task. As Father Hesburgh emphasizes: "The Catholic university must be all that a university requires and something more."

"What, Then, Does Dr. Newman Mean?"
The Vision and the Views

MARY KATHERINE TILLMAN

I

At a recent symposium held at Notre Dame on the current plight of the university, two successive speakers began their papers, de rigueur, with allusions to the educational thought of (the now Venerable) Cardinal John Henry Newman (1801–1890). The comments of one speaker contradicted those of the other, and both were misleading. One spoke of Newman's "virtually exclusive concentration . . . on the rigors of teaching and research," in contrast to the American belief "that higher education had a transforming value [or moral function] in addition to its charge of imparting knowledge." The paper of the speaker who followed said that Newman "explicitly repudiated" research as a key part of a university's mission and "almost violently rejected" the integration of career education and liberal learning. The aim of a recent book on the university is to make Newman's educational thought more relevant to the contemporary scene by eliminating from the discussion the theological and religious content of Newman's classic work, *The Idea of a University* (1852). Excluded, then, is the bearing of over half of the work, those portions which contain its raison d'être—namely, the early discourses on theology which argue for its essential place as an intellectual discipline and the concluding discourses which present

339

Newman's critique of the exclusively secular, liberal education of "the gentleman," who need be neither moral nor religious.

Evoked like the muse, Newman is the fall guy, the straw man, or the knight in shining armor, depending on the purpose at hand. For better and for worse, he seems to find a place in every discussion of Catholic higher education—indeed, in any substantive discussion of the modern university. The not uncommon disengagement from the inherently Catholic dimension of Newman's educational vision and the all too common extrication of isolated points from Newman's intentionally limited view in *The Idea of a University*—distortions congealed and fixed by repetition—understandably lead one to reapply Charles Kingsley's famous words: "What, then, does Dr. Newman mean?"

The fault of the confusion is partially Newman's own, because of what he chose to do in the discourses that make up what we now call *The Idea of a University*. That work is not, and was never intended to be, the expression of Newman's vision of Catholic higher education; it is an eloquent, rhetorical sketch of but one view or aspect according to which the university is there being considered, namely, to use his own words: its "bare and necessary idea." Stating in his introductory discourse the "mode in which I propose to handle my subject altogether," Newman writes: "I am investigating in the abstract, and am determining what is in itself right and true. For the moment I know nothing, so to say, of history. . . . I am here the advocate and the minister of a certain great principle."

"Investigating in the abstract"? Anyone who has read Newman (or about Newman) beyond *The Idea of a University* knows that a concrete, commonsense approach and a developmental method (historical, psychological, autobiographical, spiritual), not the abstract investigation of a static idea, were Newman's natural and favored modes of writing. His views were always directly related to experience and imagination, and his writings appeal to the whole personality, not just to the mind. He had a horror of the "unreal," a distaste for metaphysics, and a love of what is personal and particular. He regarded everything abstract or "notional" as incomplete until it was "realized," made real, however inadequately, in human life. In addition, Newman's practical temper of mind, his principled actions as student, tutor, and fellow at Oxford and as founding rector (president) at the Irish university, and the weight and bearing of his other major writings lead one to suspect that he must somewhere have other views on the higher education of Catholics that are not included in this intentionally "bare and necessary idea." (After all, he himself had said: "from first to last, education has been my line.")

For example, one might reasonably expect to find (and would not be disappointed) something on the origins and history of the university; on the legitimacy, limitations, and politics of ecclesiastical relations; on the restricted role of the state in church and university matters; on the university's direct service to the church, its contribution to the intellectual life of the clergy, and its application to the newly emerging laity; on participation in governance by lay faculty; on the offering of professional studies, of evening classes for workers; on academic freedom; on the university's encouragement of publication and the professional life of the faculty; on the relation of the university and the college—of the professor, lecturer, and tutor; on the personal influence of the teacher; on the relation of the university to the indigenous culture in which it finds itself; on structure, staffing, and finances. And might it not be reasonable also to expect, from this renowned religious leader and holy man, something, somewhere, on the Catholic university's pastoral role in cultivating morality and religious faith in its students?

None of these are aspects of the university that Newman considers in *The Idea of a University*. What needs to be added and taken into full account, however, is that Newman realized and intended the abstraction of the *Idea*, and that every one of the above aspects of university life (and many others) are addressed and promoted elsewhere in his writings (which now amount to almost eighty volumes). The omission of their consideration in the *Idea of a University* is deliberate and methodological, not in any way an oversight, or a "virtual exclusion," an "explicit repudiation" or a "violent rejection" of these important dimensions of the life of a Catholic university. Newman uses the distinction Aristotle makes between a thing's "essence" and its "integrity" (wholeness, well-being, completeness). Aspects such as politics, mission, governance, moral and religious education, and all the rest, are absolutely indispensable elements (sine qua non, he says) in the healthy life and integrity of a Catholic university. The essence of what *university* means, however—what makes it a university—is exclusively the intellectual enterprise of cultivating in every way possible, that is, theoretically and practically, all knowledge for its own sake; this and only this is the content of the idea *university* and of the work about that idea. In Newman's words: "Knowledge . . . is something more, it has a result beyond itself. Doubtless, but that is a further consideration, with which I am not concerned. . . . [It] is a matter foreign to my subject" (discourse V).

The Idea of a University presents a view (an angle or a slant, we would say), an aspect of Newman's large-minded vision of the dynamic reality and potentiality of higher education for Catholics. The aspect under which the university is here viewed, is *idea* as such. Only as such does it here omit other important considerations that are not general or typical but, rather, concrete, particular, and varied. What Newman means by the idea *university* has emerged from history, as he emphasizes in his *Rise and Progress of Universities;* it is an elastic kind of type to which particular institutions more or less correspond, with great diversity and range, in many different cultures and ages. No single university, including his own, could or would ever instantiate it. (By analogy, we might ask: Is there a single individual who, in all particulars, is "Renaissance man"?) Perhaps Newman's idea *university* functions as an ideal for an individual institution, but if the institution is only true to type, it may already be dead. In addition to its conserving action on the past and its continuity of principles, the institution must also be able to take into its substance new elements from its particular time and place in history. It must itself be influential and effective, and it must advance the idea *university* in its gestating anticipations of the future.

The great variety of realizations of the idea, each with its distinctive tradition, mission, and emphases, actually defines, elastically, the type or idea that thus emerges from history in our time. Like the particular institutions which more or less correspond and contribute to the idea, all thoughtful approaches to the idea likewise illuminate it precisely by means of their unique, particular points of view. As Newman writes in the *Idea:* "variations imply, instead of discrediting, the archetypal idea, which is but a previous hypothesis or condition, by means of which issue is joined between contending opinions, and without which there would be nothing to dispute about" (Discourse V).

If we would know more of Newman's capacious vision of a Catholic university, we would have to explore his other views of it; namely, those found in the other two volumes of lectures and essays on university education that were composed while Newman was actively rector of the Catholic University of Ireland (not before, as were the discourses of the *Idea*); also the volume of sermons preached before the university in 1856–1857, the year of the opening of its church. Certainly pertinent are the brilliantly original sermons he preached on the relation of faith and reason when he was tutor and fellow of Oriel College, Oxford, and vicar of the university church there; as well as other particularly relevant essays and sermons, notebooks, diaries, and letters. In other words, because Newman was not a "systematic" writer, *The Idea of a University* must be placed in the context of his other educational writings, and they in the context of his other major works. Then and only then do we get the educational vision of one of the most subtle and penetrating Catholic minds of all times, a man universally celebrated as a distinguished churchman, eminent scholar, and prolific man of letters.

The relation between religious faith and human understanding, as they originate in nature and are developed by education and practice, was the central intellectual preoccupation of Newman's long life. This is the living nucleus around which all of his views on university education revolve; it is the kernel from which they germinate and grow. Integral to his vision of a Catholic university is the essential role of an educated Catholic laity in the doctrinal (as well as the ministerial) life of the church; the importance of the formation of conscience which, in part, entails intellectual education and an understanding of one's relation to legitimate authority, ecclesial and political; and the "sacred duty" incumbent upon every human being to develop the talent of our minds in accord with our natural gifts and particular station in life.

As an intellectual and spiritual pilgrim, Newman was seeking the complete vision of truth, even as his eloquent words and works stammered and stuttered in its behalf, circling round about what he glimpsed, carefully articulating, one at a time, every partial view.

Now the intellect in its present state, with exceptions which need not here be specified, does not discern truth intuitively, or as a whole.

> We know, not by a direct and simple vision, not at a glance, but as it were, by piecemeal and accumulation, by a mental process, by going round an object, by the comparison, the combination, the mutual correction, the continual adaptation of many partial notions, by the employment, concentration, and joint action of the intellectual powers. . . . (Discourse VII)

Now I want to attempt to articulate explicitly one view, limited and partial, of what Newman might mean by the idea of a distinctively Catholic university when more of his writings than *The Idea of a University* are taken into account. It is my contribution to this wonderfully conceived, Newman-like book, an assemblage of views perfectly demonstrating that the idea of a distinctively Catholic university (like the idea, *university*) is also "a previous hypothesis or condition, by means of which issue is joined between contending opinions, and without which there would be nothing to dispute about." Altogether these views enact, develop, and help realize that idea of a Catholic university which ever eludes us, though we ever make progress. To use Newman's words, we "say and unsay toward a positive result."

As for Newman's vision, we need look no further for its contemporary expression than the introductory essay of this book and its author, Father Hesburgh.

II

Deep in history, the relationship of *university* and *catholicity* seems always and everywhere to be tensile, ever seeking, never reaching, the stasis of full and perfect equilibrium. Inherited and inhabited perspectives by means of which to attend to a particular, historical reality, *catholicity* and *university* constitute important, if implicit, horizons of thought and belief, each of them surrounded by an aura of traditionally sacrosanct principles.

Like a multicolored marble in a giant bowl, pulled toward then passing through the center, traveling outward toward the limit, breaking through the horizon of a previous circumference, then stopped short and drawn back by the pull of yet another polarity—just so is the thinking, believing intellect, of both the individual and the community, dynamically centered in the incarnation of Jesus Christ, whom T. S. Eliot calls "the still point of the turning world." Restless at heart, the thinking, believing intellect is caught up in the play of seeking and finding, of assumption and discovery, of faith and understanding, of knowledge and mystery. It tacks to the left and then to the right, drawn now by the sway of memory and the lessons of the past, now by the beckoning of imagination and the challenges of invention—ever creating, ever conserving, back and forth again. This is the dance of Sophia, Wisdom, the first-born of God, ever at play in the divine presence and delighting to be with the children of Eve.

Historically centered about the notions *university* and *catholicity* are clusters of principles, by which I mean not a priori opinions arbitrarily imposed to canonize the status quo but, rather, congealed, communal meanings, recondite sources of traditionary wisdom, which, if made explicit and examined, can serve as starting points for thought and conversation, keys for interpretation and understanding, even guides for decision and action. I here observe the historical attachment of three such principles to the notion of *university*.

1. The principle of intellect and influence. University qua university is the home of the intellect. A university is true to type if it is concerned essentially and first with intellectual cultivation as an end in itself before it is concerned with professional, vocational, moral, and religious education. From Socrates to Simone Weil, the love of learning, the pursuit and contemplation of truth, is seen to be so precious, so absolute in and of itself, that it is worth selling all of one's possessions in order to attain it, and to live and die in its service. As such, the life of the mind is not a means to any other end or product or pursuit, however naturally that product or pursuit may be informed by, or inform, or follow from the intellectual life. The only practical activity fully commensurate with the intellectual life is its own transmission and development, that is, the teaching or broad casting of the seeds and fruits of thought in speech, in writing, and in culture.

2. The principle of universality and freedom. The university welcomes all truth, encourages freedom of inquiry and the advancement of knowledge to the furthest reaches of the human mind.

Correlatively it is self-correcting in its disciplines and methods, its communal life and measure. *Universitas* implies a radical, nonterritorial openness to the whole and complete circle of knowledge, to the checking, balancing, adjusting, rounding insights of all avenues of liberal learning taken together: namely, the sciences, the arts, and the humanities, including theology as knowledge. (We are not speaking here of religion.)

3. *The principle of community and institution.* Even as it concentrates fully and essentially on the development of the intellect and the imagination, the university recognizes the rootedness of mind in the whole person, of person in community and culture, and of this community and culture in the near and far-reaching communities and cultures of our world, mindful that multicultural and ecumenical differences and dialogues are deeply embedded in history and cannot be skimmed in a myopic blur off the surface of the present. Now the practical, productive, and applied knowledges of the university take their rightful place concentrically moving out from and serving the nucleus life of the mind: vocational and professional education, moral and religious formation, the residence life of the institution—and all of the human services according to the mission, tradition, and resources of a particular institution. As institution, a university establishes libraries and laboratories, museums and conservatories, institutes and centers, seats of administration and chairs of learning—all with the primary aim of assuring the preservation and creative continuance of its inmost life of the mind.

This living idea *university,* as the house of intellect and influence, as established intellectual center of the local and global communities, has survived the onslaughts of the epochs, strengthened by the growth, variations, and adaptations of its aspects, just as the idea *state* and the idea *church* have endured and evolved from antiquity until today—each communally recognized instance the adumbration of a pattern true to type yet ever new.

It is necessary but not sufficient that a Catholic university be theistic, that is, that it profess intellectually the existence of a God or gods. This is the order of reason, shining Athens. It is also necessary but not sufficient that a Catholic university be a community in covenant with a personal, self-revealing God. This is the order of reason in relation to faith, Athens and Sinai. It is further necessary but not sufficient that a Catholic university be a Christian community partaking in the relational life and love of the triune God-for-us in Jesus Christ and the Holy Spirit—a life of self-emptying, suffering, and transforming service of others. This is the order of reason in relation to charity, Athens and Jerusalem.

Lastly, it is necessary (and probably still not sufficient) that a Catholic university be a community of teacher-scholars whose practice of the intellectual life originates in, and is animated by, Catholic principles or wellsprings of thought, belief, and action. Here are a few of those principles of the Catholic faith, all of which encroach on one another and refuse to be fixed and final: the sacramental or mediational principle; the principle of the unity of faith and reason; the doctrinal or dogmatic principle; the principle of tradition; the ecclesial or *communio* principle; the Petrine principle. This is the order of reason in relation to authority, Athens and Rome. I shall here emphasize only certain aspects of but a few of these principles of Catholicity, the ones that I think correlate most directly with the three principles of university.

The principle of sacramentality or mediation. Catholics believe that this visible world is alive with invisible presence and ultimate significance. Because of God's creation, incarnation, and sanctification, the good earth, the bodily, material, physical universe, is holy and mediates grace to us, through such of its elements as water and oil, bread and wine, speech and gesture—in particular through the incarnate Christ, his visible church, and seven special, religious sacraments. We believe that all of human history, past, present, and future, our stories and philosophies, our cultures, sciences, and religions, as well as the minute, particular circumstances of our everyday lives, are sacred instruments and meeting places of God. In sign and symbol, word and number; in music, art, and dance; with candles and incense, liturgies and devotions; we indirectly, but really, encounter God and mediate God's presence to one another. Perhaps the most ordinary, intimate, and overlooked sacramental presence of God in our lives is the mediating processes of our own minds: imagination and memory, inference and assent. Reasoning and believing, both processes by which we hold this by means of that, lead us from what is known to what was unknown, from premises to conclusions, from probabilities to certitudes. Inductively and deductively; analogically, hypothetically, and dialectically; truth itself, one of the names of God, is mediated to ourselves and to others through the ordinary and disciplined activities of the mind.

Already I am speaking of *the Catholic principle of the unity of faith and reason*—unity, not identity or coextension. Because of our belief in the wholeness and dignity of the acting person, in whom the life of faith and of reason is one life of the spirit, Catholicism has always held to a peculiarly close relationship between thinking and believing, each an act of the intellect capable of informing and furthering the other. For us, faith is not so much, as with Kierkegaard, a blind leap into darkness. Rather, faith is, with our *doctor*, Teresa, the ecstasy of knowledge, excess of kindly light, to which the inner eye grows ever more intimately accustomed, eternally. We do not place faith over here as subjective, individual, and private, and reason over there as objective, common, and public. We believe that the communal faith in which we partake has rational grounds which, if I do not know, the ecclesial community does (and into which I ought to inquire so that, with St. Paul, I may know the reason for the hope within)—that our faith has rational grounds and that our reasonings possess a fiduciary horizon and informants. We hold not only that we can believe what we do not understand, which in fact everyone does all the time anyhow, but the even more astounding truth that unless we believe, we shall not understand. We see faith as a way of knowing, as yielding religious truth that is not only a portion, but a condition, of general knowledge. "Faith is the reasoning of the religious mind," writes Newman, in agreement with his holy predecessors Augustine and Aquinas.

Next, *the dogmatic or doctrinal principle.* As Catholics we hold that there is an intellectual content to what we believe, that there are propositional truths that exist independently of our minds and of human reason, and that, *pace* Protagoras, human beings are not the measure of all things. Through the reception of, and adherence to, certain creedal and conciliar doctrines of faith, which have developed over centuries by means of a living tradition, the proud rationalist and the self-righteous dogmatist in all of us is stopped short and humbled, for we are asked to contemplate truths we could never have made up or owned as personal possessions. American Catholic writer Flannery O'Connor notes:

The intellect will takes its place in a larger context and will cease to be tyrannical . . . —and when there is nothing over the intellect it usually is tyrannical. Anyway, the mind serves best when it's anchored in the word of God. There is no danger then of becoming an intellectual without integrity.

I began with the principle of sacramentality, and I conclude with *the principle of authority,* for I think these two may be the most distinctive principles of catholicity, and the ones most invigorating of university. It is in the tensile relation to authority that the intellect is at its best, and it is upon intellect that authority entirely depends for its substance and rationality. The creative intellect thrives on conversation and contest with the authors, the authorities, the authorizations that constitute the facts and resistant realities of our lives. Authorities provide standards and rules, parameters, and limits—sometimes in excess; and reason forges ahead, unchecked and progressive—sometimes in excess. Reason and authority were made for each other.

French Catholic writer Alexis de Tocqueville observes:

A principle of authority must then always occur, under all circumstances, in some part or other of the moral and intellectual world. Its place is variable, but a place it necessarily has. The independence of individual minds may be greater, or it may be less: unbounded it cannot be.

Were reason not tempered by authority, by even other authorities within the self, we might go mad, or at best end up victims of that peculiar malady that G. K. Chesterton ascribes to those who have lost everything but their minds. And wherever authority is not illumined by reason, it quickly becomes arbitrary, tyrannical, and abusive.

Conscience is the first place where authority and reason struggle for equilibrium and are joined by judgment into one. *Ecclesia* is perhaps the final place where authority and reason struggle for equilibrium and are joined by judgment into one. The age-old dialectics, of theologians and magisterium, of laity and clergy, of universities and bishops, are illustrations of this compelling play of reason and authority.

In the magnificent final chapter of his *Apologia pro Vita Sua,*

Newman articulates in dramatic detail not only the compatibility but the requirement, each for the well-being of the other, of authority and reason.

> It is the vast Catholic body itself, and it only, which affords an arena for both combatants in that awful, never-dying duel. It is necessary for the very life of religion. . . that the warfare should be incessantly carried on. Every exercise of Infallibility is brought out into act by an intense and varied operation of the Reason, both as its ally and as its opponent, and provokes again, when it has done its work, a reaction of Reason against it; and, as in a civil polity the State exists and endures by means of the rivalry and collision, the encroachments and defeats of its constituent parts, so in like manner Catholic Christendom is no simple exhibition of religious absolutism, but presents a continuous picture of Authority and Private Judgment alternately advancing and retreating as the ebb and flow of the tide. . . .

I should like for a Catholic university to be as unapologetically Catholic as it is warmly ecumenical; as proudly intellectual as it is caring and compassionate; as concerned with the individual and communal life of the mind as it is with publications; as valuing of inference, imagination, and assent as ways to God, as of social justice; as committed to liberal education as it is to professional education; as eager in the pursuit of truth and of Catholic culture in the arts as it is of moral goodness; as steady in its own convictions and traditions as it is appreciative of diversity; as humbled and gratified by the spiritual work of mercy that is rendered in instructing the ignorant as by the corporal mercy performed in sheltering the homeless. The noble activity of cultivating the life of the mind is the first, though not the only, profession and praxis of a Catholic university; that very cultivation is its first and best service to the church, the academy, and the world.

The greatest threat to the catholicity of a university is neglect of the intellectual life—not of its products and applications, its services and technologies—but of thought and culture as eminently worthwhile in themselves and as the raison d'être of its institutional life. To be a Catholic university is above all else to energize and to celebrate the mediating, sacramental powers of the human mind.

I conclude with a brief excerpt from a sermon entitled "Intellect, the Instrument of Religious Training," which Cardinal Newman preached in the university church in Dublin, on the feast of St. Monica, 1856. Part of this same passage was printed for many years on the frontispiece of the University of Notre Dame's Bulletin of Information:

> I wish the intellect to range with the utmost freedom, and religion to enjoy an equal freedom; but what I am stipulating for is, that they should be found in one and the same place, and exemplified in the same persons. . . . I wish the same spots and the same individuals to be at once oracles of philosophy and shrines of devotion. It will not satisfy me, what satisfies so many, to have two independent systems, intellectual and religious, going at once side by side, by a sort of division of labour, and only accidently brought together. It will not satisfy me, if religion is here, and science there, and [students] converse with science all day, and lodge with religion in the evening. . . . I want the same roof to contain both the intellectual and moral discipline. Devotion is not a sort of finish given to the sciences; nor is science a sort of feather in the cap, if I may so express myself, an ornament and set-off to devotion. I want the intellectual layman to be religious, and the devout ecclesiastic to be intellectual.

Catholic Higher Education:
Historic Past or Distinctive Future?

JOHN VAN ENGEN

To *educate* means, in the root sense of the word, to rear, or more literally in its Greek form (pedagogy), to lead the young. For the ancient Greeks, *paideia* meant discipline, education, cultural formation. Every human society has devised means to form its young, to prepare them for the tasks they are to inherit. But until recently most human beings were reared and shaped apart from any instruction in letters. They were trained to farm, to fight, to sail, to cook, to nourish and to pray—but not to read. Those who acquired the ability to read, initially opened far more to men than women, applied their letters mostly to specific ends, keeping accounts, ordering documents, learning the holy books. Only a tiny minority in a few of the world's cultures pursued a higher education, reserved for an elite who served in government, religion, or education itself.

Virtually all present-day institutions of higher education worldwide derive ultimately from the European model, first established around the year 1200 to train churchmen in the north (Paris and Oxford) and lawyers in the south (Bologna). Down to the nineteenth century, church authority framed higher education in Europe and America. It was "Catholic" (later, "Lutheran" or "Reformed") in no small measure because those who authorized, taught in, and attended those universities were Catholic (Lutheran or Reformed). In the early twentieth century many older institutions moved away

353

from specific religious allegiances to mirror a multireligious and secular society. At the same time, numerous new institutions in this country took up the swelling task of offering higher education to immigrant masses under religious auspices. The question is whether this coalition between "Catholic" and "university" was simply a passing (albeit eight-hundred-year!) historical phenomenon or remains a distinctive possibility in the future.

Christianity has an inherent stake in education, for believing is not alien to learning nor learning to believing. The community of Christians inherited from Judaism, its parent, a vital concern to rear its young in the faith. In antiquity and the Middle Ages Jews generally did better instructing their boys in the Bible and the Law, with Christians content to let much of the learning take place in the doing, by way of community participation in ritual worship. But from the beginning, and especially after the year 1100, a small body of clerics—a term which came to mean both "lettered" and "churchman"—explored the depths and structure of the faith with the best resources available to them, meaning ancient Greek philosophy, especially Aristotle. Their work became normative for the university and sometimes for the church, with a philosophical term (*transubstantiation*) applied to the very heart of Christianity's redemptive mystery. After 1550 humanist Reformers demanded higher standards of learning for the faithful as well, embodied in catechisms and sermons and devotional tractates but also in the full humanist education set for ordinary clergymen, represented in its ideal form by Jesuits and certain Calvinists.

If in the late twentieth century the relationship between Christianity and higher education seems more troubled, it is not—as agnostic humanists have argued—because religion and learning are inevitably opposed. On the contrary, religion has often oriented learning or opened to it stunning new vistas, while learning has often deepened or structured religion. Church and university are, however, distinct institutional and cultural realities. The university is a human institution, even if its earliest founders and promoters were mostly churchmen. From the beginning much of its learning involved non-Christian texts, even if they were often made to serve Christian purposes. The university was never a parish, though its teachers have often assumed a kind of clerical attitude and authority. Details of organization or curricula were left mostly, if not entirely, to masters. Popes and bishops were more concerned about boundaries than debates. On occasion, masters transgressed, sometimes to face correction, sometimes to have the boundaries redefined (to admit Aristotle into theology in the thirteenth century, humanist philology into biblical studies in the fifteenth, and so on). Such give and take was—and is—unavoidable, even when the university men are churchmen. For Christian educators—if not necessarily for the ordinary faithful in the pew or the prelates and administrators who must live with the aftermath—such tensions represent merely the byproduct of an ambitious effort to combine religious commitment with intellectual understanding.

For those who do not repudiate learning altogether in the name of faith (a type always present) or faith in the name of learning (a common modern type), for those, in sum, who seek forms of mutual enrichment, two general patterns have obtained among Christians, though the lines have criss-crossed through the centuries with extreme representatives of each and many shades in between. The first sees the world disclosed by learning and reason as more or less coterminous with that revealed by faith and grace. Here creation is effectively the central doctrine: The forms and structures embedded by God in the world can be perceived and interpreted by human beings, themselves the crown of God's creation, made in the image of God. This outlook presupposes an implicit order in the universe, the relation of that order ultimately to God, and the ability of human beings to read and understand that order truthfully. Creation itself, rightly perceived, can even yield a natural theology and a natural law, that is, a general knowledge of God and of right and wrong. Whether such knowledge leads to saving truths is a matter of dispute. Medieval churchmen, in the wake of Thomas, reserved knowledge of God as triune or Jesus as the incarnate Son to revelation. But both in early Christianity and in various modern forms the Christian order has been rendered as true philosophy or the true reason of things, Christ as the ultimate human being. Either way, the whole world of learning, including education offered in universities, can proceed on the assumption that its humanly reasoned truths are continuous with the ultimate truth, that humans created in the image of God perceive and teach the creative work and order of the divine made flesh. Learning and faith become intertwined as naturally compatible, without denigration to either.

In the second pattern belief is held to yield a new person with a new vision of the world illumined by grace. Here redemption becomes effectively the central doctrine: The gifts of grace and faith, becoming remade like Christ, begin to renew the whole person, including the mind. Associated most closely with Augustine and his teachings about a divinely illuminated cognitive power, this outlook has found intellectual expression throughout Christian history. In an extreme form it holds that only Christians truly know; all other knowledge is flawed, darkened, prone to error and dissolution, like the moral and physical attributes of unredeemed human beings. In practice this approach focuses more upon the subjective than the objective side of human perception. It doubts, implicitly or explicitly, whether any subject matter exists in some wholly objective state to be apprehended fully or truly or immediately by any person with rational capacity. People of this persuasion are not surprised by the shifting paradigms disclosed in Kuhn's scientific revolutions or the fragmented and subjective epistemology that informs much of postmodern thought. But there is a crucial difference: They would not hold that all knowledge is rooted in subjective projection, that all knowing curves back in again upon the subject—though perhaps conceding that much knowledge is of this sort. They hold that in Christ there is a way of seeing the truth in things, and it is this that Christian educators must discover and pass on. This outlook allows more space for a specifically Christian outlook within the work of education and therefore finds such an education all the more invaluable. It correspondingly yields less space to a world of knowledge common to all engaged in the work of education.

Catholic learning, in retrospect, has rich examples of both strains within its educational history. There is a powerfully inclusive strain that has emphasized the place of human reason, the unity of truth, the contribution of non-Christian thinkers to a common work; in the Middle Ages it absorbed into Catholic teaching and practice ancient philosophy, in the Renaissance ancient literature and history, within memory much of modern science and psychology. But there is an equally powerful exclusive strain: Papal condemnations of Aristotle's use by theologians and episcopal suspicions of Thomas, matched by Thomas's own philosophical refutation of the pagans, the Galileo affair, anti-Modernism, the forming early in this century of separate professional organizations—all this to protect certain truths which, ironically, were held to be natural or common. Catholic educators today look back upon dramatic swings: Two generations ago the exclusive strain tended to predominate, partially to foster and protect Catholic learning in what seemed an overwhelmingly Protestant or secular environment, much of this centered around a neoscholastic vision of the universe. In the last generation the inclusive strain has predominated, initially an act of confident interaction with all forms of knowing, going over subsequently, some worry, into uncritical compromise with prevailing trends in education.

If the relationship between Catholic Christianity and higher education seems more troubled in the late twentieth century, that owes less to inherent contradictions or generational swings than to the deep change both universities and the Catholic community have undergone, with the full consequences still to be sorted out. Such change may be noted in four areas, each of which presents its own challenge if Catholic higher education is to have a distinctive future: the constituent community, the leadership, the professorial community, and vocational education.

At its origins the European university was a tiny island of learning within a vast community of baptized Christians. Within more circumscribed settings such conditions obtained still in the early twentieth century when a privileged Catholic university served a large, minimally educated Catholic constituency (or a Jewish yeshiva/university the Jewish community). Under such conditions university men (as they mostly were) fulfilled two general roles: They led the community with their learning (whether as clerics or as educated laymen); and they acted as intellectual gadflies, pushing against the boundaries of what seemed a large and invincible world of belief (or sometimes, of ignorance). These conditions have been largely reversed. The world of believers may still be relatively large in number but it is hardly unified, confident, or invincible. The world of higher education grows ever larger and more influential. A "secularizing" Catholic university may accordingly only mirror a more assimilated, less uniform or distinctively Catholic constituency, with university intellectuals leading the way in defining or describing that more assimilated, more ambiguous relationship to a larger non-Catholic culture and society. In such a setting the intellectual gadfly (a role professors have played almost instinctively and with great pleasure ever since Socrates) may appear simply to fall in with the surrounding secular order by questioning elements of the faith or of community life, by creating more space for intellectual play and less for religious commitment, by doing as all others do fostering skepticism and cynicism. It may be that the professor who tries to transmit elements of tradition, who attempts to perceive coherence against all odds, who looks for faith or charity, is, in the late twentieth century, the person working against the grain. And yet such teachers will still encounter many students, more in the last decade, Catholic or evangelical or ortho-dox Jew, who have been reared in a world of strident belief, their stridency in part a reaction to a perceived secular stridency. Those students must be brought, at the very least, to grapple with the larger world in which they will mostly operate. In such ambivalent classroom settings, professors sensitive to questions of belief and learning find themselves doubly caught. It would imaginably be easier to act as the Catholic gadfly in a secular setting than to act as both guide and gadfly for an ambiguously Catholic constituency.

Second, the leadership in Catholic universities, both adminis-trative and professorial, is being transformed. Until the 1960s all Catholic higher learning was in the hands of religious or bishops—just as Protestant schools two or three generations earlier drew mostly on ministers. But the Second Vatican Council together with the so-called cultural revolution of the 1960s blew through Catholic institutions like a windstorm. Religious orders went from expan-sion to contraction; lay Catholics of the 1960s generation (roughly 1963–1976) often went from loyalty to suspicion. The result is great generational disparity. Those administrators and professors now nearing or entering retirement remember one kind of institution and its loyalties, however much they themselves worked for change. The middle generation, which should now be assuming leader-ship, is sparsely represented in religious orders and, if not adrift altogether, often still too skeptical of institutional authority to pledge themselves and their careers to the upbuilding of a specifi-cally Catholic institution. A younger group, come to adulthood in the 1980s, knows from within neither the old order nor the spirit of reform/revolution but wants a new stability, some with an ag-gressive new allegiance to tradition. Few, however, become religious.

The real transition therefore has just begun, if it is not too late: the passing of intellectual and administrative leadership to lay Catholics pledged to a religious form of higher education, something promoted in part by the Second Vatican Council. This almost certainly will never go as far toward laicization as it did among Protestants. Yet there is no model for it at all in the Catholic tradition, and as yet virtually no concerted planning or preparation.

Third, the professorate is rarely anymore an in-house group whose chief allegiance is to teach and study within a specific community of belief—though this may remain more common in parts of the evangelical world and a few conservative Catholic institutions. Professors come out of graduate school formation and look to other professors in their fields of inquiry as their natural colleagues. They may still teach in-house, so to speak, but much of their reading, writing, grant getting, and thinking takes as its manifest point of reference the larger world of physicists, literary critics, or historians. This is particularly true for Catholics, who—unlike Orthodox Jews or certain evangelicals—have only fitfully thought of themselves as separated out; they have typically thought of themselves as part of the whole world, even the dominant presence (and represent still a growing 20 percent of the American population). Even Catholics committed to serving their community as believing professors would hesitate to propound some wholly separatist view of philosophy, psychology, or whatever that bore little or no relationship to what generally goes by that name. So too at the level of personnel, Catholic institutions, with fewer and fewer religious, look readily to large secular graduate schools rather than to Catholic universities for faculty. In this arena of the professionalized professorate, to be in this world but not of it, in St. Paul's phrase, is a difficult challenge with no simple solutions or handy tags. Indeed such a stance is one that many Catholic faculty members see no reason to adopt, actively resisting the notion of some distinctively Catholic learning.

Fourth, the student body is now large, various, and ever more vocationally oriented. Mass-produced higher education permits less of that careful attention to thought and action which was one traditional mark of Christian education. Indeed, with higher education becoming an important social and monetary factor in America, acquiring that education has built into it ambitions that in themselves have little to do with charity or community. Those goods may still be instilled, but only with a conscious working a-gainst the grain. To be sure, a vocational and specialist orientation is not entirely new; in some ways it has been inherent in higher education from the start. But the roles for which people are specially trained, important to the maintenance of a complex modern society, bear no obvious relationship to traditional Chris-tian roles. What is the Catholic component in preparing experts in computer science? This question could be multiplied through dozens more instances. To say that it has to do with the person's values is virtually to cry despair, since most people have or would claim values. The issue is whether there are values specific to Catho-lic Christianity that can still inform or enter into a mass-produced, highly specialized educational process.

Religious institutions of higher education in America come in a great variety of forms. In the smaller college setting it may be easier to shape an environment in specific ways by policies of student recruitment, faculty appointment, or curricular demands. This es-say will explore the harder case, where a university aims to achieve all those things proper to universities and where Catholics seek to have their beliefs inform their intellectual work. The questions are hard ones: What is it that makes a university Catholic? What hap-pens there different from any other university? Why should a pro-fessor, given a choice, work in a Catholic university?

Higher education and Christianity both aim at personal trans-formation, of the mind or of the whole person. At times in European and American history the two, becoming educated and becoming Christ-like, have become confused culturally or socially, as in vague notions of the Christian gentleman or the cleric as intellectual. That is less likely to happen these days, especially when learning is vaunted as hostile to religion. But Christian educators expect these two forms of personal reshaping to prove mutually supportive. Catholic institutions were founded to educate Catholic students, partly as sources of recruitment for the clergy, mostly to care for people intellectually who still faced prejudice elsewhere in Ameri-can higher education. Catholic universities generally presumed a parochial formation, upon which they were to build. Today Catho-lic institutions can assume neither that Catholic students will choose them when many other colleges beckon, nor that entering students will have a parochial formation. Indeed Catholic universities face the grave danger of seeing the finest Catholic students enter institutions of long-standing prestige if they do not themselves offer the finest possible university education.

But is it conceivable to form students, Catholic or non-Catholic, with no previous commitment or openness to an educational process considered Catholic? There is, admittedly, a fair amount of self-selection by student applicants. There is also, in some cases, heavy recruiting to fill space and generate tuition revenue. Much depends upon how students are thought of educationally. Are they empty vessels waiting to be filled? In that case a Catholic education, begging the term for a moment, can be offered irrespective of the makeup of the student body, with the expectation that forms of Catholic learning will result and prove productive for the future. Or are they half-filled vessels, where, so to speak, certain ingredients must be present in order for an educational reaction/interaction to take place? This is the more common assumption, the more fitting recognition of students as young adult subjects. But this means that a significant portion of the student body must be so predisposed if the interaction is to produce Catholic learning. My point is not to encourage restrictive recruitment policies but to discourage fuzzy thinking. Is it a label, a baptismal certificate, a certain ethnic group, that makes a university Catholic? Or is it the educational process itself? Or the interaction between the two? Catholic students come in all varieties, from the devout to the indifferent. To require that all entering students be Catholic is in effect to deny the power and quality of the education itself, to doubt implicitly whether anyone not already predisposed would take away from it any form of Catholic learning. But to deny the contribution of a predisposing cultural tradition or faith would be educationally naive.

This same dilemma confronts Catholic institutions with respect to the makeup of their faculty. Does learning have a quasi-formal character which all professors, irrespective of their personal or religious predispositions, bring to the educational process? Or is it inevitably a subjective interaction, in which case what the professor brings to it makes all the difference in the nature of the learning that students take away? Or is this formal/subjective distinction a misleading one, with some measure of each in every educational situation and that measure variant not only by person but also by subject matter? Here the answers inevitably intersect with predispositions toward the first or second philosophical pattern described above. That is, is truth itself formally open to all and continuous with Christian truth, or is its perception radically personal? With some exceptions Catholic universities during the last generation, consistent with their more capacious traditions and their formal epistemologies, have leaned more to the first than to the second approach. They have selected the finest possible faculty, on the implicit assumption that the truth is coterminous with ultimate truth, to which every human creature can contribute, including those who do not profess Jesus as the Christ. (The more pragmatic argument would point up as well the need in university settings for vigorous intellectual debate coming from all quarters.) But these universities have also sought out Catholics, fitfully and sometimes with varying definitions of who fits the term, in the conviction plainly that a faith allegiance will make a difference in the classroom and in the nature of the learning offered by instructors.

The question is whether at some point the scale is tipped irretrievably toward the secular when too many of the faculty have no personal disposition toward contributing to Catholic learning. The difficulty when this question—rightly, in my view—gets raised is to define what that personal contribution is. Are there not many Catholics who show no signs of making or caring about it? Are there not many Jews and Protestants, also agnostics, whose intellectual empathies contribute decidedly, both in formal and in personal ways? How should the *Catholic* in *Catholic learning* be measured? By ecclesiastical markers such as baptism or communion or confession? Or by intellectual markers such as thought patterns or moral empathies or critical openness to certain kinds of issues and discussions? Much of recent Catholic higher education—as distinguished from more sectarian forms found among a few Catholics and many evangelical Protestants—has become almost intentionally ambiguous on this point, a matter partly of tradition, partly of ecclesiology, partly of epistemology, and partly of opportunism and compromise in the present American climate. It seems inevitable that institutions not already tipped entirely one way or the other—particularly in this moment of renewed cultural assertiveness or tribalization and of more subjective theories of knowing—will sway precariously and ambiguously between ecclesiastical and intellectual definitions of appropriateness when acquiring new faculty.

The intellectual and religious makeup of persons, students or faculty members, is central, but it is by no means the whole question. Christian educators presume to help shape the whole person, not just the mind. The moral and spiritual dimensions therefore receive as much attention as the intellectual. This goes back not only to theological anthropology but to institutional practice. When universities welcomed a predominantly clerical clientele in the Middle Ages, colleges were formed not only as boarding facilities but as religious structures with related moral oversight and religious obligations. Protestants carried on in the same vein, usually with strict moral codes and compulsory chapel attendance. Except in very conservative evangelical settings, this supervision has taken looser forms in recent years, partly in response to the cultural revolution of the 1960s, partly as a matter of maturing insight. As one English friend put it (who, like me, had experienced it at one point in his life), compulsory chapel is a superb program for "de-conversion."

When such moral and religious guidance is offered on a voluntary basis or within looser constraints, it often proves more effective. Many students throughout the 1980s, without joining the priesthood or religious orders, have become deeply involved in religious organizations or volunteer work, have participated regularly in worship, have reflected upon the moral expectations that come with Catholic profession. The point here is not to draw too rosy a picture or to gloss over deep moral inconsistencies but simply to note that this aspect of Christian education has often gone forward, sometimes even with renewed energy, at the same time that the intellectual has wavered or been called into question. Indeed, one frustration to interested Christian educators is the apparent chasm that has opened up between a religion rooted in experience or the will and a learning anchored in the mind. It is not only an institutional problem; it may assume ideological shape when those who guide or supervise the religious try, consciously or unconsciously, to keep the professors of the intellectual at bay. In its extreme form, this must signal failure, not perhaps in keeping someone Catholic, so to speak, but in helping form a person imbued with a productive Catholic intellect.

If the work of a Catholic university is rooted in persons, faculty or students, and must go beyond worship, devotion, or moral rectitude to effect something uniquely educational, what is that and how is it to be achieved? To this many answers have been given. Several still hang in the air, so to speak, without being subjected to more careful scrutiny. One is to have sufficient numbers of clergy in the classroom or administration from the relevant order. This fails today, not only because there are at the moment declining numbers of clergy available, but because the intellectual formation of clergy—itself in transition and often deemphasized—is no longer presumed the model for the intellectual formation of Catholic laypeople, this direction set in motion both formally and informally by the Second Vatican Council. This is not to deny an important continuing place to the clergy in Catholic education. Both hierarchical notions of authority and a clergy professed for life to a religious vocation can function, beyond their theological rationales, to anchor Catholic education in considerations, both other and older and more spiritual, than those of current intellectual fashion and thus help lift fellow scholars and students above the overwhelming crush of skepticism, national myopias, or secularism.

A second common answer is to have student minds formed in philosophy, understood as propaedeutic to or preparatory for an intellectual grasp of the whole divine order in created things. This, like the presence of clergy, came directly from the medieval university where the preparatory arts degree was much like what would be called a philosophy major today. This worked well as long as various forms of philosophical theology (Thomism, for instance) were regarded as the ultimate expression of Catholic belief. Two developments in the last generation have unsettled the focus upon philosophy still found in the curricular requirements of many or most Catholic universities. The emphasis upon the Bible coming out of the Second Vatican Council and various forms of biblical theology have displaced philosophical theology, for which philosophy acted as the proper intellectual preparation. Required courses in theology—biblical, historical, ethical, or systematic— seem accordingly more likely, as in most Protestant settings, to get at the heart of distinctively Catholic teachings, assuming a faculty of theologians interested in transmitting Catholic theology as such. Philosophy itself at Catholic universities, moreover, has entered into dialogue with the main philosophical currents of our time. It may focus upon ethics or philosophy of religion, but even these emphases to some degree move away from the tradition that logic and metaphysics prepared human minds for the understanding of the divine mind. For the last century or so philosophy has often been among the most secularized, or even anti-Christian, of the liberal arts disciplines—partly because, especially in Protestant settings, it first asserted itself as a self-conscious rival to theology. A full dose of philosophy in this mode would achieve exactly the opposite of what philosophy requirements at Catholic universities were once expected to accomplish. Overstated, the dilemma might be put this way: When Catholic philosophy pursued its own path from Aristotle to Thomas, it was treated as largely irrelevant to modern philosophy, despite the success of some neo-Kantian and existential versions, though supremely relevant to Catholic intellectual formation; as it absorbs and interacts with modern philosophy, it risks becoming irrelevant to the shaping of a distinctively Catholic mind. This is not to suggest that a philosophically formed and critical mind should not still be one mark of a Catholic education, nor that Christian philosophers could not formulate answers to some of my quandaries. Indeed, what is most needed, historically speaking, are figures like Thomas who can sort through contemporary philosophy and rescue its best or most congruent features for Catholic learning. But this is to suggest that the philosophical patterns of secular academe and the divinely formative purposes of Catholic thought are sufficiently disjunctive to raise real questions about the continuing viability of this approach in its present mode.

A third answer is to require more generally a pattern of courses with a liberal arts or ethical or theological dimension to awaken minds to divine paradigms, ethical questions, or godly humanism. This has proved a common approach, also in good evangelical schools, since at least the nineteenth century. Here the present difficulties are of two sorts. One is to object that there is nothing distinctively Catholic about a liberal arts approach; many other schools with no professed religious purpose do it as well or better. Catholic educators have frequently replied: But all that is good and true and beautiful is also Catholic. Granted, but why then attend a Catholic institution? The only possible answers, it seems, are to return to the matters of personnel, the student community, the faculty's personal contributions. A second and potentially greater difficulty derives from the fact that much of higher education has become so technical and specialized that the kinds of general considerations characteristic of a liberal arts education, Catholic or otherwise, no longer dominate the curriculum. Specialized knowledge has become the order of the day: What, to repeat, is Catholic about a major in computer science?

The Catholic university of the twenty-first century will not easily locate its peculiar mission in one or two simple marks. To function fully as a modern mega-university serving mass education a Catholic university must do well all that universities do: This means a constant striving after quality; this means quality work in a full range of disciplines; this means academic freedom (whether there is any special meaning for that concept in a Catholic setting is another matter, but for most people most of the time there is not). Ideally, and as one measure of achievement, the finest Catholic students and scholars should be pleased to begin and/or end their careers at such an institution. At the same time, to function fully as a distinctively Catholic university, certain areas peculiar to Catholic thought and tradition must be guaranteed a worthy place, such that other scholars or universities seeking help would readily turn there. It is not that such a university would represent or speak for America's fifty million Catholics but it must provide a place where such matters continue to be studied, even if they fall out of fashion elsewhere, and where all their possibilities and difficulties and contradictions would be aired out in disciplined debate, research, and teaching.

But this still begs the question of whether, beyond theology or ethics, there is anything substantively Catholic in the general educational work of such a university. Some would simply say no. Some would fear intrusion or oversight from another department such as philosophy or theology. Some would say that the answer could only be worked out in discipline-specific ways within departments or subdepartmental specialties; there is no general intellectual answer. Some have pointed to a community of scholars that breaks through the fragmentation and isolation of mass universities, transcends the ambition and egotism of the professorial profession, to discuss a range of common social, scientific, metaphysical, and religious issues. From such discussions those interested in the project of a Catholic university and the kinds of work and teaching it might foster would stimulate one another.

The intersection between Christianity and higher education, properly considered, is not a matter of social or political or ecclesiastical power but of intellectual animation. Those who have felt its pull pursue structures or principles that help shape teaching and research, forms of learning that might allow teachers and students to catch some glimpse of the divine work in creation and creatures. In an age of political cynicism, intellectual skepticism, and individual subjectivism, this sounds quaint. But some such intellectual motivation must be at work—and accessible to all—if the notion of a Catholic university is not to degenerate merely into a social label or ecclesiastical politics.

Two larger conceptual frameworks, among others, should be present in a Catholic university—with their precise bearing upon individual scholars or disciplines left to debate and intellectual discernment. The first is a sense of being connected in concrete ways to other peoples and a larger story, not just the abstractions of humanity but the human richness of people, even, in Christian terms, of brothers and sisters. There are, to begin in the present, some seven hundred million people of all different cultures and societies joined in Catholicism, not to speak of Protestant and Orthodox Christians. There is, moreover, from the past, the larger story of all the faithful reaching back to Scripture. A Catholic education must affirm that all people count as bearers of a divine image, that what people do and think always counts, for good or ill. But it will place what people do and think into a much longer tradition of people doing and thinking in the name of the gospel, sometimes fruitfully, sometimes harmfully. The Catholic community affirms tradition as a theological category and retains in its theology, its worship, and its organizational forms—despite recent updating—nearly two thousand years of history, much as has Orthodox Judaism and parts of the Islamic world. But it has also lifted out privileged elements in its history (Thomist philosophy, papal pronouncements) as timeless, and often regarded the historicizing of those elements and others as intellectually hostile. Yet the Bible itself is fundamentally historical in its narratives and orientation, and the Christian community can operate, albeit imperfectly, only in time. Coming to terms with the storied nature of human existence, even or especially in its relations with the divine, is essential to attain glimpses of a wisdom that transcends the merely human. Much of the modern world, and of modern education, is trapped in an unrelieved present which can only make idols of momentary social or scientific or philosophical agendas, together with an unrelieved historicism which relativizes the past as one damned thing after another, one ever-transient way of doing or thinking. Someone formed in a Catholic education should learn to think about human beings and the human story in part by studying the stories over time of the faithful, should learn to think critically and reflectively by examining the past results of thinking, believing, and doing within the Catholic community and the whole human community. That sense—of belonging to a more ancient whole, of striking critical stances toward it, of gaining wisdom from it, of treating all human beings and human creations as related to it— was not always, it must be conceded, a part of Catholic education in the past, though it was at the heart of the thinking of many of the intellectual leaders at the Second Vatican Council (Rahner, Congar, de Lubac, Danielou). Such a storied mind is grayer in tone, more nuanced and various in its judgments, than the black and white towards which philosophical or theological thinking has often strived. But it fits the character of both Scripture and tradition, takes seriously the human condition, and may well befit the educational situation of the twenty-first century.

The second larger principle is to draw out the meaning of the divine become human in Jesus of Nazareth. This must be grounded first in the single, transcendent, unnameable God of Abraham, Isaac, and Jacob—and perhaps by extension the God of Islam—with all its implications for the understanding of creatures and the creation. But that must be transformed by Christianity's conviction that in Jesus there dwelt the fullness and the image of the invisible God. Within the Christian world, the Catholic community, more consistently than the Orthodox or Protestant, has affirmed the full reality of the Word become flesh, of the Spirit of the risen Lord still present and at work in the faithful understood as a mystical body. In its predilection for institutions and laws, for rituals and communities, for visible images and devout expressions, the Catholic community has sought to make the Word present in this life, not just to lift people out of this life into that beyond. Especially in recent times it has affirmed this world, not in its evil manifestations, but in its divine presences; and may affirm that such presences come particularly by way of human beings, as Christian theology has it, created in the image of God and indwelt by the Spirit of the risen Lord.

This may sound altogether too abstract or homiletic, but it conveys the essentials of an attitude, a stance, that an educator may adopt. An expanding world of learning is not to be feared or to be accepted uncritically. The two options noted at the outset still exist: learning may still be approached as clearly continuous or as radically discontinuous with the divine made human. Learning is to be examined conceptually in terms of the full meaning of the incarnation, of the wisdom embodied in the gospel. What that might entail for different aspects of the intellectual life—the possibilities are not one but many, and not to be predetermined by one for another—could well serve as one animating force in the classroom of a Catholic university.

Afterword

One general conclusion of this book is that Notre Dame faculty members see the challenge and the promise of a Catholic University in a wide variety of ways, all different but all valid.

The Catholic university is perhaps most easily seen as a community of service to those less fortunate, locally, nationally, and internationally. This caring has both an intellectual and a practical aspect. The community does not only study phenomena like poverty, migration, refugees, homelessness, hunger. We also try to cope with these problems in a hands-on fashion through personal service in a variety of practical ways both here and abroad. Seeking just solutions and working to implement them is Christian concern at its best but is hardly the defining activity of a Catholic university. Service to others less fortunate is worthy, expected, but not totally defining. Other institutions do the same.

Then there is the idea of a Catholic university as a broadly liturgical community where beginnings and endings of the academic years are marked by splendid liturgical celebrations, Masses, homilies, and common prayer, especially the invocation of the Holy Spirit for inspiration and grace. There are also other liturgical celebrations, especially on Sundays and special feast days. Communal liturgies are normal for the beginnings and endings of special academic and historical occasions, in times of special crises, at the untimely deaths of students or faculty. Even during the student revolution, draft cards were destroyed during Mass on the quad. In a word, the church and its liturgy are central to our joys and sorrows. We are at ease and together while engaged in common prayers, especially as an academic community academically garbed for the occasion.

Another theme is a generally accepted interest in the philosophical and theological implications of the many intellectual concerns of our colleges and professional schools. Particularly, this special interest is manifested in the work of many centers, institutes, special programs, conferences, and symposia that demonstrate that this indeed is a place where the church does its thinking. One should add that most of this is done in a broadly ecumenical fashion as contrasted with a narrowly sectarian approach. We do try to be both Catholic and catholic.

Most basically, this is a place where reason and faith intersect and influence each other, even reinforce each other, as they grapple with all of the problems that face the transmission and growth of knowledge and the multiplication of new and complex moral problems. It would also be fair to say that we are here particularly concerned with the quest for justice and peace in our times, a continuing and increasingly elusive quest for both intelligence and faith.

All of this is seen not only in the classroom, unabashedly, but also in the conferences held here, the books published here and abroad by our faculty and administrators too, the organizations to which they belong, the awards they receive.

All this is not characteristic or expected of all universities, but taken together these essential aspects of Notre Dame do begin to describe the challenge and promise of a Catholic university. It is not so much a matter of the numbers of committed Christians and others, but the depth of their commitment to the interplay of faith and reason, their intellectual acceptance of the "primacy of the spiritual," to quote Maritain's phrase. It is not that all must be philosophers and theologians but all should have some concern about the philosophical and theological implications of all human intellectual activity. There ought to be some universities where all of this is true and appreciated if both the challenge and the promise of the Catholic university are to be met in our times. Such a university must also manifest the same degree, or more, of intellectual and academic freedom that any university requires. One can argue forever about the limitations of freedom, but it remains a basic requirement of honest and tolerant and constructive intellectual activity as befits a university. If discussion about slavery had been foreclosed, we would probably still have it.

This book is hardly the last word on the challenge and promise of a Catholic university but it is a good beginning and should continue.

One last word from me. I have always been inspired by the fact that our inner dignity as men and women derives from the fact that we were created in the image and likeness of God, because God endowed us with intelligence and freedom. The university is totally dedicated to enlarging these divine qualities to their fullness, for the glory of God and the enlargement of humanity everywhere. This is especially at the heart of the special challenge and promise of a Catholic university.

I am grateful, as editor, for the enlightened intelligence and faith that characterizes my colleagues in this present endeavor. I was particularly gratified by their willingness to give open and personal observations on many prickly problems that beset the challenge and the promise of this place, our Notre Dame. With such a valiant company, and many other equally dedicated colleagues, I am confident that we will, all together, meet the challenge and enjoy the promise.

I am also deeply indebted and grateful to the distinguished director of the University of Notre Dame Press, Dr. James Langford, and to his and our very intelligent and hard-working editor, Dr. Jeannette Morgenroth, without whose extraordinary mutual efforts this book would only have appeared a year from now.

THEODORE M. HESBURGH, C.S.C.

Contributors

HAROLD W. ATTRIDGE is Professor of Theology and George N. Schuster Dean of the College of Arts and Letters at the University of Notre Dame. A graduate of Boston College, Cambridge University, and Harvard University, he is a specialist in the study of the New Testament and Christian origins. His publications include work on Hellenistic Judaism, Christian Gnosticism, and a commentary on the Epistle to the Hebrews.

OTTO BIRD came to the University of Notre Dame in 1950 to establish the Program of Liberal Studies, a course of classes based on the great books. He has been an editor for Encyclopaedia Britannica, Inc., and a frequent contributor. Director of the Program of Liberal Studies from 1950 to 1963, he retired from the university in 1977.

DAVID B. BURRELL, C.S.C., is the Theodore M. Hesburgh Professor of Philosophy and Theology at the University of Notre Dame. He has served as chair of the Department of Theology at the university (1971–1980) and as rector of the Ecumenical Institute for Theological Research (Tantur) in Jerusalem (1980–1981). His current work is in the area of Jewish-Christian-Muslim philosophical theology, as is shown in his most recent publications issued by the University of Notre Dame Press: *Knowing the Unknowable God* and *Freedom and Creation in Three Traditions*.

FREDERICK J. CROSSON is the Cavanaugh Professor of Humanities at Notre Dame, where he has served as Dean of the College of Arts and Letters. He is a Senator of Phi Beta Kappa and has been a Commissioner of the North Central Association of Schools and Colleges.

LAWRENCE S. CUNNINGHAM is Professor of Theology and Chair of the Department of Theology at the University of Notre Dame. The author of fifteen books, he is also a columnist for *Commonweal* magazine.

FERNAND N. DUTILE, Associate Dean and Professor of Law at the Notre Dame Law School, was graduated from Assumption College in 1962 and from the Notre Dame Law School in 1965. He has published several books, including *State and Campus* and *Sex, Schools, and the Law*, and many articles.

SONIA G. GERNES is Professor of English at the University of Notre Dame. She has published a novel, three books of poetry, and a series of six videotaped lectures on *Women Writers: Spirit and Society* in the Great Teachers series. She has taught in Australia, New Zealand, and England, and was the 1990 winner of the Charles E. Sheedy Award for Excellence in Teaching in the College of Arts and Letters.

PHILIP GLEASON, Professor of History at the University of Notre Dame, is a specialist in American intellectual history, ethnic history, and the history of American Catholicism. He has taught at Notre Dame since 1959 and is completing a history of Catholic higher education in the twentieth century. His most recently published book is *Speaking of Diversity: Language and Ethnicity in Twentieth-Century America* (Johns Hopkins University Press, 1992). In 1994 he received the University of Dayton's Marianist Award for distinguished achievement by a Roman Catholic in scholarship and the intellectual life.

WILLIAM G. GRAY is the H. Massman Professor of Civil Engineering and Chair of the Department of Civil Engineering and Geological Sciences. He received his B.S. degree in chemical engineering from the University of California at Davis and his M.A. and Ph.D. in chemical engineering from Princeton University. He is in his tenth year at Notre Dame, following ten years on the Princeton faculty. His primary areas of teaching and research include the physics of multiphase flow in porous media and computer simulation of environmental flow and transport.

THEODORE M. HESBURGH, C.S.C., is President Emeritus of the University of Notre Dame, where he was President from 1952 until 1987. He received his doctorate of theology from the Catholic University of America in 1945 and has served at Notre Dame since then. Currently he also serves on the Board of Directors at Harvard University and the Board of the United States Institute of Peace in Washington, D.C.

CATHERINE MOWRY LACUGNA is Professor of Theology at the University of Notre Dame, author of *God for Us: The Trinity and Christian Life*, and editor of *Freeing Together: Essentials of Theology in Feminist Perspective*. She has contributed over thirty articles to various theological, pastoral, and liturgical journals and recently was awarded the university's Frank O'Malley Undergraduate Teaching Award.

DAVID C. LEEGE is Professor of Government and Director of the Program for Research on Religion, Church, and Society at the University of Notre Dame. He served as founding director of the Hesburgh Program in Public Service, 1988–1993, and Director of the Center for the Study of Man in Contemporary Society, 1976–1985, and of the Notre Dame Study of Catholic Parish Life, 1982–1991. His books and articles are in the areas of research and methods, religion and politics, cultural politics, the sociology of religion, and higher educational administration.

CRAIG S. LENT, Associate Professor of Electrical Engineering, has served on the faculty at Notre Dame since 1986. He received an A.B. degree in physics from the University of California at Berkeley and a Ph.D. in solid state physics from the University of Minnesota. His research is in the area of device physics, nanoelectronic devices, and quantum effects in small electronic structures. He has received research grants from the Air Force Office of Scientific Research, the National Science Foundation, the Advanced Research Projects Agency, Texas Instruments, and IBM.

RICHARD P. MCBRIEN is the Crowley-O'Brien-Walter Professor of Theology at the University of Notre Dame and former Chair of the Department of Theology. He is the author of the Christopher Award–winning *Catholicism* (original edition, 1980; revised edition, 1994). He served as President of the Catholic Theological Society of America and received in 1974 its John Courtney Murray Award for distinguished contributions to Catholic theology.

RICHARD A. MCCORMICK, S.J., is the John A. O'Brien Professor of Christian Ethics. He has written hundreds of articles and many books, most recently *Corrective Vision* (1994). He holds thirteen honorary degrees and is a member of the American Academy of Arts and Sciences.

RALPH MCINERNY is the Michael P. Grace Professor of Philosophy, the Director of the Jacques Maritain Institute, and former Director of the Medieval Institute at the University of Notre Dame. The recipient of several honorary Doctor of Letters degrees and the co-founder of the journal, *Crisis*, he is a prolific writer of novels and scholarly works.

GEORGE M. MARSDEN is the Francis A. McAnaney Professor of History at Notre Dame. He has also held positions at Calvin College and the Divinity School of Duke University. He is the author of *The Soul of the American University: From Protestant Establishment to Established Nonbelief* (Oxford University Press, 1994).

NAOMI M. MEARA is a fellow of the American Psychological Association and a past-President of its Division of Counseling Psychology. She recently received an Alumni Citizenship Award from her alma mater, the Ohio State University, and a Special Presidential Award from the University of Notre Dame. In 1992 she co-authored a book with Michael J. Patton entitled *Psychoanalytic Counseling*.

WILSON D. MISCAMBLE, C.S.C. ,is a member of the Congregation of Holy Cross. He was ordained a priest in 1988. A native of Australia, he serves presently as Associate Professor of History and Chair of the Department of History at the University of Notre Dame. He is a specialist in American diplomatic history and the author of *George*

F. Kenan and the Making of American Foreign Policy, 1945–1950 (Princeton University Press, 1992).

THOMAS V. MORRIS, Professor of Philosophy at the University of Notre Dame, graduated from the University of North Carolina at Chapel Hill and received his Ph.D. in philosophy and religious studies from Yale University. The author of numerous articles, he has also written or edited twelve books, the most recent of them being *God and the Philosopher* (Oxford University Press) and *True Success: A New Philosophy of Excellence* (Putnam). He has served at the University of Notre Dame for thirteen years. He has received the university's award for excellence in teaching in the Freshman Year of Studies and has been named Indiana Professor of the Year by the Council for the Advancement and Support of Education in Washington, D.C..

MARVIN R. O'CONNELL is Professor of History at the University of Notre Dame, where he teaches and studies the history of Christianity in Europe and America from the Reformation to the twentieth century. He is the author of *Thomas Stapleton and the Counter-Reformation* (Yale University Press), *The Oxford Conspirators* (Macmillan), *The Counter-Reformation* (Harper and Row), and *John Ireland and the American Catholic Church* (St. Paul).

THOMAS F. O'MEARA, O.P., is the William K. Warren Professor of Theology at the University of Notre Dame. He has been President of the Catholic Theological Society of America and has received its John Courtney Murray Award. Among his recent books are *Theology of Ministry* and *Church and Culture: German Catholic Theology, 1860 to 1919* (University of Notre Dame Press).

TIMOTHY O'MEARA, a native of South Africa, is the Howard J. Kenna Professor of Mathematics and, since 1978, Provost of the University of Notre Dame. Before coming to Notre Dame in 1962, he served on the faculty at Princeton University. He was also a member of the Institute for Advanced Study in 1957 and 1962. He has held visiting positions at American, Canadian, and European universities, including the Carl Friedrich Gauss Professorship at the University of Göttingen. A mathematician with interests in modern algebra and the theory of numbers, he has published several books. He is the 1988 recipient of the University of Dayton's Marianist Award for distinguished achievement by a Roman Catholic in scholarship and the intellectual life. In 1991 he was elected a Fellow of the American Academy of Arts and Sciences.

Alvin Plantinga is the John A. O'Brien Professor of Philosophy at the University of Notre Dame. He taught philosophy at Calvin College for nineteen years and has been at Notre Dame for the last twelve years. For the last ten years he has served as the Director of the Center for Philosophy of Religion. Most of his work has been in philosophy of religion, metaphysics, and epistemology.

Morris Pollard is the Coleman Director of Lobund Laboratory and Emeritus Professor of Biological Sciences. He takes special interest in virology (poliomyelitis, influenza, psittacosis) and in experimental pathology (cancers of the colon and prostate, leukemia, and the phenomenon of metastasis).

Robert E. Rodes, Jr., Professor of Law, came to the University of Notre Dame in 1956. He has taught courses in the fields of corporations, procedure, jurisprudence, and ethics. His most recent books are *Law and Liberation* (University of Notre Dame Press, 1986) and *Law and Modernization in the Church of England* (University of Notre Dame Press, 1991).

Timothy R. Scully, C.S.C., was ordained a Holy Cross priest in 1981, and he taught at Saint George's College in Santiago, Chile. He received his Ph.D. in political science from the University of California at Berkeley in 1989. He is currently Associate Professor of Government and International Studies. He is also Faculty Fellow of the Kellogg Institute at the university, where he directs the Latin American Studies Program. He is the author of *Rethinking the Center: Party Politics in Nineteenth and Twentieth Century Chile* (Stanford University Press, 1992) and the co-author of *Building Democratic Institutions: Party Systems in Latin America* (Stanford University Press, 1994). In 1993 he received the Charles E. Sheedy Award for Excellence in Teaching.

LEE A. TAVIS is the C. R. Smith Professor of Business Administration at Notre Dame and the Director of the program, Multinational Managers and Developing Country Concerns. He studies, teaches, and learns about the technical models of resource allocation in the multinational corporation and how these resources can be channeled better in order to alleviate poverty in developing countries while maintaining the global economic viability of the firm.

MARY KATHERINE TILLMAN has published and lectured on the thought of Cardinal John Henry Newman in six countries during the past decade. Associate Professor in Notre Dame's Program of Liberal Studies, she has served a term as Assistant Provost of the university and is the 1985 recipient of the Charles E. Sheedy Award for Excellence in Teaching in the College of Arts and Letters.

JOHN VAN ENGEN is Professor of History and Director of the Medieval Institute at the University of Notre Dame. He completed his undergraduate work at Calvin College and his graduate studies at the University of California in Los Angeles and the University of Heidelberg. He is the author of *Rupert of Deutz* (University of California Press) and *Devotio Moderna: Basic Writings* (Paulist Press) and the editor of *The Past and Future of Medieval Studies* (University of Notre Dame Press).